THE CHINESE JOURNALS OF
L. K. LITTLE, 1943–1954

THE MAKING OF MODERN CHINA

THE CHINESE JOURNALS OF L. K. LITTLE, 1943–1954

An Eyewitness Account of War and Revolution

Edited with Narratives by
Chihyun Chang

Volume I
The Wartime Inspector General,
1943–1945

LONDON AND NEW YORK

First published 2018
by Routledge
2 Park Square, Milton Park, Abingdon, Oxon OX14 4RN

and by Routledge
711 Third Avenue, New York, NY 10017

Routledge is an imprint of the Taylor & Francis Group, an informa business

Editorial material and selection © 2018 Chihyun Chang; individual owners retain copyright in their own material

All rights reserved. No part of this book may be reprinted or reproduced or utilised in any form or by any electronic, mechanical, or other means, now known or hereafter invented, including photocopying and recording, or in any information storage or retrieval system, without permission in writing from the publishers.

Trademark notice: Product or corporate names may be trademarks or registered trademarks, and are used only for identification and explanation without intent to infringe.

British Library Cataloguing-in-Publication Data
A catalogue record for this book is available from the British Library

Library of Congress Cataloging-in-Publication Data
Names: Little, L. K. (Lester Knox), 1892–1981, author. | Chang, Chihyun, 1979– editor.
Title: The Chinese journals of L.K. Little, 1943–1954 : an eyewitness account of war and revolution / edited by Chihyun Chang.
Description: Abingdon, Oxon ; New York, NY : Routledge, 2018. | Series: The making of modern China
Identifiers: LCCN 2017036073 (print) | LCCN 2017047317 (ebook) | ISBN 9781315536293 (set) | ISBN 9781315537290 (1) | ISBN 9781315537283 (2) | ISBN 9781315537269 (3) | ISBN 9781848934870 (set) | ISBN 9781138758049 (vol. 1) | ISBN 9781138758056 (vol. 2) | ISBN 9781138758063 (vol. 3)
Subjects: LCSH: Little, L. K. (Lester Knox), 1892–1981—Diaries. | China. Hai guan zong shui wu si shu—Officials and employees. | Customs administration—China—Officials and employees. | China—Officials and employees—Biography | China—History—Republic, 1912–1949– | China—History—1949–
Classification: LCC HJ7071 (ebook) | LCC HJ7071 .L55 2018 (print) | DDC 951.04/2092 [B]—dc23
LC record available at https://lccn.loc.gov/2017036073

ISBN: 978-1-8489-3487-0 (Set)
ISBN: 978-1-1387-5804-9 (Volume I)
eISBN: 978-1-315-53726-9 (Volume I)

Typeset in Times New Roman
by Apex CoVantage, LLC

Supported by Chinese Fund for the Humanities and Social Sciences (Chinese Academic Translation project reference number: 16WZS010).

CONTENTS

VOLUME I

Acknowledgments	vii
Foreword	ix
Preface: A forty-year delay to publish Lester Knox Little's diaries	xv
Introduction to Volume I: Lester Knox Little and the Nationalists	xxi

Diaries

1943	3
1944	35
1945	99

Appendix I: Summary of Ting's letter to H. H. Kung, 28 March 1944	155
Notes	157

VOLUME II

Introduction to Volume II: The Forever Deputy of China's Customs Service, Ting Kwei-tang	vii

Diaries

1946	3
1947	49
1948	89
1949	149

CONTENTS

Appendix I: Inspector General's interview with Dr. T. V. Soong, 7 March 1947 — 249
Appendix II: Interview with Hon. George C. Marshall, Secretary of State, 12:30 to 1:00 on 22 October 1947, at 2 Park Avenue, New York (Office of American Delegation to United Nations) — 251
Notes — 253

VOLUME III

Introduction to Volume III: L. K. Little and the Chinese staff in China after 1949 — vii

Diaries

1950	3
1951	39
1952	127
1953	173
1954	199

Appendix I: Interview with Sun Li-jen, 9 December 1951 — 235
Appendix II: Interview with Sun Li-jen, 3 June 1952 — 237
Appendix III: Interview with C. K. Yen, Minister of Finance, 23 June 1952 — 241
Appendix IV: Interview with K. C. Wu, 22 April 1953 — 245
Appendix V: The Taipei Inspectorate's Service List in 1955 — 247
Notes — 251

ACKNOWLEDGMENTS

This work began as a post-doctoral project after my graduation from University of Bristol in 2010. For the past seven years, I owe too many thanks and apologies to my colleagues in the world. First and foremost, I would like to thank Dr Elizabeth S. Boylan, Lester Knox Little's granddaughter, and Professor Robert Bickers, who received the original files of the diaries from Dr Boylan, Richard R. Shippee, and the late Mrs Elizabeth Shippee. Without their permission and support, this work would not be able to publish.

The completion of the editorial works attributes to three teams: the transcriber who transcribed Little's handwritten diaries to a typed file in the 1970s, the team which transcribed the typed manuscript to the Word file in 2010 and the editorial team which annotated the diaries, edited the appendix and supported the research. Although I only superintend the second and third teams, words cannot express how much I appreciate the first transcriber and Little's initiative, as this allows me to restart their work now.

As for the second and third teams, my gratitude goes to Dr Yung-chen Yuan, the team leader of the former team, and to Dr Yen-po Hou, the team leader of the latter team, due to their extraordinary skills of implementation and management.

I am also grateful to the editorial team at Routledge for helping me in this venture and for his professionalism in the publishing business. The publishing of this book has been much more efficient than anticipated.

I am profoundly grateful to my friends and colleagues, Mr Enchao Yang, Rougang Li, Hsing-ming Chang, Shao-fu Chen, Cheng Cai, Dr Alan Crawford and Ms Yunyan Wang, who provided me with enormous assistance and tolerated my preoccupation during the revisions of this work. I also owe many thanks to Professor Yung-fa Chen and Professor I-chun Fan at Academia Sinica, and Dr Zhiyong Ren at the Chinese Academy for Social Sciences for seeking for opportunities to publish this work; to Professor Richard J. Smith and Professor Hans van de Ven for their academic advises with rich experiences in the field of modern Chinese history; to Mr Cheng-yu Hu, my beloved uncle, for helping me get primary materials from the US. Of course, my best friend, Dr Barak Kushner, who has been encouraging me with his peculiar style of scholarship and of sense of humor.

Most of the research for this book was carried out at the Second Historical Archive of China in Nanjing, the Shanghai Municipal Archive, the First Historical

ACKNOWLEDGMENTS

Archive of China in Beijing and the Archive of the Institute of Modern History of the Academia Sinica. I would like to thank all my friends at these places for rendering me with help and suggestions when I first arrived and for introducing me to the archives staff. I would also like to thank, most of all, my grandparents, my parents and my families in Taiwan, America and Mainland China for their unfailing support.

Chihyun Chang
Department of History, Shanghai Jiao Tong University

FOREWORD

The time has nearly come to write a complete history of the Chinese Maritime Customs Service (CMCS), and when it is written, the documents and analysis provided by Dr. Chang Chihyun's three-volume work, *The Chinese Journals of L. K. Little, 1943–54: An Eyewitness Account of War and Revolution*, will loom large. So will his other scholarship on the CMCS—including not only his pioneering 2013 book titled *Government, Imperialism, and Nationalism in China: The Maritime Customs Service and its Chinese Staff*, but also his ongoing team effort to transcribe and annotate the journals of Robert Hart (1835–1911), who served as the Inspector-General (I.G.) of the CMCS from 1863 to 1911.[1]

The time is about right for such a history because scholars now have unprecedented access to relevant primary and secondary sources in both English and Chinese, including most of the 77 volumes of Hart's journals and literally tens of thousands of other documents (see below). And why is such a comprehensive study necessary? The answer, quite simply, is that the CMCS stands, both symbolically and substantively, at the center of the four major themes of China's nineteenth and twentieth century history: imperialism, nationalism, modernization and revolution.

The foreign-run and Chinese-staffed CMCS, which was established locally at Shanghai in 1854, became a "national" institution in the 1860s, headquartered in Peking (Beijing). From this point into the 1950s, it was China's foremost revenue-collecting agency, and an effective, perhaps even indispensable, mechanism for facilitating trade between China and the rest of the world. But it was much more than this. Its representatives in Peking and in an ever-growing number of treaty ports, gave advice and assistance to Chinese officials about a wide range of issues, and acted in certain respects as diplomatic officials of the regime in power. The CMCS also supported various educational enterprises (most notably the so-called Interpreters College, or Tongwen guan), undertook surveys of coastlines, harbors and rivers, improved coastal and inland communications, supervised measures for the prevention of shipborne diseases, collected meteorological data, organized nearly 30 international exhibitions, and created what became the National Post Office of China. In addition, the CMMS published invaluable trade statistics and trade reports, as well as "scores of monographs dealing with such varied subjects as opium, tea, silk, Chinese music, collection and disposal of revenue, medicines, jute, furs and skins, hospitals, ginseng, [and] timber rafts."[2]

In short, the CMCS played a foundational role in China's modernization, providing useful models for China's political, economic, educational, diplomatic and even legal development. It also facilitated China's acquisition of military, naval, and industrial technologies. Over time, however, the CMCS came to be seen as a tool of Western interests, with the result that a large body of nationalistically driven Chinese Marxist scholarship arose—work that considered the CMCS to be nothing less than an instrument of Western imperialism. One important index was the publication in the period from 1957 to 1965 of fifteen volumes of collected translated primary materials in a series titled "Imperialism and the Maritime Customs" (*Diguo zhuyi yu Zhongguo haiguan*).[3]

Two pioneers in the study of the CMCS during this time were Professors John King Fairbank (1907–1991) of Harvard University and Chen Shiqi (1915–2012) of Xiamen University in the People's Republic of China, each of whom represented, in a certain sense, one of these interpretive poles.[4] Fairbank emphasized the modernizing role of the Chinese customs administration while Chen devoted more attention to the issue of foreign imperialism. As Fairbank put the matter in 1975:

> We in the West are . . . confronted with a bifocal perspective – that of the Maoist world view and that of the Western record, which has of course been less responsive to the compelling sentiments of China's political revolution. There could hardly be a greater contrast between [the] two views. In the People's Republic today the treaty era stands out as a time of foreign privilege, imperialist exploitation, and Chinese suffering and humiliation. . . . In the Victorian view of Robert Hart's day the treaty system in China stood proudly as a product of the beneficent spread of commerce and progress, bringing modern science and civilization to a heathen and backward land. Times have changed. The historical scene in Shanghai of the late nineteenth century as pictured by foreigners at the time and by Chinese today, seems like two utterly different worlds. A wide gamut of interpretations is thus offered to the inquiring student, and much ambivalence hangs over the history of the late nineteenth century in China.[5]

During the 1980s and 90s I had the pleasure and privilege of working closely with both Professor Fairbank and Professor Chen, collaborations that resulted in three books and several other publications.[6] But after Professor Fairbank's death, and with the decline in Professor Chen's health, I turned to other research interests and partnerships. And for a time, I feared that the work done by these pioneering scholars might not be continued with as much energy and dedication as they had exhibited.

These fears were misplaced. Unbeknownst to me at the time, Professor Robert Bickers of Bristol University and Professor Hans van de Ven of Cambridge University were carrying on the illustrious traditions of Professors Fairbank and Chen. Building on their earlier collaboration, and with funding from the Arts and Humanities Research Council (AHRC), they partnered with the Second Historical Archives at Nanjing, PRC in the period from 2003 to 2007 on a project designed "to further understandings of the modern Chinese state, British imperial history, and the history of modern globalization in China, by focusing on the role the Chinese Maritime Customs Service and its staff played in these historical processes."[7] And thus, the "History of the Chinese Maritime Customs Service" project was born at Bristol University, with Professor Bickers as its director.

In building his team of researchers, Professors Bickers and van de Ven attracted established scholars as well as talented graduate students.[8] One of the most accomplished of these students was Mr. (now Dr.) Chihyun Chang, the author/editor of the three-volume book in hand. At some point, I'm not sure exactly when, Dr. Chang and I began to correspond, and although I was too enmeshed in other projects to return to research on the CMCS, I began reading Dr. Chang's published and unpublished work with great interest. So when Dr. Chang asked me to write this foreword I was not only honored by the request but also gratified to be able to serve as a link between three generations of Customs scholars—those represented by Fairbank and Chen, those represented by Bickers and van de Ven, and those represented by Chang and various other younger members of the Bristol University team.

What is it that Dr. Chang has accomplished in putting together *The Chinese Journals of L. K. Little, 1943–54: An Eyewitness Account of War and Revolution*? In essence, he has done for the last foreign Inspector General of the Chinese Customs, Lester Little (1892–1981), what Fairbank and others began to do with the second, Robert Hart.[9] Like Frederick Maze (1871–1959), Hart's successor and Little's predecessor, who headed the CMCS from 1929 to 1943,[10] both Hart and Little left substantial, albeit heavily edited, records of their careers in the CMCS.[11]

A systematic comparison of these three extensive forms of personal reminiscence is obviously beyond the scope of this foreword, but in all three accounts we see able, conscientious individuals coping with the myriad problems of overseeing a unique Sino-foreign institution, one that was an integral part of the Chinese central government but one that was also subject to pressures by various foreign powers and especially representatives of their own countries—Great Britain in the case of Hart and Maze, and America in the case of Little. What these journals/diaries reveal in particular are the complexities and difficulties of operating in an "alien" political, economic, social and culture environment. Hart, Maze and Little were all fluent in Chinese, all had the best interests of China in mind, and all appreciated certain aspects of Chinese culture (especially Maze). But in the end, they were "outsiders," who had to work within the framework of Chinese bureaucratic factionalism on the one hand and the exigencies of foreign imperialism on the other. Complicating matters, not surprisingly, were rivalries and personality differences within the ranks of both Chinese officials and foreigners. Dr. Chang's three-volume study admirably documents and explains these problems from the perspective of L. K. Little, and careful readers will learn a great deal from it.

Richard J. Smith
George and Nancy Rupp Professor of Humanities
emeritus, Rice University.

Notes

1 See https://blogs.qub.ac.uk/sirroberthart/diaries/. See also Henk Vynckier and Chihyun Chang, "The Life Writing of Hart, Inspector-General of the Imperial Maritime Customs Service," *Comparative Literature and Culture*, 14.5 (2013) (http://docs.lib.purdue.edu/clcweb/vol 14/iss5/10; accessed 9–17–17), and Henk Vynckier and Chihyun Chang, "Imperium in Imperio: Robert Hart, the Chinese Maritime Customs Service, and Its (Self-)Representations," *Biography*, 37.1 (Winter 2014), 69–92.

2 B. E. Foster Hall, *The Chinese Maritime Customs: An International Service, 1854–1950* (Bristol: University of Bristol, 2015): 7–8. This small book was originally published in 1977. For some other works that discuss the multi-faceted functions of the CMCS, see Martyn Atkins, *Informal Empire in Crisis: British Diplomacy and the Chinese Customs Succession, 1927–1929* (Ithaca, NY: East Asia Program, Cornell University, 1995); Robert Bickers, "Purloined Letters: History and the Chinese Maritime Customs Service," *Modern Asian Studies* 40.3 (2006), 691–723, "Revisiting the Chinese Maritime Customs Service, 1854–1950," *The Journal of Imperial and Commonwealth History* 36.2 (June 2008): 221–226, and *The Scramble for China: Foreign Devils in the Qing Empire, 1832–1914* (New York: Penguin Books, 2011); Donna Brunero, *Britain's Imperial Cornerstone in China: The Chinese Maritime Customs Service, 1854–1949* (New York: Routledge, 2006); Catherine Ladds, *Empire Careers: Working for the Chinese Customs Service, 1854–1949* (Manchester: University of Manchester Press, 2013); and Hans van de Ven, *Breaking with the Past: The Maritime Customs Service and the Global Origins of Modernity in China* (New York: Columbia University Press, 2014); and Robert Bickers and Jonathan J. Howlett, eds, *Britain and China 1840–1970: Empire, Finance and War* (New York: Routledge, 2015). For a more complete bibliography of recent works, see http://www.bris.ac.uk/history/customs/customsbibliographies/publications.

3 Discussed in Dr. Chang's as yet unpublished article "The 'Hart Industry' and the Writing of Modern Chinese History."

4 See Chang's "The 'Hart Industry' and the Writing of Modern Chinese History," and Dai Yifeng, "Chen Shiqi yu Zhongguo jindai haiguan shi de yanjiu (Chen Shiqi and research on the modern history of China's maritime customs), *Jindai Zhongguo shi yanjiu tongxun* (Newsletter of research on modern Chinese history) 19 (1995): 60–67.

5 John K. Fairbank, Katherine Bruner and Elizabeth Matheson, eds, The I.G. In Peking: Letters of Robert Hart, Chinese Maritime Customs, 1868–1907 (Cambridge, Mass.: Harvard University Press): I: xii.

6 The books were: Katherine Bruner, John K. Fairbank and Richard J. Smith, eds, *Entering China's Service: Robert Hart's Journals, 1854–1863*. (Cambridge, Mass.: Council on East Asian Studies, Harvard University, 1986); Richard J. Smith, John K. Fairbank and Katherine Bruner, eds, *Robert Hart and China's Early Modernization: His Journals, 1863–1866* (Cambridge, Mass.: Council on East Asian Studies, Harvard University, 1991); and John K. Fairbank, Martha Henderson Coolidge and Richard, J. Smith,

H. B. Morse: Customs Commissioner and Historian of China (Lexington: University of Kentucky Press, 1995. See also Chen Shiqi, *Zhongguo jindai haiguan shi wenti chushen* (A preliminary investigation into questions about the history of China's modern maritime customs) (Beijing: Zhongguo zhanwang chubanshe, 1987) and *Zhongguo jindai haiguan shi* (History of the modern Chinese Customs) (Peking: Renmin chubanshe, 2002).

7 See http://www.bris.ac.uk/history/customs/about.html.
8 http://www.bris.ac.uk/history/customs/team.html.
9 See note 6 above and note 11 below.
10 See Nicholas R. Clifford, "Sir Frederick Maze and the Chinese Maritime Customs, 1937–1941," *The Journal of Modern History*, 37.1 (March 1965): 18–34 and Martyn Atkins, *Informal Empire in Crisis: British Diplomacy and the Chinese Customs Succession, 1927–1929* (Ithaca: Cornell East Asia Series, 1995).
11 See Bickers, "Purloined Letters" and Chang, "The 'Hart Industry'."

Lester Little, the last chief of the Chinese Maritime Customs Service, was a close observer of the death throes of a cosmopolitan Nationalist China and the emergence of a Cold War East Asia. Determined to the best for his staff and shepherd the Service through a period of intense upheaval, Little recorded his impressions of many leading figures as well as key moments as the world in which he served in high office came apart at the seams. Carefully edited, comprehensively annotated, and thoughtfully introduced, all historians of modern China and of the emergence of the USA as a world power will be grateful to Dr Chang Chih-yun's painstaking efforts to make the Little diary available in convenient form. It provides us with a rich and intimate record of one of the great shifts in Chinese and world history.

–Hans van de Ven, Professor of Modern Chinese History & Fellow of St Catharine's College, University Cambridge

It was in 2005 that I first heard from Richard Shippee that the family had in their possession a 'detailed diary of visitors and daily events'. Eighteen months later I was able to visit Greenwich, Connecticut and copy these diaries, which were far more detailed than I had imagined. I would like to add my personal thanks to Dr Elizabeth S. Boylan for her patience and interest in this project. For their kindness and hospitality I am grateful to Dr Elizabeth S. Boylan and Dr Robert J. Boylan, Richard and Debbie Shippee, and of course the late Mrs Elizabeth Freeman Shippee, née Little, who patiently allowed me to take over her dining room and copy the materials. I was surrounded as I did so my many reminders of her father's career in China – items of furniture, photographs, and even a little Chinese Maritime Customs flag, that had once stood on his desk in China, and of course by souvenirs of her own years in China. I would also like to thank Dr. Liza Little, who provided a copy of her grandfather's earlier appointment diaries. I was unable to set aside time myself to prepare an edition of this rich source, and was very pleased when my former student Dr Chang Chih-yun took on the challenge. Lester Knox Little's contribution to the history of the Chinese Maritime Customs, and to the history of the Chinese republican state, has been overshadowed by the story of his predecessor Sir Robert Hart. It deserves to be told, and 'L. K.' tells it well, and his telling is very ably assisted by Dr Chang's seven years of work on this project.

–Robert Bickers, Professor of History, University of Bristol

PREFACE

A forty-year delay to publish Lester Knox Little's diaries

The publishing of Lester Knox Little's diaries from 1943 to 1954 was delayed for 40 years. In the 1970s, Little planned to publish his diaries, so he managed to transcribe his handwritten diaries to a typed manuscript (henceforth Typed Edition). This has made my job much easier. The Little diaries cover the years 1932–1954, but he only selected the period 1943–1954 when he was the Inspector General of the Chinese Maritime Customs Service and the consultant of the Ministry of Finance in Nationalist Taiwan.

In the early 1970s, Little worked with Professor John Fairbank at Harvard to inaugurate the 'Hart Industry' concerning two sets of materials – Hart's correspondence to James Campbell and Volumes I–VIII of his diaries.[1] Little was also invited by Fairbank to compose the 'Introduction'[2] for the Hart–Campbell correspondence. However, Little and Fairbank's cooperation only concerned the Hart materials, and Little chose to work on his own materials by himself. In 1971, Little planned to publish a short version of his diaries. The original manuscript is 430,000 words (henceforth the Original Edition), but Little cut it down to 337,000 words (henceforth the Deleted Edition). There were two reasons.

First, because the Nationalist Party in the 1970s placed very strict censorship on Taiwan, the publishing of these diaries would put Little's friends' lives in danger; for instance, General Sun Li-jen was still under house arrest in the 1970s on the charge of *coup d'état* against Chiang Kai-shek in collaboration with the Chinese Communists or the CIA; and Little's best friend in Taiwan, C. K. Yen, became the President of the Republic of China (Taiwan) from 1975 to 1978. Hence, he deleted most of the politically sensitive parts. Second, the part concerning his private comments and personal life were also deleted as he chose not to reveal his negative or sentimental feelings. Due to the first reason, it seemed that Little was quite hesitant to publish his diaries. In 1982, Little passed away and the Original Edition was suspended for 25 years.

In 2007, Professor Robert Bickers visited Little's granddaughter, Dr Elizabeth S. Boylan, photocopied the Original Edition and got oral permission from Dr Boylan to publish the diaries. By this time, the first reason was no longer a concern. The Nationalist Party abolished the Martial Law upon Taiwan in 1987 and Taiwan has already become completely democratised. No one would be hurt by

PREFACE

the publishing of the diaries and most of Little's friends had passed away; General Sun and President Yen respectively passed away in 1990 and 1993. The power struggles between Little's friends' and the Nationalist Party have become histories. From Little's deleted parts, historians can discover a great deal of detail for a more explicit description. As for the second reason, readers might find Little's emotional parts very interesting as historians or litterateurs can compose Little's biography and life writing based on these texts. Fortunately, he crossed out the text on the Typed Edition which gives us the ability to reinsert these parts in the Published Edition, but after Professor Robert Bickers and I consulted with the Little families' opinions most of the deleted parts are put back to the diaries, which are identified with the crossed line in the text. However, the most private and personal parts are still deleted by Professor Bickers and me and marked by [...].

The transcription from the typed manuscript to a Word file started in 2010 when I finished my doctoral thesis under Professor Bickers' supervision. I gathered a team of five members led by Dr Yung-chen Yuan in Taiwan and finished the transcription to a Word file in December 2010 (the Word Edition).

After the Word Edition was done in 2010, I started to seek opportunities to publish it. Originally, Brill expressed interest but required the Word Edition to be cut down to 100,000 words. This would compromise the value of the Little diaries significantly. Hence, I planned to find a publisher that would publish the complete Word Edition. The CASS Press and the Renmin University Press in China were more interested in translating the diaries into Chinese (which also interested me, but I preferred to publish the English version first).

In 2013, the publishing of the Published Edition became possible because Pickering & Chatto's Commissioning Editor Philip Good contacted me and stated his interests to publish the volume. In order to meet the high editorial standard of the Fairbank team's 2 volume Hart Journals and maximise the value of the Little Journals, I continue the editorial style of the Hart Journals which consist of three parts: appendix, annotations and introductions. In 2015, Routledge merged with Pickering & Chatto, and the publishing contract then moved under Routledge.

The goal of the appendix is to find good additional materials so readers will have a better idea of the histories. The sources are (1) Little's original appendix: his interviews with General Sun Li-jen and Ting's summary of the setting up of the Sinkiang Custom House; (2) archival sources: the Directorate General of Customs in Taiwan; and (3) Little's correspondence and interviews.[3]

Of all the different types of annotations, the most difficult one is to identify the names mentioned by Little. As a highly cosmopolitan service in charge of China's international trade, the Inspector General (IG) had close cooperation with his staff of over 20 nationalities and politicians from China and other countries. Without proper annotations, the value of the diaries would not be maximised. The reasons why it is difficult to identify these people are that (1) politicians from each country require a particular set of historical knowledge to identify; (2) Little used the English names or surnames of Chinese politicians, making it very difficult to identify who, for example, Mr Chen was; and (3) even with full first names and surnames, it is simply unlikely that everyone will be identified. Given these limitations, I have done my best.

The annotations of these people are from four sources, namely (1) Who Is Who: *Who Is Who in China* (1919, 1920, 1925, 1931, 1936 and 1950) and *Who Is Who in America* Vols I–VIII (1960, 1968, 1973, 1976, 1981 and 1985); (2) the Chinese Maritime Customs Service publications: the *Service Lists* and *Documents Illustrative* (1938) edited by Stanley Wright; and (3) Newspapers' obituaries: *The Times*, *New York Times*, etc.; and (4) online databases edited by the Academia Sinica and the Academia Historica. I regrets to confess, however, only 651 historical figures are annotated that over 30% of the names in the Published Edition cannot be identified.

The introductions are provided to provide readers with an alternative angle to understand the stories told by the Little diaries. This work involves a great deal of research on CMCS's history. I started the research on the customs service's history in 2006 and have been working in this field for more than 10 years. But it still took me three years to gather primary materials from Taiwan, China, Japan, America and Britain to cover three different accounts from Little, Kwei-tang Ting (Little's Deputy), and the Chinese staff who stayed in the Chinese mainland after 1949.

This is not to say that Little deliberately misled readers as to what his predecessor, Frederick Maze, did with the "Maze Papers" in possession of SOAS (the School for Oriental and African Studies).[4] On the contrary, Little was very frank and honest about what he faced and the reason behind his decisions. But Little's perspectives towards the Nationalists and Communists in disgust, his rivalry with Kwei-tang Ting and his favouritism over the foreign staff make his diaries partially true.

In order to show the three different viewpoints, the diaries are separated into three volumes.

Volume I's introduction, entitled 'Lester Knox Little and the Nationalists', covers Little's IG career in Wartime Chongqing from 1943 to 1945.. Little started to take a closer look at Nationalist China's high politics. He familiarised himself with powerful politicians, such as T.V. Soong, H.H. Kung, Tai Li, etc. In this complex political network, Little found himself stuck in the Nationalists' factionalism. In order for readers to understand Little's role in the Nationalists' political network, Volume I's Introduction analyses the connections between Little and different Nationalist Presidents, Financial Ministers, etc.

Volume II covers Little's IG career mainly in post-war Shanghai and his final days in Canton and Taipei from 1945 to 1950 and includes an introduction entitled 'The Forever Deputy of China's Customs Service, Ting Kwei-tang'. Little endeavoured to consolidate the Nationalist government's financial stability and to smoothen Sino-American relations. The more he endeavoured, the more he was discouraged. Little confided his frustrations, depressions, anger and anxiety to the journal, as he encountered endless difficulties of bureaucratism, sectionalism and factionalism. However, Volume II's introduction narrates a different viewpoint

PREFACE

through the eyes of Ting. Ting was also a sensible candidate for IG-ship, but he was replaced by Little. He thought that Little endeavoured to protect the foreign staff's dominance in the CMCS, whereas Ting was committed to expunge the foreign presence in the CMCS after WWII.

Volume III covers Little's consultant career in post-1949 Taiwan from 1950 to 1954 and includes an introduction entitled 'L.K. Little and the Chinese Staff in China after 1949'. Little did everything he could to rehabilitate the Inspectorate General of Customs in Taipei. He brought a skeleton of staff from China to Taiwan and offered protection to them while he was the Consultant to Financial Commissioner C.K. Yen. It is fair to state that Little was the key person on the rehabilitation project. However, Volume III's introduction reveals that the staff left by Little in 1949 found it extremely unfair when they followed instructions to stay at their posts in the Chinese mainland in 1949, but Little used their pensions to pay off the foreign staff. After they made their ways to Taiwan, the Taipei Inspectorate refused to reinstate them immediately. They suspected the reasons were that the Chinese staff brought by Little to Taiwan did not want them to know 1) that their pensions were used to pay off the foreign staff and 2) that the Chinese staff brought by Little also received their *pro rata* pensions in 1950. It would not be difficult to imagine their grievances towards Little and his successors.

I have no intention of undermining the historical image of Little. On the contrary, Little was a more responsible IG than his British and Japanese counterparts, Frederick Maze and Kishimoto Hirokichi, when they prepared the retreats in 1941 and 1945. Little did his best to bring his Chinese and foreign colleagues from the Chinese mainland to Taiwan in 1949. Readers can easily understand that he could not bring everyone, but the rather unfortunate part was that he paid off every foreign employee, including himself, but only over 11 Chinese employees received their *pro rata* pensions. Thus, Volume III's introduction narrates a story about an ordinary American who was put in an impossible situation and forced make impossible decisions.

The aforesaid three parts of editorial works conclude my seven years' endeavour, but the quality of the Published Edition still can be significantly improved. The outcome of the Published Edition might have been different from Little's original publishing plan in the 1970s, but readers would realise the my editorial works are to maximise the value of the diaries and to provide a pen portrait of Little. I believe that after reading through the diaries, annotations, introductions and appendix, readers would easily find out that Little was a honorable man and a man of the Customs.

Notes

1 E. Bruner's article in memory of Fairbank, in Paul Cohen and Merle Goldman eds, *Fairbank Remembered* (Cambridge, MA: Harvard University Press, 1992), 228–229.
2 Lester K. Little, 'Introduction', in John Fairbank, Katherine Bruner and Elizabeth Matheson eds, *The IG in Peking: Letters of Robert Hart Chinese Maritime Customs, 1868–1907*, Volume I (Cambridge, MA: Harvard University Press, 1975), 5–34.

PREFACE

3 HUGFP 12.28. L. K. Little Career Box 4, Conversazione: L. K. Little, G. E. Bunker, K. F. Bruner Cornish, New Hampshire, 16 and 17 December, 1971, 43–44.
4 Martyn Atkins, who has closely read the papers for studying the Edwardes-Maze competition for the IG-ship between 1927 and 1929, states that 'Its documentation of the work of Frederick Maze appeared to tell a fascinating story. At first sight, Maze seemed to be a man locked in a constant battle with the forces of official and unofficial British opinion, fighting for credibility and facing vilification in the name of a just cause. However, the tale which the records told had to be approached with circumspection. Maze's papers are for the most part so wonderfully organised, neatly connecting one set of issues with the next, that one wonders whether the volumes were prepared as part of an attempt at self-vindication. Maze is present throughout the volumes, entering acerbic and barely legible explicatory marginalia followed by his ubiquitous monogram. While the elements of the case he presents may ring true, therefore, one has to be wary of excessive guidance by his insistent hand.' Martyn Atkins, *Informal Empire in Crisis: British Diplomacy and the Chinese Customs Succession, 1927–1929* (Ithaca, NY: East Asia Program, Cornell University, 1995), ix.

INTRODUCTION TO VOLUME I
Lester Knox Little and the Nationalists

Lester Knox Little was the last foreign Inspector General (IG) of the Chinese Maritime Customs Service (CMCS) and also the only American IG. Before him, there were two Englishmen, two Ulstermen and one Japanese. All these IGs were the 'men of Customs' – in Hans van de Ven's words – meaning they were loyal to the CMCS. The understandings of the CMCS tradition varied significantly, but overall it meant its efficiency, cosmopolitanism, integrity, unity and aloofness from Chinese politics. These characteristics were constituted in the nineteenth century and became more important in the first half of the twentieth century. Little was, of course, a man of Customs, but he was also different from his predecessors.

First, he kept a very explicit diary and planned to publish it. Judging from the records in his diaries, he was always frank and consistent on what he insisted. He did not want to manipulate how historians examine his history and he was not afraid of being judged by historians. Compared to him, Frederick Maze deliberately manipulated the 'Maze Papers' at SOAS,[1] and Francis Aglen Kishimoto Hirokichi did not leave any autobiography, diary or memoir. Although he also kept a diary, Robert Hart was relatively reluctant to publish it.[2]

Second, Little followed the Nationalists to Taiwan and rebuilt the CMCS in Taipei. It seemed that he was highly loyal to the Nationalist government. The IG's loyalty to a particular Chinese government was, actually, not a convention of the CMCS. The more consistent convention was that the staff was 'aloof from politics',[3] and the foreign IG always served the central government of China even if the previous central government he had just served under was overthrown by the current one. This phenomenon was described as the IG's 'two faced' policies by Chinese historian Chen Shiqi,[4] but in the eyes of the CMCS staff, it was their 'freedom from politics'.[5]

Little's predecessors' record of 'freedom from politics' was chequered – Francis Aglen served the Anhui, Zhili and Fengtian cliques respectively from 1917 to 1924, and he tried to cooperate with the Canton Revolutionaries in 1925; Frederick Maze took instructions from the Chongqing and collaborationist governments at the same time from 1937 to 1941. The reason they gave was that the CMCS was the asset of China and the CMCS's integrity was the key to maintain its high-quality performance.

However, Little was completely different from these two IGs. Since the first day he arrived in China in April 1943, he never talked to any collaborationist governments supported by the Japanese military during WWII or to the Communists during the Civil War. He was completely loyal to the Nationalist government no matter how incompetent it was at the later stage of the Civil War. He brought key staff to Taiwan to ensure Nationalists could reconstruct the CMCS in Taiwan. The success of the CMCS reconstruction in Taiwan relied on Little's determination, endeavour and loyalty.

However, while reading through the entries in the Little diaries, readers can easily find out that Little was actually really critical towards Chiang Kai-shek and the Nationalist government. Because he could learn information from local Commissioners, he witnessed the real situations in Free China in detail and understood that Chiang and the Nationalists' factionalism were the cause of the Chinese people's misfortune.

Hence, this introduction aims to answer the question: who and what was Little loyal to and why was he loyal?

In order to answer this question, it is necessary to explore how Little positioned himself in the networks of Nationalists from 1943 to 1949. Although Chiang Kai-shek was an authoritarian leader, the Nationalist Party was a loose alliance formed by a number of factions and cliques. Chiang was merely the Huangpu clique leader, which was frequently the most powerful clique but not always.

The Nationalist Party comprised a loose alliance of different political factions and military cliques due to its long revolutionary history before 1911. From 1911 to 1949, the Nationalist Party started from a terrorist and racist body allied to the Triads before 1911 and then became a pro-Western cabinet-style political party in 1912. In the 1920s, the party was shaped into a Leninist Bolshevik revolutionary party with a strong anti-imperial base and then became a pro-UK/US authoritarian party in the 1930s. This see-sawing of political inclinations made the Nationalists very unlikely to create an ideological consensus to unify the party.

The military cliques were another cause of crisis. Before the Northern Expedition, the right wing clique and the left wing clique in the Nationalist Party had already had several major conflicts. During the Northern Expedition, the party absorbed a wide range of local warlords and had already developed deeply rooted internal grievances against each other. After WWII, these grievances did not fade away but became more serious. Actually, by the eve of the Nationalists' retreat from the Mainland, the party can hardly be considered as a centralised, modern political party.

From 1943 to 1949, Little's relations with the Nationalists were complicated by the fact that he met different representatives from their factions or cliques. This is not to say that these Nationalists deliberately manipulated Little's understanding of modern China and the party, but they had their own particular interests which determined what they liked to discuss with Little.

The introduction aims to explore Little's relations with three groups of Nationalists, namely (1) the Presidents (Chiang Kai-shek and Li Tsung-jen),

(2) the Financial Ministers (T.V. Soong, H.H. Kung and Wang Yun-wu), and (3) his friends (C.K. Yen and Sun Li-jen). These three different natures of relationship can help us to understand why Little chose to follow the Nationalists to Taiwan.

Little and Nationalist Presidents

From 1943 to 1949, there were actually three Nationalist Presidents, namely Lin Sen, Chiang Kai-shek and Li Tsung-jen. However, immediately after Little arrived in China in April 1943, Lin Sen passed away, so Little did not have a close relationship with Lin. The following two Presidents, Chiang and Li, were lifelong enemies since 1927 and Little had very explicit observations about them. Little even visited Li twice after Li moved to the US after 1949.

Little never thought very highly of Chiang Kai-shek although he understood that Chiang's task was never easy. Little's negative opinions towards Chiang might be attributed to the timing of his arrival in China. He arrived in April 1943 and the Chongqing government had already fought for six tough years. The Nationalists had fought the Imperial Army of Japan bravely from August 1937 to January 1942 but their morale but Little could not witness Chiang's contributions to the war as he stayed in Occupied China from 1937–1941. The condition of the economy due to inflation, and the military morale were deteriorating very rapidly since 1943. Meanwhile, the American Navy had already taken superiority in the Pacific War after the Battle of Midway in June 1942. In other words, Little witnessed while the Allies were winning the war, China was losing. Little's and the American government's attitude towards the Nationalists changed dramatically. However, a rather unfortunate fact was neglected by Little – the US and Little joined the war in 1941 and 1943, but China had already been fighting against Japan solely for sixes years.

Moreover, the years of 1943 and 1944 also marked a nadir for Sino-American relations because the confrontation between Chiang and Joseph Stilwell escalated out of control. Little appreciated Stilwell's endeavours in relation to China and praised him thusly, 'Vinegar Joe is a true friend of China.' Little also knew that Stilwell 'apparently quarreled with everybody – Mountbatten, Chennault and the Generalissimo' (25 October 1944). However, Little did not agree with Roosevelt's appeasement of Chiang as he felt 'Roosevelt has been guilty of a great deal of "improvised meddling" in the China situation' (10 November 1944).

After he heard the news that Chiang stepped down and gave way to Vice President Li Tsung-jen, Little felt that:

> At least, the door is now open for compromise and bargaining, although the Gimo has waited so long to take this step that the Communists can pretty well lay down their own terms. The great question underlying any settlement seems to me to be: will the Russians, through puppets and stooges, control whatever new government comes in, or will it be a

purely Chinese show? If the former, we are in for serious trouble; if the latter, we'll be here a long time.

(1 January 1949)

But Little still felt that:

> This is good news, because, although his [Chiang's] departure will not of itself solve China's problems, no solution was possible as long as he stayed at the helm. I proposed a toast to the Generalissimo, and said that, while we were all glad that at last he had seen the light and stepped aside, and although he is responsible for most of the misfortunes of the country during the past 3 years, nevertheless the people of China and the Allies owe him a great debt of gratitude for what he did between 1930 and 1945, and especially for stubbornly refusing to give in to the Japs between 1937 and 1941.
>
> (21 January 1949)

After Chiang stepped down, Little started to put his faith in the Guangxi clique leader, Acting President Li Tsung-jen, but he also knew that 'it will not be easy, and the Communists' terms will be hard, because they have all the cards' (8 January 1949). At this moment, Little still hoped that Li could 'make peace with the Communists' to protect the integrity and continue the CMCS. He stated:

> If a coalition government is established, I see no reason why the Customs should not continue. Whether the new government will want us to remain, and whether I shall care to remain, are questions that time will answer in due course, and are minor questions. The important thing is that the Service will not be split, but will be intact and ready to carry on as we have done for 95 years, if we are wanted.
>
> (22 January 1949)

After Li took over the Nationalist government, Little had 'great admiration for Li Tsung-jen' (25 February 1949) and followed the Financial Ministry to Canton. Little's opinions towards Li were also shared by British Ambassador Ralph Stevenson and American Ambassador J. Leighton Stuart (18 March 1949). Little even praised that:

> Li Tsung-jen is making heroic efforts to prevent a break-down of the peace negotiations. He has done a great job since he took charge, and has emerged as an outstanding leader. If there is a bust, it will not be his fault... Li Tsung-jen can hold on; he has done a good job, and is the only leader so far who can raise a standard to which honest men can repair.
>
> (8 and 25 April 1949)

But when Li realised that the peace negotiations had failed/were failing, Li went to Hongkong and then to the US. Little felt that:

> This looks as if he has thrown his hand in – as Fang Tu has predicted might happen. Or possibly he will sulk in his tent. Anyhow, the next few days or weeks will see the finish of the Nationalist government on the mainland.
>
> (20 November 1949)

After he realised that Li would not come back for the Nationalists, Little again worked under Chiang for bringing the CMCS to Taiwan. Chiang was very grateful because at the end of 1949, most of the civil servants of the Nationalist government had already deserted their posts or switched to the Communist side. The American IG still refused to talk to the Communists and insisted on bringing the CMCS with the Nationalist government. Hence, Little was invited by Chiang to his residence.

> The interview lasted 45 minutes, and the Gimo could not have been more gracious to President Truman. He looked well, and was perfectly calm and entirely free from any sign of nervousness or worry. He obviously has a great reserve of strength – spiritual, perhaps – or a complete lack of sensibility. His calm poise at a time like the present struck me forcibly. I could not help admiring him, even though he must be held principally responsible for the tragedy through which China is passing.
>
> (22 October 1949)

This was the last time Little met Chiang as the IG and he never changed his opinion towards Chiang in his life. After he retired from the CMCS, Little came back to the US but he started another sort of relationship with Li Tsung-jen. As he had an extraordinary knowledge of Chinese politics, Little was put in charge of helping the Nationalists to build up Free China's 'anti-Communists' coalition. And the first task was to reconcile the confrontation between Chiang and Li.

Little was invited by Ling Tao-yang to visit Li (4 September 1951). On 12 September Little went to visit Li:

> The object of my visit was to point out to Li Tsung-jen the necessity for unity among all free, anti-Communist Chinese. He, of course, hates Chiang Kai-shek like poison. The "President" (as he was addressed by Dr. Ling) took all I said in a polite and courteous manner. He said he agreed entirely with what I said, but that it would be difficult to bring about. We were there 1-1/2 hours. Dr. Ling told me that I had planted a seed which may produce fruit. I hope so.
>
> (12 September 1951)

After this interview, Little asked around if Li and Chiang could 'bury the hatchet'. But even Archbishop Yu Pin thought it was 'very difficult'. Little was 'most discouraged' because he felt that:

> If that anti-Communist Chinese cannot unite under a common banner at such a critical time as this, how can they expect whole-hearted support from the United States? How can they expect to retain the confidence of Chinese on the mainland? How can they expect to drive the Communists from power?

One month after Little's visit, Li sent his 'secretary and brain-trust', Kan Chieh-hou, and Kan told Little that Li 'spoke highly of the conversation', 'any reconciliation must provide Li with an "important place" in the government', and Li thought that Little 'may have the key'. Little then suggested Wedemeyer was the best candidate for this task and Kan asked Little to set up a dinner for them (16 October 1951).

A week after Kan's request, Little went to visit Wedemeyer and suggested that he 'meet Marshal Li Tsung-jen and urge the necessity of a united Chinese anti-Communist front'. Wedemeyer 'agreed to see Li in Wedemeyer's office for half an hour'. Little, however, did not attend this meeting but he still hoped that he 'helped plant another seed' (23 October 1951). Unfortunately, Little did not write down anything relating to the Li–Wedemeyer meeting and we do not even know if they had met, but the crucial point revealed by these arrangements is that Little was very keen to reconcile with the Nationalists and this was notably not because he was loyal to the party.

Little and Nationalist Financial Ministers

Although the CMCS was put under the Kuan-wu Shu, which was under the Ministry of Finance, Little usually bypassed the Director General (DG) of the Kuan-wu Shu and talked directly with the Financial Ministers. He despised most of the DGs (Loy Chang, Li Tong, Chou Te-wei, among others, with the sole exception of Chang Fu-yun) although he respected (if disliked) most of the Financial Ministers. Some of these financial officials were considered as the sources of Nationalist China's corruption, but interestingly, in the Little diaries, these officials have a completely different face. The most notorious one was T. V. Soong, who was Madam H. H Kung, Madam Sun Yat-sen and Madam Chiang Kai-shek's brother.

When the Nationalists were about to collapse in 1949 and the whole country blamed the 'Big Four Families' (*Sida jiazu*) for Nationalist China's corruption, Little still defended Soong against his friend who thought 'Soong, the biggest crook unhung'. Little 'had a warm argument on this point, and agreed to disagree' (25 February 1949). Little never changed his opinions towards Soong throughout his life. When Little returned to the US after 1949, T. V. Soong and H. H. Kung were considered the most corrupted Nationalist politicians and along with Chiang

INTRODUCTION TO VOLUME I

Kai-shek and Chen Li-fu they were labelled the 'Big Four Families'. However, Little obviously did not think so. Little liked, even respected, Soong. In 1971, Little still kept this pro-Soong stance:

> I liked him. I could tell you a lot about T. V. Soong. He's not spoken of well now, of course, because Soong, Chiang, Kung, and so forth. But I always found him a very fine man to work with. He was a great executive, one of the few top Chinese who could say yes or no and mean it. He was his own worst enemy; he was a very hard man to work for.[6]

Before Little's appointment to the IG-ship, Soong had already been a very strong ally of the CMCS in the 1930s and was pragmatic enough to give all IGs his full support. It seemed that Soong always believed that the CMCS's foreignness was essential to China's financial security, so he never allowed nationalism to influence the practice of the CMCS. In 1933, when Sir Frederick Maze was the IG, before he stepped down from the post of Financial Minister, Soong stated:

> Upon leaving the Ministry of Finance, it will, I think, be pertinent for me to mention certain facts which have not been well understood by the general public. At the time that the National Government was removed to Nanking, many grievances were harboured against the Customs Service by the Government and people. It was said that the Customs had become an *imperium in imperio*; that it as an adjunct of Legation Street; that the word of the Inspector General had become law in national finances; that the Inspector General had played the *rôle* of king-maker to every finance Minister at Peking; that Customs funds were deposited almost *in toto* with foreign banking institutions and had served merely to build up their strength and credit to neglect of Chinese banks; and that the higher ranks of the Service were exclusively occupied by foreigners and were not open to Chinese. In consequence of these grievances, there is/was? as a deep-seated desire both within and without the Government to completely reorganise the Service. It was my belief, however, that the political character, which the Service was allowed to drift into, was not indigenous to it, that there was so much that was sound and wholesome in the Service that the abuses or anachronisms could be removed without injuring the organism itself. I am glad to say that my opinion has proved well-founded.[7]

This statement was given when Frederick Maze was the IG, and Soong clearly expressed his determination to keep the 'sound and wholesome' CMCS. When Little became the IG, Soong's opinions towards the CMCS remained the same.

Soong was infamous for his short temper and impatience, but he seemed particularly tolerant of CMCS foreign staff. For instance, Nathan S. Y. Yuan, former librarian of the Customs Reference Library, recorded an interesting interaction between Swatow Commissioner R.C.P. Rouse and Soong in 1948:

> Once when haughty Mr T.V. Soong, then Minister of Finance, passed through Canton, he sent for Mr Rouse. Before the Minister could open his mouth, Mr Rouse had started on a speech which lasted the full twenty minutes allowed for the interview. He was justly proud of this feat because he was the only Customs officer who had ever dared and succeeded in making T.V. a helpless listener.[8]

The other notorious Financial Minister was Wang Yun-wu, but he was completely opposite to Soong. Wang was a scholar with very high integrity and completely incorruptible. He was also a very incompetent Financial Minister in 1948 as he initiated the 'Gold Yuan'.[9] Little had complex feelings towards Wang Yun-wu as Little was obviously more experienced and inclined towards a more moderate and pragmatic currency policy. Nevertheless, Little obviously could see Wang's incorruptible integrity from the first time they met, when Little was invited by Wang to 'his very modest rented residence (one of the block of old, red-brick buildings in a rather shabby neighbourhood on Wei-Hai-wei Road . . .)'. Little was impressed by Wang's integrity compared to the residences of other Financial Ministers, such as Soong, Kung, *et al.* (21 September 1948).

Although Little's friendship with Wang was not as close as the one with Soong, Little still endeavoured to work with Wang and to stabilise the *Gold Yuan*. Once Wang asked Little's advice on a new proposal 'to make use of the foreign exchange', 'snap up a lot of Gold Yuan' and 'tend to stabilize it', Little said it 'sounded sensible', but Wang had to talk to 'two or three responsible importers and bankers and see whether it was workable'. However, Little's conclusion was that 'so long as the Government armies kept on losing city after city and battle after battle, no economic measures, no matter how sound and desirable, could succeed'. Little said that 'I must say I admire the old goat's courage; it is a pity that there are not more like him in the Government' (22 October 1948).

However, Wang's proposal did not stop the depreciation of the Gold Yuan and the failure of the currency became the last and most devastating blow to the already bankrupt Chinese coffers. As he could not keep his Customs Service and staff in good shape, Little wished to see 'a change of minister' as Little knew Wang was 'chiefly responsible for introducing the Gold Yuan, which is now weak at the knees' (19 October 1948).

Soong and Wang were the two most notorious Financial Ministers, but they were two completely different kinds of people. Soong was Westernised, straightforward, extravagant and pragmatic, whereas Wang was a traditional Chinese scholar, reserved, modest and idealistic. Nevertheless, they had one similarity – they were very determined to see through some changes. In his life, Little always paid respect to this kind of people. What Little disliked and despised most was the kind of negligent, fossilized and idle civil servants which unfortunately was typical of civil servants in Chinese political culture. The two characteristics that Little liked the most were competence and incorruptibility. Little seemed to prefer the former to the latter but he could respect a person with the latter. If a person had none of these two, Little would not reserve his sense of depreciation; on the contrary, if a person had both of these characteristics, Little would not reserve his sense of appreciation. He met two Nationalists in Taiwan and one of them became his lifelong friend.

Little and his Nationalist friends

Little's two best friends in the Nationalist Party were Financial Commissioner of the Taiwan Province C.K. Yen (Yen Chia-ken) and General Sun Li-jen, both of them are considered very highly in Taiwan nowadays. Yen and Sun were both Nationalist liberals and pro-US, but their fates were completely different. Yen was extremely successful in politics – when Little met Yen, Yen was just the Provincial Commissioner of Taiwan, but he became the Governor of Taiwan, the premier of the Executive Yuan, the Vice President, and finally the President of the Republic of China. Sun, however, was put under house arrest from 1955 to 1988. In order to protect his two best friends, Little chose not to publish his diaries in the 1970s.

Compared to Soong, Wang or Little, Yen was much more junior and 13 years younger than Little, but Little had a very good impression when he met Yen on 26 July 1949. The first time they had a private meeting, Little said, 'he is one of the most able and sensible officials I have talked with' (29 October 1949). After the half-year-long leave beginning on 1 January 1950, Little cabled Yen his resignation and Yen accepted 'with great reluctance' and appointed Little 'Advisor to the Ministry of Finance at $1,000 a month. This is a very courteous and generous gesture, and I replied and accepted the appointment' (29 June 1950).

The advisory role for Yen was not just a 'courteous and generous gesture'. As all the experienced and qualified financial officials were dismissed or retired, the only expert Yen could rely on was Little, so he was 'keen to have me visit Taipei 3 or 4 times a year to advise on financial problems and help with liaison with the American government'. However, Little 'did not intend to live abroad again, but that, if I could help both the U.S. and China, I'd be glad to consider his request' (29 August 1950). The importance of Little's advisory role for the CMCS future can be demonstrated by the following discussion between Little and Yen:

> We then discussed amalgamation of the K.W.S. and the Inspectorate. After talking of the history of the question, Mr. Yen said that he was determined to preserve the staff system. . . . He also said that K.C. Wu and George Yeh and Gen. Ho Shai-Lai had all supported the Customs and urged him not to "destroy" it. . . . I then said that, in my opinion, Mr. David Chou [Chou Te-wei, the DG of Kuan-wu Shu] lacks the experience and ability to run the administrative side of the Customs – a job

> which should be done by a Customs man. I said that his appointment [if Chou had been appointed the IG] to run the Customs would shake the confidence of the staff and undermine morale. I then suggested that the proposed Customs administration in the Pu [Financial Ministry] should be divided into two sections or departments: (1) a policy section, to deal with economic questions, tariff policy, trade policy, etc., and (2) an administrative section, to run the Customs. Section (1) could be put in charge of David Chow. Section (2) in charge of Lo and Fang. Both sections to be separate and to serve under a Vice-Minister. Mr. Yen did not commit himself, but I think his mind is working along these lines.
>
> (30 August 1950)

Little's advice on Section (1) was not carried out immediately, but the Kuan-wu Shu gradually transformed itself along this direction. In 1981, the Kuan-wu Shu was finally reorganised to the Department of Customs Administration (關政司) and was put in charge of Customs policies, still much smaller than the Inspectorate was.[10] Yen's competence and integrity made Little believe there is still some hope, and he was even considering the idea of the 'Third Force'. Little expressed this idea with Foreign Minister George K. C. Yeh:

> George asked me whether Chiang Kai-shek was better appreciated in America recently and if the American public's attitude towards him had become more favorable. I replied that, as far as I could judge, no change had occurred, and that most Americans who follow the situation in China feel that Chiang has been completely repudiated by the Mainland Chinese, and that he cannot become the rallying-point for a real "Third Force" to combat Communism. He asked me where this "Third Force" (the expression was first used by him in our conversation) was to come from. I said from men like K.C. Wu, C.K. Yen, etc. In Formosa!
>
> (31 August 1950)

If this conversation with George Yeh had been disclosed in the 1970s, no one could have imagined what sort of consequence would have confronted Yen. In fact, K. C. Wu, the other possible candidate for the Third Force, was expelled to the US by the Nationalist Party in 1954. But the cooperation between Yen and Little still continued smoothly, and Little's role changed from that of a Customs advisor to being a budget advisor. In 1951, Little arrived in Taipei and immediately met Yen. Yen:

> Gave me an over-all picture of the government financial position, which he summed up as "superficially good, but close to the end of resources." The budget for 1950 was Taiwan $1,350,000,000, and he expects the 1951 budget will be about the same. Gold reserves: 1,000,000 ounces, which the government wants to keep intact against extreme emergencies, such as an

attack by the Communists, air-raids in Taiwan, etc. The U.S. is going to supply military equipment, which will take a lot of extra money to operate and service. ECA will provide U.S. $40,000,000 of goods, and possibly China will get an additional $15,000,000 from this source. The Minister mentioned the various taxes, national and provincial, with their proceeds. They don't add up to enough to balance the budget, and it was obvious to me – although not put in words – that the Minister hopes for further U.S. aid.

(1 March 1951)

It was also possible that Yen treated Little as an unofficial channel to the US, as Yen usually showed Little 'the *real* budget' instead of the '*published* budget' (this sort of records could put Yen in great political danger in 1970s Taiwan) (6 March 1951)! Due to Little's contributions to the US aid to Taiwan, the CMCS staff was also protected by Yen, as Yen was 'most satisfied with the Customs, and with the way Lo and Fang are running the Service. He said that the Control Yuan are complaining about the salaries paid to Customs employees, but that he has defended them vigorously' (21 November 1951). In his diaries, Little gave Yen the highest commendation: 'My opinion of C.K. Yen is that he is just about the finest official I have ever met. His modesty, integrity and ability set him head and shoulders above most of the others. And, he is a real gentleman' (10 December 1951). Little never said any other similar comment to other officials, American or Chinese.

When Little was interviewed in 1971. Little still remembered Yen vividly. Little remembered that Yen said, 'I can only talk to you. You're American but you are a Chinese official. I can't talk to the American Ambassador this way; I can't talk to Chiang this way'.[11] Little stated that:

> And my golly, he did! Really, it was very interesting, because he trusted me completely, and he told me everything that there was to be known, and he was a wonderful man; as I say, he is now Vice-president. I don't think he's a member of the Kuomintang; I don't think so. A brilliant man.[12]

****

C.K. Yen's career in the Nationalist Party was considered amongst the most successful, but Sun Li-jen's one was amongst the most disastrous. From Little's friendship with Yen, Little witnessed a competent and open-minded official's endeavours to improve the a dire situation in Taiwan; but from his relationship with Sun, he witnessed how the ruthlessness and cruelty of Chiang Kai-shek and Chiang Ching-kuo brought down his best friend.

Sun's educational background was much more westernised than C.K. Yen's. Yen graduated from St. Jones, Shanghai, and had no experience studying abroad. Sun's educational record was more distinguished. He first went to the Tsing-hua College, which was the predecessor of the Tsing-hua University in charge of students' preparation for studies in the US with the Boxer indemnity studentships. With the studentship, he transferred to Purdue University and majored in Bridge Engineering. After he graduated from Purdue in 1924, he applied to the Virginia Military Institute from where he graduated in 1927. During WWII, Sun served under Joseph Stilwell in the China-Burma-India Theater and commanded the New First Army. Sun's military achievements in WWII and the Civil War made him the Nationalists' 'Ever Victorious General'.[13]

Little first met Sun Li-jen on 2 December 1949 – 'I met – and liked – General Sun Li-jen, who was introduced by General Ho Shai-lai.' Sun's pro-American and liberal style immediately attracted all the Americans' eyes in Taiwan and unfortunately this brought him a series of troubles. When Mrs Cooke, the wife of Admiral Cooke, urged 'Madame Chiang to give Gen. Sun Li-jen power and authority commensurate with his ability', Madame Chiang 'replied that Gen. Sun talked too much with Americans' (3 March 1950). Even the US military attaché, Colonel Dave Barrett, also thought 'Sun Li-jen the best soldier in China, but says he talks too much, especially with Americans' (5 March 1950).

But in the eyes of Little and the American militants, Sun was

> one of the few top Chinese military men who is definitely pro-American and pro-democracy, and it would be disastrous if one side pulls him down, and it would be playing directly into the hands of Sun's enemies among the Chinese. And he has plenty, who do not like his Western ideas.
> (9 June 1952)

From 1951 to 1952, Little interviewed Sun twice, and these two interviews make a rich addition to the already existent studies on Sun and his relations to his American friends. From these two interviews, it was obvious that Sun was dissatisfied with the 1950s' White Terror against the Communists in Taiwan, which was also politicised by the Chiangs to suppress their political enemies, Chiang Kai-shek's secret polices and Chiang Ching-kuo's sovietisation of the military commissar system. However, most catastrophic of all was the case of K. C. Wu.

K. C. Wu was another US-educated, liberal Nationalist who shared a broadly similar educational background with Sun. Wu also went to the Tsing-hua College, he received a master's degree in economics from Grinnell College in 1923 and a doctoral degree in political science from Princeton University in 1926. Then he was appointed the mayor of Chongqing and of Shanghai, then Governor of Taiwan after 1949. He was the leading figure of the Nationalists' pro-America force. After he stepped down from the Governorship, he went to the US to give public lectures. Allegedly, he bought a large amount of US dollars at a very low exchange rate, drawing criticism from the Nationalists in Taiwan. Then Wu wrote an article in Look magazine entitled 'Your Money Is Building a Police State in Taiwan'. Unsurprisingly, Wu never went back to Taiwan.

Little 'could not believe that K.C. was dishonest' and Yen also thought that 'while K.C. (like any responsible administrator) might have made mistakes, they

INTRODUCTION TO VOLUME I

were honest mistakes' and Yen 'believed K.C. to be innocent but . . . the Gimo and K.C. have gone so far that they are saying too much and talking too violently'. However, Sun's reaction to the Wu incident was much more severe. Little recorded:

> He [Sun] is completely discouraged, and seemed to me to be ready for desperate measures. What he proposed to me was that I should go to the State Dept. and urge that the U.S. government suspend all aid to the Nationalist government until reforms are made. He was very disappointed when I told him I was going home by ship and could not get to Washington until late April. "Too late", he said . . . Gen. Sun considers Chiang Kai-shek *solely* responsible for the loss of China to the Communists, and for the consequent war in Korea and the cost to America in men and money. I have never heard him speak quite so bluntly. He said that, unless the Gimo is eliminated, "the Chinese race is hopeless" . . . I detected in his attitude and language (although he said nothing on the subject directly) that he would not hesitate at desperate measures to get rid of the ruling group if he could see any chance of success.
>
> (18 March 1954)

One-and-a-half years after this meeting, Sun was accused of collaboration with the Communists and put under house arrest for 33 years. Little had not met Sun again and he left no further records concerning Sun.

This aim of this introduction is not to research whether or not Sun planned to take 'desperate measures to get rid of the ruling group', which was an ever-controversial subject. Through the eyes of Little, the competence and integrity of these Nationalist liberals were still highly venerable, and the post-1949 stability was by all means constituted by them. On the other hand, Yen's and Sun's destinies were completely different. Although Sun was not executed, his case and the Wu case become the most infamous political scandals of the Nationalists in the 1950s. To Little, the happenings of this period must have been completely unacceptable.

Conclusion

After reading this introduction, readers might have raised a fair question: Why would Little accept the 'Gold medal of the Order of the Brilliant Star',[14] accept the advisory post of the Financial Ministry and keep coming back to Taiwan until 1971? On 15 February 1967, Little arrived in Taiwan; 'Our old friend is back!' *The China Times* said, 'Little, as a true friend of China, devoted his most valuable 30 years to the CMC and cultivated a lot of Chinese employees.'[15] It was not surprising to see the mouthpiece of the Nationalist Party highly praise Little, as he brought the CMCS from Shanghai through Canton to Taipei, and he had never had any contact with the Communists. Only judging from the above evidences without reading his diaries, it seemed that Little was loyal to Chiang, the Nationalists and the Republic of China. But after reading his diaries, it is clear that Little was definitely not loyal to Chiang and the Nationalists. Hence, the question is why was he loyal to the Republic of China?

Little resented the Chinese Communist Party (CCP) but he never believed that the Nationalist Party, at least the Chiang clique, could be competent enough to restore China's prosperity. For a short period, he put his faith in Li Tsung-jen. But after he witnessed Li desert the post of Acting President and remain in the US, Little then put his faith in the Western-educated Nationalist liberals. He believed that these liberals were the hope of a Free China. In other words, Little was loyal to the notion of a Free China and this was also shared with most other Americans who supported the Nationalist Party and the Republic of China after 1949.

The belief in a Free China made Little always stand alongside the Nationalists during WWII and the Civil War and after 1949. With a very strong sense of who he liked or disliked, he never talked to the collaborationists, Japanese or Communists during his tenure as IG. In the two-volume *The IG in Peking* (1975) edited by John Fairbank's team, Little did not say anything about the Japanese staff in the 'Introduction';[16] and Foster-Hall's long article, 'The Chinese Maritime Customs: An International Service, 1854–1950' (1977), also has no information on his Japanese colleagues. This constitutes a lacuna in the historical record because Little and Foster-Hall were the only two men who might have known enough about the collaborationist Nationalists and the Japanese staff and were not under strict political censorship compared to their former Chinese colleagues. In fact, in all the three volumes of diaries, Little did not mention a word about Kishimoto, and in his interview he only said that 'Kishimoto, for example, was Chief Secretary, a very able man.'[17] Apart from this sentence, Little left no reference to his Japanese counterpart, who served as the IG in the Shanghai Inspectorate under the Wang collaborationist government.

Ostensibly, there are three major reasons why Little could have decided to follow the Nationalist government to Taiwan instead of staying in Shanghai to keep the CMCS united. First, China finally got rid of its foreign indemnities and loans during WWII, so Little did not have a duty to maintain a united CMCS for sufficient Customs revenues. Second, the CMCS's integrity had already been broken after the outbreak of the Pacific War. Third, neither the CCP nor the KMT would allow a united CMCS administering all Custom Houses in these two regimes' territories. But the underlying reason was probably more crucial, and that was Little's personality.

Little's personality was completely different from that of his predecessor, Frederick Maze, or his wartime counterpart, Kishimoto Hirokichi, who were both very astute with a great deal of political flair. Nicolas Clifford, who studies Maze's endeavour to maintain the CMCS from 1937 to 1941, met Hugh Bradley who told Clifford a story: Maze told Bradley that 'we Irish absorb politics with our mother's milk'.[18] Since Horatio Nelson Lay, the IG's influence in China and/or the world was closely related to his political finesse. Both Robert Hart and Frederick Maze's

Ulsterness enabled them to blend into Chinese political surroundings. However, Horatio Lay and Francis Aglen's Englishness failed to excerpt similar effect.

Little's diaries clearly presented his personality – determined, decent and straightforward, and he was easily attracted by the Nationalists with similar characteristics, although he did not always agree with their policies. This was why he admired the courage Chiang Kai-shek and Wang Yun-wu, whose professional judgment he, however, could never agree with. Little was always a loyal friend. In his life, he was always defending Soong, supporting Yen for the stability of Taiwan's finance, and allied with Sun for establishing a more liberal and democratic government. Little's friendships and his belief in Free China made him a unique IG, who broke the CMCS's convention of being aloof from politics and continuing the CMCS in Taiwan.

Notes

1 Martyn Atkins, *Informal Empire in Crisis: British Diplomacy and the Chinese Customs Succession, 1927–1929* (Ithaca, NY: East Asia Program, Cornell University, 1995), ix.
2 Hart stated that 'as to my journals, it is curious that they, being things which I wished to be burnt on my death, should have been preserved in the 1900 troubles when all else was lost: but that escape does not give them any special value, and I fear they would be not only difficult to read, but would also hardly repay the trouble of plodding through them: I think I am at the 70th volume now, & for even myself to read them again & strike out what is not to be used would probably require five or six years and there is not the slightest chance of my living so long.' Hart to Morse, 20 December 1906; quoted from Katherine Bruner, John Fairbank and Richard Smith eds, *Entering China's Service: Robert Hart's Journals, 1854–1863* (Cambridge, MA: Harvard University Press, 1986), 150.
3 SHAC, 679(1) 28976, Inspector General Semi-Official Circulars Vol. 1, Nos 1–100, IG Aglen Semi Official Circular No. 52, 15 December 1926.
4 Chen Shiqi, *Zhongguo jindai haiguanshi* (Beijing: People's Press, 2002) 689.
5 SOAS, PPMS2 IG Personal Correspondence Volume III, Jordan to Maze, 31 December 1937–5 January 1938.
6 Conversazione, 43.
7 Financial Minister T.V. Soong's speech, 8 November 1933; *Documents Illustrative of the Origin, Development, and Activities of the Chinese Customs Service, Vol. V* (Shanghai: Statistical Department of Inspectorate General of Customs, 1939) 176.331–332.
8 Nathan S.Y. Yuan, 'A Tribute to My Friend Mr. R. C. P. Rouse', *Free China Review* VII.5 (1957): 17.
9 In 1948, the Nationalist government could not stop the depreciation of fabi (the central government's currency), so Financial Minister Wang planned to issue a new kind of currency (Gold Yuan) that would strictly stick to the gold standard. The government forcibly sold Gold Yuan to every citizen in exchange for their gold, silver and foreign currencies. However, the Gold Yuan only lasted for less than half a year. Although the purpose was probably not as evil, this was seen as the most serious financial fraud done by the Nationalist government and it accelerated the collapse of the government.
10 This is not the end of the competitive history between the Inspectorate General and the Kuan-wu Shu. In 1991, the last IG, Zhan Dehe, reorganised the Inspectorate General and renamed it the Directorate General of Customs. In 2014, the Department of Customs Administration and the Directorate General of Customs were combined and became the Kuan-wu Shu.

11 Conversazione, 39.
12 Conversazione, 39.
13 *New York Times*, 21 November 1990.
14 AIMH, IG Circular No. 23, 18 January 1950.
15 *Zhongguo Shibao*, 15 February 1967.
16 Lester K. Little, 'Introduction', in John Fairbank, Katherine Bruner and Elizabeth Matheson eds, *The IG in Peking: Letters of Robert Hart Chinese Maritime Customs, 1868–1907*, Volume I (Cambridge, MA: Harvard University Press, 1975), 5–34.
17 Conversazione, 54.
18 Nicholas Clifford, 'Sir Frederick Maze and the Chinese Maritime Customs, 1937–1941', *The Journal of Modern History* 37.1 (1965): 20.

DIARIES

1943

The first intimation I had that I might be appointed as Inspector General of Customs was in Washington, on February 5, 1943. The entry in my diary is as follows:

"at 4.30 to State Department, a cable from Gauss[1] re Customs affairs, which are in a bad way. Maze[2] and Joly[3] both want to quit; Bradley[4] wants to go but can't. Gauss said that the Chinese Govt. might offer me the No. 1 Customs job but warned that, before accepting, I should obtain clear-cut agreement as to my authority, etc."

This was followed, on Feb. 13, 1943 by a letter from Hugh Bradley (Chungking):

"Letter from Hugh Bradley says Maze has suggested my name as I.G. Hugh paints dismal picture of Customs situation and warns me to watch my step. (Letter came through Gauss and State Dept.)"

March

March 17, Washington: I was again in Washington, and entered in my diary. To Dept. of State and 3/4 hour with Dr. Hornbeck[5] and George Atcheson.[6] They both say "go" if appointment as IG is offered.

March 24, New York: Talked with George Fitch[7] re Customs situation. He urges me to go back, but says I'll find certain people ready to sabotage Service.

March 25, Washington: Saw T.V. Soong[8] at 11 a.m. He told me that Dr. H.H. Kung[9] had cabled and asked me to return to China. "Will you go?" he asked. "Yes" I replied. To State Dept. Saw Jernegan[10] (Near East) and declined job with Millspaugh Mission to Iran. Saw Mr. Gauss, just back from Chungking. He says Customs in a bad way, but that there is an outside chance to save it. He said I was only man who could do it. Saw George Atcheson. Arranged about passport and inoculations. Lunch with Dr. Kan Lee[11] and Neprud.[12] Latter also had cable from Kung re me.

March 26, New York: Told John Hughes[13] that I was returning to China and wrote letter of resignation to Brig. Gen. Wm. H. Morrison. Miss Crystal, my secretary, cried when she took the letter!

March 27: Had conference with Shepardson[14] (Head of SI[15] OSS[16]), Washington and John Hughes. Both agreed I should return to China. At Naval Dispensary (90 Church St.) had first three inoculations; tetanus, typhoid, typhus.

April

April ?: Dentist at 1. 2nd Typhus and 1st cholera inoculations at 2. Physical examination 3–4 (Dr. Gray, U.S.N.). Except for 10 lbs. underweight and lack of part of own teeth, Dr. Gray passed me 100% on same examination given to applicants for commissions.

April 19, Washington: Saw Gen. Donovan,[17] Dr. Hornbeck, and had almost 3/4 hour with Mr. Laughlin Currie.[18] He seems to know the situation in China very intimately, and to see it clearly. Got passport. Talked with Mrs. Shipley, Chief of Passport Division. She is great admirer of Capt. Miles.[19]

April 20, Washington: Had 15 minutes with Mr. Francis B. Sayre,[20] then 10 minutes with Mr. Cordell Hull,[21] who was very cordial, interested and encouraging. He is a great man. Saw Maxwell Hamilton,[22] who was also very encouraging.

April 21, New York: To call on Hollington Tong,[23] by appointment, at 9 a.m. He was not in and left no message. Very discourteous.

May

May 8, Washington: Half an hour with Wei Tao Ming,[24] Chinese Ambassador. Very cordial.

May 13, Pawtucket: Letter from Kan Lee asks me to carry confidential documents to Chungking for Dr. Soong. This means I must go to N.Y. again.

May 17, New York: A letter from Mr. T.V. Soong addressed to Mr. Tsu-yee Pei,[25] Chungking. Query: Why, having a diplomatic pouch, does the Chinese Minister of Foreign Affairs send this document through me?

May 18, New York: Saw John Hughes at O.S.S. He said Gen. Donovan wanted to know if I'd change my mind and take charge of all Far Eastern affairs in S.I.!

May 26, Pawtucket: Someone in State Dept. asked when I was leaving. This enquiry prompted by Enquiry from Chungking.

May 31, from Pawtucket to New York: Papers had A.P. despatch from Chungking notifying appointment of K.T. Ting[26] as Inspector General. I wonder if the Chinese Govt. has changed its mind?

June

June 1, New York: Called on Henry Luce[27] (*Time, Life and Fortune*). A charming and intelligent man.

June 2, New York: Cable from Sir Frederick Maze congratulating me on my appointment as Acting Inspector General of Customs. The mystery deepens! With John Hughes, called on Gen. Donovan at the St. Regis. Gen. Donovan told me that, if I didn't like job in China, he wanted me back in O.S.S.

Back in Pawtucket: Mother told me the Providence Journal had phoned and said an A.P. despatch from Chungking announced my appointment as Acting I.G. I was glad to have this news from her, and only regret that Alice and my father weren't here to know it.

(I spent practically all April, May and June waiting for the Chinese Embassy to get me air transportation to Chungking.)

June 28, Pawtucket: Letter from Kan Lee says I'll probably get seat in plane in a few days.

July

July 3, Pawtucket: Dr. Kan Lee phoned from Washington. Said State Dept. had informed Embassy that no civilians could travel by Africa air route, and that I would have to go by boat from Pacific port. Dr. Lee, however, will make an effort through his 'internal organization' (whatever that is!) to secure air passage. He will let me know in a week. If he fails, I shall go by boat.

July 8, Pawtucket: Miss Crystal called from New York at 6 p.m. and said that Mr. Bell, of State Dept., had tried to call me. At 7:45 I tried to call him at his home, but, after 1-1/2 hours, the operator finally said 'nobody answers.'

July 9, Pawtucket: Called Mr. Bell at State Dept. He offers me passage from the Pacific coast tomorrow! Of course I told him it was impossible.

July 12, Pawtucket: Mr. Bell of State Dept. phoned and said I could sail from west coast on July 18. Called Jack, who arranged for me to leave at 8.45 TWA flight 7 for Los Angeles on July 14. Called Bell, who said that Army would grant priorities. Called Kan Lee, who called back at 5 p.m. He said he was trying to contact T.V. Soong with view to securing air passage. T.V. out of Washington, so Dr. Lee asked me to telephone him at 3 p.m. July 14 from New York! What a situation! As I can take 175 lbs. if I go by sea, I started additional packing.

July 14, New York: Phoned Kan Lee, who said "no possibility" of getting air passage for me via Africa. To TWA to get ticket to Los Angeles. To 630 Fifth Ave. to get passport extended, Australian visa, and to see John Hughes, Allman etc. I Left La Guardia on flight 7 shortly after 9. No berths; sat up all night."

July 15: Got quite a lot of sleep, but tired nevertheless. Fine trip as far as Albuquerque, after which I was beautifully air-sick over the mountains. Pretty bumpy, although good weather. Arrived Los Angeles, feeling like a dish-rag, at 3:30 and went to Biltmore Hotel.

July 16: Called on T.K. Chang,[28] Chinese Consul General, who had Andy Anderson[29] and me to lunch at University Club. Message from P.O.E. asking me to report at Wilmington at 1 tomorrow. Allman phoned that Laughlin Currie said I might get air priority after all! He'll have to work fast to do it. At Dinner at

Biltmore Bowl. I broke off half a tooth. A rather full day, but feeling better than I did yesterday.

July 17: To dentist, who pulled tooth, which proved to be abscessed. Andy drove ~~Roser and~~ me to Wilmington. Reported to Capt. Laughlin, P.O.E., a fine chap. Told we sail tomorrow. Just examining baggage when Capt. Laughlin had phone call from Washington cancelling my sailing and requesting me to come to Washington. I assume this means going by air via Africa. To Los Angeles. Left Los Angeles at 11 p.m. by TWA plane.

July 18: Slept most all night, and not sick. Fine flying weather. Arrived Pittsburgh 6 p.m., changed planes to Pennsylvania Central, but waited 3-1/2 hours. Arrived Washington at 11 p.m., and went to Roger Smith Hotel. Some week!

July 19: To Army Air Force, Gravelly Point, saw Capt. Farmer and got all instructions for journey to Chungking. I have been impressed by Army's efficiency. Lunch with Judge Allman. Phoned Laughlin Currie, who said that he had intervened regarding my air priority "in view of importance of Inspector General's position." To dentist to check extraction wound.

July 20: Talked to Jo Ballantine and Dr. Hornbeck. Both have been very encouraging and helpful. Had physical examination (Dr. Hardin) required by Army Air Force. Passed O.K. Very hot here, and I'm fatigued.

July 21: Up at 4:30 a.m.; to airport at 5:15. Weighed in, broke fast, left at 7 a.m. on a C-75 (ex-T.W.A. Stratoliner). 9 passengers, 6 of whom are civilians. Larry Adler (harmonica player), Jack Benny (radio), Anna Lee (movie actress), and Winnie Shaw (torch singer) are off to play the camps abroad. Also Roy Moore, General Motors, *en route* to India. After smooth flight reached Miami at 2, where we lunched at Battle Creek Hotel. Miami and hell differ only by 10 degrees Fahrenheit. After loading 19 military passengers, we left at 5 and reached Baranca Field, Puerto Rico at 11:30. I was a little sick, and wanted no food. Left Puerto Rico just after midnight.

July 22: Landed at Georgetown, British Guiana, at 6:30 after an uncomfortable night with temperature down in the 50's. The soldiers are a happy, pleasant crowd, and played a lot of poker. Took off at 7:30. Jack Benny and Larry Adler played for us. Adler played "Hungarian Rhapsody". He is a real artist. Anna Lee is a Hurell photograph type: small, with lovely red hair and blue eyes. Her feet were in the small of my back for 3 hours last night. Landed at Belem at 3.30 p.m. and had lunch at the Officer's Mess. Curiously, no coffee. At 5, took off for Natal, which we reached (after crossing Amazon) at 11:30 p.m. 5,000 miles in about 40 elapsed hours. Enjoyed shave, bath and bed.

July 23: Up at 8.30, breakfast at 9. I have admired the organization, efficiency and personnel of the U.S. Air Force. At 6 p.m., I was told to proceed at 8, so, after watching Jack Benny and his troupe for half an hour, I went to the field, only to be told the flight had been cancelled. This means another 24 hours here, and I am not disappointed.

July 24: Lazy day. Enjoyed meals, eaten at leisure. To dentist, who packed my "dry socket", which, he said, was the result of flying so soon after extraction.

Altitude prevents clot formation. Had a beer with Moore at PX at 5: beer line formed at 4.30. One bottle at a time, so some soldiers drank their first quart while going through line second time. I leave Moore here, because his priority is 3, mine 2.

July 25: Left Natal in "Liberator" at 9 p. m. On mattress on floor of bomb bay. Terribly uncomfortable, windy and cold and noisy. I was only civilian passenger. Reached Ascension Island at 6, and breakfasted. The bleakest place I have ever seen. Took off at 7, reached Accra (Gold Coast) at 3 Natal time, 6 Accra time. Fine supper at Officer's Mess. Fell in dark and sprained or broke index finger of left hand.

July 26: Dr. x-rayed fingers last night; not broken, but probably dislocated; severe strain and doctor put it in splint. At 1.30 a.m., woke in pain and removed splint. To field; no orders. To PX to buy tobacco, shirt, toothpaste, soap. News is that Mussolini has resigned in favour of Pietro Badoglio. Feeling among officers with whom I have talked is that Germany will be finished this year. Called on the Chinese Ministry of Information. He was with Mme. Chiang Kai-shek's[30] party, but left behind here for a serious operation. He seems to be getting better. An old man – he was with Japanese Army as correspondent in Russo-Jap War. Read in Officer's Club after dinner. Jack Benny and company gave a show, which I did not attend.

July 27: To dispensary to have wrist bandaged and finger examined. Latter very swollen. Walked in camp. Had an hour's talk on American foreign policy and Anti-Semitism. On return from War I, he wanted to ski at Lake Placid, but (although in uniform) was denied admittance at the Lake Placid Club. Painted sorry picture of Customs. Got on list at 8, and left Accra at about 11, in a DC3 (C-47).

July 28: Across Africa in a bucket seat! 21 passengers, all but me military. Supper at Khartoum and a shave and bath. Lay down on a real bed (!) from 9 until I was called (an hour too early) in time to board the plane at 1.30 a.m. Some of these places we stopped at are pretty desolate, and service there must be far from agreeable. What a wonderful job has been done in constructing these bases and intermediate stations half way around the world. And all in 18 months!

July 29: Left Khartoum 1.30 a.m. Arrived Aden at 6:30, and met Chang Fu-yun,[31] who is *en route* to Washington. Breakfasted together. Chang says Kung wants Loy Chang[32] out, but has no successor yet. Says Ting "ambitious". Said employees of other revenue departments have means of "supplementing" income, but Customs men do not (I hope not!). Agrees Customs valuable to China; thinks Kung will support my demand for adequate wages "up to a point". Not too encouraging. Lunch at Salalah (a bleak desert), where all 21 of us spent night in a Nissen Hut. No fresh water, except to drink. Bucket seats size, shape and appearance of a cafeteria tray – very uncomfortable. Plane very cold at high altitudes, but hot as the devil at stops.

July 30: After a lousy breakfast in this desolate spot, left at 7, flew across to Karachi, India, arriving at 12.30. U.S.A.F. has great establishment here. All officers and men who came with me from Accra will get their dispersal orders here. I am staying at airport, in a comfortable 2-bed room. Wired Ting "arrived India"* (not permitted to say Karachi). To Post Exchange to buy tobacco and lots of other things, but found the shelves bare of almost everything. My shave and bath (a 6-ft affair) were delightful.

July 31: What a night! At 4.30 a.m., and for what seemed hours, all the planes in India warmed up just outside my window. Got back to sleep and woke at 9.15. To Karachi by Army truck. Bought some Capstan tobacco, and toilet articles. Hour in Officer's Club, then to Air Base in taxi. Passed R.A.F. base – a huge place, too.

August

August 1: A long, lazy, warmish day. Loafed, read, wrote letters. 27 young Chinese pursuit pilots, trained in America, arrived today; pleasant to hear Mandarin again. Found that my name had not been put on passenger list here by mistake! Lucky, or I should have been here indefinitely. Will probably get away Tuesday.

August 2: One mail plane broke down so there is a delay; I expect leave Wednesday. To Karachi, and bought a pair of India-made shoes for Rupees 25 (about $8.00). Also a little more shaving soap. Bought 7 pounds of toffee for the Chinese pilots. This is desolate country – a veritable desert, flat, sandy and arid. Food here quite good, and turbaned boys very attentive. A sleepless night, at least until almost 3 a.m. Woke at 9.30 and missed breakfast.

August 3: A lazy day. Light rain, and not uncomfortably hot. To Army dentist, who packed my "dry socket" with sulphanilamide powder. Says there is some infection. Moved to new room; with a civilian named Means, a tank engineer (from a War Dept. arsenal) who has been 2-1/2 years in Africa, Abyssinia, etc., training British troops. He sounded off against the English: "cultivated stupidity". "There'll only be the British Islands left of the Empire in 20 years." "We're pointing our guns at the wrong people." etc., etc. I had back at him hard.

August 4: Called at 6, scheduled take-off at 7:30. Got off at 10 in a C-46, but had to land immediately because one wheel wouldn't come up. Got away at 10:30. Delhi at 12:15 – hot. An attractive place, from air. Hamburg sandwich. A sergeant remarked "We'll see the Taj Mahal at Agra." A Captain asked: "What is the Taj Mahal?"!! Agra at 4:30. Barracks canvas bunks. Nice Officers' Club. Constipated 3 days, so went to dispensary, where I was given a dose of salts, which acted violently. In fact, they acted while I was at the Taj Mahal, and I had to seek a secluded spot in bushes. Felt rotten after 3 movements, so went to bed. The Taj Mahal no disappointment. It is a dream frozen in marble, and set in a fairy garden.

August 5: Up at 4:30, with cramps, etc. Ate an egg for breakfast; feeling washed out. Got a dose of diarrhea medicine at dispensary. Took off at 7 a.m. If I can stand this trip – and it is terribly uncomfortable – I can stand anything. Damn that Dispenser who gave me the salts! Landed at Gaza about 12. Instead of going the usual route via Ranshi, Ondel and Calcutta, took off for Jorhat at 1, landed at 5, then off to Chabua, which we reached at 6.30. This is the jumping off place for China, and a vital junction, but very primitive. All of us put in enlisted men's quarters, but ate at Officers' Mess. Not so hot as in other Indian towns, but still not cool. ~~Diarrhea still with me.~~ Took dose of bismuth, ate almost nothing; feeling rotten. Disappointed after being so well all the trip. Took chlorodyne, also sleeping pill.

August 6: Rained hard this morning. Still weak ~~and running.~~ Shave and shower. Light lunch. Talked with several interesting pilots and navigators. Country here has extensive tea plantations, which are located under trees – apparently for shade. The troops located here deserve every praise and consideration – it is real frontier life. Loafed in afternoon. Second dose of bismuth, and feeling better. After supper, watched outdoor movie: "Panama Hattie." Told I am to leave tomorrow. Turned in early.

August 7: With luck, will be in China this morning. Called at 4:30, breakfast at 5:00. Thorough examination of all luggage by Army inspectors, to prevent importation into China of "trade goods." Finally got to airfield at 8. Lots of waiting in war! Plane is a C-46. Adjusted parachute. Hot as Hades on the ground. Take-off at 9:30. Crossing "The Hump" extremely unpleasant. Flew very high and had no oxygen masks. ~~Wore parachute.~~ Headache and slight nausea. Hour before arrival at Kunming pilot announced brakes out of order and said he'd have to ground loop. Flew around Kunming field 1/2 hour, ambulance, fire dept., all ready; removed emergency doors in plane. When we landed, however, brakes worked. Ludden,[33] American Consul-General, happened to come to headquarters and took me to his house in jeep. Most hospitable, as I was all in.

August 8: Very tired. A wonderful night in a marvellous bed! Glorious, cool weather; countryside here lovely. Groff-Smith[34] here to lunch; talked shop 3 hours. With Ludden to Air Headquarters; met General Chennault.[35] He impressed me as a really great man. He is pleased with results so far, and says he can drive the Japs out of the air and off the sea if given sufficient equipment and men. War news good. Outlook for Customs very dark.

August 9: To Kunming Customs to meet the staff. Talked a few minutes with them about the Service and its problems. Lunch at Groff-Smith's. Took off in C.N.A.C. plane for Chungking at 4:45, arrived at Chungking 7:10. A marvellous sight – in sunset – to come across the hills, with the great Yangtze below, and to land on the island in the middle of the river. Met by Ting Kwei-tang and six Inspectorate Secretaries, who took me to South Bank in Customs launch. Thrilling ride in chair up the terrifyingly steep steps. Finally arrived at my house, the bottom part of which is occupied by Banister.[36] Dinner with Banister, and talk til 10 p.m. I see that I must make a priority list of problems, and No. 1 must be the provision of living wages for staff.

August 10: Hugh Bradley got me out of bed at 7:30. He looks older and thinner. Gave him pictures of Edith and children.

To office. What a walk! Up steep steps, down ditto. Crowded, narrow, dirty, stinking streets. Talked with Ting. To call on Loy Chang, Director General of Kuan-wu Shu. He was very cordial, and promised every support. Lunch with Banister, who went to hospital for observation this afternoon. Talked with Annett,[37] who is very discouraged about Service outlook. Every man with whom I have talked curses Maze, who, they say, came back to Chungking for one purpose only – "to rob the till and run away." He took 23,000 with him, after disgorging 7,000. This in spite of having had full pensions benefits years ago. What a selfish man! Not a thought for the Service or for China or for the staff who are suffering terribly; only for himself. Shades of Hart[38] and Aglen![39] Maze is the most selfish man I have ever known. I have a terrific job ahead of me.

After tea, checked stores and supplies kindly left by Joly. All agree that Joly missed a great opportunity, and that he wasn't a big enough man for the job. Am I? I think so. ~~Maze left me a peculiar letter typical. Sent cable "Arrived safely" to Stewart.~~

August 11: Lunch with George Atcheson, Chargé-d'Affaires of our Embassy. George thinks we are witnessing general disintegration – political, economic and military. Very hot in middle of day, and very long trip to American Embassy, which is across river. 200 steps from river up to road where I took car. Worked till 6:30; walked part way home. Saw blind man on narrow street (5 foot), walking on edge with no rail to stop a 40 foot fall! Chair coolies marvellously sure-footed and strong. No electric light in house tonight.

August 12: Hot! About 100 degrees. Hugh Bradley here to lunch with me; long talk re Service. Admiral Hsu[40] called; he has been appointed Coast Inspector and is already trying to wangle a trip to America – to persuade Navy to hand over ships for Marine Dept. after war. To call on Dr. Kung, Minister of Finance. He said he had appointed a foreigner as Inspector General against considerable opposition, but he wants an efficient, reliable Customs Service for post-war collection and encouragement of international trade. Spoke in most friendly terms of America and our repeated help to China. Said Customs must change with "new era" in China, but be a "model" for other revenue-collecting organs. Saw Dr. Arthur Young[41] at Kung's office.

August 13: A busy day. ~~Hugh here to lunch.~~ To Loy Chang's home at 5:30, talked till 7. Came home to find Saxton and Munby, River Inspectors, waiting to see me. They talked till 7:50, although I was very tired. ~~Right after supper I had my old friend diarrhea and~~ I am very much discouraged. I have walked and talked and thought and sweated too much today; I've got to take things easier if I'm to keep well in this horrible climate. Oh! For a good set of intestines! Loy Chang is very insistent that I conduct Customs affairs with Minister of Finance through Kuan-wu-Shu; I can see that there has been friction between him and Ting. The founders of Rome were suckled by a she-wolf; the founders of Chungking were suckled by a mountain-goat!

August 14: ~~In bed all day, after a wretched night, during which I was "up" about 8 times. Callers: Yang Ming Hsin,[42] Fan Hao,[43] Rouse,[44] Bradley. Very weak. Slept most all afternoon. Egg at night, and melba toast and tea.~~ [. . .]

August 15: ~~Better this morning. Chicken soup, mashed potato for lunch. Banister back from hospital with clean bill of health.~~ Read a lot of Customs correspondence, and worked over remarks I shall address to staff tomorrow. Still dreadfully hot – even sitting quietly in house I sweat tremendously. Talked with Banister for an hour. He is pessimistic over China's future. I wish there were some way of getting around in Chungking; transportation is a great problem.

August 16: To weekly Memorial Service at Customs. Whole staff present. Ting introduced me and I spoke briefly. Shook hands with everybody. Took over charge of the Customs Service today as Acting Inspector General. Ting Kwei Tang, as Officiating I.G., has done an excellent job.

Annett, Banister and Rouse all held forth at length and separately on subject of omission of "leave pay" from scheme now about to be announced retiring 92 foreigners. This is a baby that I don't think it fair to leave on my doorstep.

At 7 p.m., all signs pointed to a thunderstorm, which, however, circled hills to south and disappeared. Reading "Romance of Bank of England" and "Othello". Almost finished "Decline and Fall".

August 17: Rain most all day, and gratefully cool. Bradley turned up while I was in my bath, and we talked till 9 and then went to office. He gave me a raincoat, a welcome gift. Ting tells me that charges have been brought against Loy Chang; inter alia, that he required Customs to hand over to him about 700 packs of seized playing cards which have a value of about C.N. $700 each – almost C.N. $500,000. Hall, British Consul General, called after tea. He was with me in Cathay Hotel, Shanghai, after joining the "Sungshan Marn" at Swatow, during May and June of last year. His "100 radical dictionary" idea has, he thinks, been brazenly appropriated by the Ministry of Education.

August 18: Busy day in office. Attended Secretaries' meeting and outlined my policies. Started work on post-War Customs rehabilitation. I hope it will fall to my administration to re-open Custom Houses in Manchuria and Formosa! Short walk in evening; "going for a walk" in Chungking is equivalent to climbing the Washington Monument. Reading "Post Mortem", by an Australian doctor; studies of famous people with reference to their diseases. Rather morbid. Finished "Romance of Bank of England." Again struck by similarity of conditions in 17th century England to 20thcentury China. I don't think I've ever seen so many babies anywhere as I have in Chungking! Messina has fallen, and all Sicily is in Allied hands.

August 19: At 8 a.m., with Annett, crossed river, picked up Ting and inspected Jardine's building, which we are considering purchasing by exchanging certain undeveloped land in Hankow.

With Ting, called on Vice-Ministers of Finance, one of whom was in – Y.C. Koo,[45] a good friend from Canton days. O. K. Yui,[46] the other Vice-Minister, was not in. Also called on Chief Secretary, Ministry of Finance, and several others. Waited 1-1/2 hours to see Dr. Kung, simply to report that I had taken charge of Customs. George Atcheson at Ministry of Finance to introduce a Lease-Land official to His Excellency. Home at 2 p.m., in dreadful heat. Just finished tiffin, when Dr. Claude Forkner[47] (Rockefeller Foundation) called. He says there is widespread and growing anti-foreignism in educational circles. He is leaving for tour of Northwest.

To office at 4, home at 7 p.m. Bought an ordinary teapot: $140 = U.S. $7. Same could be bought in America for 50 cents. 1 pound local tobacco, $240.

August 20: Rouse told me that Maze had instructed Cubbon[48] to hand over the original secret correspondence in the London Office (Hart-Campbell,[49] etc., correspondence) to Belfast University. Rouse does not know what has become of the copies which were made years ago. Maze has no right to give away documents which belong to the Chinese government. Maze told Rouse not to tell me about this matter. A contemptible little man!

Walked to British Consulate General to call on Hall and Nixon at 7 p.m. Both out, but met Hall on way home. Stopped on my way home, and visited River Inspectorate Office. Had a chair coolie with a lantern to show me the way.

August 21: After lunch, by chair to Second Ridge, for week-end with Bradley and Rouse. 1-1/2 hours by chair, and a very steep climb. A lovely house in the pines, with a magnificent view. A cool place, too, and grateful after the heat of Chungking. Loafed and talked and read. Hugh and Rouse walk up here – and down – every day. I think it is much too strenuous in summer.

August 22: Delightful day in hills. To Lott Wei's[50] for tea. Loy Chang, D.K. Wei and several others – including 3 ladies – also there. Walked back to Hugh's.

August 23: Up at 6:30 and to office at 8:45. Hopstock arrived yesterday from Watlam (Kwangtung); staying with me. Air raid 10–11:30. Saw a lot of planes, high up, and heard some A.A. fire, and saw what was apparently an explosion in distance. Whole staff with documents, typewriters, etc., taken into air raid shelter in ledge back of office. Shelter crowded – men, women, children, babies – and stinking. Except for 5 minutes, I sat outside on a rock. After tea, took Hopstock to call on Loy Chang. Wind and lightning at night – a fine display. Japs have evacuated Kiska.

August 24: To North Bank at 9. Met Ting, and made about 15 calls before 12:30. Plenty of exercise, climbing up and down in the rabbit warren of Treasury Offices. Met many officials, all of whom were cordial; the Chinese have delightful manners. Met Francis Pan (Dartmouth '26); he has a brother Quentin, also Dartmouth. ~~Hugh here at lunch with Hopstock and me. Busy afternoon at office.~~

Inspected site for proposed primary school for Customs staff children 7 to 12 of whom there are 120! I must live alone most of the time in order to avoid eternal shop-talk. Russians took Kharkov yesterday. Air-raid warning at 7:30; no planes. Had to take coffee to shelter. Ting says American planes withdrawn to eastern front, so Japs think they can bomb Chungking; only Chinese planes here.

August 25: Crossed river in downpour of rain, met Loy Chang and called on O.K. Yui, Vice-Minister of Finance. Talked frankly of financial difficulties facing Customs. I told him Service morale lowest in history, corruption highest, and that adequate pay for staff is essential if integrity is to be preserved.

Dropped card on Gen. Wu Teh Cheng,[51] who was out. Called on Baron Guillaume, Belgian Ambassador (doyen), who is in hills for summer. To office in afternoon, busy until 6:30. Everybody expects air-raids on every clear day from now until winter fog sets in. Hopstock moved upstairs today. I am still undecided whether to let Banister go in December or to retain him. Reading "Water on the Brain" (reminds me of OSS) and "Eminent Victorians".

August 26: Ting told me Kung wired to America last year for his son David[52] to return to China as Inspector General, but T.V. Soong objected. Kung not keen on appointing foreigner, but Generalissimo instructed him to appoint "an American" – "for the time being." At time Kung wired T.V. to ask me to return, he had not decided to appoint me Acting Inspector General. Maze not told of my appointment until end of May. (Ting's information, plus my appointment as 代理 (tai li) (officiating) Inspector General in the Chinese Order (although "Acting Inspector General" in English!) indicates the thinness of the ice on which I am skating!) Ting is very loyal to Maze; all the British in Customs curse Maze at every opportunity.[53] Ting knows he is – as he said – "an Irish politician", but insists that he did much for the Chinese staff. Ting himself thinks Chinese staff capable of running the Customs now.

August 27: Confucius' birthday; Government holiday. Woke with slight cold in head, and in a rather depressed frame of mind. Heavy rain in morning; big drop in temperature; wore a sweater all day. Re-wrote letter to Cubbon in light of Ting's comments, hints and suggestions. Drafted letter to foreign Commissioners re prospects for Customs.

It is hard to be optimistic when all my foreign colleagues – except Bradley – take it for granted that all is lost, even honor. I wish they would ease up on their constant belly-aching. Lonely today; have thought a lot about home [. . .] Fantastic price: Loy Chang paid $480 for pound of coffee = U.S. $24.00.

August 28: To office, feeling rotten. With Hugh, crossed river and went to buffet luncheon at American Embassy in honor of Senators Mead[54] (N.Y.), Russell[55] (G.A.) and Brewster[56] (Me.). Last very delightful; he agreed to mention American interest in Customs to Kung. Mead typical insincere, mush-mouthed politician. Met General Stilwell,[57] Sir Horace and Lady Seymour,[58] Capt. Miles USN, Dwight Edwards, and many others.

August 29: Spent day in bed until tea time. Read until I was sick of books. A lonely day. I have no pictures, no papers, no radio, no music, no company!! "No papa, no mama, no whiskey-soda." I planned to spend day with Lott Wei in hills, but couldn't go. [. . .]

August 30: Met Ting on North Bank and made 9 official calls before noon. Pleasant visit with Victor Hoo,[59] (Foreign Office), whom I knew at Geneva. Called on Garrison Commander, Chief of Gendarmes, Director General of Ports, Ministers of Finance, of Education, etc., etc. To office in afternoon. Cold better, but still troublesome. Letter from Ludden says his amah says she never was given my seersucker suit to wash! It looks as if she has simply stolen it; I suppose it would bring about C.N. $5,000 in the market right now. Chen Yu-kuan, who is slated to succeed Bradley, has T.B. in both lungs and must take sick leave; this is a tragedy for him and a blow to our plans. I had a haircut yesterday; C.N. $30.00 = U.S. $1.50. Formerly, it would have cost about U.S. $0.15.

August 31: Called on Gen. Odlum,[60] Canadian Minister. A very enthusiastic friend and supporter of the Chinese, yet he says that the Chinese army officers are most corrupt, – padding pay-lists, selling soldiers' rice, trading with enemy. What he can't understand is the fact that high government officials know all this but tolerate it. Banister interrupted my breakfast to complain that my chair bearers had "blocked" front door! Paid servants; they are not satisfied with $1,200 each a month!

September

September 1: Annett has chronic dysentery and must go to hospital for observation and treatment. Very heavy rain at 1:30; couldn't leave for office until 2. Wrote memorandum re seizure of Canton Customs by Japanese. Finished letter to foreign Commissioners on present and future position of Customs; I hope it will allay discontent and uncertainty. Finished "In My Time" by Sisley Huddleston;[61] I agree with much but not all he writes. He certainly foretold present war, but apparently puts all blame on democracies – a false and untenable thesis. Russians seem to have Germans on the run in several places. America built 1,200 vessels 12,000,000 tons from January through August 1943.

September 2: Ting now suggests that we can pay *pro rata* leave pay to foreigners on special list about to be paid off.[62] My view has thus prevailed, and I am sure it is the correct one. Bradley still opposed; I cannot understand his stubbornness in this case. Anyway, the worst headache to date is cured! With Hugh, to the 2nd Range in afternoon. He walked all the way; I rode in chair to top of 1st Range, then walked. Country lovely. Late tea, late dinner and talk till 11.

September 3: No electricity; back to 2-candle-power nights!

American task force commenced operations against Marcos Islands on September 1. Over half way to Tokyo from Honolulu! Home from hills at 9. Crossed river at 10, expecting to meet Ting and make calls. Through misunderstanding, he did not come. I waited in heat of day until 12, but no Ting and no car. Borrowed O.C. Co.'s car to take me to Y.C. Koo's house for tiffin. Returned to South Bank at 2:30; found my chair-bearers had been taken to Police Station because they had no license. Hire public chair; en route, knocked down bag of rice. Plenty walla-walla, and bearers had to pick up spilled rice. Ting reported at Ts'ai-cheng Pu meeting today (50 present), Dr. Kung said American senators have told him U.S. government pleased that American had been appointed Inspector General. Millard Arnold and Nixon here to tea. Nick says senior clerk at British Consulate gets more pay than Consul-General. Blunt coming here for relief work.

September 4: Busy day at office. *Pro rata* leave pay question finally settled, I hope! Bradley took his name off the special list to be paid off and insists on voluntary retirement, thus depriving himself of pro rata leave pay. Quixotic but typical. Quiet evening with a couple of dull books. Ought to write letters, but too tired. British 8th Army has landed on Italy. Hope the war ends soon so I can leave Chungking!

1943

September 5: George Atcheson and Ed Rice to lunch. George said that Senator Brewster had expressed to the Generalissimo (in Dr. Kung's presence) the gratification of the American government over the appointment of an American Inspector General. Ed Rice leaves for Lanchow next Tuesday. I haven't had a single letter from home yet; George said that 150 bags had been jettisoned from a plane last week; possibly a few for me?

September 6: Baron Guillaume (Doyen) returned my call at 2 o'clock. An intelligent and charming man. At 5, the Customs staff gave a garden party for me at the Inspectorate. Ting was master of ceremonies, and spoke well. I made a plea for unity, and for loyalty to the Service. Loy Chang and several of his staff were present, and he also spoke.

September 7: Much cooler today; wore flannel suit. Heavy rain last night, overcast today. Slow day in office, ~~so wrote John and Margaret. I haven't had a single word from home yet, or a line from John since he left for Africa.~~ I'm finding it most difficult to decide whether or not to accept Banister's application for voluntary retirement. Last Friday, Y.C. Koo's 18-year old daughter left for America to study music. In his house was a piano – an upright, probably 20 years old. Koo said he was going to sell it, and that he would get enough in Chinese dollars to pay U.S. $3,000 – which he said, would pay for his daughter's expenses in America for 2 years. I doubt whether the piano would sell for $50.00 at home.

September 8: Dinner with Hall, British Consul General. Other guests: Admiral Hsu (Coast Inspector); Mr. Lo; Mr. Williams (British Embassy); and Porter (Deputy Commissioner).[63] Admiral Hsu was on Beatty's flagship ("Lian" Lion) at Battle of Jutland. He also served as Italian submariner during World War I. An interesting and polished man. The Plenary Conference now in session may prove a most important event, as there is a possibility that the provisional constitution be changed, and the "Chairman" – hitherto a figurehead – may be made Commander-in-Chief on the American model.

September 9: Italy surrendered!! Hope John is O.K.!!

Ting conferred with General Sheng, Governor of Sinkiang Province and arrived at preliminary understanding regarding opening of Custom House on Russian frontier. Worked on post-war reconstruction scheme. With Italy out of the war, the day we can go down river is drawing near. Called on Annett at Canadian Mission Hospital. He is being treated for amoebic dysentery, and will be out of office another 10 days at least. Found that old Mr. Pratt, whom I met in hospital in Accra (*vide* July 26), is here in Dr. Allen's home, and had a nice chat with him. U.S. Army sent him all the way to Chungking in a bomber, with an orderly and a nurse! He is writing "Autobiography of a Nobody", to be published by Harper.

September 10: At 11, with Rouse, crossed river and took car to British Embassy, a hodgepodge of old, new, temporary and repaired (after bombing) buildings. Sir Horace Seymour laid up with food poisoning; met Berkeley Gage, 1st Secretary and lunched with him, 2 other secretaries, Lady Seymour and Miss Irene Ward,[64] M.P. This lady is visiting China to inspect women's wartime work (in China, there is little difference between women's peace- and wartime work.) She is broadcasting to America tonight. I gather she fancies herself as a politician. Quite pleasant and "jolly".

Also called on General Grimsdale,[65] Chief of British Military Mission, Mr. Richardson, India Government Agent; Sir Frederic Egglestone,[66] ageing and affable Australian Minister, and Mr. _____, Turkish Minister (who is out of town). Back to office at 4 p.m.

September 11: Up at 6, met Ting and Admiral Hsu at Wang Lung Men [望龍門] at 7:30 and went to Dr. Kung's house at 8, where about 100 officials gathered to congratulate him on his 63rd birthday. He was very expansive and genial. ~~Busy day in office, but got a lot done. Dr. Allen found moderate number of pneumococci in my sputum; advises 5 days of Sulfathiazole.~~ My sprained fingers still give me trouble, although I have been soaking them in hot water for 2 weeks, twice a day. Reading "Susan Lenox".

September 12: To Lott Wei's house in the hills. Delicious Chinese tiffin, plus excellent Hills Bros. coffee. Loy Chang, D.K. Wei, and 4 or 5 other Chinese present. A delightful company and a perfect day. Walked down from top of 1st Range; home at 4:30. Rev. Canon G.F. Allan, National Christian Council, called. Knew him in Canton; a most intelligent man.

September 13: Weekly Memorial Service at 9. Ting explained Chinese government's attitude towards Chinese Customs employees in occupied ports: Deputy Commissioners and Commissioners to come to Free China before December 31 or be dismissed; subordinate ranks will be retained, but puppet promotions disregarded.[67]

Hugh Bradley came to stay with me. He has been selling off his few remaining possessions; for a blue suit for which he paid $20 in America he got equivalent of U.S. $200 (C.N. $4,000). Hugh gave me "Pocket Oxford Dictionary," a roll of surgical cotton, an enamel cup, etc. – priceless gifts!

Mussolini "rescued" by Germans; most of Italian fleet in British hands. The Japs won't like this!

September 14: Ting and Loy Chang to "Ministerial Conference". H.E. [His Excellency, i.e. Kung] criticized Customs (he was in bad mood) and Ting told him (1) most of our staff are new men – taken over from Inspection Bureau, and (2) sanctioned "barter" of Jardine's building, Chungking, for Customs vacant land, Hankow.

Today is moon festival. Went to big feast at Lott Wei's house in hills. 16 or 18 present. The kind of food I don't like, i.e., banquet chow. Very gay party, pleasant company, several ladies present. Glorious ride in chair down mountain in moonlight, with lights of the city below.

September 15: Ting has written memo on reorganization of staff, which promises to be interesting. Hugh talks shop all the time; I think he will miss the Service when he retires! [. . .]

American 5th Army seems to be having a hard time in the battle of Salerno near Naples. Wonder where the 7th Army (and John) are? They haven't been mentioned for weeks.

1943

September 16: Brooks Atkinson,[68] New York "Times" correspondent, to lunch here, and talk till 3. Harvard 1917, taught at Dartmouth one year. An attractive, well-balanced man. He has made 3 trips on bombing raids. Feels Chinese Army is very corrupt at top, but sound from Majors down. Thinks war will be over in 1946. Says we are making plans for overwhelming military action vs. Japan. Says Kunming and "hump" air route very vulnerable. Lots of ill-feeling between American troops and Chinese.

News from Italy disturbing: 5th Army having hard time on beaches at Salerno.

Plenary conference decided capital is to be at Peiping: I may finish my career where it began!

September 17: With Ting, called on Minister (Lin [Yun-kai[69]]) and Vice-Minister (Liu Chi-wen[70]) of Audit. Latter I knew as Civil Governor of Kwangtung; latter as Mayor of Canton. Also called on Chief of Police and several other officials. With Rouse, to "North-South Club," guest of Berkeley Gage. Miss Ward, M.P., also with us. 75 or 80 foreigners and Chinese; choice food, served outdoors. Dr. Forkner is informing Kung that Chinese Medical Board (Rockefeller) is withdrawing from China entirely unless something is done about currency.[71] Others may follow suit. Home at 10:30; at landing, saw torches being sold: (woven grass, about 3 feet long and 2 inches thick.) An interesting sight, as they were carried up the steps.

September 18: Eleven here to lunch: Loy Chang, D.K. Wei, Hugh Bradley, and other Secretaries. Loy Chang talked solo for 1 1/2 hours. Very hot. Finally initialled Circular paying off 92 foreigners. To dinner with Admiral Hsu and Ting. Hugh, Hall (British Consul General); Gen Hsu, head of War College, his lovely wife and her sister, Mr. and Mrs. Hsi. Dinner must have cost $5,000, but I'd rather have ham and eggs anytime.

September 20: To Marine Department Memorial Service, and spoke to staff. Admiral Hsu (Coast Inspector) gave me nice introduction. Rouse sounded off in office in a very rude way – shouting and gesturing. "These miserable people" etc., etc. I kept my temper with difficulty. Loy Chang had dinner for me. All Secretaries, and all his own senior staff. Hugh had plenty of Shaohsing wine, and was garrulous. He insisted on bringing Hsu home, where they talked shop for an hour or more. I went to bed. This is Hugh's last day in the Customs; a rather sad day for both him and me! I hear T.V. Soong may be in Chungking within 2 weeks.

September 21: After lunch, took Hugh to American Embassy to say good-bye to George Atcheson. Then called on Gen. Stilwell, and had tea and long talk with him. He is very annoyed because of Chinese currency restrictions.[72] United States is giving China millions of dollars worth of goods free, but, when U.S. army tried to buy an old truck last week, Chinese asked U.S. $10,000. A new Buick recently offered for U.S. $60,000. Stilwell said if it continues, China can pay us all she owes "with a bag of oranges". Left Hugh at British Military Mission, where he will sleep and leave tomorrow at 5 a.m. He left C.N. $2,500 with me; I am to send equivalent in U.S. dollars at 20 or 30 of whatever rate I get. Very sorry to see him go; a great guy!

17

September 22: Hot as the hinges; as bad as August; 92 degrees. Crossed river at 11:30. To lunch with Fowler, head of Office of Economic Warfare in China, and staff. Among latter is John Waldron, whom I picked for OSS. He got fed up (I don't blame him.) and switched to O. E. W. (Office of Economic Warfare) Rotten food; poorest I've seen in Chungking.

Dropped card on Tseng Yang-fu,[73] Minister of Communications, my old friend who was Mayor of Canton. Called on Mr. Gray, Hongkong and Shanghai Bank. Tried to see Randall Gould,[74] who was out. To office at 4, then worked at top speed until 6, and walked home through this stinking, disease-ridden suburb. It is a depressing trip, 4 times a day.

September 23: Lunch here for Col. Brown, U.S. Marines. Also Fergus Johnston (H & S) and Rouse. Col. Brown brought me 1 lb. Hills Bros. coffee, 1 package Edgeworth, 1 package Half & Half, 3 cigars and a package of pipe cleaners. What a gift! If obtainable, these things would cost at least Chinese $1,500 in Chungking today. Mr. Gauss arrived yesterday. Heard that a C-46, with 20 passengers, exploded in air just after taking off at Calcutta a day or two ago; all killed.

Electric light goes off every night now, for an hour or all night. A damn nuisance. Can't read. Have two tea-oil open-wick lamps.

September 24: Ting sick; bacillary dysentery. Porter sick; fever. Spoke to foreign staff (Banister, Annett, Hopstock, Rouse) for about an hour, re their attitude towards Chinese and towards each other. Read part of Hart's Circular No. 8 of 1864. Spoke very plainly, and said I would insist on correct attitude towards Chinese and appealed for friendly relations all round.

Ting being sick, Fang Tu[75] attended P.P.C. (People's Political Council) meeting. Said delegates went after government monopolies hammer and tongs, and gave Pu's defenders a bad two hours. Customs interpellation will probably be made tomorrow. This P.P.C. may contain the germs of democratic representative government for China. Telegram from Bairnsfather[76] requests detachment for war service. I don't want him to go, but can't pay him enough to keep him.

September 25: Saw Ting at 5; he is pretty weak. Sent him 20 tablets sulfaguanidine. Office again in afternoon. Crisis in Customs rapidly approaching. For 48 hours I have thought of nothing else, racking my brain for some way out of difficulty. I think I'll suggest a loan, secured on Customs property in occupied China.

September 26: Cold, rainy; ceiling zero. Called off lunch with Lott Wei in hills. Worked on memorandum re wage crisis in Customs. To big dinner at American Embassy for Gauss. Talked with: Gen. Wu Teh Cheng; Liu Chi Wen, K.C. Wu[77] (Minister of Foreign Affairs), Victor Hu, Sun Fo,[78] Gen. Pai Chung-hsi[79] (I like him!), Tseng Yang-fu, O.K. Yui, Y.C. Koo, etc., etc. Crossed river in sampan with Col. Depass[80] and Capt. Farmer.

September 27: Memorial Service. Ting still very sick; I am worried about him. Very busy every minute of day.

Conferred with various secretaries regarding plan to secure immediate additional relief for staff. I am convinced that we shall have a crisis in Service before end of year, unless funds are forthcoming.

1943

I was cold in bed last night, and had to get up and put on bed socks and a kimono. What shall I do in the winter? ~~Mr. Roser, of American Embassy, phoned and told me my suitcase is in Calcutta, at Customs. Wired Hugh to try arrange ship it here.~~ Worked on additional funds scheme after dinner.

September 28: Consultation of doctors for Ting, who seems improved. Finished preliminary draft of petition to Kung re loan to tide me over until 1944. Got Audit and Financial Secretaries on job of calculated amount of money required, and its distribution. With Loy Chang 5–6:30; he agreed to support my request for loan. Loy says Ting is building up a clique in the Service. This is no news to me, as I used to hear of the "Ting Tong" years ago.[81] ~~Rained almost all day, but I was too busy to notice the weather.~~

September 29: Ting better today. Annett moved into mess downstairs. Revised preliminary draft re loan. Tso[82] says it is illegal (Treasury Law) to borrow for administrative expenses. Bad news, but I'm going to put the scheme up. Loaned "Marine Dept. Report 1936" to Col. Brown. Cold, and the fourth day of rain. Very cheerless in Chungking! War news good; Russia going strong. Are the Germans deliberately withdrawing or are they being pushed back? 8th Army took Foggia and its nexus of airfields. Looks as if we'll soon have Naples. Where is the 7th Army – and John?[83]

Not a single word from home since July 21. ~~Signed a check for $7,000,000 today just as easy as signing one for $7.00.~~

September 30: Another – the 5th – day of gloomy rain. Lunch here: Randall Gould says they've been "kicked around", more by Americans than by Chinese. Says Stilwell antagonistic; unless they will simply write stories glorifying American Army; he threatens deprive them of status as correspondents. Outlook for paper not promising. They have reported to New York, and are waiting for Starr's decision.[84]

D.K. Wei came in just as I returned from office and we talked an hour. I pass a new house en route to office. It is built, without windows, of layers of mud and plaster about 1 ft × 1 ft × 8ft. The roof is on, and windows are now being opened by cutting holes in the walls where needed.

October

October 1: hour with Sir Horace Seymour, British Ambassador, with whom I discussed the Customs situation in extensor. Then to see Mr. Gauss, the American Ambassador, for the same purpose. Told them that Customs has only one thing to fear right now and that is starvation from lack of funds.

Reading "Adventure in Journalism", Sir Philip Gibbs.[85] Good. "The Art of Writing", Quiller Couch[86] – excellent.

I am becoming somewhat hardened to the squalor and filth and stench of the trip I have to make 4 times a day to and from my office. At first, it was dreadfully depressing; now, I try to find a picturesque door-way, an interesting shop-front, or a glimpse of the river. Always the bearers of burdens, up and down the worn steps, interest me, and make me a little sad and humble.

October 2: With all Secretaries, discussed plan to ask Kung for $14,000,000 for next 3 months. Finished draft of letter to him, and gave to Tso for translation. ~~Sunshine in middle of day, yesterday and today. Cook informed me that the pots and pans he is using are his personal property, having been giving to him by Joly. This is possibly a hint that I should buy them – at about $ 20, 000 or thereabouts, I presume.~~

October 4: A very busy day, but a happy one, because I got my first mail from home – ~~a lovely letter from Betty and a note from Jesse Stillman. Betty says John may be transferred to China!~~ Sidney Au (Bank of Communications) called on me today. His son Jackie is going to America to train as a pilot. Wrote Foster Hall[87] re release of Jap. Indemnity funds to pay off foreign staff on July 31. H & S Bank apparently very sticky about it. Hear that Dr. Kung is sick – just when I want to see him and ask for $14,000,000. When I do see him he'll have a relapse!

October 5: Called on Soviet Ambassador, Mr. A. S. Paniuskin.[88] Very cordial, but asked me: "What about a 'second front'?" I told him that the Italian campaign and the bombing of Germany are a "Second Front". I might have mentioned – but refrained – the material assistance Russia is getting from the United States and Great Britain.

Called on K. Huang, Bank of Communications. Admiral Hsu with me from 3 to 4:45. Conditions in Marine Dept. staff critical because of low pay. Crews of work boats (surveying) practically threaten to strike and refuse duty. ~~Tseng Yang-fu (Minister of Communications) phoned at 4:30 and asked if I was coming to dinner with him tonight. Seems he sent me invitation last week which I never received. I declined: too tired.~~ Sent letter to John through U.S. Army P.O. here.

October 6: With Loy Chang, to see Y.C. Koo and O.K. Yui, Vice-Minister of Finance. Presented my case, and both agreed to support my request for a loan of $14,000,000. Arranged to put it to Dr. Kung tomorrow, but I still have my fingers crossed!

Rainy, wet and muddy. Busy afternoon at office, and very tired, but had to go up to Gen. Wu Teh-cheng's for dinner. Gen Hsu, just back from Washington, where he was Military Attaché, two men from Foreign Office and one or two others.

October 7: With Loy Chang, drove an hour through beautiful country to Dr. Kung's house. Waited an hour to see him. He was most courteous, listened patiently to my statement, asked a question or two, and then approved my request for a loan of $14,000,000. This will fill thousands of rice-bowls! My first major crisis is passed! Loy Chang told me whole history of Maze's premature resumption of duty and extreme displeasure of Dr. Kung and the government.[89] Home at 2:15; H.E. Mr. Lovinck, Dutch Ambassador, here to lunch; he and Hopstock (who took my place as host) had finished, so Loy and I ate while Lovinck and Hopstock sat and talked with us. To office, and very busy till after 5. A tiring but satisfactory day.

October 8: Tough day in office; many torturous staff problems, mostly having to do with resignations handed in during past 2 weeks. Drummond has delayed so long coming to Chungking that I have cancelled his transfer and am bringing Bairnsfather here instead. Drummond's dentures cannot interfere further with Service requirements.

October 9: To British Consulate to tea for Miss Irene Ward, M.P. Hall (Consul General) made an excellent speech, and pointed out how a handful of British (and Americans) in China – missionaries, officials, merchants – have in 100 years forged an "invisible link" between China and the West which, today, brings China on our side and prevents a Japanese "Pan-Asia" and a Chinese slave-state. Dropped brick: called Lady Seymour "Miss Ward".

October 10: The "Double Tenth". Chiang Kai-Shek inaugurated President, succeeding Lin Shen.[90] Heavy fog all morning. Worked 4 or 5 hours on Customs problems. Tried walking before tea, but roads and steps filthy slippery with mud. Read Mr. Saxton's account of the development of the Customs Yangtze River Inspectorate.

October 11: Fully occupied all day, with a succession of people in my office. Rouse seems to spend half his time in the office writing private letters. I wonder how much of the defeatism I have found among the foreign Commissioners at the ports is traceable to his correspondence. Perhaps I misjudge him, and maybe he has tried to encourage, but in any case, there is defeatism, and he has written voluminously. It's about time for a change of Personal Secretary.

Rain and fog all day. It has been a long time since we have seen the sun.

October 12: Annett heard radio report that Portugal was about to abandon neutrality. I wired Fay[91] at Macao to evacuate to Free China if necessary. T.V. Soong arrived yesterday morning from Washington via New Delhi. Reading "Daily Life in Ancient Rome". The narrow crowded streets, the filth, refuse, smells, public latrines, lack of privacy, just the same as in Chungking today.

October 13: Minister of Finance recently ordered dismissal of an Assistant named Shan, who had openly committed adultery with wife of another Customs man, to public scandal. Three days ago, Shangjao (上饒) Commissioner wired and asked me to advance $12,000 to permit Shan to come to Chungking and plead his case. I refused. It now appears that Ting had wired privately to Shanjao Commissioner suggesting that he wire me! Wheels within wheels. Crawford, of British Embassy, came to see me re detachment of Customs Marine officers for service with British Navy in India.

Jardine's building here, which we are acquiring in exchange for Hankow undeveloped property, today found to have a notice on it indicating that the Army will occupy it. Sent Annett across to see Dupree of Jardine's. To Loy Chang's Birthday dinner, his 54th. About 25 there, and all happy and gay.

Ting and Lu Ping[92] ganged up on me over Shan case (*vide* October 12), but I turned them down and sent telegram refusing advance. Duff gave me full story of his experiences here, and of opposition from Capt. Miles USN (OSS). He is going home, and will have interesting story. Says Miles brought out 12,000 radio sets for Tai Li and that A2 at Kunming had great difficulty getting 2 sets. Great air victory at Rabaul. 120 Jap ships sunk, 200 planes destroyed.[93] Italy declared war on Germany.

October 15: No lunches, dinners or teas today, thank goodness! A full day: work at the office; – home at 6. Admiral Hsu spent almost an hour in my office; he is a bit long-winded. Despatch from Minister of Finance authorizing me to borrow $14,100,000 came at 6:30.

To Loy Chang's to hand him checks for about $960,000 proceeds of fines and confiscations. At 10 p.m. he came to see me about the "new" and "old" procedures, and, with Banister, we discussed question until 11:30. The letters I wrote to John and Nate last week were returned to me by Col. Depass. Seems the censor objects to names of cities and people, etc. mentioned the "fog" in Chungking, but must not refer to weather!

October 17: My new shaving brush is missing! I think the rats have taken it. Tragedy! A post-card "Benny the Bum" today, through A.P.O. First word from him! Evidently sent (Sept. 11) from Sicily. At 12, word from Gauss and Atcheson that they are tied up in conference (Mountbatten[94]) and can't come to lunch today.[95] To a rotten movie at the Salt Cooperative.

October 18: Found shaving brush! Rat had taken it under box in bathroom. About 1/2 of hair gone. It looks like a rat's nest.

With Ting, called on Dr. Eng Wen-hao,[96] Minister of Economics. He is a famous geologist; told me that Szechuan is "young" geologically. To call on K. K. Kuo, Manager of Central Bank. Arranged to borrow $14,100,000 at 6% per annum. As market rates for interest now run from 5% to 10% per month in Chungking, this isn't bad! Called on Dr. Chen, Manager of Central Trust, and a Mr. Chung, also of Central Trust. I knew latter in Canton. Central Trust willing to lend money to Customs Cooperative at 2% per month – as a special favor. Dropped cards on Tsu-yee Pei.

Busy in office till 5, then crossed river again to cocktail party at British Military Headquarters. Neither our host – Gen. Grimsdale – nor the guest of honor – Lord Louis Mountbatten – was there. Probably "in conference" with Generalissimo. (I was right in my guess as to Gauss's conference yesterday.)

October 19: To office, then with Ting to see Minister of Finance. Waited 2-1/2 hours for him to come back from meeting of Executive Yuan. Thanked him for $14,100,000 and gave him letter of appreciation. Ting told him that he and Customs party are all ready to proceed to Sinkiang to open Custom House on frontier. Lunch at 2:30. Dr. Arthur Young to dinner and to spend night. Also had Dr. John K. Fairbank[97] (OSS). He is still a little too "Harvard" for my taste. "Barney" Bairnsfather arrived unannounced from Lanchow. He is to be my Personal Secretary. Had Banister into dinner, and a pleasant evening of discussion. Weather still rotten, fug, drizzle, rain and mud. Electric light very weak from 4 p.m. to about 8.

1943

October 20: Arthur Young left after breakfast. We talked of the situation in the Customs. He left me a memorandum of extracts from the "Inter-Allied Commission on Post-War Requirements" (Report to Allied Governments – June, 1943). Customs may be able to help in case of China. ~~Good day in office, and got quite a lot done.~~ Decided to send Drummond to Wuchow as Administrative Commissioner under Yang Min-hsin; hope the combination works, but I've got my fingers crossed.

~~Took Bairnsfather down to see Loy Chang at 7:30, but he was out.~~ Reading "Daily Life in Ancient Rome" by Jérôme Carcopino[98] – excellent. Also "How Green was my Valley" by Llewellyn.[99]

October 21: Walter Fowler and McGovern (Board of Economic Welfare) to lunch here, with Hopstock and Bairnsfather. 13th and 14th day of rain. Dr. Young sent me copy of Kung's cable to Soong, dated March 1943. This cable directed Soong to offer me post of Acting Inspector General, yet, when I asked Soong in Washington what job Kung wanted me for, he replied: "I don't know." H.E. Dr. Soong, Minister of Foreign Affairs, lied. I also want to find out what Kung cabled to Neprud at about the same time.

Took Bairnsfather to call on Loy Chang. Bairnsfather explained to a new Chinese cook how to make haggis. The cook replied, smiling: "Oh, I know how to make this dish: I used to cook it for the "Yang tu hui" (羊肚匯) (sheep's stomach society) = St. Andrew's Society ("An du").

Annett told me that he discussed with Sir F. Maze the pay I was to get. Freddy mentioned a sum, and Annett remarked that Little might not be willing to come out for such a sum. Freddy replied: "He'll come out for anything he can get". Nice baby, Freddy! He was little better than a pickpocket.

October 23: 21 to buffet lunch here: Sir Horace and Lady Seymour (British Ambassador); Canon and Mrs. Allen; Mr. and Mrs. O.K. Yui; Mr. and Mrs. Y.C. Koo (Vice-Minister of Finance); Mr. K.K. Kuo (Mgr. Central Bank); Loy Chang; Col. C.C. Brown (USMC); Commander (Dr.) Harrington, USN; Berkeley Gage (Counsellor of British Embassy); Banister; Annett; Bairnsfather; Rouse; Porter; Hopstock. Good food and talk. Paul Blunt arrived last night.

Busy in office until 6, still working on distribution of $14,100,000 loan. A very complicated task. Worked for an hour after dinner on same task.

October 24: Tragedy! Lost my wonderful W.C.D. pipe today. It dropped out of my pocket while on the road to the hills!

With Capt. Lightbody (British Military Mission) and Miss Jardine (Embassy), walked to Annett's house on second range. Frightfully muddy and slippery. Nice picnic lunch, and back about 5:15. Ting came in at 8. He has been ordered to stand by to go to Sinkiang. He told me that Dr. Kung had appointed him Deputy Inspector General. I am very pleased, and it is a well-deserved honour. Also, it will make it more difficult for the government to appoint an "outside" politician to succeed me. He said that I would be confirmed before long.

October 25: First letter from Mother came today! At Memorial Service, I announced Ting's appointment as DIG.[100] Attended opening of Customs Staff

Primary School – a nice group of children (about 75) from 5 to 12 years. Spoke briefly. Conference from 2:30 to 4:30 arranging final details of distribution of "Emergency Subsistence Loan." Telegrams will go out to all ports tomorrow – a great relief! Spending the money has proved much harder than getting it! The deputation to open Custom House in Sinkiang came to bid me final good-bye and "ask for instructions". A.P. Blunt, British Red Cross, here to tea, dinner, and to spend night. We talked from 5:30 to 10:30 with scarcely a pause. I was tired at bed-time!

October 26: Paul Blunt left after breakfast. He has lost over 30 pounds, and looks slightly emaciated and older. He is just over 60. His title is "Commissioner" and he says he ranks with a Lieutenant General! God bless his aristocratic, simple, good soul!

Had a letter today from Mrs. W.W. Willoughby, wife of former Secretary to Francis B. Sayre, whom I met *en route* to China in 1939. A bright and attractive young woman. She says she has written a book: "I Was On Corrigedor", which is selling well. It was nice of her to remember me and to write. Hopstock gave me a magnificent checked woollen scarf! A marvellous gift, which I put to immediate use, as I was chilled through when I got home from office.

October 27: Ting and his party left today for Sinkiang to open Custom Houses on Soviet Frontier. They will go west of Chungking further than Chungking is from the sea. It is more a political move *vis-à-vis* Russia than a revenue concern.[101]

Loaned $100,000 to Customs Cooperative to buy coal for sale to staff. Much against my will, because I find that the Coop has been badly mismanaged. Home at 5:30, with makings of a cold, so went to bed to get warm. Lott Wei sent me a cat – "Jennie" or "Jenny", to scare the rats away. Paul Blunt dropped in for a chat. Read long memos re reorganization of staff – a most complicated business.

October 28: In bed all day, trying to break up a nasty cold. About everyone in Chungking has one, and I expect to leave the place with chronic bronchitis and catarrh – if no worse. Quel climat! And yet, the sun shone today – first time in weeks.

October 29: To office, although still full of cold. In afternoon, to Turkish Embassy (a Legation until today), for celebration of 10th anniversary of something or other. Awfully crowded, and a small place. Had short chat with Quo Tai-chi, who looks the same as when I saw him in Geneva in 1932. Saw Gauss, Atcheson, and several other friends, in and out of uniform.

October 30: Trouble, Trouble, boil and bubble! Miscellaneous staff in River Office threaten refuse duty unless they get $1000 increase instead of $600. Admiral Hsu junketing at Kweilin instead of facing the music. Saxton came to my house at 7 p.m.; suggests police protection. Lunch at Fergus Johnston's (B & S). About 14 there; very poor food (buffet). Invited at 12:45; hurried to get there; ate at 2! Finished "How Green was my Valley".

October 31: Quiet day; did not leave compound. Worked on staff re-organization. Lu Ping came at 3 and stayed till 5. Thinks Marine Dept. trouble will be settled on my terms, i.e., carry on work and present grievances through regular channels; my alternative: dismissal.

November

November 1: Marine Dept. survey ship left for duty.

With Lu Ping, Banister, Tso and Fang Tu, attended big meeting of Ts'ai-cheng Pu employees to celebrate 10th anniversary of Dr. Kung's appointment as Minister of Finance. Two hours of speeches: Dr. Kung, Gen. Ho,[102] T.V. Soong (in some awful Ningpo-Shanghai dialect), Hsu Kan,[103] etc., etc. Shook hands with Gen. Feng Yu-hsiang.[104]

C.C. Huo[105] to tea at 5:30; he stayed till 7:45. A charming and intelligent man; a pity he is so lazy. I am transferring him to Nanning and replacing him with Liu Ping-I who has recently escaped from occupied China.[106] Decided to refuse Banister's application for voluntary retirement; he is very happy, because he doesn't want to leave. A man fell overboard from the ferry this morning. By the time we picked him up we had drifted downstream a mile.

November 2: My cold still bothersome; it is like chronic bronchitis. Results of Moscow Conference published today,[107] and they seem very satisfactory. Chinese will be pleased; they are now definitely one of the "Big 4", as they should be.

Paul Blunt to dinner, also Annett and Hopstock. Good food, and good talk. D.K. Wei here before dinner. First letter from John, dated Sicily, Sept. 30. He seems to be living in luxury for the moment. One morning at 5:15 he made breakfast for Larry Adler, Wini Shaw and Anna Lee (Jack Benny was sick), with whom I travelled from Washington to Natal last July.

November 3: To Loy Chang's house after lunch. He doesn't like Ting's appointment as D.I.G. Agreed with my draft despatch to Pu (Financial Ministry) protesting against attempt of Preventive Board to horn in on Customs examination. Also agreed to support the detachment of 12 Marine Dept. officers for war service with British Navy in India. Slightly annoyed because he wasn't consulted when recent transfer of Commissioners was made. Called on Tsu-yee Pei, Bank of China, and had an hour with him. He said Dr. Kung was very annoyed with Maze for not having come to Chungking before Pacific War.

To cocktail party given by Bousfield and Dick Frost (A.P.C.) at Sino-British Cultural Association. Gauss, Atcheson, Seymour (he leaves for England tomorrow) and many others. Met Prideaux-Brune, who has come to be Chargé while Sir Horace is away.

November 4: Quiet day in office. Admiral Hsu back from Kweilin where he attended engineering conference (1400 delegates). He said one of the topics of discussion was ideal depth of water in Shanghai approaches; that several delegates (who, he said, knew little) suggested 40 feet minimum low water. Admiral Hsu proposed 35 feet. Instructed Admiral Hsu to order second survey boat to proceed. If crew refuses, they are to be dismissed.

November 5: Single ~~Service-listed~~ men in Customs quarters don't want to take subsistence loan; this hurts, because it indicates a bad spirit. They are best off of all Customs employees, and need help least. They object because men living in rented quarters get $300 more! Inspectorate Miscellaneous staff also refuse loan; they want $1000 instead of $600. Saxton (River Inspector) came to see me at 7 p.m. He wants $1000 more! Lu Ping, acting as Chief Secretary during Ting's absence, is doing a very good job. He claims he is a "lazy fellow", but I could use a few more like him.

November 7: Chilly, damp day. With Hopstock, paid my first visit to Chungking Club, of which I am an honorary member. Randall Gould here to lunch; he and Opper have got the Chungking edition of the "Shanghai Evening Post and Mercury" started, and he is leaving for New York on Tuesday. Told me that Carson had behaved badly, and had run off to America. Kiev has fallen; Japs have lost heavily at Rabaul. Maybe Germany will be finished next spring.

November 8: Sung Ko-chang, at Memorial Service, gave amusing account of his escape from Tientsin and journey to Chungking. He arrived with nothing but the clothes he wore. Case of the 3 Frenchmen – Fay, Cousturier and d'Ozouville – worrying me. Ting impulsively recommended, and Pu approved, paying them off last July. Que faire?

To cocktail party for Randall Gould at Press Hostel. Met most of the correspondents in Chungking – American, British, Russian, Chinese. Teddy White[108] ("Time-Life") made amusing speech. Mr. Cross, Dean of the new Journalism School, had a son in John's class at Dartmouth. He's now flying a bomber. (He is C. & G.). A.P., U.P., London "Times", etc., all there. Atkinson (New York Times) is out of town. Gould gave me one of his pipes! K.K. Kuo, Central Bank, let me choose a pipe from 3 brand new ones. I lost one pipe and now have two.

November 9: Three months in Chungking; the time has gone quickly. Lunch at Dr. Rappe's house with Dr. Arthur Young. Bond (C.N.A.C.) and Dr. Claude Forkner also there.[109] Talked 1-1/2 hours with Arthur Young about China's postwar import needs, as called for by the international relief organization [UNRRA] which meets today at Atlantic City. We are handicapped by scarcity of Customs Trade Reports, but will be able to furnish most of the statistics. Very cold today. I had my first fire of the winter in my study, and it felt good.

Called on Mr. Hsieh, Chairman of the Bank of Communications. K. Huang there. V. C. Hung, Superintendent of Shangjao Customs and Tsai Cheng Pu Inspector, called after lunch and we talked 1-1/2 hours. Liu Ping-I, Deputy Commissioner, arrived last night. He escaped from Shanghai, where he was Chinese Secretary at the Inspectorate. Lost all his baggage en route. I shall appoint him Commissioner at Chungking, vice C.C. Huo, who will go to Nanning.

To dinner here: George Atcheson; Eichholzer (Standard Oil); and Capt. Meirling, USA (G-2), who used to be with North China Daily News and A.P. Pleasant evening's conversation.

November 11: [. . .] Big fire on North Bank, opposite Customs; whole staff spent an hour watching. Noise of fire clear and loud across Yangtze; hundreds of families homeless, poor creatures, as row after row of houses burned.

1943

November 12: Holiday; Sun Yat Sen's[110] birthday. To lunch with Bairnsfather and Rouse on Second Range. Rode up to first range, then walked. Sun almost came out; a fine winter day for Chungking. Home at 5. ~~To dinner with Paul Blunt, who is living with Hall (British Consul General) and Porter (Customs). Cold as ice, but I wore woollen skull cap, a vest, sweater, and long underclothes. Pleasant evening of talk with Hall and Porter; Paul slept most of the time. Up to his old tricks.~~

November 13: Lunch at Chinese-American Institute for Cultural Relations, given for Mr. Li (Treasury) and Mr. Chang (Chief Secretary, Minister of Finance). Latter failed to appear. Others present: Loy Chang, Arthur Young, Sze-too,[111] and six of us from Inspectorate. Lunch cost $150 a plate exclusive of cocktails. Quiet evening of reading: "The Greek View of Life."

November 15: A helluva day – finished working at 11 p.m. Had Chang, Sung and Liu to lunch, then took them to meet Loy Chang. Masses of work in office. Just about everybody is dissatisfied with relief loans and grants. No Chinese could have gotten the loan as I did, but all are yelling "Gimme more". Even my cook and coolie join the chase! Reports from Capt. Sable and Mr. Oppen from Goa disclose terrible conditions in internment camps in China and Hong Kong. Japanese are damned barbarians! Reading "First Person Singular."

November 16: Busy, and a succession of headaches, but the skies are clearing momentarily. Most of my problems so far have been heritages of the Joly-Maze regimes – as Hugh B.(Bradley) said: "One had a heart without a head; the other a head without a heart."[112] I took charge of the Service on August 16, 1943, and am responsible for everything since that date but not before. My big suitcase finally arrived. From Los Angeles by sea to Calcutta, thence by plane. Now have heavy overcoat, 2 more winter suits, woollen underclothes, Vitamin B tablets, additional shaving soap, and a pound of American tobacco. Dills & Edgeworth. Millionaire!

November 17: Rain and fog again – or yet. Mr. Chang Yung Nien[113] arrived from Tientsin.[114] He was in jail for 5-1/2 months in Peiping, on charges of espionage. Fortunate to be alive. He will be Staff Secretary. Admiral Hsu – very long-winded – told me how firm he had been with the crews of the surveying boats who had threatened to strike, and then told me he had loaned each of the 35 men $1000 out of his own pocket! I was mad clean through, and gave him hell; what can one do with people like him? I hope government won't foist any more outside politicians on the Service.

November 18: After so many unpleasant occurrences of late, it was a pleasure for me to promote 3 good men to be Commissioners: Sung Ko Cheng, Chang Yung Nien and Liu Ping I. After Lu Ping read Sabel's and Oppen's reports on conditions in Shanghai and Hong Kong, he came into my office with tears in his eyes! Lu told me the story of his arrival here in December, 1941, and of the efforts that Peng[115] (Kuan-wu Shu) and some of the Chinese Commissioners (C.C. Huo, et al.) made to abandon all foreign and Chinese employees in occupied China. A disgraceful interlude, but Lu helped save the situation. ~~Spent hour at night reading letters to Rouse from foreign Commissioners over past 2 years.~~ Drafted letters to British and American Ambassadors and Minister of Finance asking them to help get Customs men repatriated. Terrible weather; cold and rainy.

November 19: Still cold and damp. Had lunch here for Sir Humphrey Prideaux-Brune, British Chargé. Other guests: Loy Chang, Lu Ping, Banister, Admiral Hsu, Chang Yung Nien. Sir Humphrey came at 12, and we had an hour's business before lunch. He wanted particulars of British Customs Staff. ~~Slight diarrhea after lunch, and again at night. Discouraging. The only thing I fear is my own body: will it take the strain? Ill-health can lick any man. So far, except for continuous colds, I have been well here; good appetite and excellent digestion. Recently, however, I have been conscious of slight dizziness and loss of balance at times. These faint attacks pass of quickly, and I have no nausea or pain with them.~~

November 20: ~~Stayed home; diarrhea. Lonely until 3 p.m., when~~ Loy Chang called and told me that he is leaving Kuan-wu Shu and will be "Counsellor" of the Ministry. He says this is an "Irish promotion", and is very disappointed. Mr. Li Tong,[116] now head of the Treasury Department, will succeed him. I am sorry to see Loy go, but I feel that it is his own fault. I wonder what kind of Director General Li Tong will be?

November 21: Blunt came in to tea. He feels that situation has deteriorated in every way. Chinese armies hopeless; troops have to be "chained" on way to front, and then 40% desert.

November 22: To office. Change in Director General, and other changes in Ministry, subject of much discussion and speculation. Paid Mr. V.C. Huang £59,000 for car bought from Kweilin, repairs and fuel. It is a Customs' car, and payment made on Loy Chang's instructions. Seems to me about 75% squeeze.

A short letter from Joly – the first word I've heard from him. The sun tried to come out for an hour this afternoon, and was actually strong enough to cast a feeble shadow! A wonderful winter's day in Chungking.

November 23: A troublesome day, full of many problems; I sometimes don't know where to turn. At 5 p.m., after I thought everything wrong must be finished for the day, Lu Ping came in with news that Kuo Ku Shu [國庫署] (Treasury Bureau) wouldn't sign the contract ($14,000 with Central Bank of China) because Chang, the Pu's Chief Accountant, hadn't initialled the draft! And I need $4,700,000 day after tomorrow! To Sir Frederick Eggleston's (Australian Minister) to dinner. His No. 2, Waller, has attractive young wife. Others: Lady Seymour, Gauss, O.K. Yui and Mrs. Yui, Tsu-yee Pei, Col. Marsh Kellett. A very pleasant evening, and a delight to be with two nice women again. I miss women and music.

November 24: To see Loy Chang at 10, to ask him to fix up the question of my $14,000,000 loan, and right away! He wants his share of the fines and confiscation money in 3 days. Said he has to pay off several of his men who will leave Kuanwu Shu with him. Also, he will repay the U.S. $12,000 that Joly loaned him ($500 a month for his wife for 2 years) in Chinese currency at official rate (20) = C.N. $240,000. A very busy day. Mr. Kuo (Tidesurveyor) and Mr. Chang (Appraiser) came to ask me about staff reorganization scheme.

November 25: Office in morning. Thanksgiving Service at Chiu Hsiu School. Big turnout of civilians and military. Gauss read proclamation. Rev. Daniel Poling prayed. Dr. Earl Cressy spoke. Reception at Chinese-American Institute of Cultural Relations. Met lots of people, including J.B. Powell[117]'s son (J.W.), "Bucky" Freeman (Mansfield's son).[118] A good time. At 6, to Francis Pan's to dinner. 11 there, and a good evening. Mrs. Pan is absolutely charming – good-looking, intelligent and talented. She is an excellent pianist (Oberlin and Columbia), and played accompaniment for Francis' singing. He has a sensitive and very pleasing tenor. Delightful host and hostess. Missed 10 o'clock ferry and had to wait till 10:45. [. . .] ~~Millard Arnold said that Milton Bates had married "his Russian girl" and that they have baby.~~ [. . .]

November 26: ~~Busy day, got a lot done.~~ To Loy Chang's after lunch, to hand him $348,000 share of fines and confiscations: he seemed a little disappointed that it wasn't more. He said that Ting spiked the scheme to give post-1920 foreigners same treatment as pre-1920 men – and that Maze supported Ting! Lt. Shoyer, USA, came to office in p.m., and talked with Liu Ping-I and Chang Yung-nien about conditions in Tientsin and Shanghai. He is interested in assisting prisoners-of-war to escape.

November 27: Decided to pay off Fay, Cousturier and d'Ozouville. What to do about the Macao Customs is a problem! ~~Very busy all day, and dead tired at night.~~

~~November 28: Loafed. Walked to Club with Hopstock to get some books. Roads slippery and covered with 1/2 inch slimy mud.~~

November 29: A fighting, tiring day. To Loy Chang's house at 9:30. He wants more money, to give his staff who will leave the Shu. Yet he owes us U.S. $12,000 (= C.N. $240,000) and his staff owe us C.N. $62,000! Got a stenographer at last; Miss Ho, from Hong Kong, whom Gawler discovered at Kweilin. If she's any good, she'll be a big help. She has a voice like a leaky valve.

[. . .]

November 30: Got repaid $62,000 from Kuan-wu Shu staff, and Loy Chang returned the U.S. $12,000 he owes us at 20 = C.N. $240,000. That's money many thought I'd never see! Cook tells me that prices of almost everything are rising steeply again. Milk from $16 to $20 a bottle (less than 1 pint); jelly from $85 to $110 a glass, etc. Where will it all end? Coal is now $3780 a ton!

December

December 1: Have appointment with Minister on Friday, and spent most of day preparing what I want to tell him and what I intend to ask him to do. This time, it is my foreign staff (who have been very patient) for whom I intend to speak. Ting is still held up at Chengtu; he is on the way to the Sinkiang frontier, and has travelled 80 minutes in a month! No sun for a long time, but no rain, either, so we think it's good weather.

Bought 2 tons of coal – $7,560!! (U.S. $189.00 a ton). Reading *Tobit Transplanted* by Stella Benson;[119] excellent book. Also *The Island Beyond Japan* by

John Paris. English sign on Wang Lung Men steps (North Bank): "Please go by the left way side." (= "keep left").

December 2: To North Bank. Called on Minister of Information, Dr. Liang. He speaks little English, but we did well enough in Chinese; a Cantonese. Dr. Hollington Tong out; actually, in a huddle over release of news re Generalissimo's meeting with Roosevelt[120] and Churchill[121] at Cairo; Press Compound "see thing with excitement". Saw several correspondents. Called on Lu Ching-hsuen, now Chief Secretary of Pu; only Chinese spoken. A delightful Shantung man. Called on Lu Pei Chang,[122] new Treasury Department head, but he was out. Had half hour with O.K. Yui concerning main subjects of my interview with Dr. Kung tomorrow. He agrees with my proposed approach and suggested line of action. Saw Koo and Arthur Young. Dr. Herrington, USN, treated my cold in the head, and Col. Brown, U.S. Marines, gave me 1/2 pound of tobacco, 2 packages of Philip Morris, and 4 cigars! Christmas time! Signed transfer of property (Chungking and Hankow) with Dupree of Jardine's.

December 3: To see Dr. Kung at 5; about 15 people were waiting when he came in, but he saw me first. To talk to him is like conversing with a moribund carp, but I guess he's pretty tired! I reported October revenue; $104 millions; record. Told him about our plans for rehabilitation. He instructed me to submit particulars of Customs vessels to be required after war. He wants Ting to return from Chengtu. Then I asked for re-assurance to foreign staff re continuity of employment and post-war pay revision. He agreed to let me pay off foreign Customs staff now in Free China, and give extra high cost of living allowance to remaining foreign staff. Dead tired at night. Had nose treated at USN Sick Bay.

December 4: Foreign staff gave luncheon here to Loy Chang (and D.K. Wei); Loy will hand over charge of K.W.S. to Li Tong on 6 December. Mr. Warringer, new Counsellor of the British Embassy, called (with Paul Blunt and Berkeley Gage). To office at 4, and home at 5. Ting writes re his pay as D.I.G., and suggests allowance of £100 a month. I replied strongly advising him not to ask pay in foreign currency. Very cold tonight.

December 5: Our landlady's cousin – Professor Fen – came re next year's rent. Now $10,000 a month (plus $100,000 deposit), he asks $40,000 a month for next year. Told him to go jump in the Yangtze.

December 6: At 8:30, went to Huang Kuo Yeh to speak at Memorial Service at Central Mint. Introduced by Mr. Hsi, head of Mint and General Manager of Fu Hsing Co. Lott Wei interpreted. To office at 2:45. Lovely, sunny day – a rarity in Chungking, and a bright moon at 7 when I went out for my pace on the "Quarterdeck".

December 7: Easy day in office. Dictated long memorandum re status of foreign staff. I fear the post-1920 men will be disappointed, but I cannot initiate fundamental changes in the Pensions Scheme now.

American Embassy sent me copy of a letter Maze wrote (from Durban dated 24 August 1943) to Sabel re status of foreigners. Banister's comment was: "*Suppressio veri, suggestio falsi,*" with which I agree. Freddy is a thorough going Jesuit!

1943

December 8: Ting returned from Chengtu, leaving rest of Sinkiang party there. Talked with him from 5 to 5:45 p.m. [...] Hear that Stabilization Board has been abolished, and that government banks will handle exchange in future.[123]

December 9: To Rotary Club, where I spoke on the Customs Service. Findley Andrew was chairman; I was introduced by Dr. Rappe. Findley Andrew told of the Postal Hong courier who, many years ago, arrived at Lanchow with the missionaries' mails, but found nobody there to take delivery and pay him expenses of return journey. The courier then pawned the mails, took the money and left the pawn ticket for the missionaries! [...] Gardener arrived from Wenchow, wearing a full, black beard. A monstrosity, which draws crowds. He must get rid of it.

December 10: With Hopstock, to call on Alf Hassel,[124] Norwegian Ambassador. A very delightful man. Then to call on the Polish Ambassador, who seemed to us to be a little touched in the head. He did not conceal his hatred of Russia!

Chinese report that they have re-taken Changteh. Hope it's true, and that Japanese drive will be averted.

From the "Herald": A: "Has your baby called you 'daddy' yet?" B: "No, my wife isn't going to tell him who I am until he's a little stronger."

December 11: A sunny day, with little fog. Lunch at Hall's (British Consul). Lady Seymour, Sir Humphrey Prideaux-Brune, Kitson (Chinese Secretary) and Paul Blunt. I told Paul of death of Hugh Hilliard; they were old and good friends. Gardener went up to Rouse's in the afternoon to spend a few days. Ministry sanctioned my proposal to detach 12 marine officers – volunteers – for service with British Navy in India.

December 12: ~~Called on Mr. and Mrs. Munby; found them at Club. Chinese chow with Banister. Hour's walk in p.m. Paul Blunt here after tea.~~ Hear that U.S. Treasury will pay government employees here in U.S. currency, and permit them to sell on black market, and that Kung told Gauss that he had no objection! Alice in Wonderland!

December 13: With Ting and Lu, called on Li Tong, now Director General of Kuan-wu Shu. He told us that the Gimo [Generalissimo] had raised our 1944 receipt budget from $1,500,000,000 to $2,000,000,000. We now have to devise means to raise the extra 500 million. Also found out today that our expense budget of about $212,000,000 will probably be passed.

December 14: Gave Gardener list of charges against him, and asked him to reply to them. Two hour conference with Ting, Lu and Fang Tu re pay, advances and grant for 1944. Ting showed me English draft of letter he is sending to Dr. Kung and Li Tong suggesting my prompt confirmation. A nice letter, and an encouraging move; I wonder if it will succeed?

River is down to 4 feet below datum, and has been falling a foot or more every day for weeks. Entire appearance of river, rocks and banks changed. Finished "Mexican Adventure". Good history of Maximillian's tragic experiment.

December 15: To lunch at Victory House, guest of Alastair MacKenzie (Chartered Bank). 14 there: O.K. Yui, K.P. Chen,[125] Tsu-yee Pei, Blunt, etc., etc. To see

Li Tong and ask him if he wants house now occupied by Loy Chang. Fortunately, he doesn't; and it will come in handy for my staff.

December 16: To Rotary Club to hear Dr. C. T. Wang,[126] who spoke on his trip to the Northwest. ~~Lunch at Methodist Hospital, very~~ slow service. Room cold; somebody sat all through lunch on my brown hat, which was pressed flat as a pancake. Dr. Wang said that Sinkiang and Kansu can support a population of 50 million in districts now containing less than 60,000 people.

Busy in office with many important problems – post-war preventive vessels, pay and allowances for 1944, foreign staff questions, etc. This is the orange season, and the streets are lined with hundreds of stands on which the fruit is displayed. The local oranges are excellent, but not quite up to the Canton-Swatow varieties. I long for our papayas, lychees and bananas of Canton!

December 17: To lunch with Mr. and Mrs. Hassel, Norwegian Ambassador, at Chialing House. About 20 there – Chinese, American, British, Mexican, Polish, Belgian, Australian, etc. I sat next to Victor Hoo. To go to lunch on the North Bank takes 3-1/2 hours; leave office at 11:30, get back at 3. And to a desk piled high with papers! Decided to let Bairnsfather go for special war work in Burma for 6 months.

December 18: ~~Busy day in office.~~ 4:30–6, conference with Ting, Lu and Chang for final decisions re staff reorganization. I laid down principle for Service: "Equality of opportunity, aristocracy of achievement." (Prof. Richardson's famous phrase.) We shall abolish "Indoor" and "Outdoor" division and substitute "Administrative", "Executive" and "Appraising" branches – all on equal social and salary footing.

December 19: Walked up to Tien Men [天門] and back. ~~To lunch here. Lu Ping, his wife and 4 year old adopted daughter – a lovely child. Also, Ting, C.C. Huo, Banister and Hopstock. Paul Blunt here to tea.~~ Read Nov. 1 "Time", which I seldom see.

December 20: Memorial Service. [...]

At 4:30, reception and tea-party for Li Tong, new Director General of Kuan-wu Shu and his staff. I spoke in Chinese for first time. Sung Ko-chang did the translation for me, and I had most of it committed to memory, but read it nevertheless! Li spoke 35 minutes, and Ting 15. The Chinese love to let themselves go! The function was very successful; about 120 present. Americans seem to be doing well on New Britain Island, but having hard sledding in Italy.

December 21: Ting told me that Li Tong advised him not to send in letter to Minister suggesting my prompt confirmation (*vide* Dec. 14). Instead, Ting saw Kung today and made verbal recommendation. Ting said Kung promised to "see to it after New Year". Ting says confirmation early next year certain. Nous verrons! I'll believe it when it happens. Letter from Foster Hall shows that Sir Frederick Maze has "appropriated" (stolen?) most of the important London office archives. I've got to try to get them back.

December 22: Ting left this morning for Chengtu on his second attempt to get to Sinkiang. ~~Diarrhea this morning, so stayed home. Rotten lonely in this barren, empty house. Had a hot brick at my feet, and cook's stone bottle of hot water on my stomach. Wish I had a real hot-water bottle!~~

1943

Loy Chang came to call at 7. Reading *The Greek View of Life* (good soporific) and Keynes' *The Economic Consequences of the Peace*.[127] I hope the delegates to the peace conference after this war will all be required to read this book.

December 23: K.K. Kwok asked me if we have depths of coastal waters. He said he can get my personal effects out of Macao easily and safely. I think I'll take a chance and let him try. Nick sent me 2 packets of Capstan tobacco for Christmas – a welcome gift – and Loy Chang sent me a great jar of Shaohsing wine [紹興酒] – a princely gift. I'll enjoy the baccy and my guests will enjoy the wine.

December 24: At 4 o'clock, all my Secretaries and Assistant Secretaries came to wish me a Merry Christmas. This touched me! Had several gifts: 2 packets of tobacco from K.K. Kwok; 1 pound Hills Bros. coffee (!!) from the Chow; oranges from Tsai Hsieh-tuan. Still waiting to hear from Dr. Kung regarding my recommendations concerning foreign staff. ~~Banister came in for a chat after dinner.~~ Today's "Herald" in the editorial, wrote that a certain event "showed that Japan was in her last straw." How can she, then, grasp at it?

December 25: To office in morning. Buffet tiffin at Col. Depass' and Capt. Lincoln Brownell's. About 18 there, mostly British and Americans. A very pleasant time – with chocolate ice-cream for desert and Bourbon egg-nogs before lunch. Saxton and Munby called in p.m. Banister dined with me, and we had a nice chat.

December 26: ~~Walked to British Consulate in a.m. and called on Paul Blunt, who is in bed with a cold. To Masonic children's party at 5.~~

December 27: Fang Tu attended meeting of dept. chiefs in Tsai Cheng Pu. Dr. Kung spoke, and referred to Customs in glowing terms. We were only tax program which paid into Treasury its entire collection. Dr. Kung also praised Sir Robert Hart's work for China, and said that he might, instead, have worked for himself. I fear that Customs will not be popular with other organs: teacher's pet gets black eyes from the other boys. Col. C.C. Brown, USMC, sent me 1 pound S & W coffee and 1 pound Sir Walter Raleigh tobacco as Christmas present!

German "Scharnhorst" sunk by British Navy off North Cape. Americans made second landing on New Britain (Cape Gloucester).[128] Russians broke through 25 miles on Dnieper bank – all good news![129]

December 28: Telegram from Foster Hall says Jap Indemnity Funds (£500,000) released to me for paying of staff retired July 13. This is excellent news, and will ease my financial burden for foreign staff. Li Tong wants me to pay for his house servants, and provide 40 gallons gasoline a month for his car. I am disappointed; I hoped he wasn't that kind.

Wrote to K.K. Kwok, who will get my 5 case personal effects out of Macao – I hope! It's risky, but I think it's better than leaving them there. Crawford, British CG to lunch; talked re Marine Dept. recruits.

December 29: At 9 a.m., Hopstock, Bairnsfather, Rouse and Gardener – with Banister – came and we discussed position of foreigners in Service. In afternoon, Gardener talked an hour about his case in Wenchow. At 5, a letter came from the single men on the staff threatening to take their case to other quarters unless they get satisfaction!! (Relatively, they are best off of entire staff, foreign or Chinese). I wonder if anybody in the Service today is even moderately satisfied. I was played out at 6 when I got home. Weather unpleasant; steps covered with 1/2 inch of slippery, oily mud.

December 30: Lu Ping attended 1st "conference" at Kuan-wu Shu; 3-1/2 hours of reports. Took him all morning. V.C. Hung (Shanghai Supt.) asked Lu wire Shangjao Commissioner advance $20,000 to "his man" through Tidesurveyor. Lu says he has no man there!

December 31: Admiral Hsu just back from a political-personal junket to Wanhsien on a Customs ship (which probably cost us $300,000), spent one hour in my office. A windbag.

To big party at Victory House given by Dr. and Mrs. Kung. About 400 there of all Allied nationalities. Excellent food, in profusion – ham, chicken, fish, 3 desserts. Francis Pan told me it cost C.N. $500 a person. I was next to Cecilia Pan at dinner – the loveliest and most charming woman in the room. Crossed river home at 10, with a happy, singing crowd of American officers, bound for the Club. I was invited there and to American Embassy, but came home.

Talked with the man downstairs (where I had been invited to dine) and then came up to my study at 11, while they went to Club. 1944: will it bring victory? Looks that way now.

1944

January

January 1: Started to cross the river to call on Minister of Finance, but found about 500 people waiting for the ferry, so called it off and came home. At 11, all the Secretaries and Assistant Secretaries came to call on me. About 30 or 40 here. We had biscuits and tea, and several of us made remarks. Banister spoke well, as did C.C. Tso. At 3, I got Customs launch and crossed river. Called at Fan Chuang, and wrote my name in the Visitor's Book. Also went to Li Tong's house, but he was out. Picked up an old chap named Dr. Liu, who was a boyhood friend and schoolmate of Dr. Kung at Tungchow (American Board School). He knew Dr. Martin, Dr. Smith and all the Peking old-timers.

At dinner, had a glass of French claret. The boys down-stairs saved half a bottle for me – a very thoughtful gesture!

January 2: To Lott Wei's house at Huang Kuo Yeh. Found out that it is Lott's 54th birthday. T.V. Soong, Tsu-yee Pei and Dr. Li Shu-fan there when I arrived, but did not stay for lunch. We were about 20 for lunch (all Chinese but me) and had most delicious noodles-fine, like vermicelli-in chicken broth. I wish all Chinese food was like that! After lunch, sat around and talked, while most of the guests played Mahjong. After coffee and birthday cake, I left at 4:30 and walked home in 45 minutes. They asked me to stay to dinner, but I find 4 hours of the talk and laughter and bustle of a party are quite enough. Had a nice steak dinner all by myself, and read most of evening. "Society Racket", – an English appraisal of English society in the 1930's; not flattering.

January 3: Spoke at Memorial Service and gave a little pep talk. To Ministry to call on Y.C. Koo and O.K. Yui, and congratulate them on their New Year's decorations. To dentist, Dr. An, who charged me $900 for replacing 3 porcelain fillings. At official rate, this = U.S. $45. At special rate (which I get), = U.S. $30. Pretty steep, but C.N. $100 has less than G.Y. [Customs Gold Yuan/Unit][1] $1.00 pre-war purchasing power,[2] so, from the dentist's point of view, he didn't overcharge me. ~~My invitation to Tsu-yee Pei's for luncheon next Saturday went by mistake to Gen. Pai Chung-hsi, Chief of Staff and the Generalissimo's No. 2, who thought it was intended for him, and replied. Fortunately, he declined.~~

1944

January 4: Had Li Tong and four of his staff to lunch. Also, Lu, Banister, Fang and Sung. Russians have crossed old Polish Frontier. ~~Wrote to Hugh Bradley, from whom I have not had a word since he left Kunming at end of September.~~ Gardener sick for several days; he is at Rouse's house on Second Range. Rouse tells me his boy threatens to leave if Gardener stays! Eichholzer (S.V. Co.) sent me "Time" of December 6 and 13 yesterday; this is by far the quickest of any magazines I have seen from America.

January 5: ~~Quiet day in office~~. Lu told me that draft (Chinese) of my dispatch to [Tsai Cheng] Pu and [Kuan-wu] Shu re staff reorganization had been altered by a Clerk in Chinese Secretary's office! Lu gave Sung hell, and fixed everything up. If it comes to me officially, I'll have to dismiss the clerk concerned.

January 6: American Embassy sent me a curious telegram from Maze, sent through the Consulate at Capetown via the State Dept., enquiring whether I wanted the documents that he took away with him! He offers them on condition that I regard them as "secret, confidential and personnel." Lu Ping's health is not good, and I am worried about him. I hear that the bachelor Clerks and girl Typists have all certified that they are about to be married (in order to get emergency grant at married rate).

January 7: Damp and cold. Had calculation of what we paid Loy Chang, D.G. of K.W.S., last year. Altogether, C.N. $6,000,000, of which he retained at least $2,000,000. (Lu Ping claims he retained over $4,000,000). This is in addition to the official budget of his office and of the Customs College. I wonder how much of this he has safely banked or invested? Some of it, of course, went to his own clique of retainers, and I suppose, some was "split" with other officials, but the job of D.G. must still be one of the sweetest plums in China.

January 8: Buffet luncheon here; Gauss, Atcheson, Col. Brown from U.S. Embassy; Mr. and Mrs. Hassel (Norwegian Ambassador); Sir Frederick Eggleston (Australian Minister); Gen. Wu Te-cheng (Sec. Gen. of Kuomintang); Tseng Yung-fu (Minister of Communications); Andrew Lu; Tsu-yee Pei (Bank of China); and daughter Mrs. Chan; K.K. Kwok (Central Bank); Li Tong, (D.G. of K.W.S.); Francis and Cecilia Pan; and from Customs: Banister; Hopstock; Liu Ping I and Chang Yung Nien. Sir Frederick Eggleston, the old ass, came across river at Hai Tang Chi without letting me know, with result that my launch, with all other guests aboard. Cook made delicious food, including baked beans. All left at 3, and at 4, Frank Howard of Chase Bank came and talked semi-business for 1-1/2 hours. I was tired at 5:20!

January 9: Walked up to Tien Men [天門] and back in morning; spent rest of day quietly in house. Saw nobody.

January 10: ~~Busy day in office, with usual crop of headaches~~. Stopped in at Navy Signals Mess to get my size in shoes. Col. Brown thinks he can get a pair of Army brogans for me. I hope so, because ordinary shoes aren't tough enough to take the strain of Chungking mud and steps.

January 11: Lu Ping told me today that, although he is a "sworn brother" to Ting Kwei-tang, he will refuse "to work under him". Lu said that he would work for me indefinitely, but that he cannot get along with Ting, and, when Ting returns, he (Lu) will have to be given another job. Lu's health still worries me, and I urged him to take a holiday. He is going to put in his application for retirement, but will stay in Customs until the end of war if I also stay. Hsuan Te-ching, Deputy Commissioner, in charge at Lungchow now under transfer to Luichow, wrote to Admiral Hsu and asked him to get Dr. Kung to disapprove the move! Adm. Hsu showed letter to Chang Yung-nien, Staff Secretary. Shades of Hart and Aglen! Rouse and Bairnsfather to lunch. Latter leaves tomorrow for 6 months' special service with Brit. Army (Burma). Rouse had bad fall on way down from hills, and was badly shaken up. Fell flat on his face, with his nose striking a rock. Gardener still sick, so my foreign staff is badly shot!

January 12: Presided at Secretaries' meeting – 3 to 6:15 – when each Secretary gave a report if his department in 1943 and plans for 1944. Interesting and encouraging. Some reports too long-winded, but all sincere and some stimulating. My Secretaries have certainly given excellent support; the Assistant Secretaries, also are a promising group of men.

January 13: Large number of staff petitioned for issue of February pay before Chinese New Year (January 25). Same old story of improvidence, debt and the desire to make a showing. I really don't think that most of these people know or care that there's a war on; they think America and England will do the fighting and pay the bills. Meantime, they do as little work as possible, complain about their hard lot, and generally fail to cooperate. I had to refuse their request. I wish the esprit de corps shown by the senior Chinese and foreign staff could percolate down through the junior Chinese staff, who are relatively best off yet do most of the belly-aching.

January 14: After moderately busy day in office (got off report on reconstruction and post-war needs to Kuan-wu Shu), crossed river to attend Lodge meeting, consult with Arthur Young, and spend night as his guest at Dr. Rappe's house. After very nice buffet supper attended by the Lodge (C.N. $100 = U.S. $5.00) for meal that could not cost more than 50¢ at home), I went to the meeting and saw the 1st Degree worked on an American Army candidate. The lodge room in a school-room was cold as an ice-box, and most of us kept our coats on. I also wore my wool skull cap. The work was fairly well done, and I enjoyed the ritual. There were two candidates, but I left after the first, and went up to the house to talk with Arthur Young. We managed to get over most of the ground – a discussion of Young's proposal that the government should purchase abroad, on credit, certain goods for civilian use (nature as yet undetermined) for import by plane from India as transport becomes easier (C.N.A.C. expect additional planes soon) and sale at market prices. Objects: (1) gross sale price to wholesalers would go to Treasury as current revenue; (2) public would get badly-needed goods; (3) imports would tend to prevent hoarding, loosen up stocks already hoarded, and slow up inflationary price-rises. Young said Dr. Kung favors plane, but Generalissimo strongly disapproves, because he considers all available plane space must be used for direct munitions of war, etc. I myself think that Young's plan would have to be very carefully handled if strong public criticism – especially in U.S. – is to be avoided. A good case can be made out for his point of view that the economic and currency fronts are of vital war importance. In any case, as the Generalissimo is opposed, the plan is automatically dead. We are not, however, burying it; we'll put it on ice, and keep on thinking of means to implement it, just in case!

With regard to our preliminary work on UNRRA, we agreed that, as Dr. Tsiang,[3] China's representative at Atlantic City, is soon expected back in China, it will be best to postpone further work on the subject until we can consult with him. To bed about midnight.

January 15: After a fair night in a strange bed – and relatively hard bed – had a swell breakfast, talked with Arthur Young till 9:30, and then came across river to office. Had a busy day, but got plenty done, and left at 5 p.m. with a clear desk and a clear conscience, although with plenty of problems in the offing. ~~Had 3 fat envelopes from John, and thought he had at last written me some long letters. The envelopes contained no word from him, but at least passed along a letter from Mother, a few letters to John from other people praising his "Journal" article, and two very interesting Dartmouth "Bulletins". Anyhow, I was glad to see John's handwriting and to know he bears me in mind.~~

Arthur Young told me last night (1) that the Sino-British loan arrangements (£50,000,000) are not even yet finished; that the Chinese want the money for currency backing and without any strings, but that the British say they can't afford to lose such a bug lump of sterling, and insist on specific uses such as purchase of British goods, etc. (2) that almost 20,000 tons a month are now being flown over the hump – more than the Burma Road ever carried; (3) that the U.S. Army are now doing a good job of this transportation, after a ~~very~~ bad start; (4) that it is the Generalissimo even more than Kung who refuses to consider any change in the official Chinese $ – U.S. $ rate; (5) that he (Young) fears an almost certain panic when the inflation and exchange rate situation reaches the breaking-point.

My nice cat Jenny is missing! Blame laid at door of a mysterious black stranger. (Probably stolen; worth $500).

January 16: C.C. Kuo, who is transferred from Chungking to Lungchow, came to see me this morning and talked 1–2 hours. A most personable and intelligent man, but not trustworthy, and lazy as can be. Very subtly, he indicated the wheels within the wheels at the Inspectorate and throughout the Service. I have constantly to fight against the sectionalism, clannishness and "cliques" which I find in the Customs; and I am fighting against age-old Chinese characteristics! Jenny returned! Boy's daughter discovered her in a neighbor's garden.

January 17: Rouse is applying for detachment for war service. He has handed in a dispatch, addressed to me, to Lu Ping, with whom he seeks a conference, but he has not yet given me the slightest indication of his intention. V. C. Hung, Shangjao Superintendent, is shortly leaving Chungking. Lu invariably refers to him as "W.C." – and I agree. An unmitigated nuisance and crook. Gardenerhas sacroiliac trouble, and will be laid up another 16 days at least.

January 18: To Ministry, to see O.K. Yui, Vice-Minister, re my request on behalf of foreign staff (handed to Dr. Kung early in December). Yui out, but gave story to Y.C. Koo, Vice-Minister, who promised to find out what is happening. I hope to get some action soon; a crisis cannot be too long postponed. Loy Chang is still in the Chungking Commissioner's house, which I asked him to vacate before Dec. 31. I have offered to let him have half the house until Ting returns, but he shows no signs of getting out. Letter from John says he's in England. (Dated 20 November). A lovely letter describing the English countryside. He is very discouraged and disheartened about his job, however, and says he'd like to make a shift.

January 19: Rouse told me he doesn't want detachment but feels that he has been pushed around, etc. He is badly spoiled. I told him that if he leaves his application for detachment I shall grant it; if he wishes to withdraw it, he must go where he is sent without question. My plan is to send him to Foochow and bring Pouncey here. Rouse withdrew his application.

Very busy in office. Banister gave me addresses of his sister in England and cousin in Ireland to send to John. Coolie brought Jenny's friend, the big black Tom cat, up to my room and suggested locking him in the drawing room with Jenny! After I had been trying to keep them apart – against nature – the coolie suggests letting nature take the course. I consented.

January 20: With Lu Ping, to see Li Tong. Satisfactory visit. Li said Kung rather alarmed at cost of opening of Sinkiang Customs and asked me wire Ting to pull in his horns. Porter AWOL: hear he was tight last night at big party, and not home at 6 a.m. Shall speak to him tomorrow.

To big buffet dinner given by American Military and Naval Attachés (Cols. M.B. Depass and C.C. Brown) at Col. Brown's house, #3 Chialing. The swellest affair I've been to: American and British Ambassadors (and Lady Seymour); Gen. Wu Te-cheng; Dr. Kung; Tseng Yang-fu (Minister of Communications); Gen. Chang Chen[4] and 2 or 3 other 3-star Chinese generals; Admiral Yang;[5] Gen. Carton de Wiart[6] (one-arm; one-eye; 2 Victoria Crosses); K.C. Wu (Vice-Minister of Foreign Affairs) and his exquisite cameo of wife; 4 or 5 members of the Free French Military Commission (and a couple of wives); George Atcheson; the staffs of the attachés and several others. Col. Depass brought me across river at 11 in his sampan, and I was half frozen. Home at 11:30, fire out, so roused boy to re-build it. Sat and thawed out until after 1 a.m.

January 21: Very busy day. Loy Chang, who is still in Commissioner's house, had nerve to ask me to lend him my car! I like him, nevertheless. Warned Porter that if he gets drunk and disorderly again, and it is reported to me, he will be discharged or dismissed. He promised to go on water wagon for good. Nous verrons!

January 22: Quiet day in office. Rouse attended Red Cross Benefit performance of "Forever and a Day" last night and said it was rotten. I'm glad I didn't go (I gave my $200 ticket to Col. Depass).

January 23: Dr. Claude Forkner and Arthur Young arrived at 11:30, just as I was changing my clothes in front of the drawing-room fire. Cook gave us a nice lunch, which all enjoyed. Dr. Forkner finds strong anti-foreign feeling in many quarters. He says we must be realistic, and not simply hand out every-thing the Chinese ask for to curry their "good-will". Ministry of Education he finds progressive and reasonable, but National Health Administration extremely nationalistic and unreasonable. At lunch, Dr. Forkner asked us if we'd heard of the sulfa-drug used as a contraceptive. We said: no. He said: "Sulfa-control." Talked with Arthur Young about his scheme for importing necessities, to be bought by the government on credit, and sold in fapi in China, entire proceeds to go to government.

January 24: ~~In letter to John yesterday, gave him addresses of Lady Seymour's house in England, which he hopes he will visit. Also, addresses of Banister's sister and cousin.~~

Lu Ping sick. Li Tong sent me a box of New Year's gifts – cigarettes, birds' nest, chopsticks, etc., and a glass of nursing bottle complete with rubber teat!! Of all the gifts I've ever had, this takes the cake. Maze gets the K.C.M.G.; Little gets the nursing bottle. Yes, Maze gets the K.C.M.G. Annett's comment: "Instead of giving him further honors, the King ought to take away the one he already has." The British members of my staff derive a slight solace from the fact that Freddie got only the K.C.M.G. while Aglen got the G.C.M.G. This will probably make Freddie very annoyed.

Read *Old Times and New* – excellent memoirs of Lord Ernest Hamilton.[7]

January 25: Chinese New Year. Officially, no holiday, but for 3 days we shall have only skeleton staff in office, and little work done. The day is generally observed as a holiday, just as it has been for thousands of years, in spite of threats and pleadings of government. After my chair-coolies took me to office in morning, I let them go for the day. Being almost uninterrupted, I got a lot done. 2 new words in "The Sawbucks" (Masefield): barton = barnyard; stuggy = stocky.

January 26: Another quiet day at office, with most of staff on unofficial New Year's holiday. Col. Depass sent me a "Field Ration" = cake of Peter Cailler Kohler chocolate, etc. – delicious! Finished "The Sawbucks (Hawbucks)" by John Masefield.[8] Just about the flabbiest tripe I have ever read. It is incredible that Masefield wrote such a book.

River down to 1.4. It was on December 3 that I saw Dr. Kung and made proposals re foreign staff in Free China, but I have heard nothing from him, although I have been 3 times to see Yui and Koo, who promised to look into it. I wrote to Koo again today.

January 27: Last day of "semi-official" holidays, and people are beginning to return to work. ~~For two days, I have been cutting down smoking, and am very proud that I have limited myself to 6 (small) pipes each day. I found that I was smoking over 20 pipes, and my tongue was sore most of the time. I think I enjoy smoking more when I smoke less.~~

January 28: "Traumatic arthritic" fingers (Dr. Forkner) of left hand sore today as result of typing last night. Lu Ping sick all day; Chang Yung Nien pinch hit for him. Reading "Green Mansions". At 5 p.m., yesterday, had dispatched from Kuan-wu Shu asking me to give details of anything the Customs requires under

Lease-Lend by today! 24 hours to do a job requiring weeks! Fortunately, we have been working on post-war needs of our preventive and lights fleets, so were able to send in complete requirements at 5 p.m. today. I bet no other department of the government could have done it.

January 29: Gardener, still sick at Rouse's house, says he thinks he may have to lie up another 4 weeks. Rouse says he doubts that he is sick; in any case, Rouse is sick of him! I told Rouse that Gardener could come down and use my spare room. He is a problem.

To lunch at Hall's. Paul Blunt back from his trip to Changsha, etc., looking fitter then when he left. Also present: Mr. and Mrs. Hassel (Norwegian Ambassador); John Morris (U.P. Correspondent) and Porter. My God! Of all the females I have ever met, she's the limit! She is supposed to be correspondent of certain English newspapers; God help their readers if they have many such correspondents! Rude as a chimney-sweep and most demanding. She practically, no actually, asked to come to lunch or dinner with me. She said to Mrs. Hassel: "You know, I always try to cadge invitations to the South Bank, because I expect to be given a bath!" Then she asked me if I had a "long bath" in my house! Where she is staying (Press Hotel) she said the baths were "filthy." She thought she'd like to "do a story" about the Customs.

I fear I didn't rise easily to her bait, but, if sometime I have a crowd here for lunch, I'll put her at the far end of the table between two of my enemies. Her tongue never ceases wagging; wot a woman!

Back to office at 3, but came away at 4:30. Lu Ping still out sick. New words: "leasing" (z) = falsehood "Thou shalt destroy them that speak leasing" (Psalm V,6); "Osborne" a sweetened biscuit.

January 30: Col. Brown (USMC) sent me a pair of Army shoes, 8-1/2 D. They fit like gloves, and I wore them to Club and back. They will require a little breaking-in, and will be ideal for Chungking's steps and Chungking's weather. ~~Paul Blunt here for lunch~~. Big mail in from London Office. Two telegrams from Fay at Macao via Foreign Office. First, berates me for his compulsory retirement and begs me to stay on. Second, reports that [Macao re] Borras (whom I intended to succeed Fay) has confessed to embezzlement of Service funds! This is incredible; Borras is last man I know who would steal. Fay's mind is possibly affected. "Lord, how are they increased that trouble me! Many are they that rise up against me!" (Psalm III,1)

Walked up to Tien Men in afternoon. Saw dozens of beggars (a rare sight here) who spend New Year's week begging money from the thousands of people who visit the hill

January 31: A busy day. At 2:30, to Kuan-wu Shu. Talked 2 hours (in an unheated room) with Li Tong, re disposal of seized "luxury goods", Sinkiang Customs, Customs pay and allowances, and staff reorganization scheme. Li is a hard worker, and takes a live interest in all Customs' matters. I hope I can win him as a friend and supporter if our Service. At 4:30, to British Embassy, to chat with Sir Horace Seymour (and Thomas, ex-Chartered Bank) until Lady Seymour came, when we went up to their house on top of Chialing [嘉陵] hill. Guests at dinner were: Dr. and Mrs. Sun Fo; Mr. and Mrs. Andrew Liu (old Canton friends); K.K. Kwok and sister-in-law; Wallinger[9] (Counselor of Embassy). A delicious meal, and good talk. To bed at 11. I left my woolen underclothes on, wore bed socks, a skull cap and a scarf over my head. The bed was damp and cold; the sheets like ice. Had a big overcoat of Sir Horace's over the top of the blankets.

February

February 1: Didn't die last night after all! About perished at breakfast; no heat, windows open. I wore my overcoat; Sir Horace a lambskin robe. Excellent coffee. Road down hill like grease; car skidded nauseatingly. On ferry, stood at engine-room door and got warm. Fell once on way to office along foreshore. Arrived office 10 a.m.; had people in every minute until 12:15.

To Fan Chuang [范庄] to see Dr. Kung at 4:30. 20 people waiting: I went in first. Spoke about: post war requirements of Customs vessels and officers; 1943 revenue (over 1 billion dollars); assurances to foreign staff, etc. (which I first proposed on Dec. 3, last).

Dr. Kung annoyed that his office had not attended to this question, and promised to do something about it. Spoke to Daniel Chang (Dr. Kung's Secretary), and had a few minutes with Arthur Young and Bond (C.N.A.C.). ~~Home dead tired at 6 o'clock~~.

February 2: Dr. Kung certainly kept his word! I got the letter I have been waiting for so long this morning. It is exactly word for word what I drafted; it was actually typed last night in the Ministry. Twice, now, I have gone to Dr. Kung when faced with a crisis: last September (when he gave me $14,100,000 loan) and now again. He has, on both occasions, given me 100% of what I asked. Today's letter should restore confidence in the future for the foreigners in the Service.

To Buffet lunch – about 40 – at Col. Depass', a nice party. Lu Ping back in office, although still looking weak and ill. Admiral Hsu talked 1-1/2 hours this morning. He is a damned rascal, although a charming one. (I found out that the costs of his recent trip to Wanhsien was over 1/2 million dollars). Another very busy, but good, day.

February 3: Another crowded day, Munby (River Inspector) very disquieted when I told him we will not be allowed to be detached, now that I can pay him a living wage. Foreign Secretaries very pleased with Dr. Kung's letter to me (possibly Rouse is an exception; nothing seems to please him!)

February 4: Chinese staff, or most of them, called a meeting during morning to discuss request for issue of February pay in advance. This was reported to me, and I sent orders that they must return to work before any consideration would be given their request. They did so, but I found them meeting again at 2:20, when I returned to office. I interrupted, and personally ordered them back to work. They asked to see meat 5, and I spoke to them after listening to their three requests: (1) Advance of full February pay and allowance at once; (2) increase in pay or allowances; and (3) "equalization of treatment between seniors and juniors (whatever that means). I told them that I would consider (1) and (3) if presented through regular channels, but that I could make no promises except, with regard to (2), to continue to represent their needs to the government when necessary. With regard to (1), I made a bargain with them. On my side, I agreed to issue February pay and allowances as soon as possible, to issue 1/2 March pay on March 7; 1/2 on March 20; and to issue 1/2 April (and succeeding months') pay on April 15; 1/2 last day of month. On their side, they agreed not to request advance issue of pay in future. I hope this troublesome question is settled, but only time will tell. Lu Ping thinks I handled the crowd well, but that my decision was weak, and that more trouble will follow. My reasons were (1) many of the staff are entirely "broke" after Chinese New Year; (2) paying now (I'm thinking of the ports) will tend to remove temptation to "squeeze"; (3) to ease the burden of Lu and Chang (who were exhausted); and (4) to put an end to constant requests for pay in advance, and to put into effect a semi-monthly pay day, to be fixed once and for all. We shall see; I know I took a risk, but the risk seemed justifiable. It all depends on whether those "requests" are legitimate and honest, or whether they are "Bolshevik" in intent, and the work of agitators anxious only for trouble.

February 5: Busy morning. I was tired after yesterday, but got a lot done. Stayed home in afternoon, rested, and walked for 1/2 hour. Foul weather, and steps and roads dangerously slippery, being coated with 1/2 inch of mud of the consistency of gudgeon grease. (Is there such a word as "gudgeon"?). Reading *The Foreigners in China* by O.M. Green.[10] Title should be "The Britisher in China". Green says 3 foreigners have left their marks and are remembered by Chinese (1) Hart, (2) Gordon,[11] and (3) Sir Richard Dane.[12] It is, I think, fantastic to include the last; I doubt if 1 Chinese in a million even knows the name. Gordon saved, or helped to save, a decadent dynasty for another and final lease on life; Hart alone stands head and shoulder above any foreigners who ever came to China.

~~Col. Brown sent me a can of Sir Walter Raleigh tobacco. He is a very generous man. V-mail letter from John, dated Oct. 14, 1943; came via New York. [...]~~

February 6: To 17 Kou Fu Lu (國府路) to buffet lunch. Richards (American Commercial Counselor) my host. About 30 present, including [John] Hall Paxton recently arrived from Teheran. Dr. Eng Wen Hao, Minister of Economics, O.K. Yui, Y.C. Koo, etc., etc. my chair bearers go, as usual, so walked to ferry; then walked up 250 steps at Wang Lung Men to car. On my way back, car broke down near river airdrome, whence I walked to Wang Lung Men, and then climbed up home from Lung Men Hou. Equivalent of the Washington Monument – and then some! ~~Paul Blunt here to tea, we discussed Heim's case; Paul thinks he might be able to use him in British Red Cross and Hospital at Changsha.~~ Drafted letters to Gauss and Seymour re Dr. Kung's letter concerning foreign staff. Also started draft of Circular on same subject. Noted in dictionary that "falcon" is pronounced "fawkn"; never know that before.

February 7: At Memorial Service, spoke briefly (1) announced that at Ts'ai-cheng Pu Training Camp, out of 180 students from various Departments, the 13

Customs men were all in the top brackets and that 1st and 2nd honors went to a Customs Clerk and Assistant! (2) told staff of arrangements made for February, March and April pay; and stated that holding of meetings of staff during office hours, unless prior permissions is obtained, is prohibited; (3) announced death of Mr. Tu, Revenue Accountant.

At 3:15 to Li Tong's office: conferred until 5:30. This time I took precaution to wear my heavy overcoat and 2 pairs socks (first time this winter), but even so I was pretty cold: no heat in room. We discussed 7 or 8 topics at length. Li is intelligent, and, to date, cooperative, but his natural ignorance of Customs history and procedures has thrown a great additional burden of exegesis on my shoulders. From K.W.S., drove to Chialung, and found a warm refuge, a cup of hot tea and friendly welcome at the American Embassy. Had 1-1/2 hours intimate chat with Gauss, who unburdened himself to me. He has a difficult job and a thankless job in many ways, but, in my opinion, he is a valuable man in present circumstances.

February 8: ~~Got a lot done today~~. Two "Inspectors" from Ts'ai-cheng Pu visited us today to check up on our work. Both very satisfied; told me efficiency in Customs is best of any government office. (They had to inspect "sanitary arrangements" by order of the Generalissimo, who has been doing some inspection of W.C.'s himself!) Lady Seymour sent me a pound of coffee! Loy Chang again asked for the use of my car, and sent me a cordial note!!

February 9: To lunch with Arthur Young, then discussed UNRRA requirements; possibility of importing goods by plane for sale, etc., etc.

To Embassy Chancery, and had my passport extended by Hungerford Briggs Howard – some moniker! Dropped in and had chat with Col. Brown and Capt. Hitch. Stopped at Press Hostel to see John Morris (U.P.). Had 1-1/2 hours with Gen. Wu Te-cheng, Secretary-General of Kuomintang. He said that we must preserve civil service systems in Customs, and that Generalissimo wants to extend it to other departments. I told him that it is my aim to preserve our principles and civil service standards, but that the government must be prepared to let me pay my staff a living wage. I pointed out that other Departments had "supplementary" incomes which are not available to Customs. We talked of post-war planning. Home at 6:30. Dr. Kung elected Chairman of Bank of China vice T.V. Soong. What does this mean? Gen. Wu thinks (or says) that the government wishes to centralize all financial institutions under control of Ministry of Finance. Sent long telegrams to Fay, in code, through Gen. Wu. He has secret wireless stations in Macao. Gold dollar (U.S.) has gone haywire yesterday and today. From U.S. $1.00 = C.N. $80 (U.S. currency), the rate has risen to U.S. $1.00 = C.N. $180–220 according to who tells you. I wonder if it is the beginning of a serious increase of the rate of inflation. Prices have risen between 20% and 30% during the past month, and the situation among the Customs staff is again becoming critical. I wrote to Dr. Kung today, pointed this out, and suggested that customs pay be put on a sliding scale, based on the official cost of living index in the various Districts.

February 10: To lunch: John Morris (United Press) whom I last entertained in Canton; Mr. and Mrs. Stoneman (Customs); Hopstock and Rouse. Cook made

New England boiled dinner, which was very good. Morris told of a man in the Whiskey Rebellion who refused a pardon and insisted on being hanged – because he knew he'd die a less humane death if he was ever released!

February 11: 1800 employees; 11-hour day; much of machinery made in Chungking, but a few Miller automatic presses, 1 old Linotype, 2 power cutters, dozens of kick-presses. Three principal jobs (1) $100 banknotes (now being produced 1 million a day, *i.e.* face value of $100,000,000!!) (2) Postage and revenue stamps; (3) Government bonds. Letter-press, copper-plate and offset processes. Paper twists used to tie bundles of notes, etc., because rubber bands would cost over $100,000 a month. A very efficiently run plant, with every scrap of equipment in use all day long – running China into bankruptcy?

At 3, with Fang Tu to see Li Tong and discuss problems facing Customs as result of 30% increase in costs of living during the past few weeks. I think it is the most dangerous crisis the Service has ever faced, and I am very worried. Li Tong moderately sympathetic, but takes a rather legalistic or technical position. I made it clear to him that the government has got to feed the Customs staff or the Customs will simply disintegrate. We are going to work out alternative plans, which I intend to take to Dr. Kung. Dead tired at night – so much so that I refused to talk to Saxton, who came to my house after office.

Gardener came down from Rouse's today, and is in my spare room. Rouse couldn't stand him any longer, and I don't wonder. He is a difficult problem!

February 12: Annett didn't appear at the office yesterday afternoon, and nobody knew where he was at 11 p.m. I was a bit worried, but I found out today that he had been on a binge at the Club. Unusual for Annett. At office until 5; a lovely day, with sun! Until this week, we have had 35 minutes of sunshine since Christmas.

To Capt. Farner's house to a Valentine's party. About 80 people there. Bar decorated with original murals of well-developed ladies. Excellent buffet supper (including beans). I danced with Mrs. Auyang and Mrs. K.C. Lee. Came home at 10, when the party was just getting into its stride. I suppose it will last until dawn.[13]

February 13: To Lott Wei's house at Huang Kuo Yeh. Ate tremendous bowl of noodles, most delicious. Also, one of the best cups of coffee I've had in months, with Libby's condensed milk. Lott bought the milk several months ago and paid $80 a can; today the price is $600. Camel cigarettes are now $400 for 20 – $20 a cigarette. At official rates, this is U.S. $1.00 per cigarette; at "special" rate (40), U.S. $0.50. Either way, it adds up to expensive smoking. Butter (Chungking dairy) has gone up to $680 a pound.

Walked home in 45 minutes. Spent 3 hours on a corruption case from Kukong.

February 14: Lunch with Gunther Stein,[14] correspondent of "Manchester Guardian" and "Christian Science Monitor", at Press Hotel. He visited Changteh after the Japs left. Said the Chinese 57th Division did a fine defensive job, but showed not the least offensive spirit. Japs left of their own accord, and were not driven out, as the Chinese have claimed. He said the Szechuan troops are miserable; under-fed, under-paid, and always ready to loot and steal from the towns they occupy. U.S. is building a colossal air-base near Chengtu, as terminals for India-China transport, to relieve Kunming, which is outgrown. Land for base requisitioned by Chinese government, with little or no compensation. Result: riots, and official attempts to divert anger against U.S. Dr. Kung told him that the government has already advanced C.N. $10 billion for American forces in China; we paid the Chinese government at official rate (20:1), so they have built up a colossal U.S. dollar reserve. But it is an inflationary process, in China. (I am anxious about our financial relations with China; there is a lot of bad feeling on both sides, and the question is full of dynamite).

At 2:30, to Kuan-wu Shu, for weekly conference with Li Tong. Then back to office at 4 to sign and clear up my day's accumulation.

February 15: After several fairly spring-like days, it is colder again, and the fire in my office was welcome. Working on "approach" to Dr. Kung for increased pay for staff. Prices have gone up 30% to 40% in less than a month, and staff are appealing for help.

T.V. Soong uses Customs launch 6 to 7 times a month to cross the river, and he gives the crew $2,000 cumshaw almost every time. The ferry would cost him $5.00. And poor China fighting for her life! Oh yeah?

February 16: ~~Tired, and cold coming on. Stayed at home in afternoon~~.

February 17: Another terrific raid on Berlin by R.A.F. I wonder whether the Customs will survive the war. The only real danger (there are several), – the only danger I fear is Inflation. The government must permit me to raise pay as prices rise, or else (1) we shall lose most of our best men and (2) other Customs employees will steal and accept bribes wholesale. I hate to think of the senior staff, who will simply starve because they can't leave and won't steal.

February 19: ~~Still feeling wobbly, with pain in both legs and in lower part of back. Maybe I've got a slight touch of flu, maybe I'm just breaking up. To office in morning, worked at home in afternoon~~. Drafted letter to Fay at Macao. ~~Wrote to John, from whom I had note written on back of "Dartmouth bulletin". He had lunch with Foster Hall and Joly, and was dining with Jolys on the following Sunday. He had enjoyed a furlough – hotels, movies, etc. in London. Wish I'd known earlier; I'd have sent him some money to squander. I have asked Foster Hall to lend John £50 better late than never~~. Bought 1/2 ton coal: $2240. This means, at official rate (20), U.S. $224.00 a ton!! At "subsidy" rate (40) U.S. $112.00 a ton.

February 20: After wretched night, woke feeling all washed out. Showered and dressed, but at 11, had to go to bed, and leave my luncheon guests to be entertained by Hopstock, Bannister and Annett. Gauss couldn't come, he's sick. Also Tu Ping-ho.[15] Never did hear from Andrew Liu. Paul Blunt came and spent an hour with me after lunch, which he said was excellent. Dr. and Mrs. Sun Fo were my guests of honor, and Hopstock said they enjoyed the food and the party. Paul later went to Canadian Hospital, and brought Dr. Allen back to see me. He finds bronchitis and some congestion in upper part of chest. Must stay in bed 3 days! Thinks the pain in my legs was sciatica. Put me on sulfadiazine treatment.

1944

February 21: Much better night! No sciatica all night and all day: here's hoping I never have that anymore! Signed usual dispatches, etc., also about $7,000,000 in checks. When I cough, it feels as if I was being stabbed in the middle of the chest. Slow, quiet day in bed. Suddenly, in comes a large package for me – a postal parcel! (Never saw one before in Chungking). Opened, and found 20 2 oz. packages of Edgeworth sliced, and 4 of Granger, and a pipe! Parcel from "1st Lt. Edward S. Jones", A.P.O. 627. Who is Lt. Jones? Mystery solved an hour later when I got a letter from Russ Sweet, who had sent the 'baccy' out by Lt. Jones. Russ was very thoughtful to do all this for me, and it cheered me up just when I needed cheering.

February 22: ~~Another long, slow day. Paul Blunt called at 6 and had tea. We talked of Alice and that drear February three years ago in Canton. I loved her~~! Lu Ping came to talk business at 2 p.m.

February 23: ~~Sick of lying in my unheated, damp, cold bedroom so had my bed moved into my study, where I have a stove. [. . .]~~ Lu Ping and Fang Tu here for long conference at 2 re pay; Li Tong is being very unrealistic and bureaucratic.

February 24: Everitt Groff-Smith arrived at noon from Kunming for a few days' consultation. It was good to see him, even if he is primed with the difficulties facing him in the Kunming District. We talked (rather too much) most of the afternoon on current problems.

February 25: ~~Up and dressed first time since Sunday. Cold still persists, but I think congestion in lungs has disappeared~~. Lu Ping came at 10:50, talked till 12. ~~Did a lot of work at home~~. Conferences here with Groff-Smith, Bannister, Annett, Hopstock, Gardener. Mostly about how to increase staff emoluments. ~~We face the most serious crisis in Customs history~~.

February 26: ~~Cold very bad again, and feeling rotten. Li Tong, Lu Ping, Fang Tu and Everitt to lunch. Talked "relief" until 4. Li wants me to put up 3 or 4 alternative schemes for Minister's consideration. Dead tired by night~~.

February 27: ~~Feeling low and depressed. Head stuffed up. Went next door to Marines' mess and got Pharmacist Mate Dupresseault to blow out my nose. A great relief. Everitt lunched with Depass; I felt too low to go. Sat out in the sun an hour after lunch (which I couldn't eat)~~.

February 28: With Fang Tu, to see Li Tong in p.m. 2-1/2 hours' discussion of relief measures. After long consideration, Mr. Li said that he would recommend to Minister one-half the amounts of grant that I proposed. I had to take my stand, and told him that I could not agree, and that if his figures were adopted, there would be trouble to the Customs, and loss of revenue. After further argument, he agreed to my original figure of $2.000 for married people with children, but suggested 2/3 of this amount for married people without children, and 1/3 for bachelors. To this I agreed, and he promised to recommend plan to Minister. I hope it goes through – and quickly! Groff-Smith on North Bank all day, and spent night over there.

February 29: ~~Groff-Smith away all day, but home at tea. Fairly busy day in office~~.

1944

March

March 1: Had New Year's parcel from John; soap, tobacco, pipe, cigarettes, chewing gum, toothpaste! A very nice gift, and much appreciated. No word from Li Tong re relief grant; promised today to let me know his recommendations to Minister. ~~Had delicious New England boiled dinner; cook makes his own corned beef, which is better than most I've had in America.~~

March 2: Li Tong has chiseled on our agreement: instead of relief of $2,000, $1,400 and $700, he will now recommend $1,500, $1,000 and $500. Like a damned shop-keeper! To Li Tong's office at 3:30 (he asked me to come at 3:45). Found he had left for Ministry. My car under repair, so it was 4:45 before I got to Ministry in S. O. Co.'s car. With Li Tong, talked with O.K. Yui, Vice-Minister. I said $1,500 too little, recommended $2,000. O.K. Yui said even $2,000 might be too little in a couple of months, and finally endorsed Li's despatch as it stood. O.K. Yui said I could come back for more later on if necessary. I said I could not be responsible for morale of Service if staff was continuously under-paid. Li and I then went to see Minister. He read Li's despatch, and said that he didn't like the scheme at all, and that the way to handle the problem is for the Customs to buy the essentials – rice, oil, etc. – for staff! This is just what I wanted, and did Li's face fall! Dr. Kung asked me if I could draw up a scheme in 2 weeks; I asked for a month, and he consented. In meantime, Li's proposals will be enforced temporarily; Li suggested for 3 months, I suggested 2; Dr. Kung decided in my favor.

To Wang Lung Men at 7; no ferry. To Custom's House, then walked to Tung Shui Men [東水門]. Home at 8 – dead tired~~, after a helluva day. Groff Smith spending night on North Bank~~.

March 3: At Secretaries' special meeting, I gave a story of my negotiations with Li, Yui and Dr. Kung.

March 4: At 12:45, about 20 of the unmarried staff (men and women) came to the house. They said they wanted to see me about the relief grant. I told them I couldn't talk to them there, and arranged an appointment at 3:30 in my office. They came back with their old bellyaches – "dependents". I told them that I would consider no change in the method of distribution. Long walla-walla. As soon as they left, in came the 5 women employees whose husbands are in the Customs! Then the miscellaneous Staff asked to see me! Back of all this agitation are a few "radicals" who are born trouble-makers, and they are finding it easy to play on the war-weariness of the staff. ~~Groff-Smith left after tea for the North Bank, where he will spend night. He flies to Kunming tomorrow morning, in a special place, with Dr. Kung and Arthur Young.~~

March 5: ~~Everitt Groff-Smith appeared here at 11 a.m. At the airport, he was told "no room on the plane", and must wait until March 8 at the earliest. He went up to Rouse's on the 2nd Range to spend the night.~~

March 6: ~~Woke at 1 with diarrhea; 8 trips before 6 a.m. Took 2 sulfaguanidine and 3 opium pills. Felt like the devil. Spent all day in bed.~~

March 7: Up and to office; a very busy day, too. Rouse extremely annoyed because I refused Gen. Grimsdale's request for his detachment. Rouse could have been detached at any time during the past 2 years – especially a couple of months ago, when I suggested that he go instead of Bairnsfather. It is only now, when all arrangements have been made for his transfer to Foochow, that he bellyaches. I shall be glad when he is gone; he evidently would like to stay in the Customs as long as I keep him in Chungking, but becomes suddenly patriotic when I move him.

March 8: Had talk with 10 representatives of the Clerks for 1 hour this afternoon. I wonder if anybody in the Customs is satisfied?

Dwight Edwards notified me of my election by New York Board of Directors of United China Relief to the Chungking Committee of U.C.R. This Committee decides on allocation of funds sent out to China.

Hopstock has a 5-lb. can of milk powder which he is going to sell for $10,000. This equals U.S. $500 at official, and U.S. $250 at preferential, exchange rates. My boy wants a new white cotton gown; I shall have to pay at least C.N. $800 for it; before the war it would have cost C.N. $4.00.

March 9: To lunch at Mr. Loo Tsu-fu's (Mgr., Ming Shan Co., Former Vice-Minister of Communications). By request, I was given a big bowl of chicken noodles, with toast. To Kuan-wu Shu, and an hour's talk with Mr. Li Tong. Back to office at 4:30.

March 10: ~~Talked with Mrs. Pan. She has chronic appendicitis, but is as lovely and gracious as ever. Lots of nice people there. Wrote to Mother Mac-Donald. River was down to 0.1 ft. early this week, 0.5 today.~~

March 11: River up 4 feet since yesterday, and ferries again operating at night – they stopped at 6 during the extreme low-water stage.

To tea with Mr. and Mrs. Liu Chi-wen at Chialing. Also present: Gauss, Atcheson, Sir Horace and Lady Seymour, K.P. Chen and Mrs. Chen, Gen Wu Te-cheng, Quo Tai-chi,[16] Mayor Ho of Chungking,[17] Dick Lee and his pretty sister. Stopped at Naval Sick Bay, but doctor was out. Talked with Lt. Hitch. K.P. Chen is interested in writings of Sir Robert Hart, who, he thinks, is not well known among the Chinese. I agree. Hart was a true friend of China, and probably did more for her than any individual, Chinese or foreign, in the second half of the 19th century.

March 13: At 2:30, to see Li Tong. Talked Sinkiang budget; Customs College building; Dr. Kung's letter re foreign staff; permanent relief scheme. Had letter from John Hughes, O.S.S., and about 10 of my former associates at 630 5th Avenue. A very nice thing to do!

March 15: Another grave crisis has arisen: the price of official rice has practically doubled since yesterday. I was informed at noon, and we went into action at once. Our best plan for a solution – arrived at after 2 weeks' hard work – was put on paper, and I arranged conferences with the 2 Vice-Ministers, and Li Tong at 5 o'clock. Took Fang Tu with me. First hat 1/4 hour with Li Tong. As usual and as expected, he found all sorts of objections. He is a narrow-minded, budget-ridden accountant, and has no conception of the difficulties of administration or of the human values involved. We went in to the Vice-Ministers when they came back from welcoming Dr. Kung (who arrived from Kunming today), and I presented my case as strongly as possible. After 1/2 hour's discussion, Mr. Yui and Mr. Koo asked me to leave my proposal with them, and promised to give it immediate attention. I do not expect my proposal to be accepted in toto, but I think I have persuaded them that something must be done immediately if disaster is to be averted. Home at 6:30, a bit tired.

March 16: ~~To dentist (Dr. An) who replaced (for about the 10th time) one of the porcelain fillings in my left front tooth, and took impression on order to add a third tooth (or 4th?) to my upstairs plate. It is now about 8 months since I left home with all dentistry "100%"; and about the usual time to have to replace half a dozen fillings. I wish I had 100% store teeth!~~ To Vice-Ministers, to hand in additional figures they require; O.K. Yui said; "You may now wait for Minister's decision." ~~To Navy Sick Bay, where Dr. Herrington had examined my stool this morning. No amoeba, no cysts. Busy afternoon in office.~~ Sugar for which we have been paying $46 is now $76.

March 17: A big mail from London office; about 3 letters and memos, besides copies of many of Sir Frederick's letters to Cubbon. Will he be pleased when he finds out that I have them![18]~~Included was a good letter from John. He is still troubled with his back, which worries me. Foster Hall wrote very nicely of John, whom he entertained at Chinese chow. John also visited Cecil and Edith Joly.~~

March 18: ~~To Dr. An, dentist, who replaced one amalgam filling and added a tooth to my upper plate. Total cost (3 fillings, one new tooth) $1,300.~~

To Fan Chuang, to see Arthur Young. He said government has almost no control in Yunnan, where corruption is flagrant. The Governor's sons own the largest gold shops, and they – the banks – are speculating heavily. Hoarding and profiteering by officials is universal. Arthur is pretty apprehensive – and so am I! After waiting 1-1/2 hours saw Dr. Kung for three minutes. I asked him if Maze had had his permission to transfer the confidential London Office archives to his private name. He was angry and asked: "How could Maze do such a thing?" He instructed me to see that the archives are returned forthwith, I mentioned current negotiations re relief for Customs staff, and asked for sympathetic consideration. I then enquired whether the government is satisfied with my administration and expressed the hope that, if it is, my confirmation will be considered. His Excellency grunted and said "Yes". I hope he means what he grunts. To office until 5:45. Telegram from Ting says there is rebellion in Sinkiang, that Mongolian "bandits" have invaded province, aided by Soviet planes! And that situation is serious. That may turn out to be an under-statement.

March 19: Munby family (2 sons) and Dr. Allen's family (2 of their 4 daughters) and Annett to Lunch. They left at 3:45 and Paul Blunt arrived at 4. Stayed to tea, and I walked part my way home with him. Wrote two or three letters to Foster Hall.

1944

March 20: [. . .] I had 2 hours with Li Tong, and have finally won out in my long effort to get him to recognize the necessity of staff relief on sliding scale. The "budget" was not mentioned once during our talk. We shall supply actual rice, oil, fuel and salt or their market equivalent in cash. Also, a sliding scale cash supplement to take care of sundry expenses, probably the cash equivalent of 2 tou [斗, 1 tou = 7 kg approximately] of rice. Altogether, I feel much encouraged, and hope that a new day is dawning for the Service.

Home, tired, at 5, and then in comes a birthday parcel from my Johnny! 2 pipes, a pouch, 2 books and a lot of pipe-cleaners (also 2 doz. air-mail envelopes). All welcome, and very thoughtful on his part.

At 7, went to a buffet supper at the Navy Enlisted Men's Mess next door, and had excellent food and a very pleasant evening. Mr. Joseph Lucas, C.R.M., USN came to China (Peking) in 1906, A real old timer. Told me that he has raised 7 Chinese orphans – girls picked up out of the gutter. Two have been educated in America, and married rich Chinese in Shanghai.

March 21: Another birthday present. Bannister gave me a bottle of Bordeaux, and I had a glass at dinner. It was delicious, and a great treat. Sent two letters via American Embassy to Maze calling for restitution of the "Purloined Letters".

March 22: Rain and needed. River: 0.5. Busy day, but uneventful. Lu Ping back after 2 weeks' leave.

March 23: Rouse told me of the queer death of Forest, the botanist, years ago at Tengyueh. Forest had a weak heart. One day, while out shooting, he had a heart attack. He sat down, and his chair-bearers wanted to go home. He refused. As he sat, a flock of snipe came by. Forest jumped up, fired, killed a snipe – and dropped dead! Wrote Foster-Hall regarding the "Purloined Letters". Admiral Hsu in my office for 1-1/2 hours; he is a dreadful bore – also a politician to be watched!

Dined at Netherlands Embassy. Lovink,[19] the Ambassador, is an old Customs man. His Counselor, Vanderberg, is soon leaving for California, where his wife is staying (Carmel). Other guests: Gen. Shang Chien[20] (who is leaving next month to be Chief of the Chinese Military Mission to America) and wife; Dr. and Mrs. Wang Chung-Hui[21] (she is from Tientsin, and speaks beautiful Mandarin); Sir Horace and Lady Seymour; Gen. Carton de Wiart. Gen. de Wiart, unlike most Englishmen, likes Edgeworth tobacco. Nice dinner, and all over and away at 9:10, but I sat on the wharf at Wang Lung Men for 35 minutes waiting for the ferry.

March 24: Felt cold coming on, so went to bed at 3:30 after a busy 3/4 day.

March 25: To office in morning, got a lot done. To lunch at American Embassy: Gauss, Atcheson, Paxton, Sir Horace and Lady Seymour; Francis and Cecilia Pan; Dr. and Mrs. Han Li-wu;[22] Mr. Segeart (Belgian Minister or Charge) and Mr. Smets, Belgian Counselor. Dr. Han just back from "good-will" visit to England. Much impressed by Churchill, whom he asked: "When will war in Europe end?" Churchill replied: "I don't know; maybe this year." Dr. Han was responsible for saving 12,000 cases of "Palace Treasures" when Japanese attacked Nanking. He stayed till the last minute. Out of the 12,000 cases, not one was lost, and only two breakages occurred when a case containing 2 porcelain bowls fell of a truck. China – and the world – owe a lot do Dr. Han's courage and management. With Fang Tu, to see Li tong re relief. Since Monday, he has "changed his mind", *i.e.*, he considers out new plan – to which he agreed only after long argument and several con-cessions on my part – will cost too much money. I could have kicked his budgetary bottom with utmost pleasure! He wanted, apparently, to cut our plan in half. I let him know that I could not consider such a change, so he has agreed to let the (1) rice and (2) oil, coal, salt sections stand, but I had to agree to cut the "sundries" section in half. This was our weak spot, because (actually at Li's own suggestion!) we had included additional Rent Allowance at equivalent of 1 tou of rice. If he doesn't change his mind again, the final arrangement is satisfactory, and will establish the "sliding scale" principle.

March 26: Read *Public Faces* by Harold Nicolson.[23] In garden, amidst usual stiff Chinese flowers and tortured shrubs, I found some nasturtiums-like meeting friends in a strange city.

March 27: At Memorial Service, told staff of progress of negotiations for new "relief" plan. At 2, left for North Bank; waited 30 minutes for ferry; arrived at Kuan-wu Shu at 3:10. Talked with Li Tong until 4:40, while his Secretaries and Fang Tu were finishing tables of statistics, then we went to Ministry and saw O.K. Yui and Y.C. Koo. Both Vice-Ministers examined our proposals and gave them their blessing – in less than 10 minutes. Then to Fan Chuang where we were first of some 20 people in to see the Minister. Dr. Kung read through the dispatch rapidly, picked up his brush, and O.K.'d the proposal – all in less than 5 minutes! Li Tong's written presentation was excellent. Thus, after 4 months preparation, and two weeks' hard work and argument, I have at last put Customs pay on sliding scale. No matter how high prices now go, my staff will be fed. I can now re-enforce discipline, and our revenue will benefit. Incidentally, 75% of my worries ought to disappear – at least temporarily. Fang Tu, C.C. Tso and one or two others on my staff have helped me greatly during this campaign.

March 28: At 5, spoke to entire staff and told them of new plan for rice, etc., allowances.

March 29: Customs holiday: "72 Martyrs". Took things easy. Drafted letter to Commissioners re new relief scheme; also letters to Dr. Kung, O.K. Yui and Li Tong. "cynosure": from the Greek name ("Dog's tail") of the constellation which includes the Pole star.

March 30: Ca Hok Gi to lunch. He is getting old – about 59 – and has lost his fat. Looks a sick man; working for Anti-Opium Bureau. D.K. Wei came in at 7 p.m. and stayed to a pot luck – leaving at 10. All very nice, but I've had no time to myself. D.K. Wei says that American bombers will be able to fly from the new air-field at Chengtu non-stop to Tokyo! I wonder. He said that there has been great opposition by dispossessed farmers against building of the new field. The American soldiers murdered, etc., etc. Prices have gone sky-high at Chengtu:

1944

1 egg, $10.00. Another bad accident on river above Chungking: steamer sank and over 200 passengers lost.

March 31: Li Tong invited all Inspectorate Secretaries, and his own Kochang [科長], to dinner. About 24 present, food excellent, prepared by Customs cook. I took my staff over in Customs launch.

April

April 1: Busy day. At 3, a letter from Ting giving particulars of situation in Sinkiang. Ting fears another "Manchurian Incident". Soviet – 8th Route Army – Mongolian – Chinese Communists apparently allied to drive Chinese government influence out of Sinkiang. Took Ting's letter over to Fan Chuang and handed it to Dr. Kung. As usual, I got in ahead of about 15 who were waiting. Dr. Kung instructed that Ting is to complete his programme in Sinkiang. Home at 7, and found Paul Blunt here. He had had tea, and we talked till 8 o'clock. Local prices are getting entirely out of hand: night ferry ticket today went to $14.00, vs $8.00 yesterday. 1 lb. Biscuits (cheapest kind): Sept. 1943 – $46; Dec.–Jan. $68; March – $88; April 1, $115.

April 2: Wet. To Club to get books. Wrote, read and generally loafed. Officer came today said Gen. Hu Chung-nan,[24] is *en route* with troops to aid Gen. Sheng. He thinks there is Soviet-Japanese understanding.

April 3: Letter from Betty, dated Feb. 13, said that Mother had had another severe heart attack about 2 weeks earlier when it looked as though she could not live. But, as before, she refused to give in, although she was still in bed, and, apparently, not out of danger. That letter was written 1-1/2 months ago, and no news is good news.

Capt. Setman, A.U.S., brought me 12 packages of Edgeworth from Russ Sweet. Capt. Setman (Chemical warfare) here only a few days, and leaves tomorrow for Washington. Gave him card for Russ, and a new $100 bill with a message written on it to Betty. Reuters carries first news of the Sinkiang trouble, – Moscow's side of the case, which is about exactly the same as China's – in reverse. The Chinese are mortally afraid of the Russians and believe that Russia and Japan have come to some agreement that bodes ill for China. Russia and Japan have just signed an agreement re Saghalien [Sakhalin][25] and the fisheries; and Japanese troops said to be pouring into China from Manchuria. I find it difficult to credit any agreement against China. Hear that Japs have built large new airfields at Hankow and Ichang. I correct, we can expect some heavy bombing this summer. To K.W.S., and half an hour with Li Tong. Then to Chungking Customs to talk to Liu Ping I. Then to U.S. Army Headquarters, where I met Capt. Setman in Col. Brewster's office. Lu Ping said his wife sold a U.S. $10 gold piece for Chinese $10,000 last week. Loy Chang still living in Commissioner's House. – 3 1/2 months after leaving Customs job. I should think he'd be ashamed, but it doesn't seem to worry him. He is pontifical in his criticisms of others, but as unscrupulous as the rest when his own pocket is affected.

1944

April 4: A very busy day in the office. Mr. Utting, Tidesurveyor, from Lanchow, called. He is being retired. Says he found attitude of Chinese staff very off-hand and inconsiderate. Reading a typical English book of "Memoirs", – Maj. Gen. Adze. I wonder how many such clutter the shelves of libraries? Yet they help pass the hours. Started *The Mind in the Making* tonight, and find it stimulating and well written.

April 5: Dined at Gen. Grimsdale's, 17 Kuo Fu Lu. A lot of Generals: Gen. Ho Ying Ching, Minister of War and Chief of Staff; Gen. Wu Te-cheng, Sec.Gen. of Kuomintang; Gen. Victor Odlum, Canadian Ambassador; Gen. Pechkoff,[26] Head of Free French Delegation – and the Acting Inspector General! Good dinner and good company. Afterwards with Gen. Wu, went to the second half of a concert at Chialing House. A fine baritone soloist, and a good orchestra – about the only music I've heard since last July. I sat between Gen. Wu and Dr. Sun Fo. The latter told me, in reply to my question, that the large portrait of his father hanging in the hall was not a good likeness. (It is the most widely reproduced of Sun Yat-sun's pictures). Had a word with Tseng Yang-fu, Mrs. Liu Chi Wen, the Seymours, and several other friends.

April 6: Letter from O.K. Yui informed me that he had spoken to Dr. Kung on Tuesday, and that Dr. Kung would be "pleased" to "substantiate" my appointment as Inspector General, and that "the Ministerial order would be issued in due course." Very nice.

Malcolm (ex-Marine Dept., now with British Navy in India) to see me at tea, and told me that our scheme for sending 12 cadets to India for naval training may all fall through! That will be a pretty mess if it happens after all the work we have put into it, the expense incurred, and the staff arrangements required. Malcolm said that the plans for an expedition against the Andaman Islands or Malaya, which were supposed to have been applied this last winter, apparently went all wring. The British Naval units which have been hanging about Calcutta since last May are being sent away and dispersed. Malcolm thinks that nothing will be done until after the end of the monsoon.

April 7: Good Friday. News of Japanese advance towards Imphal in India rather disquieting in spite of British official attitude that the situation is under control.[27] Hope they're right! Had hour's conference with Clerks' representatives. Got a 43-page single-spaced dispatch from Fay re Borras. I didn't know which of the two is more to blame for the trouble.

April 8: ~~Plenty busy all day, but got a lot done~~. With Hopstock, went to movie at our office at 7:30. "The Mad Empress" – quite well done. Then half an hour of excellent news reels – mostly American. Movie was shown in our "ceremonial hall", where we hold Memorial Services, and it was packed. Many children and babies in arms, – one of which was 40 days old! I suppose many of the parents have no servants and have to take their children with them when they go out. A very friendly and nice-looking crowd, Commissioners and char-bearers cheek by jowl.

April 9: Lunch here: Y.C. Koo; Francis and Cecilia Pan; Admiral and Mrs. Hsu; Lu Ping; Daniel Chang; Arthur Young; Paul Blunt and Ronald Hall. Good chow, good talk.

~~To Club to change books.~~ Col. Depass explained the meaning of John's new detachment: DEML (Detached Enlisted Men's List), and says the work is probably public relations or intelligence along the lines of the Military Attaché's office. Had 1-1/2 hours with Gardener after dinner and told him I had decided to let him go. A very difficult task for me, for he is one of the ablest foreigners in the Customs. He proved rather difficult, and I must say our talk confirmed me in my judgment. He is very conceited, and devoid of a sense of humour – a bad combination.

April 10: Crossing the river at 2 is worse than the 5 o'clock subway rush. About 100 people crowded on the steps leading to the ferry pontoon, and all try to squeeze into the 3-foot "cattle run" at once. Result, squashed babies and tempers, high words and general unpleasantness. The ferries are in terrible condition, and I fear that there will be a bad accident on one of them. All over-crowded, and I doubt whether the engines, boilers or hull have been x inspected for years. With Chang Yung Nien, to D.G.'s office, where we had 2 hours' conference with Li Tong and 3 of his secretaries on subject of staff reorganization. We are getting this complicated and long-postponed question straightened out at last.

April 11: Pouncey arrived from Foochow at 8 p.m. Dined with me, and then Banister, Gardener and Hopstock came as we talked till 10:30. It is good to see Pouncey again, and I'm sure he will be of great help to me. He is not "bloody-minded", as so many of his countrymen are.

April 12: Chit from Admiral Hsu congratulating me on my confirmation as Inspector General. This is the first I've heard of it, and don't know where he heard it! He has a nose for news, and spends a lot of time on the North Bank, flitting about among the officials and politicians. Slow day in office. It looks as though I may have a fight with Li Tong over staff reorganization, but I shall try to convince him to make haste slowly. Mrs. K.C. Li and her son came to see me at 6:30. She wanted me to give her husband, who is going to India with 2 of their children, a letter which would get him by the Customs on his return. She was disappointed when I told her that he would have to pay duty on the purchases he is to make for her.

April 13: About 11 a.m., a plane, flying low up the river, hit a lot of telephone wires spanning the Yangtze in front of our office. Sounded like machine gun fire to me. Snapped a few of the wires, but didn't harm the plane. A narrow escape from a tragedy. Cold and wet, so I had a fire – first time in a week.

April 14: Still cold and damp. Finished "Over the River" by John Galsworthy.[28] An excellent novel – honest writing, honest characters. No further news about my confirmation.

April 15: Saturday, and busy right up till 5:15. ~~Letter from John "somewhere in British Isles" indicates that he is not in England. Says his job is much pleasanter and more interesting, and living conditions a great improvement on his~~

~~former quarters. Seemed much happier altogether. Short note from Nate, who is just out of hospital after a bout of jaundice.~~ Papers say that Vice-President Wallace[29] is coming to China. The advance publicity is by far the worst I have ever seen![30] One report says he is coming to induce "the generals" to unite behind Chiang Kai-Shek! Another seems to think he is coming in order to be out of the country during the Conventions! A bad exhibition, and the net result – to date – is to nettle.

April 16: ~~To Club to change books. To Lucy Wei's at Huang Kuo Yeh in afternoon. With Hopstock and Pouncey, had delicious noodles, and then walked home together.~~

April 17: My day! To office, and rushed until 11, when I left for North Bank. (At Memorial Service, I introduced Mr. Pouncey.) When I went to Kuan-wu Shu. Settled Macao impasse; got Li Tong to agree to no reductions in total pay on introduction of new scale; discussed Sinkiang, pilotage, revenue, etc.

Mr. Li showed me copy of Dr. Kung's order confirming me as Inspector General from April 14. This was my first official news.

To U.S. Military Headquarters to see [Calvin] Joyner (Land-Lease) who was out. Called on Gen. Ferris,[31] Deputy Chief of Staff, who has just arrived after 2 years in Burma theatre. A most attractive man. Also had chat with Col. Thompson and two or three other officers, one of whom told me that he had seen my name mentioned in a book called "Sharks Fins and Millet". ~~Next, to U.S. Naval Attaché's office, to see Col. Brown, who gave me cup of tea and package of Sir Walter Raleigh tobacco.~~ Then to Chancery for chat with Ed Rice, who is here from Lanchow and leaves tomorrow for Sian. To Fan Chuang to see Dr. Kung for a minute and thank him for my appointment. Saw Arthur Young, and then went over to his house for a bit of a rest before going to dinner with Francis and Cecilia Pan. At 7:30, to the Pans for a delightful dinner. Guests: Victor Hoo, Tsu-yee Pei and daughter, Lovink (Netherlands Ambassador) and Van Den Berg.

April 18: Ministry's dispatch appointing me Inspector General received this morning. To Dr. T.V. Soong's house for lunch. He was late, so I had 1/2 hour with Dr. Victor Hoo – a brilliant, hard-working, conscientious official. He said the Chinese are a lazy people; I disagreed. He conceded that they are industrious, but only because of dire necessity and desire for gain. Contrast the Germans or Swiss, he said – they work for the sake of the work. He alluded to the tight-fisted meanness of the Swiss. While in Geneva, he worked 2 weeks to organize a fête in aid of China. In spite of lotteries, prizes, etc., the receipts amounted to about U.S. $2,000. He contrasted this with a charity meeting in a poor section of New York he attended, where, for a local charity and with no prizes, 400 people raised $4,000 in an evening. And Geneva is full of wealth. At lunch, Dr. Soong, Loy Chang and I. Delicious foreign meal: T.V. said his cook cannot make Chinese food! T.V was more cordial than I have ever seen him, but nevertheless he is still on the abrupt side. He asked me about my children, and I said that John is in England, waiting for the Big Push. T.V. replied: "I think the Big Push has started." He and Hoo (like all of us) are very worried about inflation in China.

1944

To drop cards on Dr. Wang Chung-hui and Wei Tao-ming. Latter leaves for Washington in a day or two. To Ministry, where I had a few minutes with Y.C. Koo. To Central Bank, but K.K. Kwok was out. Back to office. All Secretaries and Assistant Secretaries came to congratulate me; I was very moved. ~~Hard afternoon's work, wrote note to Mother at night, again I wish that my father had lived!~~

April 19: Tu Ping-ho, Commissioner on Special Duty at Inspectorate, critically sick. He has looked very badly ever since he came, and I shouldn't think he has much resistance. Had a very cordial personal letter from Gauss congratulating me on my appointment as I.G. He, and all the men at the Embassy, have been most hospitable and helpful ever since I took up the job here. After the past rather exhausting days, it was nice to have one whole day without entertaining or being entertained.

April 20: To Central Bank, with Fang Tu, to see K.K. Kwok; arranged for loan of $6,200,000 a month for April, May, June, – all done in 5 minutes. To Fang Chuang to see Dr. Kung. He instructed me to write him about position of Inspector General respecting Pension Scheme (I requested permission to withdraw from scheme); said he would let me know what pay I am to draw; discussed revenue outlook; he asked me to prepare statement for press re Customs;[32] talked about rehabilitation of light-houses, ships and officers; he enquired whether Maze had returned the documents which he had "stolen" (Dr. Kung's word!). Had cup of coffee at the Navy Mess next door, and bought 10 kilos of sugar from Mr. Duperrault.

Prices continue to spiral, and there seems to be no limit; a very serious outlook.

April 21: Hot! I fear the summer is about here, and now for 5 months of sweat and discomfort.

April 23: Ludden there: he is back from New Delhi and en route to Chengtu, where he will be detailed for service with U.S. Army.

April 24: Mr. Chang Yung Nien spoke cordially of my appointment as Inspector General at the Memorial Service. Chang Pai Leh,[33] Dean of the Customs College, called. Very busy all day. Called on Adm. Hsu, who I heard was sick. Found him entertaining 7 men at a dinner party. Worked 2 hours at home after dinner.

April 25: To lunch: Dr. and Mrs. Wu. He is on Supreme Defence Council, and a Dartmouth man. She is a well-known writer – Chinese literature – pen name [冰心]; (冰心) and a Wellesley girl.[34] She is Fukienese, but has lived practically all her life in Peking, where she went to, and later taught at, Yen-ching. Had Ca Hok Gi (a connection of Mrs. Lu), Lu Ping and Tsai Hsieh Tuan also.

April 26: ~~One of those busy days~~. When running to catch the ferry, I twisted left ankle. Hurt like billyoh. At American Red Cross, where I first went to see Parker, Calvin – also Red Cross – let me have a bandage, which Dr. Wu of the Chinese Red Cross applied. Parker worried over attitude of National Health Administration; he says they are hoarding huge quantities of medical supplies donated in 1941 by Red Cross. He is also worried about securing freedom of action in disturbing further supplies which Red Cross proposes to import.

To Fan Chuang at 5:45. Dr. Kung addressing a large meeting when I arrived. It amused me to see the Tingchai [聽差] (and others) standing at the open door of the room; a very informal atmosphere prevails. I wonder what Morgenthau[35] would think of it? After the meeting, Dr. Kung went into his office, but unluckily for me, the Minister if Internal Affairs, Mr. Chou,[36] arrived and was "closeted" with the Big Boss for an hour. Mr. Chou is an old gent, complete with beard and a set of dazzling and prominent store teeth which would shame a Pepsodent advertisement. I went in first after Chou left, and had 10 minutes. Minister approved my statement to press, which I read to him.

To American Embassy for dinner: Guests: Dr. Wang Shih-chieh,[37] head of the recent Good-Will mission to England; Mr. Chao, Sec. General of the People's Political Council; Mr. Clarac, Counselor of the Free French Delegation; Gunther Stein, Christian Sciences Monitor correspondent; and another Chinese. On my way home, rain started. At Lung-nan-hou, waited in downpour for my chair. Coolies finally appeared and I guess I sort of boiled them out. I find that the vocabulary of invective remains bright although long unused.

April 27: Very busy day at office, with plenty of grief. S/O servants all dissatisfied with new pay scales which, although considerably higher than before, are not as high as those of miscellaneous staff. Working on Liesching etc. cases – resignation for war service; a hard nut to crack. Finished statement to press. Worked until 10:30 p.m. on rehabilitation of light-houses, etc., etc.

April 28: Water-coolies and chair-bearers struck work. On account of my twisted ankle, I had to hire an "outside" chair, which cost me $400 for 4 trips. Water coolies on duty again in afternoon. Lovely spring weather – just to tease us and remind us of more delectable climes. Rouse's brother, a colonel in Indian Army, killed in Burma. Oxlade, Deputy Commissioner, (Customs) also killed in action.

April 30: To Air Commodore Bartholomew's and Squadron-Leader and Mrs. Gridley-Baird's to lunch. Gen. Perrin[38] and several other American officers there; also a Polish and 2 Russian Colonels (they didn't mix!), Admiral Chen, Gen. Cheng Chen[39] and his wife, Van Der Berg, and several British officers. Gen. Perrin and Cheng tried to play the bagpipes; very amusing. ~~Jan. "Alumni Magazine" from Russ Fetté. Wrote John.~~ Wrote draft circular re furnishing 2/3rds cost of medicines for staff.

May

May 1: My first newspaper statement appeared today. Had a tough 1-1/2 hours with Adm. Hsu. We are facing a showdown: he says he'll resign if Capt. Sabel is regarded as the Senior Coast Inspector. This is a crisis of the first water. ~~A really hectic day. Nice tea with Mr. Geoffrey Smith and several others at the Canadian Mission. Dead tired.~~

May 2: With Chang Yung-Nien and Sung Ko-chang, drove to Customs College at Shanting. Spoke to students (Customs history). Had pleasant visit with old Chang Pai Leh (Dean) and others of faculty. Lovely country, and enjoyed the "morning off". Desk piled with work at 2, and I was extremely busy until

5:30. Malcolm (ex-Marine Dept.) came at 5:15 and said that India scheme for Marine staff is all washed up. This will be an unpleasant job to untangle! Letter from Randall Gould. A parcel containing 2 lovely pipes from a Washington shop delivered to my office (out of nowhere). Inside, a card "from Lt. William ("Bill") Drummond. Only this and nothing more. Who is Lt. Drummond?

May 3: 1-1/2 hours with Adm. Hsu this morning. He is still sticky; I don't know what sort of intrigue he will be up to, but I have sent my telegram recalling Capt. Sabel to active duty as Coast Inspector (on special duty in America and England). Maj. Crawford, and Malcolm came in p.m. to tell me that scheme for sending Marine officers to India is all off. This is a kick in the pants, after all the work we've put into it. Bungling; but there is always bungling during a war.

~~To installation of F.A. Nixon as first Master of Lodge of Star of South China (Canton Lodge, just re-established here). Excellent ceremony; dinner at Club afterwards. Officers Chinese and American of Fortitude Lodge (Cal.) present.~~

May 4: Adm. Hsu came to see Lu Ping and talked over 1 hour. Refused to come and see me. He is still very stubborn, and it looks like a showdown. D.G. (Li Tong) is going to build offices for Pilotage Board on Customs property Tai-ping men [太平門] – apparently without consulting me. More of Adm. Hsu's doings, I fear. ~~To dinner at Andrew Liu's house. Big party about 24, including Gen. Wu Te-cheng and his local wife. First time I've ever seen her! A pleasant evening, although I was very tired.~~

May 5: Hot!! Summer is here. Tiring day. Had luncheon for Canon and Mrs. Allen. Also present: Mrs. Smith (pretty as a picture); Nichols (American Red Cross); Gardener; Annett; Wilfred Ling;[40] Dick Lee; Capt. Lincoln Brownell.

To Chialing House, to tea-party starting campaign for $1,000,000 for Victory Nursery. Chairman: Sun Fo. Saw Lady Seymour, Cecilia Pan, etc., etc.

May 6: Lady Seymour sent me a letter John had written to her. Adm. Hsu wrote to me re his status; I replied. A dangerous man! ~~Lunch here as guest of mess, with 5 of the Chinese staff. Saturday, but quite busy till 5:15. This has been a tiring, troubled week the kind that causes stomach ulcers.~~

May 7: By chair to first range, where I met Hopstock and Pouncey with whom I walked to our bungalow on the second range. Hot, but nice breeze at the house. Picnic lunch, and lazy afternoon, then walked home in 1-1/4 hours. ~~Tired, but rested, and the change is agreeable.~~

May 8: Had Pouncey, Hsia [Ting-Yao][41] and Fang to lunch. Took Pouncey and Hsia to call on Li Tong. 2 hours with Director General – chiefly re Admiral Hsu and Sabel. Director General quite reasonable.

May 9: Admiral Hsu again for an hour. I fear he is not yet satisfied as to his position, and that he will continue his backstairs intrigue. He is a pest and a nuisance and a danger. Cold today: flannel suit again, and a sweater at night. [. . .]

May 10: To Fan Chuang at noon to see Dr. Kung. Reported (1) revenue (Mar. $225,000,000 – record); (2) Maze restored title to "purloined letters"; (3) Loyang evacuated;[42] (4) Adm. Hsu's case: Dr. Kung agreed that Capt. Sabel is Coast Inspector (on special duty); (5) asked Dr. Kung about my withdrawal from pension scheme. He said he approved it. Where is my letter? (6) Told me I could draw same pay as Maze. He seemed astonished to hear that I was £1,000 a month and said: "That's not what I was given to understand." Promised to let me know how much I should draw.

Busy afternoon at office. Cup of coffee at Navy Mess on Way home. Cook made me delicious ginger snaps,

May 11: To United China Relief meeting at Rappe's house. Dr. Lenning Sweet gave a talk on the organization at home and here. To dinner (and spend night) at British Embassy. Seymours' had nice dinner party: Dr. and Mrs. Chang (she is a brilliant economist); General de Wiart; a young Polish artist who made some rather poor sketches during the evening.

May 12: Nice breakfast and good coffee at the Seymours, then back across the river to work. Hot as the devil today. River rising – 8-1/2 feet this morning. ~~Col. Brown gave me 1 pound "Briggs Mixture"~~; Lady Seymour gave me 1 pound coffee. I gave Col. Brown a new pipe.

May 13: Hot again, but showers towards evening cooled the air. ~~Easy day in office. Paul Blunt returned from Changsha and came to see me. He had a letter from "Easy Gamble", his cousin who had been in touch with John. John's new address is: Port Intelligence Office, A.P.O. 506. This is about the 10th A.P.O. number he's had since he left home.[...]~~

May 14: Rain in morning, so didn't go to hills, as planned. Lunch with Paul Blunt, Hall and Watterson. Lazy day. D.K. Wei called. He said that M.Y. Tang (Bank of Canton) had been executed "without trial". Suspected of too close relations with Japs in Hongkong. M.Y. Tang was one of T.V. Soong's closest followers. D.K. said "the most brilliant among them." D.K. said his name is never mentioned by Chinese – he's a forgotten man.

May 15: ~~Diarrhea at 3:30 a.m. – 5 times by 7:30. Stayed in bed all day. Usual weakness. Light diet. Felt better at night. Letter from Stewart (April) said that Mother is gradually failing and probably cannot live much longer.~~

May 16: Felt a bit weak in morning, but went to office. Acheson[43] just back from Kweilin, where financial situation acute because of bad war news from China front and heavy bank withdrawals. Central Bank had 1-1/2 billion deposits and 3 million in cash! Acheson got Gen. Chennault to fly several tons of banknotes to Kweilin and thus eased situation temporarily. Whole financial structure in China is in precarious condition.

Pouncey told me Shanghai (Hungjao) [虹橋] Golf Club had rule that 15 out of total 16 members of Club committee must vote to elect, and that 2 blackballs would reject a candidate. When Pritchard[44] went up, only 14 voted, so he was not elected but, if there had been 15 members present and one had cast a blackball, he would have been elected! (A second ballot was held and he got in.)

May 17: Quiet day in office. ~~Bright, clear day, not too hot. [...]~~

May 18: Hot, and the river is rising; 9 feet. Dined at Morris Depass' house. Buffet, with about 20 there. Have just arrived from Indo-China. I asked the latter (très distinguée, agée de 20 ans) how she got out of Indo-China. She replied

"I cannot tell you." ~~Linc Brownell gave me a tube of toothpaste, (and Gauss sent~~ me three packages of Briggs' Mixture). Mitchinaya in Burma taken today![45] And Cassino![46] Good news. News from Honan front not so good;[47] looks very serious this time.

May 19: Cold and rainy. River rose 10.7 feet, and a "strong coffee" color.

May 20: Rain; quite cool. Had to wear woolen suit and sweater. Very busy day in office: I sometimes think staff all plan to dump their week's work on me on Saturday afternoon. ~~Nice letters from Foster Hall, Hooper, etc., on my "elevation".~~

May 21: ~~Cold, overcast. D.K. Wei called and talked an hour. To Club to get books.~~ Munby's entry into South Africa has been refused because his wife is Chinese. The Dominions are pretty hard-boiled with Englishmen! ~~Paul Blunt to tea, and nice talk.~~

May 22: Still cold: had to wear woolen underwear and sweater! River rising: 13.7 feet, and the wide sand flats opposite the Inspectorate are covered, thus widening the river 100%. Rumors widespread that Dr. Kung is leaving the Ministry of Finance; that he has resigned but that his resignation has not been accepted; that K.P. Chen has declined the job; that Hsu Kan may get it; etc., etc.

Crossed river and had a chat with Col. C.C. Brown (American Naval Attaché) re training scheme for Customs Marine officers.

To American Embassy, where I had a chat with Mr. Gauss and ~~with~~ Atcheson. To Fan Chuang, where Daniel Chang said that O.K. Yui is handling my letter re withdrawal from Pensions Scheme. To K.W.S. and an hour with Li Tong. Discussed half a dozen things, among them my pay. Li said that Dr. Kung had asked him to see me about it. I told him that I thought Maze's £1,000 a month too much. He asked me to name a figure. I said "How about half?" He said that was too little, and thought we should fix a figure between £500 and £1000. I told him that anything he and Dr. Kung fixed would be O.K. by me; and he said he would speak to the Minister and let me know.

May 23: Lunch with mess; Bishop Hall[48] of Hongkong guest of honor. He is a fine man! Busy day in office.

May 24: About 3 hours conferences (plus an hour at home) with Lu, Chang, and Pouncey on staff reorganization. At 5, to Fan Chuang. Dr. Kung's eldest daughter was married today in New York, and an informal tea party was held in honor of the event. There were between 150 and 200 people present, including wives of many prominent government officials. I met the three Soong sisters – Mmes. Chiang, Sun[49] and Kung,[50] and Generalissimo Chiang Kai-shek. I was presented to this galaxy by Dr. Kung. The only other foreigners present were Arthur Young and George Fitch. The latter arrived last Saturday, after 5-1/2 months' trip from America. From Argentina to South Africa he sailed in a 75-year old square-rigged windjammer. He saw Maze in Capetown, and said he was "itching" to get back to China. (Let him itch, says I).

May 25: ~~Got a lot done today.~~ Signed checks for almost $14,000,000. Ts'ai-cheng Pu forwards secret complaint against Yu Kwai, Deputy Commissioner, Changsha. I shall send a man from here to investigate.

May 26: Ellis, Chief Appraiser from Foochow, called at office. At tea time, Houpt, Tdsvyr. from Wenchow, appeared without warning and said: "Groff-Smith told me that you could put me up." With Hopstock in my pantry, Pouncey in my study and Gardener in my spare bedroom, this means that Houpt must have a camp bed in my drawing room. I still have bedroom and dining room, thank goodness!

May 27: ~~Funny how busy Saturday afternoons seem to be in the office here! In most ports, there is little doing. I feel that the staff try to clear their desks on Friday, and on Sunday morning, with the result that the accumulation reaches my desk Saturday afternoon.~~

~~To Club to change books. War news good from Italy and Burma. A "New Yorker" from John, and a nice letter from Nate.~~

May 28: A lovely day – sunny but not hot. To lunch at Belgium Embassy, Wang Shan. By chair up the hills through new and beautiful country. The finest I've seen near Chungking. Segaert, the Belgian Minister, is suffering from some kind of anemia, and is leaving soon for Calcutta for X-ray treatment. He is a pleasant, well-mannered man. His No. 2, a young man called Jacques Smeti, leaves for Washington next month. Other guests were: Dr. and Mrs. K.C. Wu (Vice-Minister of Foreign Affairs). Mrs. Wu is one of the most charming and beautiful women I have ever known. Also, Mr. and Mrs. Menon, the Indian Agent; both very intelligent and affable. I walked home, exactly one hour to my house. Polished letter to Li Tong re reorganization, drafted dispatch to Macao re Borras, etc.

May 29: Hot today; our cool spell is over, I fear. 1-1/2 hours with Li Tong; discussed several topics. I handed him revised staff reorganization scheme. ~~Stopped at Cecilia Pan's to enquire about next Sunday's jaunt to Koloshan. To Navy Sick Bay, to get 2nd cholera shot.~~

May 30: A dead coolie, young and beautifully built, lay on the foreshore when I went to office. By noontime, someone had put a mat shelter over the body, but it had blown away when I passed at 5 o'clock. I wonder if it will still be there tomorrow. Lu Ping said that Admiral Hsu had told him that he would "make small shoes for the Inspector General." A dangerous politician, who will bear watching.

May 31: Lunch at K.P. Chen's with Hopstock. Had long talk with Kuo Tai-chi, who is very pessimistic about situation in China. He says military, political and economic situations all deteriorating. I suggested political situation was better than a few years ago and cited work and criticism of Peoples' Political Council. Dr. Kuo replied that P.P.C. was not very representative; was only consultative; had no power of impeachment or finance; and that government paid little or no attention to it.[51] He said that Chinese armies are ill-fed and poorly cared for, and that the Chinese were "routed" in recent fighting in Honan.[52] He said he hoped I'd be able to preserve the integrity of the Customs, and agreed that the government must give me the wherewithal. He said: "You're like a housewife who has to cook for a family; she must have the rice and oil and fuel to prepare the meal." He said that he thought that the Chinese generally were not opposed to having foreigners in the Customs, and that foreigners give the Chinese colleagues in the Service "stiffening" and an incentive to excel.

Hot again today; river up to 15 feet; corpse removed from foreshore. Have read half a dozen books during the last 2 weeks, none of which deserve mention: now reading "Dr. Bradley Remembers", which is fair, and Johnstone's "The U.S. and Japan's New Order".

June

June 1: Very hot – a scorcher. Also very humid. Situation in Honan and Hsi-an very disquieting. To dinner at Gen. Ferris's (Stilwell's Chief-of-Staff). All military but me. One lady: Miss Rettenkopf, a Red Cross girl. Good dinner, including the non-melting butter, and ice-cream. Movie after dinner – technicolor "Broadway Rhythm", I think it was called.

June 2: Cooler today, and fine rain at night. Passed Spring promotions today; made 5 new Chinese Commissioners, including Fang Tu and Tso Chang Ching of my Inspectorate staff. Reading "Documents in the Case", – a worth-while detective story.

Letter from Maze re "Purloined Documents," a tissue of *suppressio veri* and *suggestio falsi*. News from Hunan bad; looks as if we shall lose (besides Loyang) Changsha and Kukong. Possibly Shangjao also, and be cut off from Wenchow and Foochow.[53] Our revenue will suffer drastically.

June 3: As usual, Saturday afternoon proved to be a busy time. To buffet supper and dance at Ma An Shan [馬鞍山]. Capt. Farmer, host. Big crowd, almost entirely American and Chinese military; cocktails from 6:30 to 8:30, then mediocre chow, but excellent ice-cream and coffee.

June 4: Cleaned up my desk, sorted letters, wrote to Mr. and Mrs. David Westborg in Assam. Drove with Cecilia and Francis Pan and Russel Fetté to Koloshan, and had tea with Dr. and Mrs. Wen-Tsao Wu.[54] She is writer, "Hsieh Ping-hsin"; he is Counsellor of Supreme National Defence Council. They have two lovely daughters, 8 [Wu Ping] and 5 [Wu Ching].[55] Her brother [Hsieh Ping-chi[56]] is a Commander in Marine Dept. On way back, stopped a few minutes with Dr. Gordon King at Shanghai Medical College. On road, 8 miles from city, picked up Arthur Young and Owen Dawson, whose bus from Peipei [北陪] had broken down.

To the Pan's for a delicious dinner; they are delightful people. Took Fetté home; thereby missing the 10 o'clock ferry by 5 minutes and having to wait 3/4 of an hour!

June 5: Rome captured yesterday! Big news, sure to have important effect in Germany, Turkey, Balkans and everywhere. News from Honan, Hupeh and Hunan not so good. Situation in Laohoukow [老河口], Kweilin, Kukong shaky, and evacuation of Customs from first and last mentioned places highly probable. Changsha staff already moved to Kweilin. Lunch at American Embassy with Mr. Gauss, George Atcheson and the rest of crowd. Excellent Chinese dish, plus good strong coffee. 1-1/2 hours with Li Tong. He says prospects in Hunan, although bad, are not hopeless, and that Chinese may stop Japs.

To Cecilia Pan's for coffee and biscuits (she gave me a pot of homemade apricot jam!)

To Fang Chuang, to see Dr. Kung and get his authority to approach UNRRA and enquire whether they will replace our lighthouse after the war. ~~Banister gave me a pound of Burma coffee. Alla samee Clistmas today~~. River rose 12 feet over the week-end. Most of the great "islands" in the river are now submerged for the summer.

June 6: The Invasion has begun! God keep John safe! At 2 o'clock, I stopped at the Navy Mess and heard B.B.C. repeat the German announcement of the invasions, without confirming or denying it. At the same time, the announcer repeated Eisenhower's last warning to the civilian population of the "Invasion Coast." At 6 p.m., the invasion was confirmed.

I had 12 to dinner here: Mr. and Mrs. K.C. Lee (H & S Bank); Col. Morris Depass; Col. Wasser (New American Air Attaché); Paul Blunt; Quick (I.C.I.); Gray (H & S) and Pouncey. A pleasant evening, talk all of invasion. At 10, listened to Annett's radio and got further details of the fighting.

June 7: Li Tong told Lu Ping that my salary has been fixed £700 a month. This is very satisfactory. Also, my proposal to withdraw from the Pensions Plan has been approved. The Invasion is the great topic of the day, and all bulletins and radio reports are eagerly devoured.

June 8: Bad weather in Channel held up Invasion forces, but things seem to be going pretty well. In Italy, Civitavecchia has been taken. Called on Brazilian Ambassador at 2:45; he was asleep, so I didn't disturb him. Called on Gen. Pechkoff, Head of the Free French Delegation. A most charming man. Lost one arm. Formerly in Foreign Legion. Knows America well. Stopped at Ministry to see Y.C. Koo, who was out. Had a minute with O.K. Yui. Annett sold 3 small bottles of Quink, a tin of Mennen's toilet powder and 200 sheets of writing paper for C.N. $4,800 with which he will buy £60 of British War Bonds!! U.S. value of the things he sold is less than U.S. $2.00 – and he gets War Bonds worth U.S. $240!!!

June 9: Extremely heavy rain last night cleaned all the city sewers for one day at least. Worked most of day on reply to Maze's letter re "purloined letters."

June 10: Dined at the Menons' (Indian Agent General); he is scholarly; she is gracious; their 19-year old daughter (a student in Ginling College, Chengtu) very intelligent. Also present: Quo Tai-chi; Dr. and Mrs. Wang Shih-chieh; Mr. Wen and Jacques Smeti.

June 11: By chair to First Range, then walked to bungalow at Liang Feng Ya. Rather hot walk, but cool and airy at destination. Hopstock and I had lunch: 3 fried eggs, boiled potatoes, toast, and tea. Lazy afternoon. Pouncey came up, then Lovink (Dutch Ambassador); then Col. Marsh-Kellett; Capt. Dew; Mr. Smith (British Minister of Information) and Mr. and Mrs. Stephant (Dutch Embassy). All had tea. Walked home in 1 hour 5 minutes, after a very pleasant day.

June 12: ~~Had Mr. Ellis, Chief Appraiser, to lunch, with Lu Ping and Annett. Ellis is just leaving on retirement~~. To Kuan-wu Shu; then to a chat with Col. Brown, who is soon leaving Chungking? Was told that people leaving China for good can go to a certain Mr. Hsu, head of the exchange department of the Central Bank, and exchange their Chinese dollars up to any amount for a sterling draft at 160! The rule is that dollars are exchangeable at 80, but payment is limited to some £100 a month. If true, this is disgraceful to a degree. Who gets the other $80?

June 13: Dr. Kung is leaving soon for International Monetary Conference at Bretton Woods.[57] Arthur Young is also going, and leaves here tomorrow. Bretton Woods in July! Warming up again these days. Good news from Normandy, where the Americans seem to be doing well. News also good from Italy, Burma, S.W. Pacific and Russia, but situation in China pretty shaky. Chinese say they still hold Changsha. I hope so. Had nice letter from Betty first news from Pawtucket in a long time. Mother gradually weakening, and Betty doesn't think she can pull through this time.

June 14: Office in morning. Afternoon, called on new Turkish Ambassador, who, fortunately, was out. To Fan Chuang to see Dr. Kung, who was very cordial. Told me to keep things running smoothly while he's away (about 4 months), and said it would be a good idea to have the "American correspondents" to lunch occasionally and give them encouraging statements about the Customs. Met Bill Hunt, who arrived yesterday from New York. I asked him what priority he had, and he said: "Oh, we had a special plane!" He would! He came with the head of Universal Trading Corp.

To Wai-chiao Pu [Foreign Ministry], to a big tea party to celebrate "United Nations Day." Dr. Soong very pleasant, but I dropped a brick! Daniel Chang had told me half an hour earlier that Loy Chang was going to America with Dr. Kung, and I mentioned this to Dr. Soong. He said: "No, I'm keeping Loy here; I need him more than Dr. Kung does." Then I dropped my brick. I said: "It must be flattering to have 2 ministers fighting over you." I fear T.V. didn't quite take it as the joke I meant, for he replied: "Oh! we're not fighting about it." quite seriously.

The place was crowded with Ambassadors, Generals, etc. I met Gen. Connor,[58] U.S.A. (Engineers), who has just come from building the Alaska Highway and is going to help build roads in Burma. Bill Hunt had 1/2 pound tobacco for Dr. Kung. I said: "Why not give it to me? The Old Man's going to America where he can get plenty." Just then Martin Gold came into the room, also bearing a parcel. "Give that to L.K. Marty", said Bill, and "that" proved to be 1/2 pound of Middleton's "Walnut". A nice gift.

June 15: River down to 15 feet, from 23 last week. Worried about my tongue, the tip of which has been sort of stiff every morning when I woke. It is a little inflamed, I think. Cut out pipe today to see if I can cure the trouble. Admiral Hsu in my office for 1-1/2 hours this morning.

June 16: Chungking Customs seized a suit-case from an officer of the Military Affairs Commission at airport. It contained 9.20 kilos raw opium, worth C.N. $1,000,000, besides some woolen piece goods. Pressure is being brought on Chungking Commissioner to hand over the opium to the M.A. Commissioner "as evidence" to be used against officer concerned. Government regulations require

Customs to hand over to police. My Chinese colleagues advised me to let M.A. Commissioner have the stuff, or we shall have trouble with them. I spoke to Li Tong about it, and he supported my view, i.e., that I must follow the government's regulations. Dirty business, when young men of all countries are dying in the war, to have high Chinese officials take advantage of their positions and uniforms to smuggle opium!

To Fan Chuang to see Daniel Chang, who was out. Dr. Herrington said that there was a slight irritation of my tongue, but no "growth".

Japan bombed by Super-Fortresses yesterday! Americans land on Saipan! (Did the Super-Forts come from Chengtu?)

June 17: Lovink, the Netherlands Ambassador, had my foreign staff, Lu Ping and me to lunch. After lunch, he spoke informally, and acknowledged his personal debt to the Customs for the 3 years – the happiest he has had – he spent in the Service; and paid a high tribute to the Customs record, emphasizing especially its international, cosmopolitan nature. I replied.

To Fan Chuang, to hand Minister my comments on Maze's letter to him re "purloined letters". He approved my draft reply, but cut out the words "disingenuous explanation". Maze is getting off very lightly. ~~Stopped a minute to invite Cecilia and Francis Pan to lunch next Monday; Cecilia told me that they have had another burglary looks like an inside job.~~

To Major Farmer's to buffet supper, movie and dance. Picture "Marines at Wake Island": spectacular. Met Col. Barrett,[59] who (I think) was in a Super-Fortress over Japan day before yesterday.

Talked with Gen. S. K. Yee (Intelligence). He said Japan's present grand strategy is to give China the knock-out blow while there's time. The Japs have 12 to 15 divisions in Honan-Hunan area, and 4 or 5 in Canton. Many crack troops from Manchuria released after signing of Jap-Russian "fishing" etc. treaty. Jap Navy opposed to Tojo's[60] plan in China, and are agitating for peace with Allies. Jap Navy mostly in waters between Japan and Bonin Islands. Chinese have spies in Jap war and navy departments in Tokyo; recently got Jap coastal charts (via Peiping) and passed them on to U.S. and British Navies. Situation here 3 weeks ago most critical of the seven years of war; everybody from Generalissimo down terribly worried. Appeals for immediate assistance sent to Roosevelt and Churchill direct: bombing of Japan and landing on Saipan were answers. Gen. Yee thinks they will relieve pressure. (I wonder: possibly they'll have opposite effect and stimulate Japan's "Continental push"). Gen. Yee said that Churchill recently informed Chiang Kai-shek that Germany had only about 1200 fighter planes in France and 1500 in Germany, and that the Allies can easily take care of those. He thinks the war in Europe will be over in 3 to 5 months. Gen. Yee thinks Changsha must fall soon, and, when it does, Hengyang [衡陽] will be lost almost at once.[61] The Japs will then move north from Canton, and make a drive for Kweilin. He advised me strongly to evacuate my staff from Hengyang immediately, and to prepare for prompt evacuation of Kweilin.

June 18: With Annett and Pouncey to Liang Feng Ya [涼風涯] ("Cool Wind Gap") and a pleasant day at bungalow. Didn't start till 10, because I had to get off a telegram to Gawler at Kweilin suggesting evacuation of Hengyang. Paul Blunt joined us at the bungalow, and we all walked home together.

Annett talked with a young Frenchman who escaped from France four months ago. Out of a party of 18 who tried to escape into Spain, one was killed by a fall, and fifteen were taken by the Spaniards and handed back to the Germans in France. He said conditions are terrible, and that 30% to 50% of the French are spying on the rest for the Germans. The bourgeois class are pro-German, the rest hate them with undying fury. Unless the Allies get into the saddle with prompt control he predicts civil war. Says that the masses hate Petain;[62] also, that the new government in France after the war will be Communist.

June 19: To lunch here: George Fitch; Russel Fetté (who is soon leaving for home); Mrs. Auyang; Hopstock and Pouncey. Francis and Cecilia Pan couldn't come. Busy day in office.

June 20: To D.G., but little business. We did what we had to do without an interruption; his English is just as lousy as my Chinese, but we managed. To Dr. An, my dentist, who ground some of the sharp edges on my teeth, hoping to remove the cause of my sore tongue. Dr. Herrington looked at it last week, and said there was no growth, but only chronic irritation.

Vice-president Wallace arrived in Chungking today. Dr. Kung left yesterday – Monday – and will be in New York on Thursday! That's speed.

June 21: Alice's birthday. A nice "memorial" note from Blunt, with whom I dined at night. He was very fond of Alice. I miss her; we were supremely happy. Admiral Hsu in my office 1-3/4 hours this morning. Wired Hall to pay my pension money (29=1/2/35ths) to Hospital Trust Co., Providence – $41,861.27.

June 22: Changsha has fallen. Hengyang will go next, I suppose; and then? Kukong way, or S.W. to Kweilin and Nanning? Or maybe a drive to Chungking? Big Jap-U.S. naval battle may be developing west of Saipan. River up suddenly to 32 feet.

June 23: To reception for Mr. Wallace, Vice-President, at the Embassy at 12:30. Mr. Gauss introduced me, and explained my position, and what I was trying to do; he pointed out that the Customs was formerly run on rather "exclusive" British lines, but that I was running it for China, and in the expectation that it would be handed over to Chinese control as a going and efficient concern. Mr. Wallace asked me about cargo crossing between occupied and free China. He seemed rather surprised when I told him that there is a large legitimate trade with the occupied area, and that 1/3 of the 1943 Customs revenue came from this trade. (I imagine he had been told about the widespread smuggling – military, especially – between the two areas.) Mr. Wallace seemed a very quiet person, and had little small talk. About 40 people at the reception. (As I finished this sentence, a 1-1/2 inch flying cockroach made a crash landing on my desk; Ugh! The first of these noxious beasts I've ever seen here.)

1944

Gawler wired from Kweilin that threat to Hengyang is growing, and suggests evacuation of surplus staff to Chungking district. I fear we're in for trouble all through central and south China; a possible Jap drive from Hengyang to Kweilin to Nanning? Or a grand slam at Chungking? Except for China, war news is excellent in all theatres. Jap fleet approaching Saipan got a sock in the eye, all right! I have a hunch that the German "pilotless plane" is doing a lot more damage in England than the censors allow to be mentioned.

June 24: A busy day! Lunch with Bill Hunt at Martin Gold's, and a long talk. Bill fears that the rumors of discord between Gimo and Missimo are true; Gimo is said to have a couple of very beautiful young girls in his intimate entourage.[63] Bill said that Dr. Kung thought of taking me with him to America, but that his party was too large for the planes as it was. While I'd liked to have gone for selfish reasons, it would have been very bad for the Service. If Ting had been here, it would have been different. River at 42 feet, and for first time since last summer it was impossible to go along the foreshore.

June 25: ~~Paul Blunt dropped in for a chat. Started a letter to John, but lights went out during dinner, so couldn't finish it.~~ 5th day of 5th moon. Dragon Boat Festival. Glad it's over, because the past week we have had too much of the monotonous and tiring boom-boom of the drums in the blasted boats.

June 26: Hot; about 92 degrees. To D.G.'s at 2:30, then to Ministry to see O.K. Yui, who is Acting Minister of Finance in Dr. Kung's absence. Li Tong is Acting Administrative Vice-Minister – pinch-hitting for Y.C. Koo. ~~To Club to exchange books~~. War news excellent everywhere except in China; Cherbourg will probably fall in 24 hours or less.

June 27: Germans announce fall of Cherbourg. Dined at American Embassy. Farewell to Dean Cross, head of the Post-Graduate School of Journalism. The other three Americans on the faculty also there. Also, Capt. Jarrell, new American Naval Attaché, plus several Embassy Secretaries, and Archie Steele,[64] Chicago "Daily News" correspondent. A good dinner, as always there. Lost the 10 o'clock ferry by 5 minutes, and had to wait till 10:45. Finished "Claudia", a pleasant book.

June 28: Hot and humid. Situation in Hunan etc. looks pretty grim, and the Chinese seem to be making no serious attempt to stop the Japs. It looks as if the latter would head for Kweilin as soon as Hengyang falls, and possibly continue to Luichow and Nanning – even if they don't make a stab for Kunming and Chungking. Gauss very pessimistic last night: he says the Chinese simply aren't fighting. How can they? For two years the troops have been idling; officers corrupt, trading with the enemy and making fortunes; men ill-fed, ill-clothed and ill-treated. True, they have little artillery and no tanks, but – decently led – they could hold at many places with the arms they have. Gauss says defection is rampant among high and low; the Chinese take the position: "No matter what happens in China, the Allies are winning the war and will drive the Japs out eventually."

Comte Raoul de Sercey,[65] of the Chinese Post Office, who left Hongkong April 25, had tea with me and Annett, and gave us a full account of conditions in Hongkong. Sixteen foreigners (fifteen English and one American) from Stanley

1944

Camp were beheaded by the Japs. Torture is common; malnutrition widespread. Customs people all right so far. A very cruel experience.

June 29: Rainy and sticky. Long letter from Li Tung-hwa describing evacuation of Loyang and Lushih: sad reading. At one place, Chinese villagers – bandits – stole even the nursing bottles and milk powder from the woman in the party. The Chinese were almost as rapacious and cruel to their own people as the Japanese.

To dinner at Dick Smith's for Billy Christian, who has just arrived for OSS. Also there: Cols. Depass and Wasser, and Major Farmer. Christian described life in the internment camp at Wei-hsien [濰縣] Shantung. The Japs treated foreigners in North China much better than in South China. Bill told story of the G.I. who wrote home: "Ma, I can't tell you where I am, but yesterday I shot a polar bear." Few months later: "Ma, I c.t.y.w. I am, but last night I went out dancing with [. . .] girl in a gross ?" Two weeks later: "Ma, I c.t.y.w. I am, but I'm in hospital, and the doctor says it would have been better if I'd shot the girl and danced with the bear."

June 30: Friday. More rain, and cooler. River (which had been at 31 feet) rose to 40 feet during day. ~~Busy in office.~~

July

July 1: Hopstock sold an old gray flannel suit for $17,000; he paid U.S. $8.00 for it in a bargain basement in Los Angeles 5 years ago. To "Dominion Day" reception at Canadian Embassy. Full of Ambassadors, Generals (3, 2 and 1-star), high officials. No electricity all day and night.

War news in China very discouraging; who can stop the Japs from taking our air-fields? Hengyang already gone; Kweilin (with five or four fields) may be next stop. Unless the Chinese army puts up a fight, the Japs could even get to Chengtu.

July 2: ~~To bungalow, with Annett, Hopstock, Pouncey, Blunt. Fine day. Stopped to see Lott Wei on way home: he is just back from Chengtu.~~ San Francisco radio at 8 p.m. said Japs have started offensive north of Canton.

July 3: Summer hours at Inspectorate: 7–12, with skeleton staff 4–6. I shall probably do 8:30 to 12, 3–5. Warming up, after a very comfortable June. War news in China very bad. Gen. Yu advised me today to evacuate staff from Kweilin. Foreign opinion is that Chinese will make little or no attempt to defend Kweilin or any other place in South China.

July 4: Typical "Fourth of July" weather – hot! [. . .] To reception at American Embassy; there must have been 300 there, from Ambassadors to file clerks, and from Generals to privates. British, Chinese, Dutch, Russians, Belgians, Turks, Brazilians, Norwegians, French, etc. And I am grateful for and proud of my title and classification: American.

July 5: [. . .] Bathurst arrived from Kukong via Kweilin. Says morale very low all through South China. Troops will not resist Japanese drive. Yu Han Mou (who gave up Canton without a fight) intends to move east into Kwangtung to avoid the enemy. Criticism of Chungking government bitter and widespread, but Chiang still popular in all quarters.

July 6: Humid and sticky. Gen. S.K. Yu sent me word at 11 a.m. that Japanese are retreating from Hengyang and from west of Loyang, and that Kweilin is out of danger for the time being. S.K. says Japs have got to turn their attention to Russia! This is dramatic news – if true. Stopped at Military Attaché's office at 3:30, and Morrie Depass confirmed S.K.'s news but smiled at the mention of Russia. Morrie said that the Chinese have got the Japs on the run both at east and west of Hengyang; that the air-field there may be retaken tomorrow; that it has the makings of a great victory. I wired to Gawler and told him to suspend further evacuation of Kweilin. ~~Bathurst here to lunch.~~

July 7: ~~Took Bathurst to call on Li Tong. One hour conference on many subjects~~. Today is "Double 7th" – anniversary – the 7th day of the month – of the start of the Chinese-Japanese War. Ching-pao [警報] air-raid alarm at 9:30; all lights out in this section, but not elsewhere. To bed at 11:15, hoping the Japs won't come. It is a lovely moonlight night.

July 8: Very hot. River up again: 43 feet. Went into kitchen at 3:30 to find a servant: found boy and his wife with 4 large cups (mine!) of cocoa, and a dozen of fine slices of toast made on my fire at U.S. $200 a ton. I can't afford cocoa. These people live well; I see to that, i.e., I don't see it! Invited to buffet supper and move at Ma An Shan, but didn't feel like dolling up, so stayed quietly at home.

July 10: To U.C.R. committee meeting at Dr. Rappe's. Distributed some C.N. $20,000,000.

July 11: River rose 6 feet while I was at lunch. 52 feet – highest this year. News today that Japanese are evacuating Changsha and Tungting Lake [洞庭湖] area. Hope it's true.

July 12: ~~Count Raoul de Sercey to tea here. Boy, who told me yesterday that he was going to Chengtu for 3 months, told me tonight that he was not going, yet~~. Today is the 90th anniversary of the Chinese Customs Service. I wrote a brief message to the staff to mark the occasion.

July 13: Reuter reported that John Morris, U.P.'s Far Eastern Manager, was killed by falling from a 12th story window in New York. He had lunch here with me a few months ago, and was the life of the party. Mr. Yao very optimistic about the Hunan war situation: says the Chinese can take back Hankow! Said rice has dropped from $2300 to $1700 in past few days: hoarders fear big Chinese victory and are unloading.

July 14: Telegram from K.T. Ting said he left Tihwa [迪化] yesterday by plane. Sent to meet him, but plane didn't arrive. ~~Today it has been HOT. This is the real Chungking summer, and I hope it doesn't last!~~

To a reception at the French "Délégation". Gen. Pechkoff, whom I address as "Delegate of the French Committee of National Liberation", signs himself "Ambassadeur". Big crowd; all sweaty. Mr. Yao told me last night that China and Russia have recently signed a pact whereby the 8th Route Army (Communist) will take Manchuria with Russian assistance! I wonder if there's anything in this rumor. Did Wallace's visit have anything to do with it?

July 15: Ting didn't turn up. His plane said to be in Lanchow. HOT! HOT! Must be over 100. Heat reflects from road and strikes you in the eyes under the hat brim.

July 16: ~~Diarrhea at 6 and 7. Spent morning in bed, fasting, and missed my Sunday at the bungalow. Checked d., and had beef tea, poached egg and custard for dinner. Hot all day. Paul Blunt came in for hour before dinner.~~ Note from somebody on my staff begging for ice for a man dying of typhoid at Canadian Mission Hospital. Mr. Duperrault, Chief Pharmacist mate, gave me the entire stock of cubes from the Navy mess's refrigerator.

July 17: Fire at Inspectorate at 2 a.m.: Peng outside Ting's house caught fire – probably cigarette – but boatmen etc. from Customs hulk put it out. I gave them $1,000 apiece as reward – 26 of them. Ting still held up at Lanchow. On the 14th, at the French reception, Dr. Quo Tai-chi said to Keith Officer, the Australian Chargé d'Affairs: "Mr. Little is our first American Inspector General." Not a highly tactful remark from a former diplomat and Ambassador to the Court of St. James! Mr. Officer, in reply, smiled and said: "Well, you had to take an Anglo-Saxon, anyhow!" ~~My stomach seems to be O.K. again today.~~

July 18: ~~Still hot. To a movie "King Ho", at the Salt Inspectorate. Very exciting story of "Carlson's Raiders" on Makin Island.~~ To the Seymours' for dinner (Mr. Gauss and Gen. Ferris also there) then to a movie show at the British Embassy. First, "First Comes Courage", – an excellent propaganda film, based on spy and commando warfare in Norway. Then a lot of exciting film of the Normandy landings.

July 20: Spent night at Seymours', and, after excellent breakfast, crossed river to office. ~~HOT. Crossed river again at 7, and dined with Mr. and Mrs. _____ (Jardine's). The Seymours, Berkeley Gage, Francis and Cecilia Pan, Lovink also there~~. Tojo Cabinet resigned!

July 21: This week the temperature has varied between 98 and 102 degrees. Things are rather slack in the office. An accusation has been made that six questions on the recent examination for clerks leaked out! Attempt made on life of Hitler! Pity he escaped! It looks as if the war would reach a climax this year, and be won, both in Europe and possibly in Far East.

July 22: Two hours with Li Tong and Admiral Hsu, mostly on subject of pilotage.

~~To "Friends of the Allied Forces" to meet Jim Henry. He looked well, although thinner than of old; as ebullient as ever. Busy afternoon in office. Jim Henry brought me letters from Stewart, Jack and Miss Crystal.~~ Told Gardener this evening that Ministry of Finance had decided his case: (1) charges against him dismissed; (2) he is to be compulsorily retired on 31 July. He was heavily sarcastic about the seven days' notice, but I refrained from pointing out that he has been on full pay for a year and never done a stroke of work.

1944

July 23: ~~With Pouncey, to bungalow. Nice dinner with the Birches and Smiths. They are 2 exceptionally attractive Canadian missionary couples both wives, incidentally, American-born. To church next door, where Mr. Birch preached well. Heavy thunderstorm in afternoon, followed by strong wind and dense fog. A fitting background for murder.~~

July 24: River up to 49.2 feet again. Hot as Hades. ~~Lu Ping back at office after 4 days malaria.~~ Lott and Lucy Wei to dinner here (also Pouncey and Hopstock). Lott told me reason for Chiang-Soong break: when T.V. came back from America, he had tea with Chiang, who asked him why he, as China's representative, had been unable to prevent widespread criticism of China in America. T.V. replied: "What could I do, when things were so bad in China?" Chiang flew into a temper and knocked over the tea table. Hence lots of tears! Lott says that T.V. wants to quit as Minister of Foreign Affairs, but that Generalissimo won't let him go. Lott is resigning from the Mint after 15 years, because the newly-appointed Director of the Mint will make it impossible for him to carry on. After 90 years of the Customs Service as an example of civil service, the Chinese government still seems incapable of rising above a cynical spoils system.

July 25: ~~Heavy rain at 6:30 cooled things off a bit. Had a lovely letter from Betty, first from Touisset, where she seems very happy to be. Letter also from Carl Neprud and Randall Gould. My boy is sick, chill.~~

July 27: Dined at Club as guest of Annett. He had an Australian correspondent – Speight[66] – who has just been with Stilwell in Burma. Says the Chinese fight as well as any troops, they are very brave. Gen. Merrill[67] had some kind of a stroke the day before the attack on the Mitchjnags airfield, and his American No. 2 – a Colonel – took command, and 2 Chinese Generals in the force didn't like it. The whole of the city might have been taken in a day except for a mix-up: Chinese troops in 3 units fought one another in the dark and lost over 300 killed! He said the American transport and supply system was the finest in the world: "No country except America could have done it." Said the situation of the Indian frontier (Imphal-Kohina) was touch-and-go for several days and, if the Japs had succeeded, the result would have been more disastrous than the fall of Singapore.

July 28: ~~Invited to dinner and dance at Capt. Dew's, but declined. Ting returned from Tichow. Very glad, too, because temperature was 104 and no electricity.~~ Ting returned from Tihwa.

July 29: With Ting called on Li Tong and O.K. Yui. HOT! 107 degrees at 5 o'clock. B-29's bombed Mukden [瀋陽].

July 30: Very hot again! At 10, to Lott and Lucy Wei's house at Huang Kuo Yah. Fine chicken noodle lunch. Loafed and chatted. At 4, several friends came in, including "Stone", i.e., "Col." Shih Yueh Pin, who calmly said that his "Commission" – Air and Water Standards Commission (or something like that) of the Ministry of Communications is going to take over the Customs Marine Dept., Pilotage, etc., etc. He also talked big about what the U.S. is going to provide after the war for China's airways. Well, maybe he'll get it!

July 31: At Memorial Service, I welcomed Ting back from Sinkiang, and he spoke for 10 minutes. At 1 p.m. we had a cyclonic storm, which did a lot of damage. My bedroom was flooded, desk soaked and paper damaged. Peng ripped to shreds; kitchen chimney down, many trees blown over.

To office at 3:30. Two huge trees at entrance uprooted – fortunately without injuring anybody. The tiles on the school building half off, and the 45 Customs College student's beds and bedding soaked. A disconsolate-looking lot! No electric light. ~~Played a double card game with Hopstock after dinner.~~ Just after breakfast, Lovink (Dutch Ambassador) brought Heinzler (Dutch Bank) to see me.

August

August 1: ~~16 people killed in yesterday's windstorm. Busy day in office.~~

August 3: 1-1/2 hours with Li Tong. ~~Hot again! In office till 6, very busy, and tired.~~ I am sick of the filth and stench and latrines and pigs and sewers by which I have to pass 4 times a day. I wonder whether these conditions will remain. Lady Seymour left today for England.

August 4: ~~Paul Blunt stopped at my office en route to hospital; he has dysentery, poor chap! [...]~~

August 5: Had Lovink, Dutch Ambassador, to lunch, with Ting, Lu, Hopstock and Bathurst. Lovink stayed and we talked an hour. He feels that the whole political situation here is deteriorating; that Chiang is not as strong as he was; that he has "monarchical" leanings; that he is very much under the influence of the "Two Chens" (Chen Li-fu[68] and Chen Kuo-fu.)[69] Lovink says that the Kuomintang is increasingly anti-foreign, and extremists in the party are already dreaming and writing of overseas expansion after the war: they will insist on free Chinese immigration into Malaya, D.E.I., etc.; control of overseas Chinese from China; "thought control", etc. I think Lovink is unduly pessimistic, because there are many Chinese who want real democracy after the war, and are strongly opposed to the Chen brand of Fascism.

Ting told us a lot about Sinkiang; he says the Russians are backing the 8th Route Army (Communists), and that there is little prospect of any agreement between Chungking and Yenan [延安].

~~Didn't go to office this afternoon. No electric lights or fans! Hot and sticky. Played double solitaire with Hopstock. Had long letter from John Macoun; the work of an old, old man!~~

August 6: ~~With Porter, to Bungalow at Liang Feng Ya ("Cool Wind Pass"). Quiet, pleasant day. Came home a new way a precipitous, wild path from the I.C.I property.~~

August 7: Still very busy in office. Our "Electrolux" refrigerator, built to operate on kerosene, has been altered to electricity, and the first cold water ever drunk in this house in summer was delightful.

~~To Hospital to see Paul Blunt, who despite amoebic and bacillary dysentery, seems remarkably well.~~ Americans in Brest, and almost everywhere in Brittany. Russians in East Prussia.

August 8: Li Tong of Kuan-wu Shu came to enquire about accounts. They (and Banister, Tu Ping-Ho, Fang Tu and Pouncey) came here to lunch.

1944

August 9: Sudden drop in temperature, with rain and wind. Had to put on sweater after lunch! 2 hour conference with Ting, then an hour with Admiral Hsu. ~~Left office at 6:30.~~ I Arrived in Chungking one year ago today.

August 10: ~~Still cool. 72 degrees. To Francis and Cecilia Pan's for breakfast: fruit, corn-flakes (3 years old, but excellent), 2 eggs, 1 hamburger, French fries, toast and 2 cups coffee! To see Francis's new office: "Agricultural Engineering Corporation". He has excellent modern and liberal ideas, but is finding it difficult to put them across. Stopped to chat with some of the men in F.E.A.~~

To American Embassy, and an hour's talk with Gauss, who thinks that the political situation is very shaky. There is a possibility of a complete turnover here; a new coalition, headed by Li Chi San[70] (Li Chai Sum), may force the Generalissimo out. I gathered that this crowd has been sounding Gauss to the American attitude. I further gathered that we will "stand aside" in case the scheme materializes – which Gauss was careful to say may not happen.

To O.K. Yui, Acting Minister of Finance, and got his authority to pay Ting $18,000 a month substantive pay. With war-time allowances, this will come to about $70,000. This took me 5 minutes; had I approached Li Tong, it would have taken 5 weeks, and Ting would have gotten about $680 in pay and maybe $20,000 in allowances. Stopped and talked with K.K. Kwok at Central Bank.

August 12: ~~Getting warm again, but not too hot. This has been a pleasant break. Note fro, Nate. Wrote to R.I. Hospital Trust Co. re my new "Agency Account". Also to Jack, re purchase of Sylvania stock.~~

August 13: ~~With Hopstock and Pouncey, spent day at bungalow. Lovely day of quiet rest; fine weather. Home at 7 p.m., just at dark. Rice crop seems to be excellent this year – and it will be needed.~~

August 14: Ting back at office today after about 10 months in Sinkiang.

August 15: Capt. Jarrell (U.S.N.), American Naval Attaché, and Admiral Hsu to lunch. Latter has proposal to recruit Chinese ship captains, naval and merchant, to act as coast pilots for American Navy when Chinese waters are reached.

August 16: Decided today to create new secretariat at Customs: Staff Welfare Department. Here is a sentence from a British Customs Regulation." "All goods derelict, – Flotsam and jetsam and wreck." (Unconscious poetry)

August 17: A bad day: letter from Wei Kung Shao, Inspector, reports serious irregularities in disposal of seizures at Kunming. At same time, Everett Groff-Smith writes accusing Wei of "under-mining" his authority, etc. It looks like the beginning of an unholy mess, but I have to wait for official statements from both sides. ~~To K.W.S. at 9 a.m.; 1 hour with Li Tong. Hot again; over 100 degrees.~~

August 18: With Ting, called on Lovink, Netherlands Ambassador. Gave him one of my kittens. Had a nice cup of coffee. Lovink asked me if Rouse might accept appointment as honorary Netherlands Consul at Foochow; I said "no".

To see Capt. Jarrell, U.S. Naval Attaché, re scheme for sending Chinese Marine Dept. officers for training in U.S. Navy. To call on Gauss and Atcheson at American Embassy. Ting gave an interesting account of conditions in Sinkiang. He

1944

thinks Russians intend to make Sinkiang a second Outer Mongolia, i.e., a Soviet Republic with nominal Chinese sovereignty.

Dined at Billy Christian's, with Brooks Atkinson of N.Y. "Times" and Virginia and K.C. Lee. Rumor that American troops are in Paris and that landing has been made in Albania.

August 19: ~~Ting and I gave farewell luncheon for Annett, who was taken sick last night and couldn't come. We had the foreign and Chinese Secretaries. With Pouncey and Hopstock, went up to bungalow at Liang Feng Ya.~~

August 20: ~~Pleasant, restful day. Hopstock returned to city, Pouncey and I stayed at bungalow.~~

August 21: Stayed at bungalow, but very busy all day with stuff sent up from office. Ting and Chang came up to discuss the "Kunming Crisis", which looks very serious indeed.

August 22: Bad night: worried over Kunming situation: Groff-Smith has, it seems to me, handled the situation badly. Flood of letters from him and from Wei Kang Shuo, the inspector.

August 24: ~~Pouncey stayed in town tonight.~~ Paris taken; Romania quits war!! Rumored landing near Bordeaux. At this rate, Germany must give in before long. Russians having heavy going, even retreats, in Baltic states. ~~Hopstock writes that my boy and coolie have left, to go to Chengtu, where wages are sky high.~~

August 25: Busy most all day on office work. Kunming situation worsening, and I must go to office tomorrow to attend to it. ~~I wonder, or as I sit on this verandah, whether Jean has ever sat here. Possibly; she came here to Chungking as a bride some 25 years ago, and this bungalow is 30 years old.~~

August 26: To office all day, to discuss and decide next step in "Kunming crisis." Came back to bungalow at 7 p.m., exhausted. Hopstock came up tonight.

August 27: ~~Annett came up to the bungalow for lunch. Poor chap, he thinks that he has dysentery again, and is feeling miserable. He hopes to leave on retirement a week from today. The boy gave us an edible lunch.~~ Pouncey and I went to church, and it was Communion Sunday. The "wine" was pear-juice, served in Chinese wine cups; I felt like saying "Kan-pei" [乾杯] as I drank it. ~~Home about 6:30; no electricity lights or refrigerator. Hopstock and I played double solitaire for an hour.~~

August 28: At Memorial Service I explained objects of new Welfare Department. Pretty soon, it will be the foreign Commissioners who need ~~some~~ Welfare work: ~~my boy is getting $20,000 a month in his new job and my coolie $10,000! 101 degrees today.~~

August 29: ~~Busy day at office.~~ "Kunming crisis" still worrying me more than anything that has happened during the past year.

August 30: ~~Cooler today. River rose 17 feet night before last. My 8 days at the bungalow cost me $7,700. Worst food I have ever had for such a long period, and most expensive. At official rate, this cost U.S. $385.00; at my rate, U.S. $192.00.~~

August 31: To conference with D.G. at 9. 1-1/2 hours; an uncomfortable, suspiciously polite atmosphere – as usual.

To dinner at Chinese-American Institute. About 200 present. ~~Had to wait 40 minutes for return ferry. River up again.~~

September

September 1: ~~Annett, who retired yesterday after 30 years, came to say good bye. I hate to see him go. He is eating with me until he leaves on Sunday.~~ News from France wonderful; British armor is now getting rolling from Channel ports; Americans five miles from Belgian frontier; whole German position in France crumbling; Russians take Bucharest.

September 2: ~~Busy day in office.~~ Drafted opinion and decisions on Groff-Smith's handling of disposal of "embargo goods" seizures. ~~Hopstock left at 5 a.m., with Maj. Farmer (A.U.S.) in jeep for Kunming. Said good bye to Annett, who leaves at 5 a.m. tomorrow by plane for Calcutta. I shall miss him.~~

September 3: ~~Heavy rain most all morning, so abandoned plan to go to bungalow.~~ [. . .] Today is the 5th anniversary of England's declaration of war, and it looks as though the next celebration will be the Victory. Americans reported in Belgium; Finland has told Germans to leave; no flying bombs over England for 48 hours.

Ting, in a recent conversation, was very bitter about the Kuomintang, and said that, if they extended their influence in the Customs, efficiency and integrity will disappear, because Kuomintang members would be more interested in promoting the influence of the Party than of the Service. His remarks were prompted by the news that the Customs College is to be amalgamated with the Political Training Institute which, Ting said, is a "thought-control" organization spending much more time on political ideology than on education.

September 4: 1-1/2 hour conference re Kunming crisis. In afternoon, to British Embassy to arrange (with Mr. Giles) for conversion of pay at open-market rate. Then, at 4, to meeting of U.C.R. 3-1/2 hours solid work on budget for 1944–5 (C.N. $897 million), and I was dead tired when we adjourned at 7:30.

September 5: [. . .] Saw a rat, nailed through a hind leg to a post, head down, being tortured by a couple of kids.

September 6: Finished my S/O letter to Groff-Smith, after waiting 5 days for an answer to my telegram. I'm afraid my letter will be a shock to him, but had I said anything less than I did, I should not have done my duty. Finished reading "Sharks' Fins and Millet" by Rolf Sues. Lots of exaggeration, yet an uncanny "inside" knowledge of many things in China.

September 7: Donald Nelson[71] and Gen. Hurley[72] arrived last night. ~~Rain all day.~~ Dined at American Embassy. Guest of honor, Bishop Walsh, Maryknoll Mission. Others: Gen. Ferris, Sun Fo, Calvin Joyner (Land-Lease). On ferry, met Gen. Tsang, who came up from India yesterday with Nelson and Hurley. They left Chabua at 9 a.m. and arrived in Chungking at 6 p.m., and had an hour at Kunming.

1944

Gen. Tsang studied at Norwich. (Vt.), V.M.I. and Cornell. He was with Stilwell during retreat from Burma.

September 8: Ate with mess; lunch for Lt. Col. D.B.V. Murray, ex-Customs, who was in retreat from Burma 2 years ago. A fine man. Very busy in office these past 2 weeks.

September 9: ~~To lunch here: Drumright, Millet and Freeman (American Embassy – all fellow "Gripsholm" passengers). Pouncey and Bathurst. Busy Saturday as usual.~~ War situation in Hunan grace; fear we shall have to evacuate Kweilin staff next, possibly Wuchow, Nanning and Lungchow, Wenchow on point of evacuating.

September 10: ~~Rain all day 10th day and had to cancel trip to bungalow.~~ D.K. Wei called and talked an hour. Pessimistic over war in China. Says Kweilin sure to fall within a month. Dr. Ernest K. Moy called. He is Special Deputy of War Area Service Corps; his job, to feed and house some 30,000 U.S. troops all over China. Described conditions in Chinese Army as appalling; troops "starving".

September 11: Still raining off and on, but cool. Wore flannel suit, and not too heavy. Pouncey was to have gone to Kunming yesterday to investigate, but missed out on plane priority; hopes to go on Wednesday. ~~Lu Ping back on duty after a month's sick leave.~~ U.S. dollar notes on black market last week were sold as high as C.N. $250.

September 12: ~~Heavy rain all day. With Ting, to tea party for Dr. McConaughy (U.C.R.) and Dwight Edwards.~~[73]

September 13: Some rain, but clearing up. Everything damp – towels, underclothes, etc. Reminds me of Canton. Pouncey left at 5 a.m. for Kunming. A difficult assignment, but he is a good man for it.

September 14: K.P. Chen, who is soon leaving for America as delegate to the shipping and business conference, said that the Chinese government has not laid down any principles for post-war business. This is exactly what [Eric] Price (B & S) had told me earlier this afternoon.

September 15: Dined at American Embassy, for Donald Nelson and Gen. Patrick Hurley. Nelson a most attractive man; typically American – friendly, communicative, simple and humorous. Gen. Hurley very distinguished-looking, tall, immaculately uniformed – more the political type. Also approachable and talkative. Nelson said that we'd be making super-Fortresses at the rate of 100 a month by December; our jet-propelled planes are now in use, do 520 miles an hour, are easier to drive and manoeuver more than the conventional planes, but are uneconomical with fuel, having radius of only 150 miles. He said the Super-Forts have 4 3000-hp engines; he rode in one with 2 engines on one side cut out and did 220 miles per hour. In reply to Dr. Sun Fo, Mr. Nelson said that he thought it would take 2 years to lick Japan after Germany is defeated. Told me he thought that the present Allied pause at German frontier is more a question of bringing up supplies than of German opposition, and that the Germans will not be able to hold us at the frontier.

September 16: Pouncey wires that Ts'ai-cheng Pu Inspector has picked up trail of our Kunming crisis, and seems to be keen to follow the scent. This is a

1944

complication that may prove very serious. ~~To see Li Tong. Met his new Deputy Director General, formerly of the Monopoly Administration. This Administration recently reorganized following serious criticism, but this guy has now been given a post in the Kuan-wu Shu. He knows absolutely nothing about the Customs.~~

September 17: ~~To bungalow, in spite of a drizzle. Blunt, Bathurst and Porter also there. Blunt brought a pound tin of Indian butter, and we gorged ourselves. Darkness overtook me on way home, and I was tired and pretty wet when I arrived. A hot bath fixed me up.~~

September 18: Sung Ko-cheng (Chinese Secretary) spoke at Memorial Service. Inter alia, he said that we have our post-war reconstruction plan, and hope to have new ships, lighthouses, planes, etc., but that the most important thing required is personal character. Right! [...]

News of air-borne landings in Holland – a great feat, which may shorten the war. Papers are full of the People's Political Council meetings, and publish the most severe criticisms of the Government. Both the questions (some of which are most embarrassing) and their publication are good signs – signs of an embryo democracy. Kuomintang-Communist negotiations are also published in extensor.

September 19: [...]

War situation in China discouraging and highly disturbing. Kweilin and its airfields seem doomed, and many people think the Japs will take Kunming. The Chinese are disunited politically and seem all tired out and defeatist. The troops will, or can, not fight. I'm afraid that a common feeling among the Chinese is: "Let the Americans lick the Japs."

Dined at Belgium Embassy, with Segaert (Minister); Rothschild[74] (Counselor); and Pieters (Chancellor).

September 20: To French church, to a Deum sung for liberation of Brussels. Diplomatic corps present in force. I sat with Dr. Wang Chung Hui. ~~Stopped a moment to see Cecilia Pan and ask her to dinner Saturday~~. Dined at the Tung Pao She as guest of Mr. Donald Nelson. Nobody else there except Gen. Hurley, Mr. Locke and Mr. Jacobson (Mr. Nelson's staff), and a couple of Chinese Secretaries. A most informal evening. I talked Sino-American trade with Locke and Jacobson. Locke says that the Generalissimo has accepted all of Nelson's recommendations; which aim at increasing Chinese production – now terribly inefficient. Also said that mist planes from Kunming to India carry rocks or sand as ballast: no exports to fill them. Mr. Nelson gave me a beautiful pipe, with meerschaum – lined bow, – a perfect "presentation piece" (which it was brought out as!) He offered to give me a lift to America tomorrow, and promised to land me in Washington by Sunday. He said that he has fixed Nov. 15 as the day the war against Germany will end. I told him I'd be satisfied with an armistice for Christmas.

September 21: ~~Glorious, sunny day almost spring-like~~. Situation at Kunming gets more complicated daily, with Supt. And Preventive Bureau and Pu's Inspector all wanting to take a hand in it.

1944

September 22: ~~Up last night at 12:30 with nausea and diarrhea. Pretty sick. [. . .] Stayed in bed all day. Better at night. Dr. Allen examined stool no amoeba, but "some little pus" and some "Giardia cysts" which may cause trouble.~~ The Allied paratroop army in Holland seems to be having hard going. Wuchow taken by Japanese.

September 24: ~~With Hopstock, to bungalow. I rode in chair practically all the way up, but walked back. Pleasant, restful day. The countryside is at "'tween seasons" – rice all harvested, and winter crops not in.~~

September 25: ~~Quiet day; got a lot done.~~ Young Mr. _____ came to see me at 7 p.m. He came from Shanghai several months ago, expecting to find a clean, healthy government in Chungking. He is thoroughly disillusioned and cynical. Says that the Generalissimo is just another warlord, aiming to pre-serve his personal power, no matter what happens to China. Kung, he says, is the most cordially man in China; vastly wealthy, entirely unscrupulous, Kung's family (wife, sons and daughter) even worse. T.V. Soong, he says (although wealthy) would be acceptable to general public as Finance Minister. Mr. _____ has a job in Ministry of Finance and gets $1,000 a month. Most days he has less than 15 minutes work. He says most of the common people would welcome the Communists. Mme. Chiang, formerly "with" Kung and "against" Soong, has recently reversed the position. Says Kung hopes to stay in U.S. permanently.

September 26: ~~To dentist. Replaced one porcelain filling, $600. He said that he charges Chinese $800 or $1,000 for the same job. He must be coining money. They say that some doctors and lawyers in Chungking are making half a million a month.~~ Li Tung Wha,[75] Commissioner at Loyang, arrived yesterday. He told me of the evacuation to Lushih, then to Sian, then to Hanyang. The people of Honan terribly bitter against the officials – all officials – and Chinese army, by whom they have been mercilessly squeezed. During evacuation, the farmers disarmed the troops and robbed all refugees who looked like officials. Li said that the corruption among civil and military officials in the province was notorious. For example, farmers were forced to pay taxes in kind and themselves bring their wheat to the military storehouses, where the storehouse men demanded squeeze before accepting the grain. Unless squeeze were paid, they would be forced to wait days, or their wheat would be declared to be inferior, etc. Li says that some of these storehouses may took $500,000 a month. When the Central Bank evacuated Lushih they took $14,000,000 in banknotes in 3 trucks, which were seized by soldiers; Li knows the officer who got most of the loot. The Preventive Bureau (closely allied with Tai Li's secret service gestapo) beat up and tortured people as a daily occurrence; also conducted searches of private homes without warrants. Li thinks that the present government will disintegrate after the war and that there will be revolution and chaos. Advises that Customs should return to coast ports under aegis of American troops at earliest possible moment! Says Communists have a clean and honest government at present, but that this is due to their restricted area, their poverty and the opposition of the Government. Thinks that if the Communists get in power they will be just as bad as the Kuomintang. Says that Chiang Kai-shek's only hold on the people is his opposition to Japan: when Japan is eliminated, Chiang will be driven out. After last night's talk with young Mr. _____, and today's with Li, I feel very discouraged about the future of this unhappy land. ~~Howard, at Consulate, told me that Neprud is coming to Chungking as "Commissioner of Customs and Technical Advisor to Ministry of Finance".~~

September 27: [...] Telegram from Neprud says he's coming out on temporary mission and asks for U.S. $2,500 advance for expenses. Ex-Gov. Sheng Shih-tsai of Sinkiang (now Minister of Agriculture and Forestry) called on me at 4:30, accompanied by several bodyguards.[76] We had tea in my office (with Ting) and a chat. The Russians drove him out of Sinkiang. Ting says he doesn't dine out because he's afraid of poison. He ate one or two pieces of cake with us, however. (The Tingchai ate all four plates as soon as we left the room!)

September 28: Allies seem to be held up on German frontier, and British paratroops at Arnheim forced to retreat

September 29: This week, got D.N. $50,000 for Rs. 833, through "British Channels" (British Embassy), who sells in open market. At former rate, $50,000 would have cost me £312; through British Channel they cost £64.

With Hopstock, to lunch with Mr. Lu Tso-fu,[77] head of the Min Sheng Co. He is going to America as one of 5 Chinese delegates to attend the international business conference at Atlantic City.

September 30: Took Li Tung hwa to see Mr. Li Tong. Li Tung hwa talked for almost an hour, giving a dramatic account of the evacuation of the Customs from Loyang to Lushih, and then to Sian. Li was taken by the Japanese – saw several Chinese assassinated, but by great luck managed to escape.

October

October 1: The 4th rainy Sunday in 5 weeks! No trip to hills today. With Hopstock, lunched with Paul Blunt and Watterson (Marconi's man). Wrote Guy Wells, Stewart, and Annett.

October 2: To lunch at Gen. Pechkoff's (French "Delegate"). Patterson, Canadian Chargé, also there. He was formerly in YMCA in Japan, and an old friend of Russ Durgin. Poorest food I've had in Chungking, and table alive with flies.

With Li Tung Wha, to call on Mr. O.K. Yui, to whom Li told the depressing story of the Honan debacle. The outlook in China is extremely gloomy; the army isn't fighting; Chang Fa-kwei's[78] troops are said to have looted Kweilin completely and burned half the city; Chiang keeps his best troops in the Northwest, watching the Chinese "Communists"; criticism of the government is more scathing, widespread and open than I have ever known it to be. I shouldn't be surprised to hear the government is overturned any day, but God knows what could replace it.

October 3: Very heavy rain during night; we have had no sun for over a week. Miss Pansy Ho, my so-called stenographer, gave me "penultated" vice "promulgated" in a draft today. ~~Had word that Drummond got out of Wuchow safely, and is en route to Kweiyang.~~ I am bringing him here to await orders.

October 4: Japs reported to have landed near Foochow. I hope Rouse is all right! ~~Cool but still rainy.~~

October 5: Heavy rain again; colder. ~~Very busy in office.~~ Fr. Smith (Maryknoll) called; he is worried about his Mission people from Wuchow. Am re-reading Carl Van Doren's[79] "Benjamin Franklin", which I think about the best biography written in my lifetime.

October 6: [...] Ting very pessimistic over future of China; he says all Chinese believe that after the war with Japan is over, there will be a civil war in China; Kuomintang vs Communists. The latter, he thinks, aided by Russia will control North China and Manchuria. W.A.B. Gardener left tonight, without saying goodbye to me. Rather odd, after having occupied my guest room for over 6 months. But I can't hold it against him: his mental state is unsound. He is filled to the skin with bitterness against me, the Service and China. He is a combination of insufferable conceit and no sense of humor.

Had a rat in drawing-room tonight, so called in Jenny, who had good hunting and soon finished Mr. and Mrs. Rat. Bought 1 pound of coffee cheap – $2,400. At official rate, this is U.S. $120; at special rate, U.S. $60; at my rate (British open market) about U.S. $12.00. Even $12.00 a pound is fairly stiff for coffee.

October 7: Ting away all morning at meetings with Kuan-wu Shu and Ministry. Pouncey returned last night from his Kunming inspection trip, and gave me an excellent report. The whole mess is fundamentally a result of Groff-Smith's stupidity; he is beautiful but dumb. And he has a large share of the stubborn obstinacy that often goes with stupidity – sort of a protective coloring.

October 8: ~~Threatened with a cold. I stayed in the house all day instead of going up to the bungalow.~~ Heard that Wendell Willkie[80] had died. A great loss to America and China.

October 9: With Ting, to wedding reception of O.K. Yui's daughter. A very pretty and attractive girl.

October 10: ~~"Double Tenth", and a Customs holiday. I spent afternoon in bed; cold worse. Weather still terrible. Parcel containing medicine, soap etc. came from Betty via John.~~

October 11: ~~In bed all day, trying to break up my cold. Wrote to Betty and thanked her for the Parcel which arrived yesterday. Did quite a lot of office work.~~ No sun for 3 or 4 weeks; Oh! for October in New England!

October 12: ~~In bed till noon; to office in afternoon.~~

October 13: ~~Seem to have conquered the cold, but excused myself from going to the Frosts' for buffet dinner and dance.~~

October 14: ~~1-1/2 hours with Li Tong in morning, devoted to "leakage" in Clerks' examination papers.~~

~~To Sick Bay, where I was told I had ringworm on sole of right foot! Phooey!! Last time I had them was in 1920, and I got them in the hotel at Williamstown,~~

81

1944

~~Mass. Busy Saturday afternoon at office – as usual. Sun tried to come out this morning but got discouraged. Rain at night.~~

October 15: Found these gems in a poem "Mother" in an American magazine:

"My evil ways helped guide the plow
That cut the furrows in her brow"
"If I had lived like mother taught
My life would be more as it ought."

October 16: Ting made long speech at Memorial Service. He is a natural orator – as are many Chinese. Had Ip Yau Cheung to lunch: he is going to Kunming as Tidesurveyor. I had him with me in Canton. ~~Parcel of medicines from Betty via Nate arrived. In a regular packing case!~~

October 17: Called on Brooks Atkinson (who was in bed with grippe), Gunther Stein and Teddy White at Press Hostel. Met Mrs. Jacoby (widow of Melville Jacoby), who will replace White as "Time" and "life" correspondent here. Gunther Stein 100% sold on the Chinese Communists after his trip to Yenan. Chungking censors cut over half his stories, however, and emasculated even what they passed.

Called on George Atcheson at the Embassy (Gauss was out), and on MacCracken Fisher at OWI. Mr. Peng (Customa), detached for study at School of Journalism, called on me; he has won scholarship to Columbia School of Journalism.

October 18: For the first time in 4 or 5 weeks, the sun almost shone at noon. By 5 p.m., however, it was again raining. ~~Very busy in office today.~~

October 19: Loy Chang came in at noon and said that T.V. Soong had had a wire from Governor Lung Yun[81] of Yunnan asking whether Groff-Smith's home leave could be "advanced" so that he could accompany Lung's son to America as – according to Loy – "guide, philosopher and friend". I think senior commissioners of Customs have better things to do these days than playing nurse-maids to Chinese youths who ought to be fighting and not leaving China on conducted tours. I wonder whether Groff-Smith seriously thinks I'd consider the proposal – especially as his leave is not due for 3 years? Some finagling and intrigue going on: I have thought from the beginning of the Kunming case that sooner or later that the Yunnan gang would intervene politically.

Tonight, big news: America landing on Solomon Island, Philippines, and big British attack on Nicobar Islands.

October 20: To 2-1/2 hour meeting of United China Relief. Passed detailed budgets for C.N. $1,200,000,000 for 1944–5. Dr. Robert Lim there: he seems to be the Great I Am. Rested at Dr. Rappe's house till 7, then went to Canadian Embassy for dinner. Patterson, the Chargé, was host (Gen. Odlum is in Canada). Besides his staff, Dr. [Leone] Liang (Wai-chiao Pu; Cassels and Hutchinson of British Embassy, etc. Good chow. Patterson an ex-YMCA man from Japan – friends of Russ Durgin. Home at 10:30. Still raining, and 6 inches of mud on some of the Chungking streets.

1944

October 21: Drummond arrived on evacuation from Wuchow. Staying with me. Had Navy Enlisted Men's Mess – about 15 – in for cocktails.

October 22: ~~Still raining, so unable to go to bungalow.~~ News of Philippines invasion has been like a tonic to all here – foreigners and Chinese. I hope it will buck up the latter!

October 23: To an OWI preview of "Report from the Aleutians", "Toscanini" and "Battle of Tarawa". Latter a very realistic picture of desperate fighting. Most sobering, especially to see the bodies of Marines drifting in and out with the tide on the beach.

October 25: With Ting, to return call on Governor Shang of Sinkiang, now Minister of Agriculture.

To lunch with Gunther Stein at Press Hotel. He read me his notes (1 hour) on the financial, revenue, taxation, etc., policy and experience of the Communist "border area". Even if only half true, the situation they reveal is 10 times as solvent, honest and clean as that of the Chungking government. Press Hostel a-buzz with news that Gen. Stilwell has been recalled. Opinion is that the Generalissimo demanded it, and Roosevelt acquiesced. This will have unfortunate repercussions: Vinegar Joe is a true friend of China, but he has apparently quarreled with everybody – Mountbatten, Chennault and the Generalissimo. He will be succeeded by Wedemeyer,[82] now on Mountbatten's staff. Stein said that, when Stilwell went to say good-bye to Chiang Kai-shek, the latter handed him the highest Chinese decoration, but Stilwell handed it back! I am plagued with trouble: (1) D.G. wants to approve promotions of Clerks to Assistants before they are made; (2) Groff Smith has made an unholy mess of the staff quarters building program.

First news of great Jap-American naval battle in Philippines. "Princeton" (7,000 or 10,000 ton carrier) lost. Flash from Pearl Harbor via New Delhi at 7 said we had sunk six battleships, one carrier, two cruisers and several other ships. Later broadcasts during evening did not confirm, but gave loss of "Princeton" and said we had sunk one large carrier, and damage five or six battle-ships. We have destroyed over 150 planes; I wonder what our plane losses have been? The battle evidently continues: the Japs apparently have decided to throw everything they have into battle. It looks as if it would be (at least, may be) one of the crucial battles of the whole war. If the Jap Navy is decisively defeated, the war will be shortened considerably. Working on question of resuming granting home leave to foreigners. Pouncey and Hopstock talked to me before dinner; Banister after dinner. He asks to be given New Resident Scale job!!

October 26: No rain, and real sunshine in afternoon! Ching pao at 7 p.m., and no light or radio.

At 6 p.m. listened to Tokyo's account of the Philippine naval battle. If true, the U.S. Navy is finished and annihilated – again. Tokyo is celebrating the great victory; McArthur[83] is being driven off Leyte, etc. 16 B-29's were destroyed yesterday (American broadcast says one destroyed). The Jap propaganda says invasion simply an election stunt of Roosevelt's. Also, that U.S. is insulting the

Philippines by talking of liberation, because the Philippines is already an independent republic!

October 27: Lovely, sunny day. Had all my clothes and shoes out in the sun, to get the mold off. Another air alarm at 7 p.m., but lights came on at 10. ~~John has been promoted to Sergeant!! Had a fine V-mail letter from him, and learned of the promotion only by the address, probably he wrote me about the promotion in an earlier letter that hasn't arrived. I am very proud of him.~~

~~Busy in office this week.~~ Reports of naval battle still confused, but apparently Japs took a good beating and have been driven away from Leyte and the vicinity. I fear our losses were not light.

October 28: Foulest weather to date: cold, heavy rain, wind. To Czecko-Slovak Independence Day reception at Victory House, about 400 present (no British officials, because of official mourning for Princess Beatrice,[84] youngest daughter of Queen Victoria). 2 hours of Czecko-Slovak music by a Chinese symphony orchestra. The large movement of the "New World" wasn't too bad, but the rest was pretty lousy. But (like Johnson and the woman preacher) the wonder about the dog who walked on his hind legs, was not that he did it so poorly, but that he did it at all. Buffet eats were served at about 9, after which I slipped out. Talked with Gauss, whose views on the Stilwell ouster follow closely those expressed by Gunther Stein: "Mr. Big" has forced Roosevelt's hand, and the latter didn't dare oppose just before election. Gauss must find his job terribly difficult with all the special big boys coming out to deal with the Chinese government. They are supposed to keep him informed, but I gather they rarely do. In my opinion, the fault lies with the President: he is too impulsive and slap-dash.

October 29: To buffet luncheon at Belgian Ambassador's at Wang Shan. Excellent food (especially the chocolate soufflé made by Mr. Segaert himself) and pleasant company. I took Rothschild and Pieters in my car: crossed Yangtze by usual ferry to North Bank; by car to automobile ferry; by ferry back to South Bank and by road to Wang Shan. After lunch, at 4, back across the car ferry to North Bank to Chialing House, to reception by Turkish Ambassador (Faud Tugay). *Tout le monde y était.* I stayed an hour, then returned once again across the river by the usual ferry and home at 6 – tired.

Air-raid alarm again, and lights out from 7 to 11. No planes.

October 30: O.K. Yui said that Generalissimo had told a recent meeting that War Time Consumption Tax is to be abolished soon.

Two main subjects of conversation these past few days: (1) Philippines naval battle and (2) Stilwell's recall. We won the first but lost the second. The latter is also a great loss to China, and does not do credit either to Chiang Kai-shek or to Roosevelt, from the evidence so far available.

October 31: Quiet day in office. River rose 12 feet in 24 hours over the weekend, and all the bamboo houses on the foreshore were under water. It is unheard of to have such a rise (to 39 feet) at this time of year.

1944

November

November 1: Before going to the Australian Chargé (Keith Officer) to dinner, I dropped in to see Gauss, who is confined to house with eye-trouble. He told me he had resigned, and we sat and listened to San Francisco broadcasting the news, with Roosevelt's statement that the resignation had no connection whatsoever with Stilwell's recall. I told Gauss that his resignation was a personal sorrow to me, would be regretted by all who know what he has tried to do here, and would certainly be interpreted as a sigh that Sino-American relations had deteriorated. He said that it would be a good thing if people realized what the real situation is. He said no idea who is successor is to be. George Atcheson will act as Chargé d'Affaires. This resignation, right on top of Stilwell's recall, plus Roosevelt's statements on the subjects, make one hell of a mess. At the Australian Ambassador's, Gen. Carton de Wiart said he saw the Generalissimo on Saturday, and that he was in "great form" and seemed very "pleased with all the changes," i.e., Stilwell's leaving and arrival of Wedemeyer. That No. 1 damn fool, the Canadian Ambassador (now in Canada – hope they keep him there!) gave out a statement to the effect that Stilwell's recall will stabilize (or some such word) the situation in the Far East!

At the Australian Embassy: Sir Horace Seymour (British); Mr. and Mrs. _____ (Norwegian); Clarac (French Chargé); Minowsky (Czech-Slovak); Lovink (Dutch); – all Ambassadors except Segaert – the guest of honor – who was absent. Rather stodgy party, but I talked with Gen. de Wiart an hour, and he is always interesting and charming. He lived in Poland 24 years, and doesn't think there's a chance of a Polish settlement unless Russia suddenly turns "benevolent." Wot a life!! Hopstock came back from Col. Depass' at 11 p.m., and says the American Officers are seething at Roosevelt's statement about Stilwell.

November 2: Rainy and cold; simply filthy weather, week after week. To dinner (excellent) at Foreign Correspondents' Club at Press Hotel, as "guest speaker". I spoke for 1/2 hour on Customs, then answered questions for an hour. Small group (about 9) because 4 or 5 correspondents are away. Home – tired – at 11.

November 3: Thank God I don't have to cross the river today; still raining. Had my first fire of the season – stove pipes only installed today. Made my decision in Kunming case: recommending compulsory retirement of Groff-Smith and discharge of Huan Pei-chan. Telegraphed to Kunming and instructed Groff-Smith to hand over to Gawler, whom I am moving from Kweiyang. Gawler will be succeeded by Drummond, who is here, refugeeing from Wuchow. It now remains to be seen whether government will support my decision. I never thought that it would fall to my lot to recommend getting rid of Everitt Groff-Smith – my best friend in the Service at present. It's a queer world!

November 4: Ting attended regular meeting at Ts'ai-cheng Pu, where O.K. Yui announced that the Generalissimo had instructed (on advice of Hsu Kan, Minister of Food) that the War-Time Consumption Tax is to be abolished. Reasons:

(1) It is troublesome to the people and (2) it produces an insignificant revenue. Actually, it is the least troublesome of all present Chinese taxes, and the mostly honestly collected one. In 1944, we shall collect C.N. $2,200,000,000. I admit that this is only 1/2 of 1% of the proposed astronomical government budget for 1945 ($380,000,000,000), but it isn't exactly chicken-feed. Personally, I'm delighted that the government is able to do away with this emergency tax on internal trade, but I'm not sure that its end result will be entirely happy. The abolition of W.T.C.T. confronts the Service and me with yet another crisis in our history, and I lie awake nights thinking out plans.

Letters from Dr. Li (Li Tong's Sec.) very disturbing; Li Tong apparently intends to insist on passing on Customs promotion before I make them.

November 5: ~~Cold, damp and rainy. Went out for a walk but the mud discouraged me after half an hour. Also did a lot of thinking about the future of the Customs~~.

November 6: Busy day, ending with 1-1/2 hour meeting with Secretaries to discuss abolition of W.T.C. [Wartime Consumption] Tax. A rather gloomy pow-wow, but I tried to give as much encouragement as possible. Ting said that there's "anti-Customs" politics behind this move, and that it could not have happened if H.H. Kung had been here. He says the attack came from three sides: (1) Consolidated Tax (who fought against having Customs take on W.T.C.T. in first place); (2) Preventive Bureau (tied up with the "Gestapo", who recently tried unsuccessfully to interfere with our examination work); (3) Hsu Kan, Minister of Food (former Vice-Minister of Finance), enemy of Loy Chang, and foe of the Customs, in a Training Camp speech, he stated: "The (Chinese) in the Customs are all slaves of the foreigner." Ting was outspokenly cynical about conditions in his own country; he said that no matter how laudable your aims and sound your arguments, unless you know the right people you had no chance. On the other hand, no matter what skullduggery you do, you can get away with it if you know the right people. I'm afraid there's a lot in what he says. Anyway, I'm going to see O.K. Yui tomorrow morning; he's "right", but a small potato compared with Hsu Kan, H.H., etc. Still, he's my boss, and I've got to place my case before him and see whether he will take it higher.

November 7: To consult with Li Tong about abolition of W.T.C.T. He said that the government would certainly retain the permanent Customs staff. I agreed to prepare a statement of the case for discussion with him next Saturday, and he will consult with his staff in the meantime.

To see O.K. Yui, Acting Minister of Finance. Mr. Yui said that he had not been consulted before-hand by Mr. Chang Li-shang,[85] Chief Secretary of Executive Yuan, and resented it. He had dinner with the Generalissimo recently, and intimated that the matter was not 100% settled. Mr. Yui realizes how important it is to retain the Customs staff, and is prepared to fight for re-consideration. I agreed to give him a memorandum on the subject by Friday. Returned to Customs House and got Liu Ping I on the job writing a statement of the various non-Customs functions (assistance to other bureaus; control of exchange; embargo goods, etc.) we perform. Called Secretaries meeting at 3, gave them an account of my interviews, and parceled out the drafting work among them. I feel much more encouraged today than I did yesterday. Li Tong also mentioned Clerks' promotion; said he had no intention of interfering with my control of Customs staff, but that he wanted to examine the proposed pro-motion in order to avoid public criticism. In future, he will keep hands off. ~~Drummond, who is leaving for Kweiyang [貴陽] in a few days, dined with me.~~

November 8: One of the busiest days of my career; plugging all day long, and driving others to plug, on the "abolition of W.T.C.T. question." My staff gave me uncomplaining support. But I was dead tired at 5.

Dined at Air Commodore Bartholomew's to meet Col. Ride, of the B.A.A.G. Also present: Capt. Douglas, Bathurst, and Drummond. 10 o'clock B.B.C. said Roosevelt elected, with Democratic majority in Senate about same, and increased in house. Popular vote (at time of announcement) about 18,000,000 Roosevelt, 16,000,000 Dewey.[86] Ham Fish[87] defeated (thank God!); Clare Luce[88] re-elected.

November 9: To "tea-party" at Gen. Wu Te-cheng's, for Mr. Gauss. About 40 or 50 there, and one woman – an American Red Cross girl. Met Dr. Chiang [Monlin], the Chinese UNRRA representative, just back from America. Chinese (and British, too) all delighted that Roosevelt is re-elected. They don't seem to understand that Dewey's election would have made no difference in the prosecution of the war. ~~On way to Gen. Wu's, stopped in to give Cecilia Pan a jar of honey and some magazines. She had a serious abdominal operation a few weeks ago, but is getting on well now.~~

November 10: Lunch at American Embassy, and an hour's talk with Gauss. He sent me word of his desire to retire by Dick Service. Nobody in Chungking knew about it. The day after Service gave the message, the New York papers had it, and connected it with Stilwell's recall. Gauss doesn't know where the leak occurred, but thinks it might have been from one of the White House Secretaries. He is fed up with the procession of American "Special Representatives" sent out to China. Donald Nelson and Patrick Hurley were instructed to consult with him, but I gather they did precious little. Nelson apparently has made substantial promises; and I gathered that Hurley was mixed up in the Stilwell affair. Gauss feels that it may be a wise thing for the government to leave the Ambassadorship unfilled for six months or so, until things settle down a little. He says Hurley is now in Yenan. (I wonder if he will try to mediate between Communists and Chungking?). Gauss said that the Generalissimo had let Roosevelt know that he preferred to deal direct with "Special Representatives" than through the Ambassador! I can't help feeling that Roosevelt has been guilty of a great deal of "improvised meddling" in the China situation. Our present rather strained relations are in large measure due to this fact.

To ministry of Finance, where I handed my statement re the proposed abolition of War-Time Consumption Tax to Mr. O.K. Yui. ~~Back to office at 3:30 and two busy hours cleaning up my desk. Gave Bathurst a bit of a dressing down for his rather irresponsible comment on a memorandum.~~ River down to 19 feet, and the first decent day (bar one) in about 7 weeks.

Yesterday, I talked with Dr. Eng Wen-hao, Minister of Economics, who said that conditions in the Chinese Army are much worse today than when the war started. The reasons, he said, were the rise in prices and the failure to pay troops and officers a living wage. The officers, he said, can and do squeeze, and are well off, but the troops are miserable.

November 11: To lunch: Hall Paxton had 22 or so to Chinese chow at Bank of Communications. ~~3 ladies, (Chinese) and rest about 1/1 Chinese and American (and Hopstock). Excellent food (if you like it) but I still prefer baked beans, or Hamburg steak, to the finest Chinese cuisine.~~ Mr. Chuk (banker) got maudlin drunk, and made a ling and tearful speech about "Mother Paxton" who, it seems, adopted him as an orphan of 8 in Chinkiang, where she and her husband ran a small missionary school. ~~Kai Liang, my old friend from Canton, who has been in Luichow for 2 years, was present.~~ Luichow airfield, which cost U.S. $70,000,000, was destroyed early last week; Japs took Luichow yesterday or the day before.

Ting attended conferences at Pu this morning to discuss abolition of W.T.C.T. Conference unanimously agreed to recommend to Minister of Finance to reconsider decision. I feel a great burden off my shoulders, and think we have safely passed (or shortly shall) a dangerous crisis in Customs history.

November 12: ~~To bungalow. Started to drizzle half-way up, but Hopstock and I bought paper umbrellas ($2.60) at Huang Kuo Yeh. Pouncey, Bathurst, Drummond and Porter also present. Good dinner. Foggy and misty all day, visibility zero. Cold, but managed to keep a fire going.~~

November 13: Yesterday was Sun Yat-sun's birthday and the 50th Anniversary of the founding of the Chinese Revolutionary movement. Spoke at Memorial Service and told staff about our negotiations concerning proposed abolition of W.T.C.T.

To American Embassy for a quiet chat with Gauss, and to say good-bye. He leaves at 6 a.m. tomorrow. Managed to scrape up 3 cigars to give him. ~~Sent note (and one of the medals Lott Wei had made) to Jack by Dr. Frank H. Herrington (Lt. Commdr.) who is leaving with Gauss.~~ [...]

To see deputy Director General (Mr. Chu) and asked him to push consideration of (1) the Kunming case and (2) resumption of leave for foreigners.

To U.S. Naval Attaché's office, to talk with Capt. Jarrell about possibility of sending some Customs Marine Officers for U.S. Naval training. HE gave me the story of the naval battle of the Philippines, with the help of the fine maps in his office.

To 2-hour meeting of U.C.R. Dr. Tsiang (head of UNRRA) is back from America and in the chair. Also just back from America is Bishop Paul Yu-Pin,[89] Bishop of Nanking. He is a big, husky northerner from Heilungkiang. [...]

November 15: Loy Chang came to see me and ask if I could suggest a place for Judge Helmick to live when he comes to Chungking. That is a job!

November 16: To Rotary Club. It was Ladies' Day, and the speaker was Mrs. Jacoby, "Time" and "Life" correspondent. She told of the invasion of the Philippines, and did it well, in spite of a weak voice. Lunch was served in a mat shed over the garden, and I nearly froze to death.

Brooks Atkinson's N.Y. "Times" article of October 31 on Stilwell vs Chiang Kai-shek. T.N.T.!! Brooks Atkinson links Ho [Ying-chin] (Minister of War), Chen Li-fu (Education) and Daddy Kung as Chiang's subservient yes-men. It is the frankest article yet written about the present mess in Chinese-American relations.

[...] The Japs have taken I-shan. Query: will they push west against Kunming? According to local gossip, the Chinese are doing no fighting at all; Kweilin is said to have been occupied by 400 Japanese troops. Kweilin was to have been defended by Pai Chung-hsi; Luichow by Chang Fa-kwei – China's two best generals. What has happened?

November 17: Presided at 2 hour meeting of Secretaries, 4–6, to discuss rehabilitation. [...] Worked 2 hours at night on Confidential Reports on Clerks for selection as Assistants.

November 18: To reception at American Embassy for Donald Nelson and the experts he has brought to form a Chinese W.P.B. About 150 present. Invitations read "4–6:30" instead of "5–6:30" as George Atcheson intended, so it was a long affair. Almost everybody there. Talked with Chou En-lai,[90] the Communist leader; an impressive and likeable man. There must have been some eyebrows raised to see him there. In the same crowd were Chen Li-fu (Minister of Education) and Gen. Ho Ying-chin (Minister of War) – two "arch-fascists". I wondered what the Minister of War was doing at a cocktail party at a time when his armies seem to be disintegrating.

Gave Locke (Nelson's secretary) a memorandum on China's external war-time trade (1943). Stayed at the Embassy for dinner and the night. The bed was hard as a rock, but I managed a fair night.

November 19: Up at 7, and, with Carl Boehringer and Tony Freeman, to the Wei I [only唯一] Theater to see a movie, as guest of Cols. Depass and Wasser. The idea of going to a movie at 9 a.m. on Sunday morning was revolting, but it turned out to be one of the best pictures I have ever seen: "This Land is Mine". After the picture, we were taken by our hosts to Victory House for 1 hour of cocktails and then tiffin. Menu: fruit cup, soup, fish, chicken pie, beefsteak, frozen dessert, fruit, coffee. (I reneged on the beef). At least 4 Chinese Generals and 1 Admiral, a sprinkling of Ambassadors, etc. Gen. S.K. Yee told me that Kweiyang cannot be held, because there are not enough Chinese troops for the job. But, he said, it will not be taken for a least 2 months. (He told me that Kweilin would hold out until the New Year (!!), so I take his intelligence with a grain of salt). Col. Depass very pessimistic; says the Japs are going anywhere, at will, and that the Chinese army is disintegrating. He has made arrangements to move his outfit to Lanchow. He says that a few hundred Jap parachutists, aided by fifth columnists, could easily create panic in Chungking and take the city. I talked with Admiral Hsu (Coast Inspector) and Ting yesterday about the possibility of evacuating Customs staff and families from Chungking in case of necessity. Admiral Hsu wants $3,000,000 to repair 3 launches, and $2,000,000 for fuel. I shall have to keep the staff (about 2,000 with families) from panicking.

November 20: Called meeting of 5 Secretaries to plan evacuation of staff in case of necessity. Gave Admiral Hsu $5,000,000 to repair and fuel his ships. Appointed

Chang, Hsu, Fang and Liu as committee to work out details of plan. Ting said that a real danger would be that the local Szechuan people and troops (who hate the Central government and the influx of "outsiders") would turn on all "non-natives" and loot, rob, and kill! Ain't that a nice thought!

7 Ministers have been changed, including Dr. Kung, who is succeeded by Mr. O.K. Yui. I'm sorry to see Dr. Kung go, but glad his successor is a good friend of mine, and, I think, sympathetic to the Customs. Ho Ying Chin (reactionary Minister of War), Chen Li-fu (reactionary Minister of Education), also get kicked out. T.V. Soong, apparently, remains as Foreign Minister. Butter is now $1,400 a pound. The U.S. one dollar bill changed for C.N. $535.

November 21: Busy day in office. Hear that a B-29 made a forced landing on the river airstrip this afternoon. If so, how will it ever get off such a short runway? Air-raid alarm at 7, but lights out only a few minutes.

November 22: With Ting, crossed river to offer congratulations to O.K. Yui at 9:30. Finally saw him for 10 seconds at 11:30. Made several other calls in between. Saw B-29 on river airport; she made the C-54 alongside look like a toy! I expect the Japs will come and bomb her.

To dinner at Francis and Cecilia Pan's – Cecilia's first appearance after her operation. About 24 present, and most delightful evening. Mr. Shen (Dartmouth) just up from Luichow; he's a railroad engineer and said they had to leave some 25,000 workmen to shift for themselves. No money, no food. Many have sold their children; some have killed them.

A Chinese friend told me tonight that the Chinese soldiers in Kwangsi are running away, and that the Japs can come to Chungking or any other place they please. He said that the Generalissimo is interested only in maintaining his political position, and knows nothing about the life and hardships of the soldiers. Such talk is symptomatic of a growing criticism of Chiang, and dissatisfaction with the administration.

November 23: U.S. dollar went to C.N. $630 today. My stenographer, Pansy Ho, who is getting about $6,500 from Customs, is leaving for a job with O.W.I. at U.S. $120 a month. She will therefore draw about C.N. $75,000 a month!! How can I keep any morale in my staff at this rate? The U.S. government ought to pay Chinese staff in Chinese currency.

Had interesting letter from Rouse, describing occupation of Foochow by 3 or 4 hundred puppet, Formosan and Korean troops, against 8,000 Chinese troops who left in good time without fighting. Chinese looted all the foreigners' houses thoroughly, and burned some of them.

November 24: Two Inspectors from the Ministry came to investigate anonymous charges against Ting. They were in my office from 11:45 to 1:20, and we went into things in painful detail. I think we convinced them that there is nothing in the charges – except malice.

Tokyo has been bombed by Super-Fortresses! That is grand news, and won't help the Japs sleep more easily. Last Wednesday, Rothschild (Belgian Chargé d'Affaires) called me on the phone and asked me to give him a lift to "Atcheson's", where he thought I was dining. I told him I hadn't been invited to Atcheson's, but was dining at the Pans', and would be glad to give him a lift. As we drove up the winding road from the river and entered Ting San Road, Rothschild asked: "Is this the usual way you go to the British Embassy?" I said, "British Embassy? Atcheson is at the American Embassy." He said: "But I'm not dining with Atcheson, but with 'Hutchison! You see," he went on, "I drop my aitches." Poor chap, he was dining with Hutchison, at the British Embassy. Anyhow, I let him have my car; and recalled that Hutchison had invited me to his house that night.

November 25: ~~To American Embassy, to see George Atcheson and Judge Helmick, who arrived yesterday and will make a study of China's business laws. The Judge looks well. He said that Garnett Gardner is now on the "lecture program", and doing quite well.~~

~~To luncheon at Victory house, given by Col. Depass. Table set in the big hall, and, with about 14 guests, it looked like a fly on a sheet. Food quite good (too much, as usual).~~

[...] At lunch at Victory House, I sat next to Colonel _____, Military Attaché of the Polish Embassy. He is very bitter against Russia which, he says, is intent on creating a "Red Poland". He says Russia is going to do the same in all the Balkan states, in Sinkiang, Manchuria and Korea. The only hope is effective. Intervention by America and England, he says. In China (Manchuria and Mongolia) the Russians will work though natives to establish their control – followed by annexations or incorporation as a "Sov. Soc. Republic". The Colonel said, "When you want a woman you don't go up to her and say 'Take off your clothes and get into bed', but you start by saying 'What lovely fingers you have!'"

November 26: A lovely day, but I had to stay at home because I had guests for tiffin: Dr. Claude Forkner (Rockefeller Foundation); Billy Christian (OSS); Teddy White (Time & Life); Mrs. Jacoby (Time & Life); Spencer Moosa (A.P.); Nuner (Shanghai Evening Post); Chen (Dartmouth '29, railroad engineer); Randall Gould (Shanghai Evening Post (N.Y.)). ~~Good chow and a pleasant crowd.~~ They said that the B-29 was on the river airport is being stripped of her armor, guns, etc., etc., and, after the runway is lengthened, will attempt to take off. It seems to me a dangerous undertaking.

November 27: Quiet day; lots done in office. U.S. dollar/Chinese dollar rate has been jumping all over the place this last week. From about 450 to 1, it went up to a high of 700 on Saturday, but is now around 480.

November 29: To house warming and Martin Gold (Wm. Hunt & Co.). Vast crowd. Asked Mr. Nelson (who told me he is leaving this week) if he had his Chinese W.P.B. all set up. He said that he had, and that he had told the Chinese that it's up to them now to go ahead and make it work. Mr. Nelson said that it's their show, and, with the American experts to help, it is for the Chinese to carry on.

November 30: To Rotary Club, where Dr. Sun Fo spoke on China's postwar economic plans, i.e., the development of industry, with special reference to the participation of foreigners. If Dr. Sun's predictions come true, the business laws will be quite liberal, foreign capital will be welcomed, and there will be a

1944

minimum of government interference. His audience smiled when he said "for example, a Minister of Finance will not be permitted to own a bank." I was guest of Roy Pearson.

To big cocktail party given by Jardine's at Victory House; then to a dinner at the Sino-American Institute of Cultural Relations for Mr. Donald Nelson, Dr. Tsiang, Victor Hoo, etc. Said good-bye to Mr. Nelson, who is leaving shortly. I wonder where he's going. Locke, his Secretary, said: "We aren't going straight home." I took Ting as my guest, gave a Miss Pong, a manufacturing chemist (soap, perfume, etc.) a lift home. She's an Ohio graduate, and an odd stick. Had to wait 3/4 hour on the pontoon for ferry; and very tired when reached home. All chair-coolies belonging to foreign staff went on strike today at 3 p.m. without warning.

December

December 1: I guess the crowded rooms, bad ventilation and hundreds of colds I've been exposed these past few days got me at last, because I woke this morning with a cold in the bronchial tubes.

To office in morning, but spent afternoon in my study, hugging the fire. Let Capt. Jarrell, U.S. Naval Attaché, borrow my launch to stand by when B-29 Super-Fortress took off. On account of bad weather, attempt postponed.

December 2: Bronchitis, and in bed all day. No fever, but the usual knife stabbing in my chest when I coughed.

December 3: Chest still very sore; talking difficult. Steele (Chicago "Daily News") came to see me, but I couldn't talk very well, and I'm afraid he found me rather dumb.

At 2:30, the B-29 got off the island air-port, and flew gracefully past my house (I said a little prayer of thanks as it passed). I hear the pilot is 22 years old. A long, dull day.

December 4: Stayed home. [. . .]

December 5: Foul cold rain, so stayed at home again. Worked most of morning and part of afternoon. Ting came at 4 and we talked shop for 1-1/2 hours. He thinks Kuan-wu Shu is trying to take more and more of Inspector General's prerogatives away from him, and become the administrative, rather than the simple supervisory Customs organ. I agree; and I can see that a time will come, sooner or later, when I shall have to have a show-down with the Kuan-wu Shu, but I must wait for a question of principle important enough to warrant a fight.

The Kuomintang has issued secret instructions that one-fifth of the Party members aged 18–35 join the "Educated Youths' Military Force." We have been told to send a list of Customs employees who are Party members within these age limits to the local KMT Headquarters. Ting says that there are between 5 and 10 such members in the Inspectorate, but that not a single member of the Customs has volunteered to join the "Educated Youths' Military Force." Here their country is in utmost jeopardy, yet the youth of China are unwilling to fight.

1944

Ting says that Mrs. Huang Pei-chan is in Chungking, intriguing through Wang Shao-lei, trying to influence Li Tong and O.K. Yui in favor of her husband. The Shu Inspector (Chang) says that the two successful bidders for the Kunming seizures were (1) the Governor of Yunnan and (2) Wang Shao-Lei! Both acted through agents of course, and both fixed the deal with Huang. I wonder if Groff-Smith was as stupid as to permit this crookedness without suspecting anything. And I wonder whether the reportedly charming Mrs. Huang will get away with it? [...]

December 6: Weather still punk, cold not too good, so stayed at home. Very dull, in spite of plenty of work. [...]

December 7: Tushan [獨山] has fallen to the Japs; 75 miles from Kweiyang, which the Customs is now about to evacuate. [...]

December 8: Fang Tu very discouraged over Customs situation. He thinks Li Tong and Chu Chi (Director General & Deputy. Director General) are deliberately trying to ruin the Service. I half agree with him! And I feel very discouraged over the outlook.

December 9: Up bedtimes, and at Kuan-wu Shu at 8:15 to see Li Tong. Discussed several questions; he has raised no objections to my selection of new Assistants. Fang Tu with me, and we went on to talk of Customs pay. Li is very stubborn, and I got nowhere – but neither did he. He said he hadn't read my memorandum of yesterday, and that he was presiding at a Pu meeting this morning to discuss pay in Salt Gabelle and several other Chi Kuan [government units, 機關].

With Ting, called on new Vice-Minister of Finance. We mentioned Customs pay to him, and he at once took the opposite view from Li Tong. He said: "In America, many firms pay their general managers more than the President." It was a relief to talk with someone who knows what we're trying to do in the Customs, and not with that dried-up German professional calculating machine! Also called on the new Chief Secretary of the Pu, and left cards on the new Treasury Director General. Drove out to Hua Lung Chiao [華龍橋] and called on T.V. Soong, who was not there. Had a chat with Loy Chang. Chinese have re-captured Tushan, and have driven 18 miles south of it. Hope they can keep it up. Minister of War announces tonight that the immediate crisis is over. Hope he's right!

At the office, we are handing out cigarettes and oranges, "troop comforts", to all passing soldiers. The Chinese Staff Benevolent Association has contributed $300,000 and I added $200,000 from my "free funds". (Staff Welfare funds).

December 10: Quiet day at home. Read a flock of memos re pensions. Walked an hour morning and afternoon.

December 11: Wrote two memorandums on (1) 7d.rate in calculating pensions and (2) issue of half leave pay to expatriates. Ormac has been taken, and it looks as if McArthur would soon clean up Leyte.

December 13: [...]

To cocktail party at the French Embassy (Georges Pidot). Major St. Giles, British Embassy, suggested that I build up a Chinese dollar reserve for evacuation expenses. The news today, however, makes immediate evacuation much less probable that it was a week ago. The Japanese have retreated 18 miles inside the Kwangsi border. Many hundreds of Chinese troops en route to the front have been passing through Chungking the past few days.

[...]

Had Mr. Shafer ~~(Dorothy Smith's boy-friend)~~ to lunch, with Pouncey and Hopstock. He is a Hungarian, and got out of Shanghai (via Peiping) in June. Says conditions are bad and deteriorating in the concentration camps. People are hungry; many deaths. He fears that, in a later stage of the war, all remaining foreigners may be massacred.

December 14: ~~Dined and stayed the night with Paul Blunt, who is living temporarily in Wallinger's quarters at the British Embassy. Also present: Dr. and Mrs. Han Li Wu (new Vice-Minister of Education); Francis and Cecilia Pan; Mr. and Mrs. Lennox. Dining room cold as Greenland. Cecilia who is not well – had her dinner by the drawing-room fire, and each of the men had one course with her.~~

December 15: News from Kwangsi front still encouraging; Japs falling back. Ormac, on Leyte, has been taken – Whitamore, British Consul General (who has taken Hall's place) called re Munby, who has left England. Embassy unwilling recall him to England, so Whitamore wants me to let him stay in India. I said "no": either he goes back to England for his leave, or comes all the way to Chungking. I think W. will support me. I also got W. to agree to put my 4 British employees on the evacuation list: the Embassy's view had, apparently, been that, as they are Chinese government employees, which government should look after them.

To U.C.R. meeting at Rappe's. Dr. T.F. Tsiang proposed to ask New York to give $150,000,000 to supplement pay of teachers in government universities. I'm not entirely sold on this idea, which I told the meeting was "subsidizing the Ministry of Education." The resolution was tabled for further discussion at our next meeting.

To Embassy, to get warm! Carl Boehringer gave me a coffee and a good doughnut. George Atcheson in bed with food poisoning. Chatted with the boys for one hour, and then Judge Helmick came. I left for dinner with Dr. and Mrs. Sun Fo. Wretched rain, and chauffeur couldn't find house, so we were 15 minutes late. Mme. Sun Yat-sen there; she is lovely. Asked me to come and have tea with her. Three other Chinese there, and Howard Coonley, American expert and advisor on the new Chinese War Production Board. Excellent food. At 9:35 I had to say a hurried good-bye and make a dash for the last ferry at 10 o'clock. I stumbled down the 350 steps at Wan Lung Men and got to the landing at 9:55. The last boat had left 5 minutes earlier! I did some plain and fancy cussing – ferry company and employees, Chinese in general, the government, country and climate – then climbed back up the 350 steps. I'd told my car to wait, and I drove to the Customs House. Mr. Huang Jan, the Tidesurveyor, happened to be there, and he telephoned to the Customs pontoon on the South Bank and had a sampan sent across to Tung-shui-men for me. After half an hour, drove to Tung-shui-men, and down its interminably long, steep, torturous and slimy steps to the river. In the sampan

1944

I found a welcome charcoal brazier glowing warmly, and I huddled over it, under my umbrella, as we crossed the river. A chair was waiting for me, but, as there was only two bearers, I walked almost all the way home. It took 10 minutes to rouse the watchman, and I finally got into the house at about 11:30, tired and damp and cold.

December 16: ~~Busy day in office. To American Naval Attaché's house for dinner. Capt. Jarrell and his staff, plus two Chinese Generals and one American captain. Excellent food (local goose and American canned turkey white meat!). [...] I was careful to leave at 9; got a ferry at 9:35; home at 9:55; hot bath at 10, and to bed with a book.~~

December 17: ~~A wretched day outside: fog, rain, sleet, and very cold. Had following to lunch: Loy Chang; Nichols (American Red Cross); Millet (American Embassy) and Hopstock. Good food and talk.~~

Went over to see Dick Frost in afternoon, to talk about evacuation of British subjects in Customs if necessary. Frost said he would add Hopstock's name to the list. American forces landed on Mindoro Island, 150 miles south of Manila!

December 18: Big day in office: (1) drafted long telegram to ports concerning revision of tariff procedure, etc. of War Time Consumption Tax. Many changes, but we are still collecting the tax and the Customs has another lease of life. This has been a close shave! (2) KWS has finally agreed on a new scale of allowances, etc., effective from Nov. 1, 1944, and has not altered basic pay. If they keep their word, I shall be able to give the staff good wages for a change, considerably above the subsistence level (or below) on which many have been existing. Ting said to me today: "We shall need a foreign Inspector General for at least 10 years!" I said: "Not me, I'm not the man!" Germans have broken through U.S. 1st Army at 3 places.

December 19: Clear and sunny for a change. Still cold; maximum yesterday (24 hour) 38 degrees. Much colder last winter.

Met Belgian Ambassador. Worked on autumn promotions; a big job. ~~Pouncey has been sick for 5 or 6 days. Sent note to John, together with a letter I wrote him last summer but returned to me.~~

December 20: German counter-offensive against American 1st Army is serious business. I wonder if the Germans have a new weapon – V-3? The speed and depth of the advance lends color to the speculation.

Worked most all day on autumn promotions, and finished them at 4 p.m. Liu Ping I came to report on his trip to Chengtu, etc., in search of buildings to house Customs refugees in case we have to evacuate Chungking. He has found a few places, but says that in most of the country districts there is no law, and that the lives and property of our people would not be safe. Even a few miles from Chungking it would be necessary to bribe the "No. 1 Bandit" – or local Al Capone – before Customs people could take up residence or even travel in safety. Ting says that Huang Pei Chen, of Kunming ill-fame, called on him this noon and told him that Mr. Wang Shan-lei, (Huang's wife's "god-father"!) was trying to influence the Minister on his behalf. Huang gave Ting a parcel of sharks' fins!!

December 21: ~~To see Minister in afternoon, but he was out at 3 and again at 5. Tea at Cecilia's with Mr. Sze (singer), Gov. Chang Chen's son, and Francis. Dropped cards on Mme. Sun Yat-sen and Gen. Hurley.~~ Dined at American Information Service (OWI) as guest of MacCracken Fisher, and spoke to staff on history of Customs Service.

December 22: Heavy fog yesterday and today until 10 a.m. Pouncey back in office for half day, still feeling rocky. German counter-offensive still going strong – little news yet about it. Super-Fortresses bombing all over East Asia. Leyte campaign almost finished.

December 23: Up bedtimes, and breakfast at 7:15, intended to see Li Tong at 8:15. Heavy fog, so no ferry until 10:15; I stayed comfortably at home, and had a water-coolie tell me when the first boat left. At Kuan-wu Shu conferred 1 hour with Chu Chi (Vice-D.G.), Dr. Li and Mr. Wu. Then to Ministry, and a cordial talk with O.K. Yui. He said that T.V. Soong recently told him that he (Soong) was not convinced that the War-Time Consumption Tax should be continued! This is a threat from the quarter from which I should least expect it. O.K. Yui asked me to see T.V. on the subject, and will arrange appointment. Saw Li Tong for a few minutes, and got home to lunch about 2. Very busy all afternoon; everybody in the office had something to show me. Left in the dark about 5:45. Approved the method of distribution of the new scale of allowances. These are very liberal, and ought to go far to satisfy all the staff, as well as to strengthen my hand in dealing with the refractory minority.

News of German counter-offensive still disturbing.

December 24: D.K. Wei sent me some tea; Malcolm (ex-Marine Dept.) 1/4 pound Capstan; Bos (Dutch Embassy) a pipe.

To Nelson Mission (W.P.B.) Cocktail party. Big crowd, nice decorations (including Christmas tree) and good food. Gen. Hurley there. Gave my chauffeur pair of thick wool socks, for which he was grateful. K. Huang told me that Lott is to be No. 2 in Nanyang Bros. Tobacco Co.

December 25: ~~Up late – 8:15 and a leisurely bath and breakfast yesterday.~~ Up early, and to office until 11 a.m. To Embassy for Christmas dinner at noon: Judge Helmick, Carl Boehringer, Tony Freeman, Arthur Ringwalt, Billy Christian and a Texan, – agricultural advisor, whose name I can't recall. Judge Helmick produced a bottle of Haig & Haig. We had turkey, cranberry sauce, asparagus, peas and butter out of tins, besides the local vegetables. And good coffee! A fine meal with a congenial group. Had several Army Christmas programs for the phonograph, and swapped stories and reminiscences. I proposed a toast to the folks at home, old and young, which was cordially honored! Billy Christian in usual form: told of a party he attended last night at Wang Shao Lai's: "whore's, diplomats, Tibetans, business men, – from top to bottom crusts." One attractive girl said she was Wang Shao Lai's "niece", and pointed out one of Wang's lady-friends who, she said, was her "aunt" or "mother" (she wasn't sure which); the latter was about 25 years old. Billy asked her if Wang could recognize all his sons. She said: "Yes, if they were all together in one room, but he wouldn't know most of them if he met them on the street!" Billy told the story of the negro who was obligingly taking girls home from a dance. He had just started from the dance-hall and said to his companion: "You is the fourth pregnant girl I've taken home from the dance tonight." She replied; indignantly: "How come, nigger, you talk that way: I ain't pregnant yet!" "No", replied Sam, "an' you ain't home yet!"

~~Stopped in at Col. Morris Depass' "at home" in the morning on the way to the Embassy.~~ At 7, with Pouncey, went to my second Christmas dinner – this time at Geoffrey Smiths', Canadian Mission. Another excellent meal. (American oysters, cranberry sauce, etc.). 10 at table, and a slightly different atmosphere from noon. But both were very pleasant, and hospitality equally open and generous.

The German counter-offensive seems to have been slowed down, and the American Army is attacking the German salient in some places. 2000 bombers, 900 fighters – stretching 400 miles – attacked the German thrust.

December 26: Busy day in office. At 3:30, Fang Tu and Ting came with long faces [upset]; Li Tong has gone back on the arrangement we concluded with the Vice-Director General, etc., in one vital particular: he has wiped out the "flexible allowances" for coal, oil and salt. Damn the man's miserly, obstructive and pettifogging ways!

~~Had luncheon for Baron Desdefranze de Phemffe, new Belgian Ambassador. At 12:30, had note saying that he was sick abed with "Chungking tummy" and couldn't come. Rothschild, who was also invited, didn't come, either. But I had Whitamore (new British Consul General), Kai Liang (my old Canton friend), Col. Depass, Ting, Lu, Pouncey and Hopstock; and we had a pleasant meal.~~

Leyte campaign finished, according to MacArthur. Jap casualties: 112,000. Ours: 11,000. Japs also lost heavily in ships, planes and equipment.

December 27: ~~Loy Chang host, plain food, excellent Shao sing, and good conversation. Got away at 3 p.m. Worked at top speed on preparation for counter-offensive vs Li Tong.~~

December 28: Wot a day! To Director General's at 8:45, with Ting and Fang Tu. Almost pitched battle with Li Tong and his narrow-minded cohorts. Ting, Fang and Li all talking at once. At first, Li refused to listen, after an hour, he grudgingly agreed to re-examine the question of allowances and pay; I left Fang Tu to fight it out with Li's Secretaries. Ting and I drove out to see T.V. Soong, who had called for us at 11. He was delayed, but we spent a pleasant hour with Loy Chang and K.C. Wu, – ~~Wu (just returned from Sinkiang)~~, and I got warm after the chill of the Kuan-wu Shu. Dr. Soong arrived at 12, and we had conference. He wants to abolish War-Time Consumption Tax because of the public opposition to the government, but he also wants to preserve Customs organization. He asked me if we could take over all the inspecting duties now performed by dozens of different bureaus. We said "Yes". Dr. Soong instructed us to let him have a memorandum in English and Chinese by noon tomorrow. (We really should have a month to do it!) It was most refreshing to negotiate with a statesman like Soong after an hour with that stinker Li Tong. We stayed to an excellent lunch with Dr. Soong, and got back to office at 3. I called conference of 4 Secretaries concerned and laid the problems before them. Ting started memorandum which he sent to my house at 7:30. I corrected and revised it and sent it back at 8:15. A bite of dinner, and then I drafted a supplementary letter to Dr. Soong. Wot a day!

December 29: Wot another day! With Ting, to Dr. T.V. Soong's house at 12. After conference with him, he saw Gen. Tai Li;[91] then all four joined in conference at the dining-room table. After long discussion (and a delicious tiffin), Dr. Soong instructed Tai Li and me to confer tomorrow and hammer out a plan for the control of all inspection posts by the Customs, assisted by armed military guards. Back to office, and another conference (in which hot differences of opinion were expressed). I left at 5, absolutely all in, but had to cross the river to go to dinner given by Mr. and Mrs. Liu Chi-wen and Mr. and Mrs. Dick Lee. Buffet, and good food. About 30 there. Boy, was I tired! Still, it probably did me good to get away from the office. Home at 10:15, and spent 3/4 hour examining latest "compromise" with Kuan-wu Shu over new allowances. They are not as liberal as I wanted, but are infinitely better than Li Tong was at first prepared to concede.

Coming down Wang Lung Man steps with Ting and Liu Ping I at 3 p.m., a barrel of cement got loose and came bouncing after us in a great yellow cloud as it disintegrated. Missed us by a few feet, but covered Liu with cement from head to foot.

December 30: With Ting and Liu Ping I to conference with Gen. Tai Li and Gen. Chang. 2:45–5:00 (with excellent coffee in between). Very straightforward talk and businesslike. Finally convinced Tai Li that Customs must be the sole control of Military Guards insofar as Customs functions are concerned (His first proposal placed the Commissioners under the command of the guards!). Agreed that we should draw up a final draft, combining agreed-on features of his plan and mine, for discussion next Tuesday. Home at 6:15, after the most hectic kind if week.

~~Had 1/2 pound of S.S. Pierce's "Our Private Mixture" tobacco, and a pipe from Russ Sweet! Also, Adm. Hsu sent me a jug of some kind of powerful Chinese liquor. K.K. Kwok sent me 2 pounds of coffee (!!) and 4 packets American tobacco several days ago. Princely gifts!~~ Ting says there are rumors of drastic changes in government: possibly a coalition, with Communist and other participation. Disaffection widespread throughout the country: if something fundamental is not done soon, Chiang may have to go! T.V. may possibly take over Finance Ministry concurrently. O.K. Yui possibly shifted to Foreign Office.

American 1st and 3rd Armies pushing back the German thrust in Belgium; news much better today.

December 31: To office at 10. Conferred with Ting. Liu Ping I, Lu Ping and Chang Yung Nien. ~~Paul Blunt called in afternoon.~~ At 7:30, to cocktail party at Dick Frosts'. Then to New Year's Party at Club. Good buffet, and a pleasant crowd. I slipped out at 10 and came home. Getting old! This has been a full year, and 1945 promises to be fuller!

1945

January

January 1: Ting came at 9 to discuss draft of proposed organization of Customs consolidated inspection and preventive work, Customs guards, etc. Staff (Secretaries and Assistant Secretaries) all came at 10 to wish me a Happy New Year. Ting and I went to Ministry of Finance, to do the same for O.K. Yui, but we had been misinformed as to the time, and arrived too late. Generalissimo, in proclamation, promises that a new constitution will be adopted as soon as military situation permits, and that Kuomintang will hand over political control to the people during the war instead of one year after the war, which has hitherto been the program. This indicates the correctness of what Ting told me on Dec. 30 regarding the situation. Dinner with mess Banister, Hopstock, Bathurst and Porter (Pouncey, poor chap, had to go to a curry tiffin which I declined). We had a swell dinner at 1:30, soup, salmon cakes, sausage, chicken, pineapple, as well as his last bottle of French white wine. I contributed coffee, butter, and the bottle of port sent to me by Horace Smith[1] from Sinkiang (good, too!). Worked 2 hours on Customs guards scheme.

January 2: [. . .] Letter from my Canton stenographer, Alma Poon, married in Australia and now Almo Goon (believe it or not). Also, a fine letter from John, with a picture of Churchill and de Gaulle[2] he took in Paris on Armistice Day. With Ting, to see Tai Li, who accepted our plan and agreed to hand it to T.V. Soong today at 5. To farewell tea for Nichols, American Red Cross Chief. Ting and I called on the New American Ambassador – Gen. Patrick Hurley. Pat is a smooth talker – and talks most of the time. He had a good line, and seemed very sincere. Says he speaks lots of times with the Generalissimo, with whom he discusses all questions in the frankest way. U.S. Object, says Pat, is a strong, united and free China. Roosevelt, he said, is determined to see to it that China becomes one of the "Big 4". "China, a great democracy in the East; America a great democracy in the West." Gen. Pat Hurley was very cordial. Reminisced about his Army career – private to major general. Said Eisenhower and MacArthur were his aides when he was Sec. of War.

1945

January 3: ~~Terribly busy in morning.~~ Had another conference with Gen. Tai Li and Gen. Chang – 3–5 p.m. T.V. Soong did not accept my plan, and insists that Customs take charge of all "security" inspection throughout China. This is, in my opinion, a serious blunder, but, if I am ordered to assume the responsibility, I shall do so and try to make a success of it. Tai Li said that the organization now attending to security work was very unpopular, and that the Generalissimo and T.V. Soong intend to place the job in better hands. All this flattering to the Customs, but I still consider the move highly dangerous. Major Hancock, RAF, (ex-Customs) to lunch here, with Ting, Banister, Pouncey, Hopstock and Bathurst.

Ting came to house at 10:20 p.m. and left at 11:30. We went over the revised plan of organization of inspection and prevention. He had prepared a good draft, which I worked over. I also drafted a letter to T.V. Soong.

January 4: With Ting, to Tai Li's at 10. Hour with Gen. Chang, then Tai Li came in and we hammered out differences and finally agreed on a document which T.V. Soong will take to the Generalissimo tomorrow – we think! In my letter to T.V. Soong, I protested against giving Customs the responsibility for detecting subversive elements, apprehending spies, arresting deserters, etc., etc. ~~Home to lunch about 1:45~~. As guest of Roy Pearson (who was called out of town suddenly yesterday), I attended Ladies' Night at Rotary (Victoria House). Pretty lousy dinner, but, as I was next to Cecilia Pan, it didn't matter. Dr. Victor Hoo was principal speaker and his subject was the Dumbarton Oaks Conference proposals. Morrie Depass, who presided, rambled and ranted and clichéd for 20 to 25 minutes in his introduction – one of the poorest I ever sweated through. I had to leave before Victor made his speech – in order to catch the ferry at 10.

January 5: ~~To see Lott Wei on his first day as Asst. General Manager of Nanyang Pros. Tobacco Co. (one of T.V. Soong's enterprises)~~.

With Ting, to Dr. T.V. Soong's house at 11. I argued most strongly against saddling the Customs with responsibility for security functions. T.V. seemed to accept my argument. Then, while Ting and I waited downstairs, Gen. Tai Li was closeted with T.V. Next, the four of us had a very frank discussion. I stuck to my guns; Tai Li stuck to his; T.V. said the problem seemed "insoluble", but supported my contention that the Customs should not be responsible for security work. Finally decided that Tai Li will re-draft proposals for T.V. by tomorrow morning, so our fate rests in T.V.'s hands for the moment. If he sticks to the principle I have fought for, I shall be the happiest and most relieved man in Chungking! That Tai Li is immensely powerful, and that he has the ear of the Generalissimo, is quite apparent. Anyway, I have put up the best fight I know how: I told both T.V. and Tai Li that the consequences of putting security work on the shoulders of the Customs might easily prove "disastrous". One thing is interesting – the excellent reputation the Customs enjoys. Tai Li said (in reply to my question: why don't you put security under a strictly military control? "If I knew of any organization capable of doing the work, I should not suggest giving it to the Customs." After the buffeting the Service has taken these past four years, our prestige is still far highest of any department of the government. T.V. has his difficulties, it was plain to see;

1945

their nature, I can only speculate on. He was eminently reasonable, courteous, and willing to listen. My regard for him as a great man has increased.

January 6: ~~To dentist, who was too busy to treat me.~~ One of the slackest days in office in a year, a welcome relief after these past 2 weeks. To lunch at Mon. Delvaux de Fenffe,[3] new Belgian Ambassador. Good food and company. BBC at 10 p.m. Said Wanting re-taken by Japs; San Francisco at 10:45 said Japs retook Wanting on January 3, but that Chinese had now driven the out! Fierce battles in Ardennes salient. Moscow has recognized Polish Lublin government. It's about time for Roosevelt, Stalin and Churchill to get together again.

January 7: A blessed day of rest! ~~Cleaned up my desk in the morning. Also revived some pretty gummy pipe-cleaners with gasoline.~~

January 8: ~~To dentist. One porcelain filling renewed: C.N. $1,000.~~ To Canadian Embassy, for chat with Dr. Patterson, Chargé. (Old YMCA man in Japan; friend of Russ Durgin). Hopstock laid up; he had a rather severe fall Saturday night. Pouncey fell this afternoon; ligament torn in foot. Bathurst warned to watch his heart: he has blood-pressure. Porter half-sick. Banister and I are O.K. – at the moment! What a collection! Government has approved my recommendation to give promotions – if due – to all foreigners paid off in 1943/44, but refused promotions to those still in captivity.

January 10: With Ting, to K.W.S. At 9. Discussed Customs College: plans for next school year; numbers; curriculum; how to attract good students. Also discussed question of appointment of Commissioners and Deputy Commissioners. Ting very conservative, and thinks we should try to retain I.G.'s nominations. Li Tong told me that the Pu had agreed with my recommendations in the "Kunming case": pay of Groff-Smith; discharge Huang Pei Chen; pay pension benefits to widow of Siu Liang. Radio at 12:30 (Delhi) announced U.S. Landing on Luzon! Following the pattern in "The Valor of Ignorance"? Great news.

January 11: ~~Quiet day but busy day in office.~~ Passed draft, written by Pouncey, to Pu requesting that post-1920 foreign staff be given same pensions treatment as pre-1920 staff. This is the most important single question – outside of pay scale – bearing on the post-war employment of foreigners.

January 12: With ting, to see T.V. Soong at 6. On arrival at Hua Lung Chiao (a half-hour drive), one of T.V.'s secretaries met us with a "tui pu chi" [對不起, sorry] but T. V. had been called by the Generalissimo, and could we come tomorrow at 9:30? We could and shall. ~~To cocktail party at Billy Christian's. Drove back in Dick Frost's car; flat tire twice, so walked last 20 minutes. Hopstock took first degree in Fortitude Lodge tonight.~~

January 13: And I am the happiest and most relieved man in Chungking! To see Dr. T.V. Soong at 9:30. He said he wanted a last talk on the subject of inspection work by the Customs. T.V. then said that he had decided that the Customs should not take on security inspection! (Those few words lifted a weight from my mind!) He said that War-Time Consumption Tax would be abolished: that Customs would continue to collect import and export duty; that we could have military guards at each Customs station. We told him we thought 1,000 soldiers enough. He said we could have more if found necessary. These soldiers will wear military uniforms, but will be paid by the Customs and be under my sole control. I told T.V. that what he said was better than a gift of a million dollars. He cautioned me as to secrecy, and said that his name must not be mentioned in connection with, the proposed developments: the announcement must come from, and appear to originate with, the Generalissimo.

T.V. was in his most gracious mood. He told me he hoped I would continue to administer the Service with efficiency and integrity, and warned against the presence of "cliques". (This was for Ting's benefit!). I assured him of my utmost support; and said that I felt more optimistic over the outlook for China now than at any time during the past 7 years. As we stood up, Ting asked permission to mention the Kuan-wu Shu, and pointed out the delay etc. caused by duplication of work, etc. T.V. said, almost before Ting had got going: "I'm going to abolish the Kuan-wu Shu and Superintendents of Customs! A historic interview: more done in 10 minutes than is usually done in 6 months.

To office; spoke to the Secretaries "in the know" and warned against talking (I did not mention abolition of KWS).

To big buffet supper and dance at Victory House, given by the British officers in Chungking. (300 plates at $800 = $240,000) I came away at 9:15, after a delicious supper and several dances with attractive partners.

January 14: Munby arrived from England today and came to tea with me. Munby said V-1 and V-2 bombs pretty bad, Food situation in England excellent. Clothing and furniture hard to get, and inferior quality. ~~To Cecilia Pan's for dinner. Her birthday. Delicious dinner and a bottle of Veuve Cliquot! I'm not especially fond of champagne, but this tasted heavenly after the rot-gut served in Chungking.~~

~~Didn't go to a cocktail party at British Embassy; had a quiet evening for a change~~. Ting (discussing possible staff evacuations) said that the danger to staff, in case of serious trouble, would not be from Japanese, but from the Chinese. I think this is correct, and was shown both in the recent Honan and Kwangsi evacuations. Ting also said that the Szechuan and Yunnan provincial authorities (military) were all prepared last month to declare their "independence", and prevent the flight of Nationalist government from Chungking in case the Japs advanced on Chungking and/or Kunming. Maj. Farmer said he saw many bodies lying along the roads in Kweichow – all stripped clean by soldiers and civilians.

January 16: Had to dismiss an Assistant, an Examiner and two junior O.D. [Out-door] ranks for engaging in trade. To dinner with Sumner,[4] Economic Attaché, U.S. Embassy. Also there: Carl Boehringer and Hall Paxton. My car didn't turn up, but luckily I met Capt. Jarrell, who let me use his car both ways.

January 17: Decided to send Hopstock to Foochow to replace Rouse, who is going on leave. Hopstock took the news very badly, said he was being "sacrificed" and a lot more of the same kind of rubbish. After a most tiring day, I was trying to have half an hour's rest at home before going out to dinner, and Pouncey came to my room and said he wanted to talk about Hopstock's transfer! I felt like telling him to go to hell, but contented myself by suggesting that I would talk with him tomorrow. Then in walked Hopstock and produced a medical certificate dated

1940 or 41, saying that he ought not to have to undergo hardships! God! I'd give $10,000 if I had a gut like his! He lives a very gay life here, but flashes this certificate when I ask him to go to Foochow! I told him it was not acceptable; if he is not physically fit, he should get an up-to-date certificate locally. To a big dinner given by Col. Depass at Victory House for Gen. Hurley and Gen. Wedemeyer. The latter didn't get back to Chungking in time. Too much food, too crowded at tables. 45 guests. Probably cost $60,000, and a rather pointless crowd. I left the table before the fruit in order to catch the ferry.

January 18: Despatch from Pu says Generalissimo has ordered all Central government organs to leave Kweiyang! This means that our Changsha Head office (evacuated from Kweilin to Kweiyang) will have to vamoose, and leaves Drummond free for transfer. I shall send him to Foochow, because his leave is not due for 3 years, while Hopstock's is due next October. Decided on leaves for foreign staff: Rouse, Porter, Gawler, Bathurst, and Banister. Banister to be voluntarily retired end of his leave. Bathurst says he doesn't want leave! After all the bellyaching I've had to stand, this takes the cake. He's going on leave, willy-nilly. I'm getting fed up with these temperamental individuals. I told him the Customs is neither a milk cow nor a country-club.

January 19: To big reception at British Embassy for a lot of visiting firemen. Party given by Findlay-Andrew and guests of honor were two top-flight British intelligence officers. To my surprise, who should walk in but Gen. Donovan – two stars now; only one when I last saw him. The gathering looked like all the Anglo-American hush-hush chiefs.

January 20: Tu Kuan-wu Shu at 8:45. Li Tong told me that government had decided to abolish War-Time Consumption Tax. I tried to look surprised. He also said that Accounts section in Ministry had refused to pass the item for fuel in proposed new scale of allowances! This, after fighting for two months! To Army Headquarters, to see Gen. Donovan, who wants any information the Customs can give him. ~~Back to office, to tell staff about abolition of W.T.C.T., and suggest that there is no ground to fear for the future of the Service~~.

To tea (i.e., 2 kinds of chiao-tzu, turnovers and peanuts) at Mme. Sun Yat-sen's house. She is very gracious and easy to look at, and I enjoyed myself. Worked till 10:45 on a letter to T.V. Soong, asking authority to tell staff that the government will not disband Service.

I had 10 minutes with Mme. Sun before other guests came. She asked me if I'd been seeing T.V. Soong. I told her that I had, and that I was greatly impressed and encouraged with the work he was doing. I said "He may have become the Churchill of China". She said: "Not Churchill, that Imperialist!" Later, when the guests were present, she remarked à propos of Emily Hahn's[5] book, *The Three Soong Sisters*, the Emily had asked for an interview but that she had refused to see her. Also, that Emily had sent her the M/S of the book, which she has returned without even "taking off the string." Mme. Sun said: "Why should Emily Hahn write a book? I might like to do it myself." Mme. Sun said what China needs is a "united front", i.e., bring in the Communists.

New American Embassy Chancery burned to ground last night. No casualties. Building only completed 3 or 4 months ago.

January 21: Had intended to go up to bungalow for first time in months, but Hopstock told me there was a party of five from the British Embassy had asked him if they might stop in and eat their lunches there! Hopstock told them that he thought "the I.G. would have no objection!" The I.G. had plenty of objections: he wanted a day of rest and relaxation; he didn't want to have to play host and talk to five strangers (one a girl who might have thick ankles); he didn't want to sit in one room with eight or nine people trying to keep warm in front of a tiny fireplace; he wanted to be able to strip on arrival and put on dry underwear. The upshot of it all was the I.G. stayed at home all morning. ~~In p.m., to Lott Wei's to congratulate him in his birthday. A lot of Mint people there, playing mah-jong [麻將]. Had a bowl of delicious noodles.~~

January 22: With Hopstock, to lunch with Gen. Donovan and two of his staff, at Gen. McClure's residence. Gen. Donovan doesn't think that the British, and certain Chinese factions, are too keen on the American policy of a "strong and united China."

January 23: ~~Busy day in office.~~ At 7 p.m., Lu Ping wrote and said K.W.S. had phoned that Control Yuan had notified Ministry of Finance that Preventive Bureau was to be abolished and its functions taken over by the Customs. This is the first of T.V.'s taxation reforms. Conformed by Central News Agency, along with several other decisions of the Executive Yuan. Looks like a busy time ahead for me! Russians driving into East Prussia and Silesia; Ardennes bulge almost liquidated; Burma Road open; Americans 45 minutes from Manila. This may all add up to the kill.

January 24: Ting away morning and afternoon at conference concerning abolition of W.T.C.T. and assumption of new inspection and preventive duties by Customs. I called meeting of Secretaries and explained situation to them.

To Canadian Hospital at 11. ~~My gums have been sore for 3 days. Dr. Allen and Dr. Service, and the dentist all think it may be caused by an ulcerated tooth, so I had an X-ray. Because of weak current, had to wait until 1:15! Result tomorrow.~~ Had 1-1/2 hours with Chang Yung-nien going over final draft of staff reorganization scheme. Pouncey very pessimistic over new Customs functions: he spreads gloom – unconsciously – but I wish he'd be a little more cheerful! God knows there are headaches ahead, but so far so good. Executive Yuan announced many major reforms in tax structure. Soong is using the broom for a pretty clean sweep.

January 25: ~~To dentist at Canadian Hospital who said X-ray negative, but found cavity near gum. This may be cause of inflammation. Filled cavity.~~

Two hour conference with Ting, Pouncey, Lu, Fang and Chang on despatch to Pu regarding abolition of W.T.C.T. and assumption of new duties. Ting drafted body of despatch; Fang Tu, Lu Ping and Chang Yung-nien worked until 3 a.m. this morning preparing data re finance, stations and staff. They did a fine and quick job! Pu's despatch today approves my decision in "Kunming case" in toto. This is most satisfactory, and will have excellent effect on staff, because it shows that

1945

the government acts honestly and fearlessly in spite of the intrigue and influence in high places of Huang Pei-chan – perhaps – others.

January 26: Ting at K.W.S. all morning. Conferred in afternoon. He said Li Tong objected to practically all the recommendations in my despatch to Pu. One or two of his criticisms were justified; all the rest were childish and churlish. I'll make a monkey out of him if he pushes me too far. Despatch to Pu re-drafted in part; it will now go direct to Pu, and to hell with Li Tong. The sooner the Kuan-wu Shu is abolished, the better for the Customs and the country.

January 27: Staff worked until 1 a.m. getting despatch written to Pu. Had 20 at lunch: Ambassadors: Lovink (Dutch); Minovasky (Czecho-Slovak); Gen. Pechkoff (French). Chargés: Keith Officer (Australian). Counselors of Embassy: Clarac (French); Van den Berg (Dutch); Wallinger and Kiton (British). Chief of Nelson Mission: Howard Coonley. Customs: Ting, Banister, Tu, Pouncey, Liu, Bathurst, Hopstock, Chang, Sung, Adm. Hsu. Good chow and a nice party. I spoke briefly about the Service, and Lovink (who started his career as an Assistant in the Customs) responded in a prepared (and sincere) talk for 10 minutes. All well-received. To office, and busy, in afternoon.

January 28: To bungalow, with Paul Blunt, Pouncey and Hopstock. House cold as Greenland; coal 2/3rd stone. Nevertheless, had a good lunch: baked beans, eggs, toast (and butter supplied by Paul) and 2 cups of coffee. Left at 3 too cold to stay! To cocktail party at Club, given by Whitamore (Brit. Con. Gen), who has just learned that his son, who was shot down over Germany and believed killed, is a prisoner of war.

January 29: Spoke at Memorial Service re new taxation reforms and their effect on Service. Gave staff as much inspiration as I could. To Dr. Chang, dentist, at Canadian Hospital who filled 2 teeth and ground down one old filling. In chair 1-1/2 hours and very uncomfortable. I hope to have all false teeth before long! First convoy over new India-China road arrived at Wanting; met by T.V. Soong and other dignitaries. The Generalissimo has named the new road the "Stilwell Road" – a great and well-deserved honor to Vinegar Joe. [...]

January 30: To Col. Depass' to check on a message received from Hong Kong. To office at 9:30, and every Secretary in the place had something for me to see or sign before 10:30, when I crossed river and had interview with Col. Dutton, USA. Talked chiefly about proposed Customs functions on Burma frontier; agreed to let Gawler recommend details of cooperation. I mentioned Army's leasing of land on Customs property at Kunming, and Col. Dutton said he thought it could be fixed up. To Gen. Wedemeyer's office, but he had left; arranged to see him tomorrow. To Embassy for lunch with George Atcheson. Pleasant break: Judge Helmick there, as well as the mess. Also, Judge Adv.-Gen's office, brother of the Captain of the "San Francisco" who was killed on the bridge of his ship. To Ministry of Finance at 2:30 and had nice talk with the Minister. Mr. Yui said that abolition of War Time Consumption Tax was principally a political move; that he had insisted that the Customs Service be preserved; that the government couldn't hope to meet its budget by internal loans or taxation; that the scale of gold was proving fairly successful in combatting inflation; that there had been a lot of corruption in the various tax offices. I mentioned my difficulty in the Customs, i.e., that all Customs pay was "on top of the table" and that we had no way to "supplement" our income. He understood, and, he said, the Customs must be adequately paid. I asked him about the Emergency Allowances (we've been fighting over them for 10 weeks!) and he said he'd approved them 2 or 3 days ago! Yet we've heard nothing. Saw Li Tong for 5 minutes – 4-1/2 too many. To U.C.R. meeting at 3. Passed a lot of grants. To French Embassy "the – cocktail" at 5:30. Everybody was there, but I didn't stay long, and I was getting tired. Home at 7. Busy day!

January 31: Called on Tsu-yee Pei (Bank of China) who is just back from two or three conferences in America. During his visit, he found time to impregnate his wife (who has been in America several years), thus leading to the remark of his colleagues that he was the most productive of all the Chinese delegates! To U.S. Army Headquarters to call on Gen. Wedemeyer. He was very cordial. We discussed Customs functions on Stilwell Road. He said that the overall control organization was still under discussion! (it's about time that was settled.) The high U.S. authorities have ordered him to see that there is no smuggling; he has a secret service detail on the job. Gen. Wedemeyer said that Delhi indicates that, if control of the new road is entirely in American military control the British will not establish a Customs on the Burma side of the frontier – if otherwise, they will. Drafted letter to Gawler re Customs functions on Stilwell Road.

February

February 1: Rang the bell this morning and told the staff that the long-awaited increase in Emergency allowances had materialized. Also told them that I expected hard and conscientious work from them, and that any who didn't deliver would be discharged. At 3, to see Mr. O.K. Yui. Reported on my interviews with Col. Dutton and Gen. Wedemeyer re Customs functions on Stilwell Road, and showed him draft of my letter to Gawler, which he read and approved. Also mentioned Ting's abortive visit to the Preventive Bureau yesterday, and asked him to instruct that the Preventive Bureau equipment (trucks, boats, radio, etc.) be handed to Customs. He said he'd instruct Li Tong to handle disposal of this stuff, and asked me to see him about it. Also mentioned Li Tong's last-minute change in the new Emergency Allowance regulations, i.e., that the question of the allowances to foreign staff would be considered separately. Told him that I couldn't wait any longer, and that I had sent out telegrams giving increases as already agreed to by all concerned. He said he approved, and added "I'll leave the pay of foreigners to your discretion!!" What a pleasure to deal with a man like that instead of that louse Li Tong!

To U.S. Army Headquarters, and showed Col. Dutton my draft letter to Gawler. He agreed with what I'd written, and will send a copy to Chen. To tea with Cecilia and Francis Pan, who showed me the ration of dehydrated food he is trying to induce the Chinese government to adopt for the Chinese troops. Reading "Strange Fruit" – an absorbing book.

February 2: To dentist at 2:30. He turned up at 2:50. His drill broke; after that was fixed, he had almost finished cleaning my teeth when the electric light went out. He finished with his assistant holding a candle under my nose.

To reception at Victory House, given by Maj. Gen. G.E. Grimsdale for his successor, Maj. Gen. E.C. Hayes.[6] Russians are within 40 miles of Berlin; U.S. 1st Army going strong towards Siegfried Line; MacArthur makes a landing 50 miles south of Manila. It all adds up to a big Victory pretty soon. But the Japs are consolidation all through East China.

February 3: Up at 7, across river at 8:15 (cold!) to Kuan-wu Shu. Hour with Chu Chi and Dr. Li, then to office. At noon, took my launch to Nan Yang Tobacco Factory, where Lott Wei and Philip Chan gave a big buffet lunch (about 40) after which we inspected factory. 206 employees; place spotless; obviously well run. Back to office about 4, and very busy for an hour. Then home to shower and change. I had forgotten to order car, but crossed river at 6 on spec: by a stroke of luck, I ran into U.S. Naval Petty Officer who gave me a lift in a weapons carrier to the Attaché's house, where I attended a pleasant cocktail party. From Capt. Jarrell's, I got a ride with Howard Coonley to Cecilia Pan's, where I dined. Guest of honor was Gen. Wedemeyer, who is a most delightful and friendly man. Other guests: the Lennoxes; William and Mrs. Wang (Cecilia's sister); Major MacGee (Wedemeyer's Aide); Prof. Sze (the famous singer); Mrs. Kwok. Francis was in good form. I was dead on my feet, and left before dinner was over, in spite of pressure to stay all night. Had offer of 2 cars to Wang Lung Men. Gen. Wedemeyer's and Mr. Wang's. Got last ferry, and crossed with Pauline Auyang, whose faithful escort (and fiancé), Mr. Hsi, had brought her to the ferry. I was glad to get back to my quiet and warm study, after a tense and buys week, climaxed by a packed and tiring Saturday. [. . .] I think I must have spoken to over 100 different people today. (5 years ago, today, I married Alice. I still love her.)

February 4: Stayed abed till 8:30 and had a long, quiet day – all done! Saw nobody except the boy when he brought my chow. Filed my private correspondence. First convoy over Stilwell Road arrived at Kunming – Americans within 15 miles of Manila.

February 5: MacArthur in Manila! Quiet but busy day in office. This week I have only one social engagement (so far), a dinner here tomorrow night.

February 6: To dinner here: Ludden (who has just returned from a long trip with the Chinese guerillas; he got within 100 miles of Peking); Jack Service; Tony Freeman; Blunt; Nixon; Bathurst; Hopstock. Lots of talk, and gossip like a pack of women.

February 7: Busy day, with plenty of important decisions taken. Wrote to all ports re status of Service after recent reforms. Also a similar letter to Foster-Hall. Still no mail from America: neither Hopstock nor Pouncey has had any U.S. mail for over a month. There must be a big bottleneck somewhere. [. . .]

February 8: With Ting, to see T.V. Soong at Fan Chuang. He said he would be there every morning (except Monday and Tuesday) and that I might come to see him at any time, without appointment. He asked how the new reforms were going, and we discussed details of stations, guards, etc. I told him I was proposing the levy of export duty on goods shipped into occupied China; he instructed me to let him have a memorandum on the subject in English and Chinese. I reported my interview with Gen. Wedemeyer. He asked us how things were going between Inspectorate and Kuan-wu Shu. I told him that the K.W.S. caused much delay; that it was responsible for endless duplication; and that I resented the Shu's attitude of suspicion and distrust. Ting said that the Shu was trying to force the Customs into line with other organizations in the matter of pay, etc. Dr. Soong ended by saying "I'll remedy all that." I hope he does: the real remedy is to abolish the K.W.S., but he didn't go so far as to promise this, as he did once before. Real snow today: 1/2" deep. The hills were beautiful (what you could see of them).

February 9: Had Elsie Soong and her oldest son (Gerald) to lunch. For the past two years she has been teaching school and running a small dairy at Tushan (Kweichow). Japanese advance forced her to evacuate, and she came here a month ago. She plans to send her four children to an uncle in Jersey City; she says she can't afford to keep them here. It is much cheaper in America if she can get U.S. $ exchange at the official rate of C.N. $20 to U.S. $1. She is a courageous and resourceful woman, and youthful-looking and quite pretty. Aloy Soong was the first Chinese (outside of the laundryman on Cottage St.) I ever knew: he was studying at Brown when I was in high school.

[. . .]

To consult Dr. Stewart (Capt. U.S.N), U.S. Army dentist. He thinks my trouble is due to recession of gum from teeth, leaving a space in which food decays. Am going to give it a couple of weeks without upper plate to see if it clears up. My fountain pen gone from my desk when I came home; horrid suspicion: did Elsie's 17 year old son (Gerald) put it in his pocket? He sat on the desk for some time, and seemed to be interested in the things in it. One of the coldest days Chungking has had. Also spitting rain and sleet, with mud an inch deep everywhere underfoot.

February 10: Ting away all day attending conferences. To lunch (Chinese chow) at K.C. Lee's. Virginia is back from India. A lovely Mrs. K.K. (or C.C.) Chen (husband, Agricultural Dept., Bank of China) a refugee from Kweilin, present. Also, Belgian and Brazilian Ambassadors, Rothschild, Dr. Neighbor (U.S. Navy) and "Arturo" Campbell, Lt. USNR. Latter drank like a fish and ate like a hog. Wrote memo on charge allowances at night.

February 12: Extremely busy day. Long argument with Ting re Charge Allowances. Letter from Foster-Hall says Queen's University declines to return Hart-Campbell correspondence unless at request of Minister of Finance. (Drafted letter which I shall ask the Minister to sign.) Had a "Xmas – New Year – Birthday" box from John, with tobacco, chocolate powder, eating chocolate, soup powder, soap, 2 books. Wrote him thank-you letter. The gifts were individually wrapped in regular Christmas paper, too.

February 13: Chinese New Year, and a Customs holiday for the first time in many years. The government has never been able to suppress the celebration of the lunar New Year. Sporadic fire-crackers last night, despite the official ban. Drafted memo re increased Sterling allotments, discontinuance of special extra $4,000 Expatriation allowance, etc. Walked 1-1/2 hours up "Pagoda Valley"; country green with new vegetables coming up. Broad beans in blossom – purple. [. . .] At noon, radio gave gist of decisions of the Big Three at the Crimea Conference. At first hearing, very satisfactory, especially a promised settlement of Polish question. Looks to me as if Russia will be in war against Japan before too long.

February 14: To U.S. Army Headquarters. Discussed (1) lease of property at Kunming; (2) Customs functions on Burma frontier; acquisition of some jeeps or trucks by Customs. To see O.K. Yui, and ~~after which I~~ discussed with the Minister (1) supply of uniforms for Customs staff; (2) jeeps or trucks; (3) re-organization of Customs functions (Mr. Yui said that, when abolition of W.T.C.T. was being discussed, he insisted that Customs be given other tasks, to preserve "your efficient and well-trained organization.") (4) Hart-Campbell correspondence. Mr. Yui read and approved my draft letter – for him to sign – to the Vice-Chancellor of Queen's University, Belfast. I think I have at least cornered these two old Irish foxes, Maze and Wright,[7] and can make Maze disgorge the documents he stole. ~~Found Dick Smith here when I got back. Talked till 7. Nice letter from John, dated. Jan. 7. Still enjoying Paris~~. Worked at night on letter to Ministry re jeeps and uniforms.

February 15: Crossed river at noon, in biggest crowds I've ever seen in Chungking. Thousands at ferrys, which were dangerously and recklessly over-crowded. About half were women, all of whom seemed to have a small baby in arms. All in all, however, a good-natured New Year's crowd.

To U.S. Army Headquarters and conferred with Col. Gato re Kunming property. He called in the legal department, and I think we've got it fixed O.K. To Foreign Economic Administration to see Bill Stanton and ask him to help me get 10 trucks and 10 jeeps. He suggested we should get in touch with W.P.B., so, when I returned to office at 4, I wrote draft letter and sent it to O.K. Yui to sign. ~~A busy day; a lot done~~. Drafted letter at night to Foster-Hall re Hart-Campbell correspondence. I hope this will be my last letter on that subject!

February 16: [. . .] Took some important decisions today re Pensions, Retiring Allowances, and treatment of internees. After months of consideration and argument, I finally decided on the specific recommendations I shall put up to government.

February 17: At 9, to see Li Tong. Long conference, with many questions. It is apparent that he dislikes and distrusts the Customs. Possibly the knowledge that Ting has written to O.K Yui suggesting the abolition of the Kuan-wu Shu has something to do with his attitude! Dictated aide memoire of my conference (4 foolscap pages!) and gave necessary orders arising therefrom. Rumor persists that T.V. Soong is going to take over the Finance portfolio. U.S. carrier-based planes in great strength bombed Tokyo this morning! Right on Hirohito's[8] front door-step.

Had 10 to dinner here. After guests left, I took Mrs. Trevor-Powell to Club dance, and danced about ten times with her and others! I'm getting old: there was too much drinking to suit me. I'm not amused. Bathurst announced his engagement to Miss West. She is a big girl – about 6 ft. Left Club about 11:45, and Robinson said he'd see Mrs. Trevor-Powell home (he is living at the APC house). He was so drunk, however, that I had to prevent him from falling and breaking his neck, so I had to climb all the way up to APC house with them. Home after midnight.

February 18: [. . .] To bungalow with Hopstock. Good fire, and our usual meal of poached eggs, toast and coffee. Also had one of the tins of sardines John sent me. No sun, and rather chilly walking. Road up to first range crowded with pilgrims visiting the temple at the top. Dozens of market stalls all the way up selling red votive candles, joss-paper, etc. ~~Paul Blunt came in for a chat at 6. We talked of Alice, who died 4 years ago today, and of what a lovely and "complete" woman she was. She had an "educated heart".~~ Worked 2 hours at home.

February 19: One of the busiest days I have ever had in the office. I wrote and dictated dozens of letters, signed innumerable checks (one for $23,000,000); saw half my secretaries, and presided at Secretaries' meeting from 4–5. I guess I did a little driving today, but drove myself hardest. Worked at home at night. Marines landed on Iwo Jima.

February 20: To U.S. Army Headquarters, where I talked to Col. Gato re Customs functions on Burma frontier. A Lt. Cohen (CID) asked me about duty on parcels sent out to civilians in China through APO. Called on Benjamin Kizer,[9] the UNRRA man just out from America, and his No. 2, Dr. Harry Price. Home at 6, and worked an hour after dinner.

February 22: Dined at new quarters of Sino-American Institute of Cultural Relations. ~~Mediocre chow, very crowded. Ducked out at 8, after dinner, and so escaped the usual meeting and entertainment.~~

February 23: Ting out yesterday afternoon, and all day today. Don't know where he is! ~~Wrote long personal letter to Barney Bairnsfather re pay, prospects, etc.~~ To big Rotary dinner at Victory House, guest of S.T. Chang. 40th anniversary of Rotary International. Principal speaker: Gen. Wu Te-cheng.

February 24: The battle of Iwo Jima continues; one of the bloodiest of the war. ~~Busy day in office.~~ To big buffet dinner at Victory House given by the Mayor of Chungking.

February 25: Lovely spring day, sunny and warm. 10 to lunch: Victor Hoo (Vice-Minister of Foreign Affairs); Gen. Olmstead; Gen. Hamden.[10] Col. Young (Judge Adv. Gen.); and Col. Gato of U.S. Headquarters; Bill Stanton and Norman Meiklejohn (of Pawtucket) F.E.A.; Benjamin Kizer and Dr. Price (UNRRA); Ting. Excellent chow and pleasant talk. [. . .] ~~Walked 1/2 hour, and~~ Went to a phonograph concert at Club. Moonlight Sonata, Bolero, L'Après-Midi d'un Faune, and Jesu, Joy of Man's Desiring. ~~Started letter to Jean in evening.~~

February 26: ~~Warm sunny day. Finished letter to Jean.~~ Sent in despatch to K.W.S. and Pu recommending rehabilitation of the pension scheme. The reception this proposal meets will be a guide to what foreigners in the Customs may expect. Paid $200 for a haircut this last week: up from $100. ($200 = U.S. $10 at official rate.)

February 27: ~~In bed with touch of bronchitis. Worked on stuff sent from office.~~
February 28: ~~Same.~~

March

March 1: Ready to leave for office at 10 a.m., ~~feeling a little weak~~, but chair coolies had disappeared, so stayed home in a.m. These Szechuan coolies (and servants generally) are extremely unreliable, discourteous and ungrateful. The "down river" Chinese dislike them intensely, and refer to them as "Sze-chuan hao-tze" = "Szechuan Rats." The feeling is, I hasten to add, reciprocated. Chaucer Wu,[11] Minister-designate to Chile, called at my office. ~~Very pessimistic letter from Bairnsfather about future of Service. Busy afternoon in office.~~

March 2: ~~Still feeling lousy. Busy morning in office.~~ To tea with Gen. Wu Te-cheng at 4. He lives near at Li-Tze Pa, in the late President Lin's big house. Pleasant and affable as ever. I asked him whether government and public opinion would tolerate having foreigners in administrative positions in Customs after the war. He was most emphatic in assuring me that government and people would not object, for example, to having a foreign Commissioner in Shanghai. He doesn't like idea of "advisers", but said foreigners should continue as active administrators, – more efficient, – Chinese staff learn more; better discipline. I mentioned P.P.C. resolution of 2 years ago (no more foreign I.G. or Commissioners). He said that policy is not to be introduced for a long time; that my appointment as I.G. is good proof of the point. ~~An hour with Cecilia Pan. She says O.K. Yui almost certain to go, and T.V. will be Minister of Finance. Rumored that Wellington Koo[12] will be Minister of Foreign Affairs.~~

To dinner with Dr. and Mrs. Tseng Yang-fu. He looks like a broken man; very feeble, and a dreadful contrast to the ebullient character I have known. He is leaving for medical treatment in U.S. Others: Sir Horace and Lady Seymour; Dr. Leone Liang (F.O.) ~~he says with T.V.S. or Wellington Koo head Chinese delegation to San Francisco conference). Andrew Liu and his petite wife; Paul Blunt. Home at 10, to an hour's work.~~

March 4: ~~Had following to lunch at bungalow: Bathurst and his fiancée Miss West; Mr. and Mrs. Geoffrey Wallinger; Pouncey; Hopstock. Sardines (last can Jack sent out) on toast; beef ball stew, baked beans, pie, coffee. Good fire, easy conversation. Home at 4. To concert at Club, and an excellent selection of records. Read and loafed in evening; too tired to write letters.~~

March 5: To lunch with Col. Young, Judge Advocate General, and Major West. Discussed importation of parcels (and smuggling) by APO. Had 2 dishes of chocolate ice-cream! Took me 1-3/4 hours to get to U.S. Headquarters. Ferries crowded. ~~Busy afternoon.~~ To dinner given by Victor Hoo for Wellington Koo. Also present: Lovink; Patterson; Officer; Brazilian Ambassador; Dr. Price; Admiral Shen; and a couple of men from the Foreign Office. Quite the finest Chinese food I've ever eaten. Dinner given at home of a Mr. Hsiao. (Adm. Shen told me it costs over $1,500 a plate exclusive of wines, cigarettes, etc.). Bird's nest one of the dishes. Liqueur whiskey after dinner. I ran away at 9:40, but missed last ferry, so had Customs night-duty sampan come for me. The evening cost me $1,000: $100 for a guide from Canadian Embassy to the host's house; $400 to Standard Oil chauffeur (I had loaned my car to Chaucer Wu to go to Wang Shen to see the Generalissimo); $500 to Customs boatmen who took me across river.

March 6: Cold rain. Neither entertaining nor entertained today. Cologne taken by U.S. troops. Rhineland battle almost over.

March 7: Porter taken sick in office this morning and sent to hospital. Munby in bed with heart trouble. Banister out with a cold. To dinner at Mr. W. H. Chu's (Taikoo House). Cold as a barn in dining room. Good food but far too much. My chair coolies had disappeared and I had to walk home. They are the most undependable crowd I've ever seen.

March 8: Fine weather. To reception at Victory House given by Paul Blunt for Lady Louis Mountbatten, – "Lady Superintendent of the Society of St. John of Jerusalem". Lord Louis also there; I met both. Big crowd.

March 9: American troops cross Rhine. I crossed Yangtze. To Ministry of Finance, but Mr. Yui was out at 3. To U.S. Army Headquarters. And saw Col. Gato. Back to Ministry of Finance; O.K. Yui still out.

March 10: To Ministry at 4. Conference with Li Tong. At 4:30, conference with Minister. Reported recent reorganization of Customs stations, taking over of Guards, etc. and asked for urgent pay order for $90,000,000. Mr. Yui said that T.V. Soong had sent him my memorandum on post-war employment of foreigners. He said he saw no reason why foreigners should not occupy administrative posts: he himself had recently suggested employing a foreigner in the Textile Bureau. I explained the pension system, and urged favorable consideration of my despatch proposing rehabilitation of the system. Mr. Yui said he would consider it sympathetically.

To U.S. Headquarters and talked to Maj. West (Judge Advocate's Office) re A.P.O. Barcels. – Li Tong told me confidentially that another increase in pay is just around the corner.

Howard Coonley and Jacobsen are going home; met their successors. To George Atcheson's for buffet supper. Almost 50 there, all nationalities. I ate with a very pretty Mrs. Chu. She had a German mother and an American father. Born in Germany, spent years in Italy, married a Chinese. Speaks English, German, Italian, French, and Chinese. I slipped away at 9; home at 10:30. George asked me to spend the night at Embassy, but I was too tired. Guess I'm getting old! Letter from Dr. Kung re Capt. Sabel and Neprud. Implies that Dr. Kung has no objection to Neprud's returning to China. Will he come?

March 11: To Canadian Hospital to see Porter who looks very well. Told him his home leave has been granted. ~~To lunch at Dick Frost's and Mrs. Trevor-Powell's. Francis and Cecilia, Hubert and Mrs. Chang, Air Commodore Bartholomew, Billy Christian, Dick Smith and a couple of others.~~

1945

March 12: [. . .] While putting on boots this morning had sudden acute pain in right side under lower ribs. After five minutes' rest, started breakfast and was half way through porridge when I almost black-out. Managed to call Hopstock, who stood by until the black-out lifted. Got into bed. Doctor Allen came at noon and said I have pleurisy and must stay in bed for a week. Had a busy day on office work – at least 4 hours of it. Little pain except when I twist my body at the waist. Ting called.

March 13: [. . .] A parcel from Russ Sweet: 5 packages Briggs' mixture and a pound of "Old Virginia" chocolate! The chocolates are the first good candy I've had since I left home: I just like to smell them; they are very fragrant. In bed all day; did quite a lot of work. Tired in afternoon, and slept almost 2 hours. Reading the "The Condition of Man" by Lewis Mumford[13] – and enjoying it.

March 14: [. . .] Another busy day, with several important questions settled. Time does not hang heavily on my hands.

March 15: Less pain today. Very busy all day (and until 10:30 p.m.) on Customs work. Staff Secretaries came to discuss proposals re £ pay for foreign staff.

March 16: Mrs. Geoffrey Wallinger, of British Embassy, sent me a tin of butter with good wishes for a speedy recovery. She is an attractive lady. Calvin Joyner and Norman Meiklejohn called and we talked business, Chinese politics and lots of other things. Fang Tu came on business. Prices have gone up again steeply: I'm more alarmed over the inflation than over the military situation.

March 18: Mr. Kizer and Dr. Price (UNRRA) called in a.m. Kizer is very precise and professional type; I fear he is going to find his job a tough one. He doesn't look to me to be the administrative type. Paul Blunt had tea with me, and we had a long talk. He asked me if I thought Marcia would have him now. I said "No." Poor Blunt, he still loves her deeply, and doesn't seem to realize that he would seem like a father or grandfather to Marcia now. Paul Blunt admired Lady Louis Mountbatten's energy, but didn't like her as a woman. Too demanding; she treated him "like a coolie", he said.

March 19: To Canadian Hospital at noon. Fluoroscoped. Left lung O.K. Right lung clear except for thickening at base (where my pleurisy was). Heart and diaphragm O.K. Worked in house in afternoon.

March 20: Celebrated my 53rd birthday with diarrhea. Probably got chilled yesterday at hospital, especially when stripped to the waist in X-ray room, which was unheated. Felt wretched all day. Stormed. Hopstock gave me a can of chocolate drink.

March 21: Better today, but no pep. Busy with office affairs. Lu Ping and Ting came to discuss various questions. Ting is very pessimistic about the future of China. He says "Manchuria is sure to go", i.e., to Communists with Soviet backing. Also, North of China probably. He sees no stability after war for present form of government. Said the foreigners in Customs would do well to be paid off now, because radical changes in government after war might result in total loss of pensions.

March 22–24: Terribly sore throat, constant temperatures between 99.5 and 101.5. Dr. Allen ordered sulfathiazole. Said I have bronchitis. Feeling rotten; eating almost nothing.

March 25: Mr. Smith, Chief Pharmacist's Mate USN, who lives next door, brought in Dr. Grief, U.S. Navy. He is a charming and thorough and competent young man. Gave me thorough examination, took me off sulfathiazole. Gave me 2 gargles; told me to eat plenty – "think of food as medicine." What a nice thing for Dr. Grief to do! To give up 3 hours of his Sunday and cross the river and climb up here to take care of a perfect stranger.

March 26: ~~Mr. Smith called. Roy Pearson called: he's leaving for U.S. In 2 days! Temperature normal all day first time in a week.~~

March 27: ~~Shaved. Throat better, though still hurts when I cough. Very "dopey" after lunch; dozed 2 hours.~~

March 28: Dressed at 10 a.m. and spent most all day in study. Felt a bit groggy at first. Ting came to discuss letter to Dr. T.V. Soong asking for urgent pay order, the same pay order I've been trying to get out of the Ministry unsuccessfully for a month. They give Customs immense new responsibilities (including 1,200 troops) but provide no cash to pay for them! Gen. Carton de Wiart (with whom I was to have dined on the 30th) sent me 2 tins of "Capstan", as an "Easter Egg." The Navy Mess next door sent me in beets! Finally, Hopstock, noticed that my undershirts are in tatters, and gave me a nice woolen undershirt! Certainly, people have been very nice to me.

March 29: Outdoors for first time in almost 2 weeks. Warm sun; trees all in leaf, many in blossoms. Spring is here. ~~Munby and Porter called. Little Mr. Tai (a brother of En-sai Tai[14]) called; he's in Central Trust.~~ Revised draft of letter to T.V. re 4 tariff proposals. Tsai Hsieh Tuan, Asst. Staff Secretary called.

March 30: Up all day, worked at house.

March 31: Up all day, worked at house. [. . .]

April

April 1: Easter. Long, quiet, sunny day. To buffet supper at George Atcheson's for Leon Henderson.[15] A very engaging and affable man. Saw many of my friends. Met Briggs, new Minister-Counsellor of U.S. Embassy – Gen Odlum, Canadian Ambassador, back. Met first girl employee of U.S. Embassy. Two girls have arrived for Embassy, and Briggs told me his wife is coming out: this is great reversal since Gauss left – he was strongly opposed to having any women here. [. . .] 10th Army and Marine Amphibian Corps landed on Okinawa this morning! This is great news: we are now within 450 miles of Shanghai, Formosa and Nagasaki, truly a key position. It will lock up Japan's southern conquests, and unlock the door into China and Japan. Heard some good Easter music from London.

April 2: Lunch with Mr. Leon Henderson. Gave me a bourbon and water, also a good cigar after lunch, and a bottle of 200 Multiple vitamin tablets. We talked from 11:45 to 2:15. He asked me whether the Chinese could set up an efficient price-control organization, "of intelligent, able, young college men." I said it would be a matter of extreme difficulty, but might succeed on one condition; viz., that the staff be adequately paid and held to strict accountability. Mr. Henderson asked me many questions about the Customs Service. He is a charming man, and a man to whom America owes a great debt. Nice to be back in office today, after a 3-week lay-off. Very hot. 91 degrees.

April 3: Ting extremely pessimistic over China's future. Says Manchuria will never be recovered, but will pass under Communists' control, backed by Soviet Russia. Korea will be independent, but under Soviet influence. Communists are establishing themselves in coastal regions as far south as Pakhoi, waiting to meet the Americans when landings are made. The Chungking government may find itself cut off, and in much the same position as the Polish government in London. Ting suggests that, in their own interests, it would be better for all foreigners in Customs to be paid off now, because he fears there will be great changes in the government after the war, and that foreigners risk losing their pensions.

April 4: 20 degrees cooler then yesterday. Rain. Got soaked climbing steps at Wang Lung Men. With Ting, to Fan Chuang to see Dr. Soong, who was not there. Drove to Hua Lung Chiao, but Dr. Soong couldn't see me, but asked us to come tomorrow. Called on George Atcheson and Mr. Ellis Briggs,[16] new Minister-Counsellor at American Embassy. George is leaving for America in a week or two, soon after Gen. Hurley returns.

April 5: To Fan Chuang, with Ting, to see Dr. T.V. Soong. He approved all my original proposals re pay, and thus saw the Customs through a serious crisis. Regarding the urgent pay order for $90,000,000 and the question of separate mess allowances for staff serving in war zones, he was a little nettled when I told him I could get no reply from the Ministry of Finance, and that I had to have money to carry on the administration. Dr. Soong then sent for Mr. O.K. Yui, the Minister of Finance. He told him he had approved my proposals re pay, and asked him to attend to the "extra money" I required. I also mentioned the post-war employment of foreigners. Dr. Soong said he favored, generally, the employment of foreigners, but that he would give me more detailed instructions on his return from the San Francisco conference. I was just putting up the question of £ pay for foreign staff when we were interrupted by Mr. Yui's arrival, and I had no chance to get Dr. Soong's opinion. I planted the seed, anyhow. To a big dinner (40) given by Tsu-yee Pei to Leon Henderson. Lots of my friends there, and many of the most beautiful women in Chungking, including Pei's daughter, Cecilia Pan, Virginia Lee, and several others. Leon was "gamlaying" like a house afire; I left before dinner was half over, and I don't know how he progressed. He had a bag of gifts: lipsticks, coffee, toothpaste, cigarettes, etc., etc. which were distributed by lottery: I drew a box of "Mum"! The dinner must have cost a fortune. ~~200 oranges were used for juice they cost nearly $20,000!!~~

April 6: With Fang Tu, to see Li Tong and try to get some cash. Li was out, but his secretary Wu said that we had been authorized to borrow $30,000,000. Had nice talk with Dr. Li, of Customs College. Took Fang in to see Mr. O.K. Yui, and thank him for supporting my requests for pay and allowances. ~~Letters from John and Nate.~~

April 7: ~~Quiet day.~~ Passed final draft of despatch to government recommending putting foreign staff on Sterling basis. ~~To see Paul Blunt at 6: he has had a poisoned leg. Myers leaves London today by air to come to Chungking as Blunt's successor. Short letter from Jean.~~

April 8: With Hopstock, to bungalow. Pleasant and restful day. Rape very lovely; saw some with light purple flowers (I think it was rape). ~~Paul Blunt in to dinner. He brought me 1 pound of coffee and 1/2 pound of tobacco. Cook gave an excellent meal, and we had a glass of Sinkiang port.~~

April 9: To lunch here: Commander (Dr.) Herrington USNR, Lt. Driscoll USA ~~(nephew of Capt. Cassidy, USN)~~, Pouncey and Hopstock. Japanese battleship "Yamamoto" (45,000 tons) sunk. Koiso[17] cabinet out; Adm. Suzuki[18] in.

April 13: Hopstock told me at breakfast that President Roosevelt was dead. The world has lost a great man, and his loss will be widely felt. Mr. Winant,[19] American Ambassador in London, said: "The greatest American of our day is dead." I agree. I wish Dewey – and not Truman[20] – was stepping into F.D.R.'s shoes.

April 14: At 9, conference with Li Tong. 10, conference with Col. Young, Maj. Wert and Lt. Driscoll in Judge Advocate General's office re Customs control of U.S. convoys from Burma. Col. Young agreed that the best procedure will be for Gen. Wedemeyer to write direct to the Generalissimo and tell him what the U.S. Army wants to do. 11:30, to talk with Mr. A.T. Kearney, W.P.B. I gather that he is faced with a pretty tough job, and that he finds Chinese ideas of management very different from American ideas. ~~12, to Cecilia Pan's for a nice cup of Nestle coffee and home-made doughnuts. 1:00: Took Cecilia and Francis to the Lennoxes for lunch. Also there: Duncan (H & S Bank), Lott and Lucy Wei, K. and Mrs. Huang, Hubert and Ann Chang. Very middling food: the duck was so high that I couldn't touch it. Home at 4, and did not go to office.~~

April 15: ~~With Pouncey and Hopstock to bungalow. Quiet, warm sunny day. (Yesterday, cable from Betty acknowledging receipt of draft for $2,000 I sent for John by Col. Wasser on April 2.)~~

April 16: Our Memorial Service was dedicated to memory of President Roosevelt. Large attendance, including many from Chungking Customs, Marine Dept. and – this pleased me – the whole Customs primary school, about 100 scrubbed and well-behaved children. Ting spoke (in Chinese) very eloquently of Roosevelt's friendship for China and world leadership. Banister, as senior British Commissioner, also spoke well. He said that not since the death of his own father had he felt such a sense of personal loss. Hopstock, as a Norwegian, also spoke of Roosevelt's concern for the smaller nations. He said that, just after the Germans hat occupied Norway, his old mother had written to him and said that she felt sure that Roosevelt would find some way to restore Norway's freedom. On the platform there was a table, on which a photograph of Roosevelt, encircled in a wreath of flowers, was placed. To close the ceremony, we bowed three times to the portrait. It was a very impressive ceremony.

1945

With Ting and Liu Ping I, attended the state memorial service given by the National government and the American Embassy. President Chiang Kai-shek presented flowers and incense before a large painting of Roosevelt, which was flanked by the flags of China and the U.S. Huge crowd: the auditorium of the Central Political Institute was crowded. Worst band I've ever heard "played" a dirge; excruciating! ~~Very busy at office in afternoon~~. Ting says "only Roosevelt could control Churchill and Stalin. We don't trust Churchill very far, and Stalin not at all." I fear this is a common Chinese reaction. The "gold scandal" is widely discussed. One rumor is that Mrs. O.K. Yui bought 1,000 ounces on the 25th of March; I hope this is not true. 1,000 ounces would have cost $20,000,000, and could have been sold next day with a profit of $15,000,000; or, if the owner waited 6 months, got the actual gold and sold it in the black market, the profit could easily run up to $50,000,000.

April 17: After lunch, crossed river. Talked with Col. Young and saw draft of letter from Gen. Wedemeyer to the Generalissimo. To F.E.A. and talked with Norman Meiklejohn about preclusive buying, etc. ~~Norman gave me 3 cigars, some candy, book matches and a package of tobacco~~. To see George Atcheson (found him at Chialing House having tea with Mr. and Mrs. Percy Chen.[21]) Said goodbye; he's off home Thursday, after having done a fine job here. He has been chargé for almost 1/4 of the last 2 years. ~~To call on Elsie Soong, who gave me a nice cup of coffee and a tin of cocoa. She says she has an American Army friend who is very generous. I'll say so: she had 5-pound tins of coffee, cocoa, catsup!~~ Home at 7, after a tiring day: it turned hot, must be over 90. Wrote to Lauchlin Currie after dinner. George Atcheson will take the letter home. Had a tin of beer (my first in 20 months) with dinner. Gift of Col. Young, and it tasted good!

April 18: ~~Very busy day at Office~~. I have been tired at day's end of late; probably due to hot weather. Also worry: the K.W.S. seems to be trying to hamstring the Service. Paid $52,000 for 2-2/5 tons of coal.

April 19: At 2:30, with Fang Tu to K.W.S. and 2 hours argument with Li Tong. He is a narrow-minded bookkeeper, and I had to be pretty outspoken once or twice. He is the world's worst chiseler. I told him frankly that, if the government couldn't afford to pay the Customs staff, the Service should be wound up.

To Central Bank, to show K.K. Kwok a letter from Tihwa (dated 14th April) saying that thousands of Chinese refugees (including government officials) had been murdered at the air-field near I-li (on Sinkiang/Soviet frontier). I fear our Customs staff may have been killed.

April 20: Lunch at F.E.A. mess with Norman Meiklejohn. Also Col. Fisher, who is pinch-hitting for Gen. Olmstead. To meeting of U.C.R. at 2, which I had to leave at 3:15 to go to Ministry. (First went to Naval Sick Bay and had tetanus booster shot, because I fell on my hand in a filthy place and broke the skin.) Mr. Yui was very busy, so I stayed only a minute, to report news from Sinkiang. To British Embassy to see Capt. Billyard-Leake, Naval Attaché. He wants to get particulars of the requisition by the British Navy of six Customs ships in Hongkong before Pacific War. Also offered to take up questions of getting ships for us for post-war use. Discussed training of Customs personnel in British Navy: he has done a lot to push the scheme, but Admiralty (like U.S. Navy Dept.) lukewarm.

April 21: Am sore from inoculation. ~~Busy day. Myers called in afternoon and saw his old Customs friends~~. On way home at noon, somebody had thrown 3 $1,000 bills on the street, but nobody bothered to pick them up. They are practically valueless. One of my Chinese secretaries said that dollar bills are cheaper than toilet paper. I paid $600 for a pound of sugar yesterday. Despatch from Executive Yuan via Pu granted everything agreed to by Dr. Soong. Li Tong must have been aware of this despatch when I talked with him on the 19th I think he hoped I would consent to bargain and compromise before I got the Executive Yuan's decision. It rather looks like an attempted dirty trick.

April 22: ~~With Blunt, Myers, Pouncey and Hopstock to lunch at bungalow~~.

April 23: Russians reported in Berlin. Despatch from Neprud applying for voluntary retirement. I cabled reply: "No." Now let's see what intrigue he'll uncover to stay away from China! Expect he'll try to talk into Daddy Kung's "soft ears."

April 25: To see O.K. Yui at Ministry at 5:30. He already knew that Neprud had applied for voluntary retirement; Neprud had written to him direct, and never mentioned it to me. I told Mr. Yui that I had wired Neprud refusing his application, and he said he would do whatever I recommended. Discussed U.S. Army's letter to Generalissimo re control of convoys on Burma frontier. I told him that I had heard from several sources that the Ministry of Communications intended to take over the Customs Marine Dept., and suggested that, if the government agreed to the proposal, the change should be made in the near future. He said he would bear it in mind. ~~Dined with Paul Blunt, Myers and Whitamore at British Consulate. Paul leaves for good tomorrow, and I shall miss him~~.

April 26: Agnes cabled me that Mother died peacefully yesterday. Although the news was expected (and although I realize that she prayed for release) it has hurt me terribly. She had a beautiful and useful life. I loved her tenderly, and I can't imagine what it will be like to come home and not find her there to welcome me. Cabled Agnes. Had a conference with Capt. Billyard-Leake, British Naval Attaché re supply of British naval vessels for post-war use in Customs. Had shots for cholera and typhus. ~~Wrote Stewart~~. So many memories crowd tonight! And they all add up to the strongest and truest best Mother a man could ever have.

April 27: ~~Have thought much of Mother all day. Busy at office~~. Had Porter to lunch; he leaves in a few days for six months in London. Ting said that the Control Yuan had investigated the "Gold Bar Scandal" and presented a detailed statement to the Generalissimo – naming names and suggesting publication. Generalissimo pigeon-holed it because it contained too many "big" names. Another reason is, I think, fear of criticism abroad, especially in America. If public in America knew that the gold loaned to China and sent at great risk over the Hump was being used by officials in the know to make colossal overnight fortunes, there would be hell to pay.

April 28: To conference with Li Tong. Discussed Customs College, rehabilitation of R/A [Revenue Account] and pensions system. ~~To lunch here at mess for Porter. Bathurst and Munby also present~~. [. . .]

1945

Dined at Bathurst's, Pouncey, Myers and I. On arrival, we were told that Mrs. Bathurst had been bitten by a dog, and had gone across river for treatment. We had nice dinner, and at 9:45 the B's returned: she had had the wound in her leg stitched, had taken 4 sulfanilamide pills, and had 1st shot of antirabies serum. In spite of which, she was very cheerful. Home in time to hear BBC say that Himmler and the German High Command had offered to surrender unconditionally to the Anglo-American armies, but that the offer had been turned down.

April 29: Worked several hours on letter to Powell replaying to his protest re his status. Joly certainly left me a dead cat in his handling of the resigned employees!

April 30: The Ts'ai-cheng Pu has turned down my recommendations for the rehabilitation of the pensions system. This is most discouraging, and the first fundamental set-back I have received. If the decision is not modified, it may well be the beginning of the end of the "Inspectorate System". I feel very depressed. A whole series of air-mail letters from Canada written in Feb/Mar 1944 are just now reaching Chungking. Mussolini, his mistress and 16 of his pals executed in Milan. Venice, Milan, Munich all taken. Fighting almost over in Berlin. Himmler reported to be offering surrender. It can't be long now in Europe. 30th day of fighting on Okinawa.

May

May 1: Started daylight saving. Lunch with Mr. Kearney, Nelson Mission. Also at our table: Bryan Eddy and Mr. Lopes of Fall River, and Maj. Lavrov, Mining Engineer, whom I knew in Canton. He and Tania are divorced; his 10-year old son is in a concentration camp in Shanghai. Talked "background China" to several of Mr. Kearney's staff until 2:30. To American Embassy. Called on the Ambassador, resplendent in civilian clothes! Gen. Hurley said that U.S. law forbids American diplomats to wear uniforms. How he loves fine feathers, ribbons and gold braid! He said: "I suppose, on special occasions, I can wear the uniform." He again spoke at length on the fact that, a few years ago, he "ranked" Eisenhower, Bradley, and all the other generals except Douglas MacArthur. He can talk a steady stream and say nothing – a typical politician, but a smooth dresser! Chatted with Briggs (Minister-Counsellor) while he had his hair out. He comes from Maine, was Dartmouth 1921, and knew Ted Marriner[22] well. Also knows Kippy Tuck. Saw half a dozen of the other boys, and met a man named Biggerstaff, who was professor at Yen-ching, Harvard, etc., and shares my affection for Margaret Gardner. ~~To Francis and Cecilia Pan's for a cup of coffee and chat~~. Thence to 2-hour meeting of U.C.R. After usual financial business, Dr. T.F. Tsiang gave his views on cooperation between U.C.R. and CNRRA.

May 2: Hitler reported dead: is he? To dinner at Victory House to celebrate Czecko-Slovak Independence Day. Saw many of my friends. About 150 there. No American Army or Embassy officials because of official mourning. No French because of a case of smallpox at the Embassy. Tired; sneaked out at 9.

1945

May 3: Took Banister to U.S. Consulate to get his visa for America. Briggs Howard, Consul, leaves for home this week. Had second cholera and typhus shots. Saw Major MacAfee (Wedemeyer's Aide) re letter re-addressed to Neprud, which I later sent to Military Attaché to go APO. Hitler (and Goebbels[23]) reported suicides. Berlin, Hamburg, Rangoon and all the remainder of Italy fell to the Allies yesterday and today. ~~Conference with Pouncey, Hopstock and Bathurst re next steps to be taken re pensions~~.

May 4: To "housewarming" at new Belgian Embassy. To dine at the Pans! Thence to concert, Excellent music. Spent night at Pans'. Note: As tickets to concerts, etc., even for charity, are subject to 40% tax, about 3/4 of the tickets to tonight's concert were in the form of "invitations", which are not subject to tax. At bottom of ticket there was a line thus: "M. . . . ". I discovered that this "M" meant $1,000! Typically Chinese.

May 5: Breakfast at Pans', where we got first news of German surrender in Holland, Denmark and N.W. Germany. I stopped in at Netherlands Embassy next door at 9, and Lovink was just coming back downstairs. He hadn't heard the news, so we listened to BBC at 9, and the first sentence told of the liberation of Holland. By this time, 4 of the Dutch staff were glued to the radio. We shook hands all around and had a cup of coffee.

To Ch'ing Shui Chi to dinner with the Eichholzers. Mr. Rae contributed a bottle of Harper's bourbon. ~~Nice dinner~~. He told of G.I.'s in South Seas who were using the hospital refrigerator to cool beer. Taken to task by medical officer for waste, they said it was much cheaper than the method they formerly used of flying their beer for a few hours in a plane at 18,000 feet!

May 7: Joly's youngest son – Bobbie – killed in action in Germany. I wired Joly and wrote to him and Edie. Had Loy Chang to dinner; he brought complete documents regarding requisitioning of six Custom vessels by British Navy in Hong Kong in 1941. 9 o'clock BBC says Doenitz[24] has announced that German High Command has surrendered entire German forces to Allies unconditionally. Situation still obscure, but this looks like the very end of the war – in Europe.

May 8: V-E DAY. ~~Busy day in office~~. Had following to dinner for Mr. and Mrs. Bathurst: Mr. and Mrs. Trevor-Powell; Dick Frost, Banister; Pouncey; Hopstock; Capt. Everest; Munby. Hopstock produced a bottle of champagne in honor of V-Day. At 9, we left the table and came upstairs to hear Churchill broadcast the official end of the war in Europe. Then part of a church service, and a series of broadcasts from London, Edinburgh, Belfast, etc. describing the celebration. ~~Couldn't get USA at all.~~ [. . .]

May 9: Ting says Chinese papers contain report of Control Yuan re "Gold Scandal" and names O.K. Yui and K.K. Kwok as two of the officials responsible for leakage of news of increase in price of gold on March 28. Dined (and slept) at British Embassy.

May 11: A rather non-committed reply from Mr. O.K. Yui to my memorandum (to Dr. Soong) re post-war employment of foreigners in Customs. Took Capt. Everest to call on Sir Horace Seymour (Brit. Ambassador), Capt. Billyard-Leake

(British Naval Attaché) and Capt. Jarrell (U.S. Naval Attaché). ~~Dropped in a minute to see Col. Joyner and Norman Meiklejohn (F.E.A.) Latter gave me 2 Baby Ruths, some cigars and 2 packages Camels.~~ To dinner at Belgian Embassy. Guests: Dr. Sun Fo; Russian Counsellor and wife; Maj. and Mrs. Everand (Netherlands Military Attaché); Minovsky (Czeck Ambassador); and two or three others. Excellent food, especially the ravioli.

May 12: ~~Lunch for Bathurst and Bannister at Ting's house. Birds' nest soup, cuttlefish, and several other of the expensive foods which I despise. I liked the rice at the end; why can't Chinese serve their every-day and excellent food? Lots of samshu drunk; a very pleasant and congenial occasion. A nice letter from Betty, also one from Mr. Dow.~~

May 13: To United Nations' Service of Thanksgiving and Prayer at Central Broadcasting Hall. Led by Bishops Chen and Bevan and Dr. Rappe. ~~Took Norman Meiklejohn and Col. Fisher (USA) by car~~ to Liang Feng Ya, ~~and had delicious beans and stew at the Bungalow. Hopstock had walked up.~~ Hills covered with coreopsis; also dwarf azaleas. Rice "seed-beds" like jade jewels sprinkling the valley. ~~All walked home together. Calvin Joyner gave me 2 new shirts and 1/2 pound tobacco. Mother's Day. I shall wear a white carnation for the first time.~~

May 14: ~~Busy in office.~~ To garden party at British Embassy for British subjects. Ambassador of United Nations, and a few high Chinese officials there. Hurley easily the best-looking and best-dressed man in the crowd, although still cursing the State Dept. for not letting him wear his uniform. Gen. Wedemeyer also fine-looking man. Met new Russian Ambassador – Petrov.[25] About 300 there; perfect weather.

May 15: ~~Clear and hot.~~ Three men from O.S.S. came to my office to enquire about navigation on Yangtze: Ting very discouraged about the situation in the Customs because of the attitude of Li Tong and the Kuan-wu Shu. I told him we must try to be patient; when Dr. T.V. Soong gets back we must have a showdown. ~~Dr. Hampshire told me he has found suspicious sounds in Pouncey's chest, and doesn't like loss of weight and continued temperature. I'm going to try to get him to go to Kunming and get properly X-rayed.~~

May 16: ~~Very busy in office.~~ A hot day; yesterday 97 degrees; it must have been 100 today. More pin-pricks from Kuan-wu Shu. This time they pass on an accusation that Lu Ping was responsible for the leakage of the Clerks' examination papers. He never saw one of them! A showdown with the Shu is inevitable if the persist in their attitude, but I hope to postpone showdown until T.V. Soong returns. Papers say he will remain several weeks in America, and stop at Moscow on way home. ~~Bathurst and Mrs. B. leave tomorrow a.m. for six months in England. Wired Gawler and asked if he would arrange X-ray for Pouncey at Kunming.~~

May 17: Yesterday: 101.3 degrees at 6 p.m. official shade temp. ~~Pouncey still in bed, my cook is feeding him this week, and P. is enjoying the change to a lighter, fat-free diet. A hard day at office, with 4 or 5 difficult questions to settle. Spent an hour in evening reading over Mother's letters from August, 1943 to February, 1944. A lovely, lively and proud record.~~

May 18: To lunch here: Palmer, new Canadian Trade Commissioner; Robinson (B & S) and Hopstock. Busy day in office. With Ting to Y. M. C. A. dinner. Todays paper said that Ho Ying Ching (Chief of Staff) proposes that the owners of the U.S. $300,000,000 belonging to Chinese, frozen in America, should be disclosed; that all money belonging to traitors, profiteers, etc. should be confiscated, and the rest "borrowed" by the Chinese government. This is a similar proposal to one made recently by Gen. Feng Yu Hsiang. I mentioned it to Ting, who said that the Chinese who have the most money in America are, in this order, (1) Ho Ying Ching; (2) Gen. Feng Yu Hsiang; (3) Madam Chiang Kai-shek; Mr. H. H. Kung. He also said that the reason Madam Chiang went to Rio de Janiero was to collect all the wealth of the family in South America – all of which was in her name.

May 19: In office till 5:45. [. . .] Excerpt from a letter from one of my Chinese Commissioners, which says a lot! "Since 1935 I had been waging the economic war with the Japs and this is my fourth evacuation. I believe I could have done far better had our men under arms been more keen in the military enterprise than the economic one."

May 20: Fierce rain and windstorm about 1 a.m. Window in drawing room broken; one tree snapped. Loafed all day; ~~cleaned out drawer in desk; wrote to Mother MacDonald and Beatrice Wakefield. Intended to go to bungalow, but it was very threatening in morning, so Hopstock helped me eat some of the beans baked for 6. Walked an hour in "Pagoda Valley."~~

May 21: With Chang Yung-nien, Li Tung-wha went and Chang Pai-leh went to Customs College at Shantung. Spoke at Memorial Service; and nice lunch with faculty afterwards. [. . .]

May 22: With Ting, to dine at Netherlands Embassy. Car broke down; walked back to Custom House. Sent for Standard Oil chauffeur and 'phoned to Lovink who said he'd send his car. In 10 minutes, our car appeared. We left word to tell Lovink's car to follow us, and we started. Half way up steep hill, stopped again. Lovink's car picked us up and we got to Embassy 3/4 hour late. One minute we had no car; next minute, 3 cars. At 10, when we left Embassy, our car was there, but we drove to Wang Lung Men with Col. Dusenbury. Our car went into the repair shop today. At dinner: Dr. Quo Tai-chi; Australian Chargé; French Ambassador (Gen. Pechkoff), Gen. Sabatier (who had just arrived from Indo-China, where he was in command of all French troops),[26] Vandenburg (Netherlands Counsellor), Colonel _____, Polish Military Attaché, Ting, Dick Frost.

May 23: Took Banister to say good-bye to O. K. Yui. Very cordial. I had 5 minutes business with him: mentioned Ting's pay (and left letter on subject); and pension and Sterling pay for foreigners. He promised to look into all questions. Saw Li Tong for a few minutes, and left copy of letter re Ting's pay with him. He won't like it.

May 24: One of the hardest days I've ever put in, of solid plugging on a variety of tough questions. Churchill has resigned, and the political pot is now boiling in England. Prices of some goods (piece goods, especially) have fallen considerably as result of good war news frightening hoarders.

May 25: Ting came to my house at 8:30 en route to Kuan-wu Shu. Ministry of Communications has proposed to take over Marine Dept. "after the war," and K.W.S. wanted Customs views. Primed Ting accordingly. With Hopstock, to dinner for 16 at Chialing House, given by Mr. and Mrs. Hassel (Norwegian Ambassador). ~~On ferry, met K.C. and Virginia Lee. He was cursing the Chinese volubly! Duncan (B&S Bank) was with them and very drunk.~~

May 26: I was glad to see end of this week, as I am very tired. Reading "Journey in the Dark" – a great book.

May 27: Invited by Gen. Hayes and officers of British Military Mission to lunch at Wang Shan, but didn't go because of an incipient cold. Wrote letters to O.K. Yui about Military of Communications proposal to take over the Marine Dept.

May 28: Cold settled in chest, so stayed in bed. A day of depression, my first bad experience for a long time. The minutes dragged; I couldn't concentrate; my mind was a loose pulley; I felt compressed, and got out of bed and walked from room to room; I couldn't face lunch. As Thomas Wolfe[27] says, in "The Anatomy of Loneliness", "There are times when anything, everything, all or nothing. . . . can in an instant strip me of my armor, palsy my had, constrict my heart with frozen horror, and fill my bowels with the grey substance of shuddering impotence." And again: "The huge, dark wall of loneliness is around him now, and bunches and presses in on him, and he cannot escape." "And the cancerous plant of memory is feeding at his entrails." A thoroughly bad day (this is written next day, when equilibrium is restored).

May 29: ~~To office; usual catarrh, but no temperature.~~ [. . .]

May 30: K. K. Kwok has resigned as Manager of Central Bank – probably as result of "Gold Scandal". Rumored that he will be succeeded by Hsi Te-mou, now in U.S. Also rumored (again) that O.K. Yui is going, and that T.V. Soong will take over Financial Ministry. (If O.K. goes, I hope T.V. will do so). Bought C.N. $5,000,000 gold certificates with Welfare Funds, at C.N. $35,000 an ounce. Chinese have retaken Foochow and Nanning this week. Are Japs retiring from South China? ~~Pouncey left 3 weeks leave and medical check-up in Kunming.~~ Government now issuing transferable "cashier checks" in $5,000, $10,000, $50,000, etc. denominations. "Inflation currency", Ting called it.

May 31: ~~As guest of Hubert and Anne Chang, to Ladies Night at Rotary Club. Dancing (I refrained) to an American G. T. band with strong lungs.~~

June

June 1: Finished draft to K.W.S. recommending introduction of League of Nations "Draft Customs Nomenclature." Lunch at Dick Smith's with S. Y. Wu, Sec. Gen. of Legislative Yuan. He is off to America to discuss legislative problems arising out of new treaty. A character: he wanted to propose to recent Kuomintang Congress that "foreign devils" be appointed "Mangers" of all Chinese government departments and political divisions down to hsien [縣]! To dinner – guest of Mr. and Mrs. Albert Lu at Nanyang Bros. office. Others: Norman Meiklejohn, Lott and Welling Wei, Hubert and Anne Chang, K. and Mrs. Huang. Missed 9:30 ferry by 30 seconds; waited 1/2hour. Bad situation in Syria: the French are making damn nuisances of themselves.

June 2: To Kuan-wu Shu at 9. Li Tong forgot the appointment, and we had to 'phone him at Ministry. He was 3/4 hour late. 1-1/2hours conference. To office at 11:40. Dead tired after lunch, so lay down. At 4:30, had one degree temperature, so decided to go to bed. 10 minutes later, I sweat a bit, and temperature to normal. Crossed river to cocktail party at Carl Boehringer's (he's going home) because I wanted to see several people. Stayed 1/2hour, and went to Nelson Mission where I had a chat with Byron Eddy. He leaves for U.S. in 2 days. [. . .] Byron is a great talker; I'd hate to have to live with him. He is done a good job in the cotton mills here. Banister says U.S. dollar has gone to C.N. $1,000 today.

June 3: With Hopstock, to bungalow. Guests: Bob Smyth, Arthur Ringwalt, Biggerstaff, Calvin Joyner, Norm Meiklejohn. Lovely, quiet day. Bought some blankets, linen and cutlery from Banister.

June 5: Lott Wei to lunch. He has had a serious quarrel with Lucy, who denounced him to a large and mixed party at their home. She is a mental case. A pity. No rain for over two weeks, and crops are beginning to show effects. If this heat and dryness continue, we shall have a bad time.

June 6: Still hot (99.5 for 3 days), and crops are suffering. With Ting and C. C. Tso, called on Wu Ting-chang,[28] the Generalissimo's brain-trust, MC, etc. 64, he looks 54. Formerly banker (Joint 4-banks), newspaper prop. (Ta Kung Pao [大公報]) and recently Governor of Kweichow.[29] His is now Wen Kuan Chang [文官長] – chief of the Civil Officials Department of the National Government. He is a relative of Tso.

June 8: Still hotter; must be several degrees over 100. A very busy day, with one "urgent" subject after another. Saw two of the principals in the "Cigarette Paper Case". One of these two is a damn liar. Treasury refused to cash my check for $5,000,000 for June 1/2 month pay, on grounds that Kuan-wu Shu had informed Ministry of Audit that our pay scale had not been sanctioned by government! Ting very excited, and wanted me to go full steam ahead vs Li Tong. I got Fang Tu to phone Wang at Shu, who said Shu had never given any such information to Ministry of Audit. Fang and Wang will go to Treasury tomorrow. Marine Dept. crews etc. threaten to strike on Monday unless their pay demands are met. I have put whole case up to Shu, and, if the men strike, I shall lose no sleep.

June 9: 104 degrees at 6 p.m. yesterday; about same today. Heluva day in office, and glad when it was over. Had farewell dinner here for Banister. 15 at table – all Customs except D. K. Wei. A pleasant occasion. No mail from home for a very long time. Last letters I had were written about middle of April, before Mother's death.

June 10: To buffet lunch at Eichholzers' at Chinshuich. Lots of alcohol; several pretty tight. Met Mrs. Green, great friend of Irving and Mary Brown. She's in O.S.S. Also a Miss Frame of O.S.S. Two Red Cross girls and Miss Morley of Fall River. Lt. Hayes (probably changed from a Polish name) who used to drink and dance at the German Club "just off Broadway, Pawtucket. He also knew "Carey's place." Pawtucket's fame! About 25 there, various nationalities. I walked home at 5:30. At 9, thunder and half hour of rain. I hope it was enough to save the rice crop. [. . .]

June 11: ~~Fairly quiet day in office. Gratefully cool. [. . .]~~

June 12: To lunch at French Ambassador's (Pechkoff). His new Counsellor of Embassy ——— gave me a tobacco pouch to replace the Scotch plaid pouch I lost recently. (Sequel: when I got home at 5:30, my plaid pouch was lying on the low tables by my chair! As I sat reading, I lighted my pipe, and dropped the lighted match on the pouch (instead of the ashtray), which was soon burned through and useless. So I started the day with no pouch; at 5:30 I had two; at 6:00 I had one). To U.C.R. meeting at Dr. Rappé's. I smell a rat in Dr. T. F. Tsiang's request for a few million dollars for CNRRA's program in Kweichow; I fear this is the forerunner to enormous requests for subsidies from the good people of America to pay for expenditures which are clearly the responsibility of the Chinese government. To O.S.S. and a chat with Maj. Stevens and Col. Happner. The latter says O.S.S. is going places and doing things out her at last. He has about 1,300 on his staff; 3 airplanes; excellent cooperation with Gen. Wedemeyer, etc. Saw Mrs. Green and Miss Frame, who work of O.S.S. My car still laid up. I rode to French Embassy in Standard Oil car; Embassy to Rappé in Mr. C. C. Chien's car; Rappé's to O.S.S. in Dr. Han Li Wu's car; O.S.S. to ferry in a jeep.

June 14: Dragon-boat Festival. Whole city celebrating, and little work done. Hundreds of thousands spent most of day on river bank, watching the dragon-boats. (Incidentally, the local boats can't compete with those at Canton). It is very evident that the Chinese are practically unaware that there's a war on; this festival is far more important to the average Chinese than any battle, whether in China or elsewhere. The war hasn't really touched them except as it has brought inflation; high wages and high prices. Mrs. Woo Chi came to see me at noon and plead for leniency to her husband. She asked me to change my decision from "dismissal" to "discharge." I told her I couldn't. It was a hard thing to have to say. She is a gentle, attractive, sweet little woman. I wish I might have obliged. [. . .]

June 15: Kuan-wu Shu has cut K. T. Ting's pay from $97,000 to about $60,000. This is simply personal revenge for Ting's suggestion that the KWS be abolished. A dirty trick. [Kuan-wu] Shu got Minister's approval of cut, I don't see anything I can do about it – yet. Sooner or later, it seems that either Li Tong or Li Tu (Lester Little) must go. ~~A hell of a day.~~ Chen You-tai, who was so helpful to me in Canton during internment, called to see me and brought me a 5-lb can of powdered milk. After he left Customs, he was Lt. Col. in Chinese army, which he quit because he couldn't stand the brutality shown to the soldiers. He saw them left to die by the roadside; 80% of the recruits died of malnutrition and mistreatment, while the officers got rich. I got Chen a job with the British Military Mission, in which he has done well and is very happy.

June 16: To K.W.S. at 9. 1 hour's rather chilly interview with Li Tong. To office at 11. Lunch with Col. Dusenburg's. ~~Home at 3. To cocktail party at Bill~~

1945

~~Stanton's (F.E.A.) at 6. Home at 8:00.~~ Ting is very much hurt and disturbed by K.W.S. action in cutting his pay. This is going to be a tough problem. Banister left at 9:30 p.m. to spend night on North Bank and fly to Calcutta tomorrow at 4 a.m. He seemed happy to be going, and thanked me for obtaining his leave. Bought 1 ton coal: $20,000, plus $10,000 coolie hire = $30,000. At official rates, this equals $1,500 U.S. – which is rather expensive coal. At British Channel (my) rate, it comes to about U.S. $48.00. ~~Sent U.S. $10.00 by Banister to Myrl Myer in Calcutta, to pay for repair to watch.~~

June 17: Raining heavily in morning so didn't go to bungalow. ~~Wrote long letter to Stewart in reply to his letter of May 22. Sent one copy via John, one via Nate.~~ Walked an hour in afternoon. Read "Red Harvest" (Hammett[30]). 200–300 cases of cholera last week. An extract from a recent S/O letter from one of my Chinese Commissioner: "Mr. Leung and his family were not molested by the enemy including his flock of hogs."

June 19: River rising rapidly, and practically all the rocks are submerged at 27 feet. Nice weather, sunny but not too hot. [. . .] General Simon Bolivar Buckner,[31] U.S. Army Commander on Okinawa, killed in action.

June 20: Busy preparing for interview with O.K. Yui tomorrow. To dinner at American Embassy with Millet. Others: Mrs. Green (O.S.S.) and Dawson (Agricultural Attaché). Excellent pien fan [便飯 supper], and pleasant talk.

June 21: A big day. To Judge Advocate General's to ask about U.S. – Chinese agreement re convoys on Burma frontier. To F.E.A. to see Norm Meiklejohn (just back from India) and Col. Joyner, who is helping me to get trucks, jeeps, etc. To Navy Sick Bay, for typhoid booster shot. To Ministry at 11:30. Had 20 minutes with Minister. Discussed: (1) Marine Dept. Minister said that Executive Yuan had decided to shift it from Customs to Ministry of Communications. There will be an outcry, I fear, from shipping circles, or, at least, a lot of apprehension, but I am glad the move is being made now if it's ever going to happen. Also, I've got quite enough headaches ahead of me without having to run that department. (2) Foreign Staff pensions and pay. Mr. Yui agreed to study the question personally; and to see Pouncey and Hopstock on Saturday on the question. I told him that a favorable decision is sine qua non of a post-war foreign staff. (3) Rumored Amalgamation of Kuan-wu Shu and Customs. Mr. Yui stated categorically that no such proposal had reached him. I told him I was relieved, but added that, if such a scheme did appear, I hoped he would let me give an opinion before it was acted on. He said that, some time ago, the possibility of amalgamation, or of abolishing either the K.W.S. or the Inspectorate, was raised, but that he had advised the Generalissimo not to make any change at present. He further said that, if either was to be abolished, it should be the K.W.S. (4) Ting's pay. "Mr. Ting should remember that he is a Chinese" (said Mr. Yui). In cutting Ting's pay, there was no intention to hurt him or to indicate dissatisfaction with his work, but the Minister has to meet criticism if too favorable treatment is extended to the D.I.G. – a Chinese. ~~Busy afternoon at office. Tired, but had Scotty Farmer and Hopstock to dinner. Gossipped till 10 p.m.~~ Maj. Farmer (Asst. Military Attaché) made a crack about the Army's attitude in not getting parts for the Ambassador's Cadillac. This crack was made to Hurley who – a little tight at dinner – represented it to Gen. Wedemeyer. Result: Scott to be court-martialled and reprimanded. Then Hurley denied the remark; result: court-martial cancelled; reprimand cancelled. But, Army has last word and is sending him home. (He is one of the few officers who wants to stay in China). T.V. Soong returned to Chungking from San Francisco yesterday. [...]

June 22: Spent most all day drafting letter to Dr. Soong – re-drafting and polishing – setting forth my difficulty in dealing with Li Tong and the Kuan-wu Sh. About 1000 cases of cholera – a day in the city; sale of peaches, plums etc. banned. 8 deaths among workers at U.S. Headquarters at Chin Ching Compound.

June 23: Hopstock and Pouncey went to see Mr. O.K. Yui and argue case for post-1920 pensions, etc. O.K. Yui was polite, sympathetic, but non-committal. This, I have found, is his usual attitude. Finished my letter to Dr. Soong re relations with Kuan-wu Shu. This may prove to be the most important document I have yet written. It may result in (1) abolition of Kuan-wu Shu; (2) replacement of Li Tong; (3) kicking Mr. L.K. Little out of the Customs. Anyway, I feel better now that I have brought things to a head, and that I am dealing with a man who can make decisions. Also wrote a report on recent Customs developments for T.V. Soong. Mr. F. Chang is back in China. River rising rapidly; 37 feet today, and all but the highest tops of the great rock ledge off shore is covered.

June 24: With Hopstock and Pouncey, to bungalow. Had Joyner and Norman Meiklejohn. Beautiful day. Rice crop apparently saved by last week's rain.

June 25: Started scrutinizing "Spring" promotions. This is always a big job for me, because I read the confidential reports of each man, and often query the recommendations of the Staff Dept. and the D.I.G. To Capt. Jarrell's (U.S. Naval Attaché) for buffet dinner and picture. Both were excellent – the latter was "Fighting Lady", the life and action of an aircraft carrier. In gorgeous color, and without a touch of Hollywood. Big crowd: Tsu-yee Pei, just back with T.V. Soong from San Francisco, French Ambassador, and that charming woman – name unknown – from his Embassy, Gen. de Wiart, Col. Gordon, etc., etc.

June 26: To British Embassy to see Sir Horace Seymour. Had only a few minutes with him, because T.V. Soong had called him. Talked with Cassels about pension question, etc. To Embassy for lunch: Gen. Yu Fei-peng,[32] Minister of Communication; Mr. Chang, Minister of Information; Mr. and Mrs. Hollington Tong, Vice-Minister of Information; Mr. and Mrs. P.H. Chang, "Official Spokesman"; Briggs, Robertson and Ringwalt of the Embassy, and our host, Gen. Patrick Hurley. I'm still wondering whether Pat Hurley is a smart diplomat or a tailor's dummy. To office in afternoon. A full hour's conference with various Secretaries; a couple of letters to dictate; despatches and cheques to sign, and then back to the promotion lists. I backed out of a cocktail party at the Canadian Embassy, and a Chinese buffet dinner on the North Bank: once a day is enough to cross the river; I'm getting wise in my old age. [...] Battle of Okinawa victory.

June 27: Pouncey damn near gave me stomach ulcers in an hour's belly-ache after dinner. He now wants full year's leave (just after I got 6 months leave with

1945

travel time!) and talks of "unfairness", "rights", etc. He is a gloomy customer if I ever saw one. One of the best men in the Service, but he certainly has a difficulty for every solution. He groaned about his job, his pay, his prospects – everything. This job is certainly teaching me a lot of about human nature! UNCIO conference ended.

June 28: To U.S. Naval Attaché's office to discuss with Capt. Jarrell the proposal from Rouse to build and lay buoys in Min River. Had 1–2 hour chat with Loy Chang, who said that T. V. had left yesterday for Macao. An important assignment, which I hope will bear fruit! To F. E. A. and saw Norm Meiklejohn and Bill Stanton. ~~Busy afternoon; left office at 5:45. To Club, to see "Fighting Lady" again. Great picture.~~ Read Truman's and Koo's speeches at closing of UNCIO at San Francisco. A historic occasion, and I hope that the "United Nations" will be able to do what the League was intended, but failed, to do. MacArthur announced end of organized resistance on Luzon.

June 29: Hot again, over 90. Finished spring promotions. [. . .]

June 30: [. . .] ~~Darn hot.~~ To cocktail party at No. 4 Chialing (Robertson, minister Counsellor, U.S. Embassy). Asked Gen. Hurley and Gen. Wedemeyer when I could call and introduce W. R. Myers, British Red Cross Commissioner. Former said at once: "Any time; fix it up with Ringwalt." Latter a bit cautious and wanted to know what it's all about. Big crowd. Met Gen. Escalante, new Mexican Ambassador. John Earl Baker is here, now with UNRRA. Saw Norm Meiklejohn. Briggs gave me a "Dartmouth Alumni Magazine" which I spent the evening reading. Gave Gen. Hurley a ride down the hill to his house. Called at Press Hostel on way to party to see Hallett Abend.[33] Had nice chat, and took him and a couple of female members of the American newspapers etc. party to No. 4, Chialing. Abend had a house in northern Vermont. While on a lecture tour, he was informed one night that the house had burned down. Next night he was in a bad railroad wreck and lost his baggage. He arrived at the New Weston Hotel, New York, with one toothbrush and a couple of Pullman blankets wrapped around him. These, he said, were his total possessions. My cook told me tonight that he wants to leave next month. I now give him $10,000, and the Service pays him almost $11,000, but it ain't enough. He says cooks are getting 40 to 50 thousand now.

July

July 1: With Pouncey and Hopstock to bungalow. Very hot day, but delightful in hills. To buffet dinner at Col. Dusenbury's for Maj. "Scotty" Farmer. Invited for 6:30 (and came home from bungalow early for purpose) but ate at about 9!! A mixed group, Chinese, British, American. Most of them got lickered up too much. Tony Freeman had a luscious Chinese actress as his companion Wong Shao-lai there with one or two of his wives. Col. Dickey and his French friend – Gen. Pechkoff's Secretary. She's the best-looking woman in Chungking, with beautiful brown eyes. Her husband (an Englishman in R.A.F) was captured in Java, and is now a POW [prisoner of war], but she doesn't know where. I talked an hour with Bob Smyth, who was just as bored as I was. If I'd known the kind of a party it was to be, I'd never have gone.

July 2: Summer hours at office: 7–12; 4–6. I shall keep on my regular hours. K.K. Kwok found guilty by court of divulging information about increase I gold price to a wealthy friend who went out and bought thousands of ounces. Several other bankers, and Mr. Wang in the Ministry of Finance, indicted for misuse of advance information. Kao Pei-fang, former head of Direct Tax Bureau, sentenced to death for corruption. Ting says this is far "too severe." And that a prison sentence would meet the case. Ting says that Kao was hated by the "Special Service", many of whose top men own businesses which Kao had to tax. This Special Service of Gen Tai-li is as ruthless – and more corrupt – than Hitler's Gestapo. The sooner it is destroyed, the better, but Tai Li seems to have the Generalissimo's ear. Scotty Farmer leaves tomorrow for America.

July 3: Over 100 degrees the past 3 days. ~~Wrote to Slater Branch, I.T. Co., and sent copy of my letter of 15 January as yet unanswered.~~ Inflation continues. U.S. $1.00 – C.N. $2,500. I paid C.N. $17, 130 for 6 bottles gin and 6 White wine – all local rot-gut. Read Drew Pearson's[34] account of Hurley-Wedemeyer fight, arrest of Jack Service, etc. Pearson is a menace.

July 4: Cooler, but still no rain. Took Pouncey, Hopstock, Ting and Chang Yung-nien to July 4th reception at Embassy. Big crowd and pleasant time.

July 5: Heard that a jeep with seven men in it went over a bank on the way from the Embassy party yesterday: none killed, but four in hospital. Also heard that 86 quarts of Bourbon were consumed at the party. To dinner at Bank of Communications; host, Lott Wei. ~~mediocre chow.~~

July 6: Some showers; I hope enough to save the rice crop. Lott Wei said last night that a local secret society had plans to kill all government officials from "Down River" last fall when it looked as if the Japs might come to Chungking. The "down river" Chinese certainly dislike the Szechuanese – and vice versa. Letter from John, most enthusiastic over Louis Bromfield's[35] "Pleasant Valley." I wrote Mr. Bromfield and sent him a copy of John's appreciation. Investigation at Wanhsien shows what appears to be a nasty case in which Customs employee, under guise of Cooperative Society, bought a large quantity of cotton piece goods from the Cotton Control Bureau at official price and resold them a market and split the profits.

July 7: "Double Seventh" 8th anniversary of Lu Kou Chiao [盧溝橋] Incident and start of present Sino-Jap War. Police, youngsters and others collecting "contributions" for troops at ferries, corners, etc. Cars stopped, rickshaws overhauled, and occupants "invited" to contribute. Looked very much like a forced levy. To lunch at F.E.A., with Whiting Williams,[36] Chief of the China Branch of F.E.A., Washington. Host, Bill Stanton. At 3, took W.R. Myers, British Red Cross Commissioner to call on Gen. Wedemeyer. Myers said he wants to bring out some 80 doctors, nurses, etc. from England for service with Chinese troops. Gen Wedemeyer said: "I don't know whether or not I can let them come in to China." I couldn't help thinking that the Englishmen I knew when I first came to China, must have turned in their graves! Gen. Wedemeyer said he'd do what he could, but that Myers must show how his plan would lick the Japs. Very humid; about 99%, I'll say. To bungalow, with Pouncey and Hopstock to spend night.

July 8: A very hot day, but comfortable in the hills. Mr. Greene (O.S.S.), Col. Joyner and Norman Meiklejohn came to lunch. Pouncey and I went to the church next door at 5. Home at 8. U.S. $1.00 = C.N. $3,000 last week.

July 9: A scorcher: 104.9 degrees at 6 p.m. Parcel from John, containing 1 bottle Bisquit Cognac, 1 bottle Grand Marnier! I don't like brandy, but my friends do, and these liqueurs will be highly appreciated. They are practically non-existent in Chungking. To dine at Chialing House, guest of Gen. and Mrs. S.K. Yee. Others: Delvaus de Fenffe, Belgian Ambassador; Rothschild, Belgian Counsellor; Brig. Kay, Canadian Military Attaché; Col. Bailey, USA; Dick Smith, B.A.T.; Palmer, Canadian Trade Commissioner, and the Polish Counsellor of Embassy. The latter said to me: "We shall probably be leaving Chungking soon." I wonder where these Poles will go? They – especially Count Poninski, the Ambassador – have been violently anti-Russian; and I shouldn't think they'd be welcome anywhere except at the Vatican. It would be suicide for them to go to Poland. Delvaux said that if the Belgian king returns to Belgium, the overwhelming majority of the people will welcome him; and that opposition to his return is engineered by a small but vocal minority of Communists. Nous verrons.

July 10: To lunch at Canadian Embassy, guest of Palmer, Canadian Commercial Attaché Others: O.S. Lieu;[37] Mr. Hsia (Shanghai Commercial Bank); Gen. Odlum (Ambassador); Brig. Kay; Col. Wooster. Odlum and Kay are both very opinionated! I'd think they might clash occasionally. When I left at 2, my car had been standing an hour in the sun, and was like an oven. To U.C.R. meeting, 2:30–5:00. Passed budgets of some five billion Chinese dollars. Last sales of U.S. dollars ("grey market") were at 1600 to 1. Our original budget was based on 600–1, so we are obtaining a gain by exchange of about 200%.

July 11: To lunch here: Dr. Price and E.T. Nash of UNRRA. Ting, Tso, Pouncey, Hopstock. Nash was formerly in Shanghai Municipal Council, and told of the Taxpayer's Meeting at the Race course when a Japanese shot Keswick.

July 12: Up at 6:30. With Ting, left Wang Lun Men at 8 a.m. to drive out to Hsin Kai Shih (1-1/4 hours) to call on Dr. Kung. I asked Ting specially the day before to make sure that Dr. Kung would be home. Ting thought he would be there, but he was in town! A long, hot, dusty, bumpy ride in vain. Back to Fan Chuang, where there were 30 people waiting to see Dr. Kung. We got in in 10 minutes. He looks better than when he left a year ago. Home at 11:30 with a cracking headache. To office at 3. Had dinner here for "Whitey" Willauer, F.E.A. Chief, Washington. Also, Norm Meiklejohn, Hoden (F.E.A.), D.K. Wei, Ting, Pouncey, Hopstock, Col. Fischer. Whitey got lost; he rode a pony from Lung Men Hao, but got started in wrong direction. We sent coolies out to look for a "big American on a pony.", and one of them found him. He had a long ride, used two ponies, and paid $2,000 to get here! A nice party.

1945

July 13: River has risen phenomenally; about 30 feet in 48 hours (27' – 57') Several hundred (or thousand) oil drums floated down the river this morning, some full and some apparently empty. A serious loss at this time. Heavy rain last night and intermittently during the day. It should save the rice crop.

July 14: Busy morning. At 5, took Ting, Pouncey, Hopstock and Fang Tu to reception at French Embassy – the first Quartorze juillet since V-E Day. ~~Gen. Pechkoff is going to Paris for 2 months, and says he'd be delighted to see John.~~ [. . .] ~~To bungalow with Hopstock and Pouncey.~~

July 15: Pleasant and restful day in hills. Rice paddies look much better after rain.

July 16: T.V. Soong left Moscow on 14th. Took Myers to call on Gen. Hurley who rambled for 10 solid minutes about Russia. He said he suggested to Pres. Truman that he (Hurley) should go to Moscow to find out what Russia's intentions towards China and the Chinese Communists were. He came away satisfied that the Russians were going to be content with mildest conditions, but found London and Washington sceptical. They felt that Russia had let them down over Poland, and had not kept her word given at Yalta. Hurley thinks the Russians are sincere, although he admits that it may be a "try-on". On the whole, he seemed optimistic. Told of seeing a man smoking just outside a dynamite storehouse in the Oklahoma oilfield. He shouted at him: "God damn it, can't you see that 'No Smoking' sign?" "Yeah, I can read the sign, but it doesn't say 'positively'". Introduced Myers to Briggs, Robertson and Smyth. Rained hard, and we got a little damp. Sent letter to John for Gen. Pechkoff, French Ambassador, to take to Paris. Gen. Pechkoff said he'd be delighted to see John.

July 17: Rained hard in morning. By noon, it stopped, and we had review of the Customs Guards on the school playground. We had about 200 officers and men. I inspected them; then they marched past and I took the salute; next, they drilled; then I made a few remarks (interpreted by Li Tung wha), followed by remarks by Ting. Then presentation of a gift of money, and we left. The Guards are very well trained, smart and strong fellows. Li Tung wha has done a fine job supervising the training.

July 18: Attended graduation exercises of Customs School. About 150 children present. I made a few remarks, and put up the money ($10,000) for the prizes, which K.K. Chen, Welfare Secretary, presented. Children looked so clean and nice!

July 19: In p.m., made calls. Bond (CNCC) is in Calcutta. Saw Willauer at F.E.A. with Bill Stanton and Norm Meiklejohn. ~~(Latter gave me some baccy and a cigar).~~ Willauer said that T.V. Soong had ordered the W.T.B. to give me 10 trucks right away. He also said that T.V. had requested W.T.B. to help procure 10 jeeps for us. I then went over to Headquarters and saw Gen. Olmstead (G-5) who advised me to get T.V. Soong to instruct the W.T.B. to give us the first 10 jeeps available. Willauer came in just then, and he said he'd get T.V. to change the order accordingly. It isn't what you know, but whom you know! To drop card on Mme.

Sun Yat-sen who was out. ~~Cup of Lea with Francis and Cecilia Pan. Cracked my head on the low lintel of the ferry pontoon.~~ Prices all up again, and we shall shortly be in another crisis. The currency seems to be out of control.

July 21: ~~Very busy in Office. To lunch downstairs as guest of mess, together with Myers. At 5:30, went from office to bungalow.~~

July 22: Lovely day on Second Range. Breeze. Birds in pines, flycatchers, orioles, etc. Drummond came up. Good lunch of C-rations, baked beans and my cook's stew. I left by car at 6:15. Waited 3/4 hour at ferry, then 1/2 hour on ferry, and got to Mme. Sun Yat Sen's house at 8:30. 1 hour late. Fortunately a film was being shown – "Battle of Russia" – and buffet supper afterwards. About 30 present, left about 10:15 and home at 11. 102 degrees in city.

July 24: Drafted memorandum to hand Sir Horace Seymour on Thursday, re pensions, pay, etc., of British staff paid off in July 1943. I shall ask him to speak to Dr. T.V. Soong. Our Deputy Commissioner at I-Ping [宜賓] Station, Mr. Wu, died in Canadian Hospital. He had taken 16 sulfathiazole tablets in half a day! Alf Hassel, Norwegian Ambassador, had cholera last week, but is recovering in U.S. Army Hospital.

July 25: [. . .] ~~Very hot again today.~~ Ting says the local Communist paper states that Central government troops have attacked the Communist troops in great strength. If true, it could scarcely be more ill-timed. [. . .]

July 26: Interview with Sir Horace Seymour regarding protests of British members of the Customs paid off in 1943. Sir Horace agreed to see T.V. Soong. If T.V. agrees, it will be my biggest coup so far. Lunch with Mr. and Mrs. Wallinger. Col. Ride also there. ~~Had 2 delicious chocolate peppermints!~~ Sir Horace said there are strong rumors again current that O.K. Yui is leaving the Ministry of Finance. Paper today says Dr. Kung has resigned as Chairman of Central Bank, and that O.K. Yui has been elected to succeed him. Very hot on way back to office at 3. 102 degrees yesterday; at least as hot today. 9 o'clock radio says Labour has won overwhelming victory in British General Election. ~~This will have important consequences everywhere.~~

July 27: Very humid and hot. Toc cocktail party at F.E.A. to meet Mr. Paul, one of the big shots from Washington. Ting went with me; he had a dozen cocktails and a thoroughly good time.

July 28: 14 here to lunch. Heavy rain, and 3 guests dropped out during morning, but I filled their places with men from my office. A big junk, fast in the mud in a small bay, broke in half when the water went the water went down 15 feet in the night.

July 29: ~~Rained last night, so postponed going to bungalow until this morning. Pouncey, Hopstock and I. Norm Meiklejohn and Col. Joyner came to lunch. Mr. and Mrs. Smith (Canadian Mission) came to tea.~~ Gen. Zau Kwang-ming (detached from Customs) waiting to see me. He has been fighting in Burma. Says U.S. equipment (artillery, planes, rifles) coming in in large quantities. Says Chinese new armies now have the Springfield. Gen. Zau gave me a Japanese battle-sword, which was taken during the fighting at Wanting – one of our Customs stations on the Burma frontier.

1945

July 30: Gen. Zau, Ting and Li Tong to lunch here.

July 31: Dr. Wang Shih Chieh appointed Minister of Foreign Affairs. Government announced that a 40% tax would be deducted from gold purchased during past few months and now ready for delivery. This looks like a breach of faith, and, I fear, won't help China's credit. My cook "requested" another raise – in U.S. $ – tonight. I now give him U.S. $20 plus C.N. $10,000, plus his Customs pay C.N. $11,500. Altogether, in July he got the equivalent of C.N. $77,500 – which is more than a Chinese Commissioner of Customs gets! In terms of the official rate, my cook gets more than I do; only £ 700 (@ 80) = C.N. $56,000. The world is upside down.

August

August 1: Dined at Walter Robertson's (U.S. Embassy). Other guests: Sir Horace and Lady Seymour; Gen. Odlum, K.C. Wu; Capt. Jarrell; Bob Smyth, K.C. told of correct diagnosis and treatment of his wife's long illness by an old-style Chinese doctor – an illness which had baffled 2 of the best western-trained Chinese doctors. Sir Horace spoke to T.V. Soong today about pensions and pay of interned British subjects Customs employees. Said T.V. seemed sympathetic. Sir Horace will send T.V. a memorandum on subject tomorrow; says T.V. is leaving for Moscow in a very few days.

August 2: The Deputy Commissioner who ate 16 sulfa tablets and died (*vide* July 24) was buried a few days ago. His total pension moneys came to $13,000 – 1/3 of a month's pay, and he left a wife and 5 children. I wrote an indignant despatch to the Ministry of Finance about the case, and said that the family is destitute.

August 3: Took Pouncey and Hopstock to a movie at Naval Attaché's office. Caught last ferry with 1 minute to spare.

August 4: Potsdam Conference communique issued. Part of it puzzles me. ~~Ting out of office all day. Nice letter from John, also some pictures, and a package containing chocolate, instant coffee, chewing-gum, tobacco, talcum powder, etc. The bungalow with Hopstock.~~

August 5: Quiet day at bungalow. Cold! I had to wear a flannel shirt and a sweater until 11 a.m. Pouncey came up for lunch. ~~Two more packages from Nate: a lb. of tobacco, and an assortment of chewing-gum and 3 candy bars. The latter had sweated, and were pretty sticky. However, I'll eat them even if I have to use a spoon.~~

August 7: Atomic bomb announced; bad news for Japan; is it also bad news for civilization? Had long conference with Capt. Everest re 2 corvettes offered us by British government in part payment for 6 Customs vessels requisitioned by British in Hongkong in 1941. ~~I was joint host with Francis and Cecilia Pan to Sir Horace and Lady Seymour, Ellis Briggs, Gen. Carton de Wiart, Nancy Lee, Prof. Sze (the singer) and one other Chinese whose name I don't know. Had half an hour with David Shaw, who was in New York office of O.S.S. with me. He came out with Gen. Donovan for a look see.~~

August 8: Bulletins full of the atomic bomb. It cost two thousand million U.S. dollars, yet we have utmost difficulty in raising 5 or 10 millions for cancer research. The "harnessing of the atom" may prove more important than the application of steam to machines, the invention of gunpowder or the introduction of electricity. Worked most of the busy day on despatch to Pure British corvettes, letter to Sir Horace Seymour, etc.

August 9: ~~A very tiring day in office on the go every minute.~~ Russia at war with Japan. Nagasaki "atomized". Dined at Gen. Carton de Wiart's house. Usual good company, good food, good conversation. ~~Capt. Echford (Gen. de Wiart's aide) told me he has become engaged to one of Hugh Hilliard's daughters.~~ Gen. de Wiart says Wedemeyer is doing a fine job; that Admiral Lord Louis Mountbatten has antagonized him and relations are not good; de Wiart says it's Mountbatten's fault. Gen. de Wiart leaves for England next Monday; I gave him a letter for Foster Hall.

August 10: Had the 2 vice-Ministers of Finance and 15 heads of departments to buffet lunch. Very optimistic over the end of the war – some said 3 or 4 days; others, three or four weeks. ~~Very busy in office; this has been a tiring week.~~ At 9 p.m. Chungking radio said peace rumors without confirmation are sweeping in from all over the world. By 9:15, firecrackers by the millions were being fired in all parts of the city. One of the coolies came up to Pouncey and me, who were standing at the top of the garden steps, and said: "Japan has surrendered." At 10, San Francisco radio said that Domei had announced Japan's willingness to surrender. B.B.C. at 11 said that the Japanese government had broadcast its readiness to surrender and accept the Potsdam terms if the Emperor's prerogatives are not disturbed. This is the end, thank God! John and Nate and millions of other boys can go home. I am devoutly thankful that all the boys in our immediate families have been spared. Ting wrote me a congratulatory note and says the government will probably declare a holiday tomorrow and that he has bought $30,000 worth of firecrackers and set them off at the Inspectorate. ~~Pouncey listened with me to the radio; Hopstock is out to dinner. Bed at 11:30.~~

August 11: A busy and exciting day. I let all the staff who wanted, take an unofficial holiday, but I was on the go all day. The tasks ahead are monumental! Jap offer to surrender confirmed, but question now is: will the Jap commanders in the field obey their own government's order to quit? I bet I made 250 decisions today! D.K. Wei came to see me at 6, and talked 1 hour. I like him very much, and he is a very intelligent man, but I wish he wouldn't stay so long. He has nothing to do. ~~Norm Meiklejohn has just offered him the job in the F.E.A. for which I recommended him, but the end of the war will, I presume, mean the end of Norm's scheme.~~ [. . .]

August 12: ~~Didn't go to Liang Feng Ya this week-end because I had to go to a buffet lunch at the Trevor Powells. About 20 there.~~ Worked on rehabilitation – what a job! River very high, and squatters' houses along bank washed out.

August 13: River to 70 feet – highest in the three summers I've been here. Several feet of water over the stone bridge near the office, and we had to cross by sampan. ~~Frightfully busy and tiring day.~~ Spoke briefly at Memorial Service; had one hour conference with all Secretaries. ~~Stomach out of order old friend diarrhea. Pouncey terribly downcast and pessimistic; he is a Cassandra – one of these men who have a difficulty for every solution. But it was hard to tell him and Hopstock that their leaves must be postponed.~~

August 14: In bed all day till 6 p.m., when I had to get up to entertain a dinner party of 12. Took 8 tablets sulfaguanidine and felt like hell. Guests: Mrs. Hassel (wife of Norwegian Ambassador, who is recovering from cholera); Mr. Rose – Anderson, Counsellor of Norwegian Embassy; Lovink, Dutch Ambassador; Mr. and Mrs. Trevor Powell; Air Commodore and Mrs. Bartholomew, Pouncey, Hopstock, Drummond. Hopstock opened his last bottle of champagne and we drank to Victory – just around the corner. I gave them Grand Marnier that John sent me; their eyes popped when they saw it! The Powells dined with me on V-E day; again with me pretty close to V-J Day!

August 15: This is The Day! Peace at last, over all the earth. ~~Lott Wei appeared just before breakfast (which he ate with me) to ask for a job for his future son in law.~~ To Ministry all morning, arguing with Li Tong over my appointments to the coast ports, pensions, pay, etc. I fear I was very frank with him. Back to office, Pouncey gloomy as usual; I haven't had a cheerful word out of him for months. Russia and China have signed a treaty, and all outstanding questions settled. This news is almost as important as the surrender of Japan, because the situation between China and Russia had the makings of another world war. Cruiser "Indianapolis" said to have been lost with all hands: I wonder if she had an atomic bomb explosion aboard! ~~Frightfully busy all day, and dead tired. I don't feel in the least like celebrating. Invited to dinner at K.C. Lee's tonight but called it off.~~

August 16: ~~Still a bit off color, and pressed every moment.~~ Had hour and half with four Secretaries drafting detailed instructions to Commissioners who are going to take charge of re-occupied ports. Also wrote circular letter to Customs internees.

August 17: Ting away all day at conferences. Came to report to me at 6:30. ~~Maj. Don Monroe and Capt. Foster Knight had tea here and a long talk. Monroe may want to re-join Customs immediately, but he has rather large ideas of his importance. He was rather deflated when I told him that I'd like him to come back tomorrow as Dep. Commissioner. Apparently he thinks he could come back as Commissioner.~~

~~*August 18:* At noon, had slight temperature (bronchitis) and had to give up trip to bungalow. Still very busy with plans for reoccupying coast ports.~~

August 19: To bungalow. Ting and Chang arrived just before lunch: I knew it must be bad news. It was; Li Tong objects to my appointing foreigners as Commissioners at Tientsin and Canton. ~~Norman Meiklejohn to lunch; he brought clam chowder, which his wife sent out. I was delicious, and nostalgic. I contributed a tin of Boston brown bread with one of beans. Went both ways by chair, because I wasn't up to walking. After dinner, had conference with Pouncey and Hopstock.~~

August 20: To Pu with Ting, to see Li Tong. On his assurance that ban on foreigners at Tientsin, etc. is only temporary and due to special circumstances, and on his assurance that after government is re-established at Nanking I can appoint foreigners anywhere, I agreed to appoint Chinese Commissioners to Tientsin and Canton. Loy Chang dined with me, and we had a good talk on Customs until 11 p.m. He intimated that China has had to make some fairly extensive concessions to Russia in the new treaty – which is still unpublished. [. . .]

August 21: U.C.R. meeting 2:30–4:30. Not half over, but I sneaked out and went to say goodbye to Norman Meiklejohn, who is leaving for U.S. tomorrow. Then to Embassy, and had a chat with Neil Gorman, who has recently come out as "Petroleum Attaché." ~~To Pan's (they were not at home), where I rested, tried to play the piano for first time in 2 years, awful(!) and changed.~~ Then to dinner at Lovink's (Netherlands Ambassador).

August 22: All sailors, tingchais, chair-bearers, water-coolies, etc. struck this morning. I'm getting rather used to these incidents; also, fed up with them. I have no use for the Szechuan native. A big crowd came to office and wanted to see me. I refused to have a mob, but consented to talk to representatives; Six came to my office, and, with Ting's help, I explained once again the whole pay situation. Ting then addressed the whole gang, who went away satisfied (for the moment.) We have been trying to get the increases for months, but it was only the actual strike that made the Kuan-wu Shu move, and, this afternoon, approve my proposals. "They yield nothing to reason but everything to fear." Ting and I broadcast short message over Station WX04 at 9:15 p.m. to staff at Shanghai and other liberated ports. The "Communist" situation is still dangerous.

August 24: ~~Quiet day; lots done.~~ Situation in Far East disquieting – especially in China. Ting says Communists enter Peiping and Tientsin daily, rob and kill. I wonder what will happen in (1) Manchuria, (2) Hongkong, (3) Indo-China, (4) China. [. . .]

August 25: Van den Berg and Ting to lunch. Van den Berg has just been promoted Minister; he is a good man. Before guests left, four Standard-Vacuum Oil Co. men from New York called: "Chief" Meyer (Director); Anderson (Geologist). Both my Dutch and American guests are speculating – and worrying – over conditions in post-war China. I myself find the future very obscure, and I think we can only live from day to day. Much depends on the Russian – Communist – Chungking – U.S. relationships. I also think that China will find some practical method of using foreign ships, men, capital and brains, in spite of present laws.

August 26–27 (Confucius' Birthday): ~~With Pouncey and Hopstock, had 2 days at bungalow. Good rest, except when P. got going on the hardships of the foreign staff. He is gloomy and stubborn. Monday rainy and cloudy. Ting and Everest, after 1 day's delay, expected to fly to Chinkiang today; 1st stop on way to Shanghai. I can't seem to shake off my bronchial cold, which gives me some discomfort.~~

August 28: Had Mr. and Mrs. Y.C. Koo, Pouncey and Hopstock, to lunch. Mr. Koo was in good form, and talked most intelligently about China's prospects, drawbacks, and opportunities. He is a great believer in rural industrialization – also birth control, which he thinks the Chinese will be willing to accept. Mr. Koo also praised the great work of Sir Robert Hart. River rising rapidly and dangerously – 20 feet in a day to 74 feet this afternoon. Saw a well-dressed Chinese go in all over at the Lung Men Hao landing. Luckily, he was pulled out – much to the amusement of the crowd. To see Col. Dusenbury, U.S. Military Attaché, who fears that American aid to China may weaken, instead of strengthening, her. I disagree – provided our aid is intelligent and not Santa-Claus aid. ~~To Naval Attaché's office, where Dr. Harrington said my chest was O.K. Saw Capt. Jarrell a minute. To U.C. Army Headquarters to see Col. Young, Judge~~ Advocate General, re seizures made by U.S. Army, from convoys and planes, to be handed over to Customs. Just as I walked down the hall to his office, I saw a large group of 4, 3, 2, and 1-star generals, led by Gen. Wedemeyer. They were Gen. Wainwright[38] of Bataan, and the General officers of his staff who were released from POW camps and flown here from Mukden this morning. I'll bet they are the happiest men in China today. I talked with a couple of them; one told me he'd lost 50 lbs. As Gen. Wainwright and the other released POW's went by, I heard a young officer say: "Boy, what pay checks are waiting for those guys!" To Dr. Rappe's house to reception to say goodbye to Sweet (U.C.R.) who is leaving for America. Met Mr. Kizer (UNRRA) who is just back from Washington and London. ~~To Pans' home, for a breather and little visit with Francis and Cecilia.~~ Then to Wang Lung Men, and a scene of confusion, with hundreds of people trying to get aboard the ferries. Steps packed half way to top. I had taken precaution of having my launch stand by and a boatman guided by a devious route to it, and I got comfortably across the river at 7 a.m. – a bit tired.

August 29: River up to 85 feet, highest in many years. [. . .] ~~Very busy in the office,~~ Ting, before he left, asked Chang (Staff Secretary) to transfer a young clerk away from Chungking because his daughter is in love with him. I refused to sanction the transfer because I consider it an abuse of Ting's position, and it would certainly be used as a weapon with which to attack him. Very hot: "Autumn Tiger" – "Chiu lao hu" [秋老虎].

August 30: ~~Very busy in office, and got through a lot of work. Hot as hell today, but river down.~~

August 31: Today I recall Silas Strawn's[39] story about the dog "August".

September

September 1: To Ministry of Finance at 9, with Adm. Hsu and Chang, to discuss opening of Yangtze, with Li Tong. He is a bit of an ass. For months, I have urged him to give us the money for work-boats, launches, etc. but with little success. Now, when the Generalissimo orders the river to be surveyed, Li Tong expects us to do it in a week.

September 2: V-J DAY. At 9:30 a.m., listened to the surrender ceremony on U.S.S. "Missouri". Heard MacArthur and Nimitz,[40] also Pres. Truman from Washington. Today, the United States stands as the most powerful nation in the world;

God grant that she may always stand there, and use her great power for the benefit of all the world. Admiral Hsu and Mr. Munby here for conference on opening of river. To office in afternoon. River dangerously high; almost 90 feet at 6 p.m. I fear bad floods further down the valley. ~~Don Monroe and Foster Knight dined in the mess, and spent night here because the ferries have stopped running.~~

September 3: Holiday. To office in a.m. River highest in 25 or 30 years; 99.9 at 3 p.m. Floods down river almost certain. Could not cross by sampan to shore road, so had to go around I.C.I. property and approach office from back way. ~~Don Monroe and Foster Knight to breakfast with me.~~ At 9 a.m., whistles and sirens, and gun salutes. ~~Lazy afternoon.~~ Searchlights at night. ~~A quit day for me. Started letter to John at 9 p.m., but lights went out.~~

September 4: Lott Wei (who has just been appointed Director of the Mint) came in as I was breakfasting to ask the use of the Customs launch to cross the river. I crossed at 2:30. Called on Mr. O.K. Yui and asked for four or five of the trucks recently given to the Central Bank to carry bank-notes. He said he'd look into it. This means "no". Saw Li Tong, and told him we've either got to pay foreigners adequately or get rid of them. He asked me how many foreigners we have and, when I said "150," he said "too many"!! The dirty louse!! We had 500 a few years ago, and if we lose many more the Customs Service will go to hell. Called on Gen. Wiart. Latter will have command in Shanghai. I suggested advisability of getting Neprud to Shanghai quickly, but don't think they grasped the point very well. Picked up passport at Consulate, ~~and had a cup of tea with Francis and Cecilia. Terrible crowd at Wang Lang Men at 6 when I crossed the river.~~

September 5: ~~Very busy all day.~~ Heard a house fall down across the river with an appalling crash and a cloud of dust. Undermined by flood. Water down to 65 feet. Four Secretaries told me they would leave for Shanghai tomorrow; at 4 p.m., told that trip is postponed!

September 6: River down to 50 feet; a drop of 50 feet in a little over 2 days. George Atcheson appointed Ambassador to Siam and political advisor to Gen. MacArthur: a well-deserved promotion. Wrote him a note.

September 7: ~~Hot and tired. Nervous indigestion and diarrhea at night.~~ [. . .]

September 9: Nixon came a 9 a.m. to talk about Fay, whom I have recommended to UNRRA for a job. ~~To bungalow (both ways by chair). My stomach aches dully and sporadically, wonder if I've got ulcers?~~ Paul Josselyn called up from Embassy; I had no idea he was coming to China. He is going to Shanghai. Had long chinwag with Neprud, Foster Knight, Pouncey and Hopstock after dinner. Foster Knight says that 9 out of 10 G.I.'s are taking away a very low and unfavorable opinion of the Chinese, principally because of corruption and theft. Japan signed the surrender to China at Nanking today.

September 10: With Neprud lunched at No. 4 Chialing with Paul Josselyn and Bob Smyth. To see Li Tong and had 1/2 hour during which I had to hold on to my temper. He is an unadulterated so-and-so! I went for him with both barrels. ~~Back to office, which I left exhausted at 5:40.~~ Preston Lee, a boat officer, just evacuated

1945

from the Wanhsien internees' camp, turned up at 6: 40; under the influence of alcohol. I didn't see him, but Hopstock and the rest took care of him. [...]

September 11: U.C.R. Committee meeting to discuss inflation, deflation, budgets, etc. ~~To dentist (Drs. Au and Chang) who replaced 1 small porcelain filling for C.N. $4,000.~~

September 12: In bed all morning, feeling like death. Dressed at noon to have Bishop Carleton Lacy,[41] Neprud, Pouncey, Hopstock, and Drummond to lunch. I starved all morning, but had 2 poached eggs for lunch. At 3, Fang Tu came to discuss Service finance. He is very discouraged and pessimistic and so am I! He said that the government officials (those below the top) are riff-raff and that China may well lose the peace. Admiral Hsu and Mr. Chang Yang-nien then came and we discussed harbor works, etc., until 6 p.m. [...]

September 13: ~~Feeling O.K. again. Busy day. Li Tong still obstructive.~~ [...]

September 15: ~~To office, and very busy day. Pouncey leaves at 3 a.m. tomorrow for Hongkong.~~

September 17: ~~Another busy day. Stoneman leaves for Canton tomorrow. Had pathetic letter from Eddie Pritchard in Hongkong.~~

September 18: To Ministry with Chang and Fang Tu to see Li Tong. Had a knock-down, drag-out fight with him over treatment of foreign staff. We yelled and pounded and shouted. I felt like punching his nose. ~~Too tied up in my stomach to eat much lunch.~~ The breaking-point has almost been reached. The best unconscious humor I've seen recently was the statement of one of the Japanese generals arrested as a war-criminal. To correspondents, he said: "We have lost the war; there must have been some mistake."

~~*September 19:* Cocktail party for "Chief" Meyer and other Standard Oil "mission" at Victory House. Hopstock dined with Neprud and me, with Loy Chang watching us eat. Loy came to ask me how his son can get out of the U.S. Army! Loy and I talked till 10 p.m. re Customs, and I gave him a bellyful!~~

September 20: Neprud flew to Nanking and Shanghai this morning. Letter from Maze re his advice to Customs neutrals in Shanghai. As usual, he lies.

September 21: Lunch at French Embassy. Host: Gen. Pechkoff. Dr. Quo Tai-chi (to whom I mentioned my difficulties with Li Tong, and who said he would speak in "certain" quarters); Keith Officer (Australian Chargé); Andersen (Norwegian Chargé); Gen. Hayes (British); and 4 Frenchmen. To see Lovink, who is sick, and congratulate him on the news of the safety in Java of his wife and children of whom he had no news for 3-1/2 years. To see Col. Dusenbury. ~~Busy at office.~~ To Loy Chang's house before dinner. Worked 2 hours after dinner.

September 22: To Ministry at 9:30. Minister presiding at meeting so made calls at Embassy (all out saying good-bye to Gen. Hurley); W.P.B. (found Jacobson in bed with fever); Swedish legation; Foreign office (to call on Liu Chieh,[42] vice-Minister – was told he comes to office at 3 p.m.!) Back to Ministry, and saw Mr. O.K. Yui at 11: 30. I pointed out that, if government desires to retain service of foreigners, pay must be increased immediately. Told him of my interview last

Tuesday with Li Tong, and outlined my proposal to issue double Sterling allotments for 6 months. The Minister agreed in 10 minutes. A good day for the Customs, but I don't think Li Tong will be happy. A very busy afternoon in office, getting off telegrams to London, Shanghai, etc. ~~With Hopstock left at 6 for the bungalow.~~

September 23: Dr. T.V. Soong returned to Chungking last night. ~~Lovely day in hills. Drummond came up. Home at 5: 30. Adm. Hsu called up an urgent business at 6 and stayed till 7: 30.~~

September 24: another extremely busy day, but with a lot accomplished. Telegrams, despatches, letters, memos, people – all day long. Worked at night on comment on Executive Yuan's proposal to place Customs under direct control Kuan-wu Shu. My comment raises the question squarely: why not abolish the K.W.S.? I have a feeling that certain high quarters (although realizing that the Shu is an anachronism) are determined to retain it.

September 25: ~~Telegram form John "Home on Spring St. Everything wonderful love." I replied by telegram. I hope Nate is home, too.~~ To Keith officer's to dinner (Australian Chargé). Gen. Maddox[43] (Wedemeyer's Chief of Staff); Mr. and Mrs. Allard (Swedish Minister ~~and kinda dumb~~); Mr. and Mrs. Liang (ex-Minister of Information); Dr. Kan (Vice-Minister of Foreign Affairs); Stoker (Australian Secretary); ~~Hot all this past week: 90 to 95 degrees.~~

September 26: To Hua Lung Chiao at 3:45 to conference with Chang Fu-yen. ("F. Chang") until 7:30! Home at 8:30. Mr. Chang has been ordered by Dr. Soong to take charge of the Kuan-wu Shu!! This is great news. No more Li Tong, thank Heavens. We talked staff, organization, ships, Dairen, Hongkong and a hundred other things. [...] Long reports from Shanghai. I have never been so busy in my life.

September 27: News of F. Chang's appointment made public. Customs staff delighted. To the Seymours' to dine and spend night. At dinner: Chen Li-fu and Mrs.; Dr. Chiang Mon-lin and Mrs.;[44] Mr. and Mrs. Menon (India Commissioner in China); Hutchinson. Had long talk with Chen Li-fu: he is bitterly anti-Communist and, I gathered, pro-fascist.

September 28: ~~Newman arrived from England. Crossed river to office at 9. Crossed again at 11~~ To consult with Mr. F. Chang (who assumed office today) about the Marine Dept. staff demands. Mr. Chang crossed with me and had lunch here. I crossed again with him, left him at Wang Lung Men, and crossed again to office. At 3, crossed again with Chang Yung Nien, and went to Kuan-wu Shu, where F. Chang, Chang Yung-nien and I had 1-1/2 hour interview with representatives of Marine Dept. crews. Mr. F. Chang handled things marvellously, and the representatives went away satisfied, and promised to sail when ordered. It is a great relief to have F. Chang to deal with; it has been like a breath of clean air for the first time in 18 months. Crossed again at 5:45, and had 3 callers at house at 6. (Li Tong Wha, Lo Ching-hsiang[45] and Tseng Kwang Chin,[46] appointed to Tsingtao, Chin Wang Tao and Chefoo, respectively, leaving tomorrow.) Last caller left at 7:15. ~~N.B. Crossed river all except first trip in Customs launch.~~

1945

September 29: [. . .] ~~Busy day in office.~~ At 10:30, one of the accountants came through a pouring rain to get Hopstock's safe key to get out $50,000,000 which 2 of our men will take to Ting in Shanghai – flying at 6 a.m. tomorrow.

September 30: Rained cats and dogs all night and this morning. Had an hour with Mr. Kizer, UNRRA Chief, and some of his staff. I had gone there to see Jim Henry, who was out. Kizer told me that Jim had joined UNRRA and was leaving soon for Canton.

October

October 1: ~~Newman spoke at Memorial Service.~~ To K.W.S. at 11. Talked with F. Chang till 1, then he came to lunch with me. Back to office at 3. 1-1/2 hours with 3 Marine Dept. officers who wish to resign. A tough proposition! ~~Dr. Jim Henry here when I got here at 6:00. We had a great gab fest until 1:10, when he went to bed and I worked on telegrams. A very busy day.~~

October 2: A coolie woman ran in to my office today, knelt and kowtowed. She accused one of the Chinese staff of beating her. We'll investigate. Lu Ping off to Tientsin; Tseng Kwang Chi to Chefoo. With Chang Yung-nien, inspected the three river launches which are about to leave for surveying the middle and lower Yangtze. Dictated at least 20 letters.

October 3: To K.W.S. and 1-1/2 hours with F. Chang. To U.S. Headquarters to see Gen. Maddox, Chief of Staff, and other officers. Lunch with Col. Dusenbury, Military Attaché. Busy afternoon in office.

October 4: Had Mr. Kwok (Wai-chiao Pu Delegate in Liang Kuang) and his Secretary, Mr. Wang, to lunch with Hopstock, Drummond and Newman. I think I've dictated 50 letters in last 2 days. Am doing quite a lot of "homework" these nights – like old times.

October 5: With Hopstock and Wu Fen (Pension Chief Accountant) to see F. Chang and discuss foreign pensions and pay. Good progress; discussion lasted till 12:15 and will be continued tomorrow. J.H.L. Turner (Dep. Commissioner), now Lt. Col. Turner called on me at 2:30. He is stationed in India, and is coming back to Customs.

October 6: Another 2 hours with F. Chang this morning re treatment of internees paid off in 1943. I think the conclusions we reached, while not too generous, are very fair to all concerned in the light of all circumstances. I hope they will be approved by the government. Very busy afternoon. A small steamer sank just across the river from my office yesterday. The paper says that 70 people were lost. ~~Worked at night.~~

October 7: ~~With Hopstock and Newman to Liang Feng Yah. Brigadier Kay gave me first letters from Pouncey at Hongkong. Foster Knight spent night here. Worked at night.~~

October 8: ~~Letter from Hugh Bradley.~~ [. . .] Crossed river. Saw Bob Smyth at Embassy. Met new Naval Attaché and Naval Doctor. Dr. Harrington has joined UNRRA. Called on Col. (Father) McNamara, of Rumford, R.I., Theatre Chaplain.

1945

~~Had tea with Cecilia Pan. Mr. Stoneman came to see me about getting to Canton. Stayed to dinner.~~

October 9: To U.C.R. at 2:30. Henry Luce there as observer. At 4, meeting adjourned and tea given for Mr. Luce. ~~Stopped at Mrs. Powell's. She has had malaria. Worked in evening.~~

October 10: Holiday. First Double-Tenth in 14 years that China has been free of the Japs. To tea party at Central government, given by Gen. and Mme. Chiang Kai-shek. Big crowd – 300–400.

October 11: Liesching walked in unannounced at 6 p.m.; just out from London.

October 12: ~~To dentist at 2:30. In one hour he replaced 3 fillings, and charged me $12,000.~~ To British Embassy to discuss corvettes with Capt. Billyard-Leake, Naval Attaché. Saw Tony Keswick,[47] Lady Seymour, etc., and had tea with Mrs. Wallinger. To big cocktail party at French Embassy for Admiral____. High Commissioner for Indo China. I guess he's got plenty of headaches these days, for Indo-China, Malaya and Java are in ferment. A great contrast to the Philippines. Ronald Hall came to see me; he is just back from home leave. [. . .]

October 13: As usual, Saturday was a very busy day. Huge mail and dozens of telegrams. Worked at home almost every night this week.

October 14: ~~With Hopstock, Liesching and Newman to bungalow. Worked at night. Also wrote letters.~~

October 15: ~~A very busy day, lots of problem.~~

October 16: ~~To U.C.R. meeting. To U.S. Naval Attaché office. Tea at Mia Lennox's. Henry Barton, of Bristol, called.~~

October 17: ~~Henry Barton to dinner. Much talk of Bristol, Rhode Island and old friends.~~

October 18: Cocktail party at Nelson Mission for Locke (Truman's personal representative) called off at last minute. Bill Stanton says there's a rift in the lute – apparently Jacobson (present head of Nelson Mission) doesn't hit it off with Locke. In any case, cancellation of the party is childish and inexcusable, and will certainly cause talk. Hyman Hodes gave me a pair of G.I. flannel trousers and a flannel shirt for U.S. $9.15. They will keep me warm this winter. ~~Called at Naval Liaison office re telegrams to Army. Coffee with Cecilia, Mrs. Trevor Powell and Mr. Lawrence there. Worked at home after dinner.~~

October 19: Struggling with two big questions: (1) new General Customs Regulations and (2) drafting regulations for free port of Dairen. Both are extremely complicated.

October 20: ~~One of the busiest days of my career.~~ Finished draft proposals for free port of Dairen. Worked at home at night. Sellett told us last night that a G.I. could buy 5 packs of cigarettes for U.S. $0.25 at PX, sell them for C.N. $15,000 and buy a CNAC plane ride to Kunming!

October 21: With Hopstock, Liesching and Newman, a glorious day at the bungalow. After a day like this, I can almost forgive Chungking's climate. Worked in evening preparing list of ports I shall suggest to government to open to overseas shipping.

October 22: ~~Busy to nth degree.~~ 2 hour Secretaries' meeting to discuss opening of ports – very interesting. Worked 4 hours at home with enormous mail in from Shanghai. ~~Loy Chang not made Director General of Consolidated Tax as first reported.~~

October 23: Another busy day. Arthur Young, just back from U.S. via Shanghai, to breakfast. Ronald Hall, British Consul General, to dinner. Worked an hour after he left.

October 24: Colder. To "American Friendship Day", a celebration at Fan Chuang, at which Chinese-American. Inst. of Cultural Relations entertained the U.S. troops, presented gifts, etc. One great book of inscriptions in memory of F.D. Roosevelt was presented by Dr. Kung to Walter Robertson. Both men made good speeches. ~~Talked business with Arthur Young, and say a lot of friends. Worked at night.~~

October 25: Malcolm (Marine Dept.) called. He is re-joining Customs after war work. His last job was to go to scene of airplane crash (air, jeep and 100 mile walk) in which Maj. McMullen (Chefoo) and 5 others (4 Americans) were killed. If plane had been 100 feet higher it would have missed mountain. Bodies stripped of rings, watches, money. Only one identifiable, but "we counted 6 heads."

October 26: Busy day getting ready to go to Shanghai tomorrow.

October 27: Up at 5:30, to island airport by launch at 6:30. All Secretaries turned out. Plane left at 9. Smooth trip to Nanking; thence rough. Majority (of whom I was one) were air-sick. Met at Kiangwan by Ting, Neprud and Kuo Yu-yung.[48] Felt rather wobbly. To my house at 1901 Ave. Joffre at 5, where I found Kenneth and May Ashdowne, with Michael and Hilary. Also Miss Foster, ex-State Dept. They took me right in as member of family. House and garden in excellent condition. At 6, to swell reception at Cathay, given by Army to Navy on Navy Day. Met a lot of brass and others.

October 28: Reception for me at Customs Club at 10 a.m. About 300 present; I spoke, emphasizing the necessity for a united Service. At 11:45, to Community Church, in time for 10 minutes of the sermon and the closing hymn. At 2, Ting, Neprud and Tso came to confer. We ended at 7 p.m.

October 30: Further conferences with F. Chang, etc. Lunch at Park Hotel given by Neprud. 12 including the exquisitely lovely Mrs. Tsu-fa Li. Paul Josselyn to dinner at my house.

October 31: Called on Admiral Kincaid[49] and Admiral Coombs[50] on U.S.S. "Rocky Mountain". Conferences rest of morning and all afternoon with F. Chang. Buffet supper and dance (U.S. Navy) at Cathay. Lots of beautiful girls. Met "neutral" foreign staff at Inspectorate at 5.

November

November 1: Called on Adm. Joy on "Nashville" and was shown around ship. Called on Mayor Chen in former S.M.C. Building. Further conference (until 11:45) with F. Chang. With Capt. Everest, discussed corvettes, etc., with Capt.

1945

Billyard-Leake. As host with Ting and Neprud, had 40 guests to a Chinese dinner given at Ting's house. Had I known the plan, I would have made it less expensive and expansive. Admirals and Generals falling all over each other; WACS (including Col. Westray Boyce,[51] the head of the organization, now on a world tour of inspection. (I dropped a brick when I called her 'Major'). Pretty girls (including Mrs. Li Tsu-fa; I danced a lot with Miss Beatrice Woo). All over at 11.

November 2: Left Kiangwan airport for Chungking at 9; excellent trip, but very cold. No heat in plane, and outside temperature 32 degrees. In office at 2 p.m., and worked until 5:30. Worked at home after dinner. This has been a most strenuous week, but well worth the effort, because I got a lot of things settled. Superficially, Shanghai looks much the same as ever, but I fear things are not going too well below the surface. The outbreak of civil war between Chungking and Yenan – is a most depressing and discouraging development. China is the only country in the world where, when things get as bad as they possibly can, they can always get worse.

November 3: ~~Very busy day. Got a lot done.~~

November 5: Spoke on my Shanghai visit at Memorial Service. Crossed river at 2:30. At British Embassy, called on Sir Horace, ~~Myers and Themes~~. Dropped card on O.K. Yui who was out. Called on Robertson, U.S. Embassy. ~~Stopped at Executive Yuan, but Arthur Young was out. Had tea with Cecilia Pan, and stopped at Elsie Soong's (out). Worked at night.~~ Sir Horace Seymour had a fire in his room; I saw no fires at the American Embassy: the world is upside down!

November 6: A hammer and tongs day; busy every minute. Letters from Gerli – that Arch-Fascist, now sings a different song, and humbly pleads his "loyalty" and "Anglo-American" sympathy! Rot, rubbish and hypocrisy. In the same envelope, a letter from his sweet wife Nina. It was nice to hear from her again. He is studying singing and thinking of going on the concert platform.

November 7: ~~Work eased up a bit for the first time in 2 months. Weather continues good, for Chungking!~~

November 9: Quiet but busy day. Worked at night. Item: This past summer is the first I have ever passed without using a mosquito net. I can't recall having been bitten once all summer, day or night.

November 10: ~~Usual busy Saturday; crescendo up till 5:30 p.m.~~ [. . .]

November 11: ~~Heavy rain all night, so did not go to bungalow. To buffet lunch at Jack Parsons. Very mixed crowd, very mediocre food. Usual program: cocktails until about 2:45. I don't like this kind of party.~~ Crossed river to give a document to Arthur Young re export restrictions, which we are trying get removed. Arthur says T.V. has asked U.S. government to send out several Treasury experts to advise on budget, taxes, etc. Arthur has told T.V. that he thinks that any such plan should include him, and that he should be put in charge. I agree. Arthur says he will resign if plan goes through as proposed. His resignation would be a loss to China and America.

November 12: Holiday. To office till 11, then to bungalow, where we had baked beans, hash (K-rations) and coffee. Hopstock, Liesching and I then walked to the other Customs-owned bungalow, which has been "commandeered" by Hsu Kan, Minister of Food, for several years, and recently given back to us. It was terribly filthy, neglected and empty. It is simply disgraceful that a Minister of State can leave a place looking like a pig-pen – and without as much as a "thank-you".

November 13: To U.C.R. at 2:30. To American Embassy at 4:30: talked to Robertson about Arthur Young (vide 11 November). Robertson doesn't think Embassy can intervene, but sees Arthur's point of view. At 5:45, had 1/2 hour with Dr. T.V. Soong, who had called for me. He was most affable and approachable. Asked me how things were going in Customs. We discussed employment of foreigners, and he said I could employ as many as I need. Arms for guards at Shanghai. Said he might take a foreigner for Salt Gabelle, and would use some in Executive Yuan, as advisers. I mentioned treatment of internees; he said "I will see that they're treated decently." Mentioned Li Tong's objection to appointment of foreigners at Tientsin and Canton. He said: "Li Tong is out now; go ahead. But don't appoint a Britisher at Canton." Mentioned Pritchard; T.V. said: "He's a good man; keep him." I raised question of "Certificate of Purchase of Exchange", and expressed hope that they could be waived temporarily in order to get trade started. He said he intended to act accordingly. I asked him when we could move Inspectorate. He said: "Next month." He asked me whether I was going to Nanking. Told him we had no property, houses, etc. there. He said Customs Inspectorate, being part of central government, should be at Nanking, not Shanghai, so instructed me write to Minister of Finance and ask for accommodations needed. [. . .] Stopped in to see Francis and Cecilia for 1/2 hour. Francis very happy because UNRRA has approved erection of 18 shops for manufacture of agricultural machinery. Francis hopes to be put in charge of program. 2 hours work after dinner; stacks of documents.

November 14: Very busy day. First letter from Chinese Customs, Taipeh, Formosa in over 50 years. Hopstock, Liesching and Newman had coffee and talk with me after dinner. Newman leaves tomorrow morning for Amoy. [. . .]

November 16: To see Minister. Had 1/2 hour with him, discussed several questions. Got his approval to declare coast ports at which Customs is functioning open to overseas trade and shipping. (Notified British Embassy and wired Pouncey at Hongkong). Told Mr. Yui that T.V. Soong instructed me that Inspectorate should move to Nanking. Mr. Yui said there was no accommodation for us. I asked him to speak to T.V. Soong on the subject. He told me Certificates of Purchase of Foreign Exchange will be waived, and that government is preparing to remove exchange restrictions in order to get trade started. Called on Li Tong. Had coffee and chat with Lovink, who is just back from India, where he met his wife and 2 children, who have been prisoners in Java during war. He said they are all in poor condition, suffering from beri-beri, malnutrition, etc. Terrible treatment: last 6 months, lived on 2 bowls of rice a day. Japanese paraded Red Cross parcels in front of the prisoners, but gave them none. Lovink's family, now en route to Carmel, California. He is very pessimistic about Communist situation; I am, too. [. . .]

November 17: Another very busy Saturday, and I was tired as I stumbled home in the darkening evening along the filthy, narrow, and uneven path. Worked at home after dinner. I wonder if I'll ever enjoy a civilized life again? That is, music, and shows and church, etc. I enjoy my job, and realize its importance, but I also realize that I am married to it and she's a hard taskmistress! Except for my mealties and sleep, I'm on the job practically every minute of the day.

November 18: To bungalow with Hopstock and Liesching. Worked before I went, and 3 hours after I returned – all on one subject: negotiations with British Admiralty concerning compensation for 6 Customs vessels requisitioned in Hongkong in 1941. A very complicated problem.

November 19: At Memorial Service, I presented Financial Medal to Fang Tu, on behalf of Minister of Finance. Very busy; worked till 10:30 p.m.

November 20: Communists reported to have occupied Changchun. It looks as if the Russians are backing them to take Manchuria, and deliberately keeping the Central government out. Had a most scurrilous anonymous letter from the "Chinese Patriots' Associates", Shanghai, denouncing the "bigamous" Chiang Kai-shek, etc., etc., and warning Americans "not to be suckers." The situation in China is far from healthy, and the forecast is "stormy weather." What a tragedy, after all these years of war! And I'm scared to death that the U.S. may get dragged into the dispute, and possibly come into head-on collision with Russia. Wrote a long letter to Mr. F. Chang: worked on it until 10:30 p.m.

November 21: Had small dinner here. Person did all the talking. 7:30 to 11, and was most interesting. A born actor and raconteur.

November 22: Hollis Gale (ex-Red Cross and O.S.S., now UNRRA) and a Scot named MacMeckin called at office and chatted about an hour. An unheard of thing in my office these days! Ting's younger son – Yao-chen[52] – critically sick in Canadian Hospital: T.B. His daughter resigned her typist job and left for Shanghai this morning. Read editorial "What Price Peace in China" from "Time", explaining why U.S. troops are still in China. A significant and well-written article, which, I hope will be widely read at home. To Francis and Cecilia Pan's for dinner. Quentin Pan, Mrs. R.C. Chen, Tillman Durdin[53] (New York Times), Stanley Smith (British Info. Service) Hamish Mackenzie (British Embassy), Prof. Sze (singer), Dr. Shan(Tsinghua) I had to leave before dinner was finished to catch the last ferry at 10. Thanksgiving Day. First time in my life I didn't' have some sort of celebration.

November 23: I have so much to do that I don't know which way to turn! Worked till 11:30 p.m. Stopped in to see Elsie Soong and Cecilia Pan. Latter in bed, and very depressed. Had a bad night, with terrible pain. I hope her operation was successful! Francis isn't worried that there is anything serious. [. . .]

November 24: Buffet lunch, at "Chief" Meyers'. Good chew. Dined at Gen. Wu Te-cheng's house. Home at 9:45 – that's one thing I like about Chinese dinners; you can get away early. Worked till 11.

November 25: With Liesching, Hopstock and Drummond to bungalow. Glorious sunny day, and had a welcome rest. Did no work except 2 hours after dinner on a memorandum concerning re-instatement of foreign staff who resigned for war service in their own countries before Pearl Harbor.

1945

November 26: ~~Very busy day. Ting's son Yao-shen critically sick (T.B.) in Canadian Mission Hospital. Telegram from Lu Ping (Tientsin) forwarding message from Tommy Little.~~ Melville Walker, of the U.S. Embassy, called to discuss import and export restrictions. No electricity today, but dug out an old "Aladdin" lamp, got some of the kerosene I bought from Banister, rigged a mantle, and soon had excellent illumination, by which I worked till 11:10 p.m.

November 27: To U.S. Embassy to see Walter Robertson and hand him letter requesting him to sound U.S. authorities on possibility of getting about 25 U.S. naval vessels for the Customs. He was very cordial and promised to push it. By luck, I met Mr. Howard, who is head of the U.S. Commission for selling surplus U.S. Army and Navy materials in Robertson's office, and gave him a copy of my letter. We two talked it over, after which Howard took me to his place and I met two of his staff, Mr. Cunningham and Brig. Gen. Johnson. All agreed to do everything possible, but they must get details of the legal position, etc., before moving. (Howard is a Boston lawyer, who used to have Dickey – Dartmouth's new President – in his law firm. He spoke very highly of Dickey, and called him one of the very best men going.) To see Capt. Kenny, U.S. Naval Attaché. [...] ~~worked 2 hours after dinner.~~

~~*November 28:* Another hectic day, with a lot done. Worked till 10:45 p.m. [...]~~

November 29: Gen. Patrick Hurley's resignation and public denunciation of the U.S. Foreign Service and State Department have created a sensation, as he undoubtedly intended they should. He tried hard to make peace between Chungking and Yenan. Had he succeeded, he would, rightly, have been famous. He failed; and it seems to me that, in his chagrin, he is looking for somebody to blame, and has selected the career men of the Foreign Service and State Department. I don't think anybody could have tried harder, or had much more success, than Hurley, but I doubt very much that his failure was due to the opposition of his subordinates. Some may have sympathized with the Communists; others not. But, if Hurley was trying to get Communists and government together (and he boasts that he did so) was it contrary to his policy if some of his subordinates did sympathize with one of the two parties he was conciliating? He himself went to Yenan two or three times and gave the Communists plenty of face. Now he turns on the Communists as if they were all devils (which I think 99% of them are – at least the Chinese brand). I have often asked myself whether Hurley was a very clever man or a tailor's dummy. I still don't know, but I consider that he was utterly unfair in his sweeping condemnation of the Foreign Service, and I hope he is compelled to prove his charges or else apologize. He was notoriously indiscreet here on several occasions – especially after a little too much alcohol. My respect for him has dropped precipitately. I wonder what he had in mind in referring to the "imperialist blocs" which, he avers, are favored by those of the career men who do not favor the "communist bloc". Is Pat Hurley the only true American left? Here's hoping that Gen. Marshall will do a better job out here. My guess is that he will. Worked till 10:30; wrote long letter to F. Chang, and asked him to make arrangements for me and my key staff to move to Shanghai. I hear that 2,500 officials (including 500 from the foreign embassies) are moving to Nanking in December.

November 30: Papers full of the Hurley mess. ~~Busy in the office.~~ Had Secretaries' meeting re move to Shanghai.

December

December 1: Luncheon here (15). Lady Seymour was my hostess. (Sir Horace is in England.) Busy afternoon, then a quick change and across the river to dine at Gen. Carton de Wiart's at Hua Lung Chiao. Cold and drizzly passage, and I was tired, but one of Gen. de Wiart's cocktails (1 rum, 1 lime juice, 1 orange juice, 1/2 brandy) helped! Also present: Mr. and Mrs. R.C. Chen, Wallinger, Gen. Ho (Chief of Military Intelligence), Col. Harmon, Col. Eckford, and Major somebody. Delicious dinner, the piece de resistance of which was fresh crabs, which Gen. de Wiart had brought with him alive from Nanking this morning. I couldn't touch them, so had 2 poached eggs and bacon for that course. Spent the night with Geoffrey Wallinger at the British Embassy. His house was the old Consular Constable's residence, and the guest room was the jail (or goal) in the old days. We talked politics till 12.

December 2: ~~Drizzled, so did not go to the hills. Home at 11, and worked and read alternately till bed time.~~

December 3: ~~One of these days!~~ Dined at Dr. Quo Tai-chi's. He had borrowed a cook and a house for the dinner; neither very good. Food mediocre, house cold as a barn. Guests: Gen. Pechkoff, Davidson, Lady Seymour, Wallinger, Prof. and Mrs. Roxby, Prof. and Mrs. Needham, Dr. Quo's brother. I left at the "sweet" in order to catch the last ferry, and caught the next to the last, and got home at 10. Gen. Pechkoff, French Ambassador, is leaving in a few days. He told me he has the choice of two posts: governor general of French West Africa or of Madagascar. Both are very big jobs, but his is a big man, and one of the most sincere and genuine people I have met. He is supposed to be the illegitimate son of some famous Russian author.

December 4: Called on Arthur Young at Executive Yuan to discuss duty treatment of U.S. surplus army supplies sold in China, and many other subjects. Worked at home before and after dinner. [...]

December 5: When I got up from the breakfast table somebody stabbed me in the back: lumbago! ~~Gosh, it hurt!~~ I had to cross the river because I had an appointment with the Minister of Finance at 10:30. I hobbled into his office, and he asked: "Lumbago?" I said: "I'm afraid so." Mr. Yui said: "You should be in bed." I pointed out that the rule regarding foreign shipping sent to Ting from the Generalissimo through the Shanghai Municipality would produce retaliations from foreign powers, etc. Mr. Yui instructed me to postpone implementing the rules (which are utterly fantastic.) This was what I wanted and suggested. To office (and very busy) all afternoon. Every move I make gives me a twinge of pain. Mr. O.K. Yui said that the situation in Manchuria had taken a turn for the better, and that our Customs men may soon be able to go to their posts.

1945

December 6: Lumbago better, but stayed home all day to shake it off. Mr. F. Chang returned from Shanghai yesterday and had lunch with me. We talked business for 2-1/2 hours. Worked at home. Chang Yung-nien came at 6 and we discussed selection of 10 men to go with me to re-establish the Inspectorate at Shanghai. Had to decline dinner invitation at the Smythes, tonight.

December 7: An hour with Mr. F. Chang. What a pleasure it is to go to the Kuan-wu Shu now! He is business-like, sympathetic practical, the antithesis of that old bull-frog Li Tong. To lunch with Arthur Young at the Red Cross Hostel. Also there: Lovink, Calvin (Red Cross) and the Red Cross girl in charge. To dentist to replace one filling; he found 2 more that had to be replaced! Worked till 10:30 p.m.

December 8: Elsie Soong's son came at noon bearing gifts: some cold turkey, bacon, potato salad and cheese. He stayed to lunch, and I didn't have any fountain pens lying around!

To see F. Chang at 3:30. We discussed pilotage, transfer of Inspectorate to Shanghai (10 from my office are authorized to leave by plane after December 15th), and many other questions. I was bitterly disappointed when he said that Dr. Soong had cut down on the ex gratia makes-up for post-1920 internees from 75% (recommended by F. Chang and O.K. Yui) to 50%. Mr. Chang said that T.V. at first vetoed the whole thing on the grounds of expense, but that he (F.C.) had persuaded him to pass the other provisions without amendment. This is an unfortunate and unexpected development. Mr. Chang said that Dr. Soong remarked that China isn't a rich country, and that the men concerned aren't "Flying Tigers." This last comment is an unfair as it is uncalled for. Back to office at 5, and very rushed. Loy Chang and D.K. Wei called at house at 6:30; stayed an hour. Loy aid that T.V. has had a bad cold, which has made him very miserable. Maybe this explains the above comment and the cut from 75% to 50%. Loy says that corruption is flagrant in connection with Tai Li's "aviation" inspection service. Our Admiral Miles,[54] USN, has helped build up this gangster with American taxpayers' money! Worked till 11, Saturday Night – like hell!

December 9: Lumbago practically gone; only an occasional twitch. Worked 2 hours in morning and 1 in afternoon sorting and packing, preparatory to move to Shanghai. Capt. Paul, of B & S, S.S., "＿＿" has kindly agreed to take one suitcase and my private papers to Shanghai. Then I must select what I shall need here until I leave – and not over 30 kilos. Next, I shall pack another box or two of stuff to come down the river when the staff moves. Wrote several letters on official subjects. Had Liesching, Hopstock and Drummond to lunch. We had sardines, turkey, and stuffing (sent by Elsie Soong), potato salad, canned corn, sausages (canned), canned apricots and cheese. Hopstock contributed the sausages and a bottle of French red wine. Over coffee and cigars we talked till 3. A good meal!

December 10: To U.S. Army Headquarters to see Brig. Gen. Randall,[55] Commanding General, Liaison Group, re surplus property to be handed over (I hope) to Customs by U.S. Army Port Headquarters, Shanghai. I suspect that other government organizations have also got their eyes on it! Stopped in at Naval Sick Bay, and found that Dr. Gudex has just been promoted to Captain, USNR. He took my blood pressure; O.K. Tested eyesight on chart, and found it much subnormal. My left eye is pretty bad, and the right not too good. I have been punishing my eyesight for a long time, and the bad light, bad paper and bad printing of Chungking haven't helped. Dr. Gudex gave me typhus and cholera booster shots, and cowpox inoculation. By 6 p.m., I was feeling a little groggy and feverish, but I think a good night's sleep will fix me up. F. Chang left for Shanghai this morning.

December 11: Felt punk in office, and stayed at home in afternoon. Temperature 101 degrees at 3 p.m., so went to bed.

December 12: 3 or 4 ghastly dizzy spells in bed between sleeping and waking. The whole house seemed to turn and spin, and I dropped into an abyss. Vertigo nauseated me, and, combined with the beginnings of a cold, forced me to stay in bed all day. Bedroom has not heat and is damp and raw. Ate almost nothing.

December 13: Better night. Hopstock suggested moving stove from drawing room into small bedroom, which was done. Busy with papers all afternoon.

December 14: Much more comfortable in warm bedroom. Worked at least 10 hours today, and so tired that I didn't sleep till after midnight. Nice letter from John.

December 15: Telegram for Betty said Nate had joined Foreign Department of Chase Bank and would probably be sent to Shanghai next fall! That's fine news, and it will be great to have them with me in Shanghai. I wired congratulations back.

December 16: I opened my sole cans of asparagus and strawberries for the occasion, although my sense of taste was so feeble that I could scarcely distinguish between them. Arthur Yong spent an hour in the morning discussing the plan of exchange, vs trade, control, and said that opinion in high places is veering towards the latter. If this is so, the Customs will play its part in any scheme: possibly it is in connection with this that Dr. Soong has called for me tomorrow. Chang Yung Nien and Fang Tu called at tea time. The Executive Yuan has, on the Gimo's orders, arbitrarily instructed a 20% cut in personnel of all government bureaus. This presents me with a very difficult situation as my staff is now at a minimum and should be increased after we get going in Manchuria and Formosa. Mr. Li Chang-cho,[56] Chungking Acting Deputy Commissioner, arrived just as I was beginning my dinner in bed. He stayed half an hour, while my dinner was kept hot in the kitchen. Wrote letter to F. Chang re pilotage after dinner.

December 17: Outside for first time for some days. To Executive Yuan to see Dr. Soong at 10. I got there at 9:45; he arrived at 11:45! I sat for 2 hours in an unheated office. My interview lasted 2 minutes: Dr. Soong said he wanted the 120 Customs Guards now en route to Shanghai to go to Tsingtao. This instruction could have been phoned to me in 5 minutes, or his Secretary could have sent me a note. Saw Dr. Chu – Deputy Secretary General of the Yuan, re 20% staff cut. Saw Arthur Young. Stopped at Naval Sick Bay to thank Dr. Gudex for looking after me. He gave me an influenza inoculation. Worked from 2:30 to 6:30, without a break, and after dinner.

December 18: To office all day, and very busy. The Chungking Commissioner, Li Chang-cho, came with a message from Executive Yuan at 9:30 p.m. Lucy Wei dropped in for half an hour at tea time, and talked a blue streak with Hopstock and me. Worked till 10:30 p.m.

December 19: British S.S. "Wan Liu" left at noon for Nanking with 200 Executive Yuan staff on board. Flew British flags, gave us a toot as she went by.

To Executive Yuan to see Dr. Kiang re air-lifting customs Guards to Tsingtao, and my staff to Shanghai. Former to leave December 22; latter, in 2 group of each, between 26th and 31st December.

With Seetoo (KWS) and Chang Yung Nien, to see Li Tong re U.S. Army's request for Chinese organization to take over port work at Shanghai. To Executive Yuan to see Dr. Kiang once more. Loafed after dinner for first time in over a month; drafted 2 short telegrams and read despatches, etc. for an hour.

December 20: All day at office, with no interruptions. Didn't go to cocktail party at Gen. Hayes' because I was tired and my cold still hangs on. [. . .]

December 21: Went to a photographer's shop on way home to get a passport photo taken; at lunch, he was out, but his wife said he'd be back at 2:30. At 2:30 he was still out, but his wife assured me he'd be on hand at 5:30. So, at 5:30, I again found my way through devious and muddy and steep alleys. Sure enough, he was there. While my four chair coolies, the photographer's wife (and nursing baby) and half a dozen neighborhood kids looked on, I sat on the stool and got ready. The bright lights were snapped on, and the professor was just about to press the bulb when the lights all went out, leaving us in complete blackness. I managed to grope my way to the door, and the photographer agreed to come to my house tomorrow at 8:30 a.m. to perform the operation. Worked after dinner.

December 22: Another hectic Saturday. Had Mr. Li Chang-cho (Chungking Commissioner) and wife, and Drummond, to lunch. Telegram form F. Chang berating me for "delay" in sending in official despatch re pilotage. I still don't know what he wants; maybe he doesn't know himself. Drafted long letter to him after dinner. [. . .]

December 23: Worked all morning on draft of a dispatch to KWS re pilotage. I still don't know whether it is what Mr. F. Chang wants, but it's the best I can do. To a pre-Christmas buffet luncheon at the Texaco Mess. Good food and a pleasant, sober crowd. Left at 3 o'clock. [. . .]

Hopstock had supper with me: can of clam chowder, can of beans, can of brown bread. He produced one (1) bottle of beer, and the last inch in a bottle of Peppermint (real stuff). A memorable meal

December 24: Terribly busy all day, I guess my staff think I'm a slave-driver! My stenographer would have a cold and have to stay off duty on a day like this. Listened to the U.S. Army broadcasts for 2 hours before dinner, and enjoyed the Christmas recordings, especially the carols. But they were rather hard on my emotions. My first Christmas without Mother. And I felt generally lonely and homesick.

Worked on hour at night.

December 25: Christmas Day. Busy Morning at office. Lunch as guest of men downstairs; very nice meal. Dr. Li Kan arrived as we ate; he stayed until 3:30, talking trade and exchange control. The great problem is: how to protect China's foreign exchange position and, therefore, the Chinese currency? I argued strongly against prohibitions and "quotas". Dr. Li wants statistics from us. ~~Stopped in for a few minutes to see Cecilia Pan and wish her a Merry Christmas. Francis was out, but Prof. Sze and his lady friend were there. He has a contract with Hurok, the producer and impresario of America, but can't get a passport or foreign exchange!~~

To Walter Robertson's party at No. 4 Chialing, for the Embassy staff, in honor of General Marshall. I had a long talk with Gen. Marshall, and felt that I had met a great man. What a contrast to Gen. Hurley! Gen. Marshall is a modest, quiet, sincere person. He feels the great responsibility of his job, and says that the hardest thing is that he is expected to do so much so quickly. I told him I thought his present job was next most important to Pres. Truman's for the future of America. I also said that he had a fine, loyal staff to help him. We have one thing in common: shrimp allergy. He said that he would be unconscious half an hour after eating one shrimp.

~~Worked a while after dinner, when my gums began aching. It has given me trouble almost every night for 2 weeks, but tonight it is excruciating. It is in the lower right gum, where there are no teeth! But it aches just like an abscessed tooth. Damn!~~

December 26: ~~When I woke, I drank a glass of orange juice with no ill effects. A few minutes later, however, I took my first sip of hot tea and boy! My whole lower jaw began to throb and ache terribly.~~ To office, then across river at 11 to see Dr. (Cap.) Gudex, USNR. He said: "Neuritis", gave me some anti-pain pills and some Vitamin B-1 tablets; said neuritis sometimes due to vitamin deficiency. Off and on all day my jaw ached, mostly on! At 5:30, staff gave me a tea party; farewell to Chungking. I spoke. Had lots of cakes. I contributed $23,000 for the wine, and gave a carton of Lucky Strikes. I estimate about 120 there.

~~December 27:~~ ~~Neuritis very much better. Busy day.~~

December 28: ~~Lunch with Mr. and Mrs. Li Chang-cho (Chungking Commissioner). Two lovely children. Other guests: besides Liesching, Hopstock and Drummond, were Mr. and Mrs. Chang. He is in the China and connected with CNRRA. She is one of the most beautiful women I have met. About 26, gracious and with lots of character.~~ Farewell calls: British Embassy (Wallinger out); saw Lady Seymour. ~~Met Trixie Leslie, who lived in Moller's boarding house when I was married in 1917. Saw a few others.~~ To American Embassy: saw Walter Robertson, Neil Gorman, Biggerstaff, Bob Smyth, Walker. Dropped card on Gen. Marshall at Niu Kou Tou; he was sleeping. Lovink had left for Shanghai yesterday. ~~Tea with Francis and Cecilia Pan.~~ Said good-bye to Dr. H.H. Kung at Fan Chuang. Packed in evening, with Hopstock's help, till 11 p.m.

1945

December 29: Last day in Chungking. Strangely, I leave with a certain regret, although glad to go. Called at Kuan-wu Shu in afternoon to say good-bye. ~~Quiet day in office.~~

December 30: Departure postponed on account of fog. To big buffet luncheon at Pickles' – British Consul. 2/3rds or people there were strangers to me. Had talk with Sir Allen Mossop,[57] formerly Judge of British Supreme Court for China. He saw the Mazes in Capetown. Freddie claims he is a refugee from China, which he claims as domicile. Ergo, he pays no South African Income Tax. That rich old so-and-so – no children and a wife with money – hasn't paid a cent of taxation to China or Great Britain or any other country during the war. ~~Dined with the mess, Liesching, Drummond, Hopstock.~~

December 31: Up at 5; by launch to island air-field at 6:30; took off at 8 sharp. Plane full. Had Hopstock, Chang Yung Nien, Fang Tu and Tsai Hsieh-tuan with me. Smooth passage to Hankow, where Fan Hao, Commissioner, and a few of his staff met me. Five minutes after leaving Hankow, the port engine began to spurt fire, so the pilot cut it out, and returned to the field. We had 3 hours to wait, and had a chance to drive around Hankow. I have never seen such destruction; the American Air Force certainly did a thorough job on the Hankow Bund; especially the Japanese Concession in which every building seemed a gutted shell. At the Custom House (which was intact) I met and spoke to the staff. Told Fan Hao that he has been selected to go to America on invitation of State Department to study foreign trade-zone system and other Customs work. At. 3:30 took off (in another plane) for Nanking, where the Commissioner came to see me. Then to Shanghai – arriving at 7:15, and met by Ting, Neprud, Sabel and Secretaries. Tired, unshaven and dressed in G.I. pants, woollen shirt and old tweed coat, arrived at my house to find a party under way – some 30 junior U.S. Naval officers and about the same number of beauteous damsels of various nationalities preparing for a gala New Year's party. I confess to a little annoyance, because I knew nothing of the party, but I stuck around, enjoyed a marvellous buffet supper (provided by the Navy), and turned in about 11:30. I couldn't sleep for the noise, which kept up till about 2. Some of the girls wondered, when they saw me, how such an old, bald, tramp gate-crashed such a swell party. End of 1945 – Annus Victoriae

APPENDIX I
Summary of Ting's letter to H. H. Kung, 28 March 1944

Hazaks;[1] nomad tribe; killers and bandits. Last autumn; Russian-speaking; formerly lived in Russia; Russians moved them into China. Hazaks on Altair border rebelled and looted cattle and foodstuffs which were taken into Russia. Sinkiang authorities successfully repressed movement early 1944. Beginning of March, K's returned with Mongolian regular soldiers (machine-guns and light artillery) and attacked Chinese garrison troops, who withdrew. Air planes with red stars (1 to 4) daily attacked Chinese troops. Soviet C.G. at Tihwa refused to accept Chinese Special Diplomatic Commissioners' protest re planes, saying planes falsely marked in order to harm Sino-Soviet relations. Central government planes at Tihwa [迪化] and I-li [伊犁] cannot operate because no gas. Gov. Sheng has sent brother to report x to Generalissimo. Up to end 1942, Sinkiang completely under Soviet influence and 8th Route Army. Soviet advisers were *de facto* authorities. Soviet spent large sums propaganda, construction, etc. Battalion Soviet troops stationed at Hami [哈密]; plane factory at Tihwa. Revolt of Ma Chang Ying suppressed with Soviet military assistance. Trade route from Hotien [和闐] to India closed. "Sinkiang was becoming another Outer Mongolia." Early 1943, with change in international situation, and Soviet abolished 3rd International, Gen. Sheng came over to Chinese government 100%. Soviet advisers discharged; Kuomintang Office opened; Communist activists suppressed; "undesirables" jailed. Gen. Sheng tried uproot all Soviet influence. Soviets stopped exportation of goods to Sinkiang and propagandized amongst tribes (especially Hazaks) against Gen. Sheng. Reported that ex-Soviet advisers, Outer-Mongolian government, 8th Route Army and Soviet people joined to drive Gen. Sheng out of Sinkiang. Present non local disturbance, but may have serious consequences unless suppressed and "properly handled by local and central governments."

NOTES

1943

1 Clarence E. Gauss (1887–1960), United States Ambassador to the Republic of China during WWII. He resigned from the post in November 1944 and was replaced by Patrick Hurley.
2 Frederick Maze (1871–1959), nephew of Sir Robert Hart. Immediately after the outbreak of the Pacific War, Maze was dismissed by the collaborationist Nationalist government and replaced by Chief Secretary Kishimoto Hirokichi. He was imprisoned in Bridge House till May 1942. After he was released, Maze went back to Chongqing as Inspector General in March 1943 and stayed in the post for three months. He ended his career in China with full pension.
3 Cecil Henry Bencraft Joly (1892–1968) was born in Macao. After the outbreak of the Pacific War, the Chungking Nationalist government appointed him Officiating Inspector General. He applied for retirement in 1943 and returned the IG-ship to Maze the same year.
4 Hugh Bradley, British Commissioner in the CMCS. He applied for short leave before the outbreak of the Pacific War, so he avoided capture by the Japanese military in December 1941. Officiating IG Joly instructed him to return to Chungking and continue as Staff Secretary.
5 Stanley K. Hornbeck (1883–1966) was an American diplomat, a Rhodes scholar and the author of eight books. He was Ambassador to the Netherlands (1944–1947).
6 George Atcheson (1896–1947) was Chargé d'Affaires of the US Embassy. He was an embassy counsellor in Chungking in 1943. In 1946 he was given the personal rank of Ambassador by President Harry Truman.
7 George Fitch (1883–1979) was an American Protestant missionary in China. He returned to China in 1939 to serve with the YMCA and later with the United Nations Relief and Rehabilitation Administration (UNRRA) until 1947. He then served the YMCA in Korea and Taiwan until 1961.
8 Soong Tzu-Ven (宋子文; Song Ziwen; 1891–1971) was a prominent businessman and politician in Nationalist China. The Soong family was closely connected to the Nationalists. His three sisters married H. H. Kung, Sun Yat-sen and Chiang Kai-shek. In 1940, Chiang appointed Soong to Washington as his personal representative. After Pearl Harbor, Chiang appointed Soong Minister of Foreign Affairs, though Soong remained in Washington to manage the alliance with both the US and the UK. During his tenure as finance minister, he managed to balance China's budget. He was promoted to President of the Executive Yuan (1945–1947) but stepped down due to the public's hostility towards his wealth and alleged corruption. After 1949, Soong moved to the US and avoided any association with politics in China or Taiwan.

NOTES

9. Kung Hsiang-Hsi (孔祥熙; Kong Xiangxi; 1881–1967) was T. V. Soong and Chiang Kai-shek's brother-in-law, and a banker and financial official in Nationalist China. Soong and Kung were highly influential in determining economic policies from 1927 to 1949. Kung was Minister of Finance from 1933 to 1944 and Governor of the Central Bank of China, from 1933 to 1945.
10. John Durnford Jernegan (1911–1981) was an American Foreign Service Officer, US Ambassador Extraordinary and Plenipotentiary to Iraq and to Algeria.
11. Kan Lee (李榦; Li Gan) graduated from Tsing-hua University in 1920 and specialised in agricultural economy. He served the Nationalist government as an economic technocrat and continued his course in agricultural diplomacy.
12. Carl Neprud, American Commissioner in the CMCS, was put in charge of investigation of the Chinese staff who had worked for Kishimoto Hirokichi from 1941 to 1945. As he was in the US during the War of Resistance, he was considered a neutral candidate for this task.
13. John Chambers Hughes (1891–1971) was an American diplomat and the United States Permanent Representative to NATO from 1953 to 1955.
14. Whitney H. Shepardson (1890–1966) was an American businessman and foreign policy expert. Following the involvement of the United States in the war, he served with the Office of Strategic Services in Washington and London. He became head of the agency's Secret Intelligence Branch in 1943, staying with the organization, which would ultimately become part of the Central Intelligence Agency, until 1946.
15. The Secret Intelligence Branch (SI) of the United States' Office of Strategic Services was a wartime foreign intelligence service responsible for the collection of human intelligence from a network of field stations in Asia, Europe and the Middle East.
16. The Office of Strategic Services (OSS) was a United States intelligence agency formed during WWII and a predecessor of the Central Intelligence Agency (CIA). The OSS was formed to coordinate espionage activities behind enemy lines for the branches of the United States Armed Forces. Other functions included propaganda, subversion and post-war planning.
17. William Joseph ('Wild Bill') Donovan (1883–1959) was a United States soldier, lawyer, intelligence officer and diplomat. Donovan is best remembered as the wartime head of the Office of Strategic Services (OSS), a precursor to the Central Intelligence Agency.
18. Laughlin Currie (1902–1993) was a Canadian-born US economist who served as economic advisor to President Franklin Roosevelt during WWII (1939 to 1945).
19. Miles Rutherford Browning (1897–1954) was an officer in the United States Navy in the Pacific during WWII and a pioneer in the development of aircraft carrier combat operations.
20. Francis Sayre (1885–1972) was a professor at Harvard Law School and High Commissioner of the Philippines. He served as foreign affairs advisor to the government of King Chulalongkorn of Siam, Assistant Secretary of State, High Commissioner of the Philippines, and US representative to the United Nations Trusteeship Council.
21. Cordell Hull (1871–1955) was an American politician from Tennessee. In 1943, Hull served as United States delegate to the Moscow Conference. Hull was the underlying force and architect in the creation of the United Nations, as recognized by his award of the 1945 Nobel Prize for Peace.
22. Maxwell McGaughey Hamilton (1896–1957) was an American diplomat and United States Ambassador to Finland between 1945 and 1947.
23. Hollington K. Tong (董顯光; Dong Xianguang; 1887–1971) was a Chinese journalist and diplomat. In 1925 he founded *Young Post*. After 1949 he became Ambassador to the United States in 1956 and to Japan in 1958.
24. Wei Tao-ming (魏道明; Wei Daoming; 1899–1978) was a Nationalist diplomat and public servant. He served as Ambassador to the United States from 1942 to 1946.

25 Pei Tsu-yee: (貝祖貽; Bei Zuyi; 1893–1982) was Governor of the Central Bank of the Republic of China. In 1947, Pei was ordered by T. V. Soong to open foreign currency exchange and gold markets which led to financial chaos, and he was impeached by the Control Yuan.
26 Ting Kwei-tang (丁貴堂; Ding Guitang; 1891–1962) was Deputy Inspector General under Inspector General L. K. Little from 1943.
27 Henry Robinson Luce (1898–1967), American magazine publisher, was called 'the most influential private citizen in the America of his day'. He launched and closely supervised a stable of magazines that transformed journalism and the reading habits of Americans.
28 T. K. Chang (張茲闓; Zhang Zikai; 1900–1983) became Minister of Economic Affairs in the Nationalist government in 1952 and was appointed President of the Bank of Taiwan.
29 Roland Bennett Anderson (1913–2010, US Assistant Naval Attaché, served during WWII as an Ordnance Staff Officer for the US anti-aircraft command in the Pacific theatre, and later joined the Department of Defense following the end of WWII.
30 Soong May Ling (宋美齡; Song Meiling; 1898–2003) was First Lady of Nationalist China, the wife of Chiang Kai-shek. On 18 February 1943, she became the first Chinese national and the second woman to address both houses of the US Congress. She made several tours to the United States to lobby support for the Nationalists' war effort.
31 Chang Fu-yun (張福運; Zhang Fuyun; 1890–1983) was Chinese politician and financier. He graduated from Harvard in 1917 and was appointed the first Director General of Kuan-wu Shu in 1927 at Financial Minister T. V. Soong's request. After WWII, he was again appointed Director General of Kuan-wu Shu in 1945 and stepped down in 1949.
32 Loy Chang (鄭萊; Zheng Lai) was the Director General of Kuan-wu Shu from 1942 to 1943.
33 Raymond P. Ludden (1909–1979) was one of the United States State Department's China experts. Ludden was interned by the Japanese in Shanghai the day after the attack on Pearl Harbor but was released the following year in what was then Portuguese East Africa (now Mozambique) as part of a diplomatic exchange arranged by the Swiss Red Cross. He volunteered to return to China and was subsequently detailed to Joseph W. Stilwell as a member of an elite political intelligence team.
34 E. Groff-Smith joined the Customs Service in October 1917. His last post was Kunming Commissioner. He retired in January 1945.
35 Claire L. Chennault (1893–1958) was an American military aviator best known for his leadership of the American 'Flying Tigers' and Nationalist China's Air Force in WWII. Chennault retired from the United States Army in 1937 and went to work as an aviation advisor and trainer in China. Starting in early 1941, with funding and control by the US government, Chennault commanded the First American Volunteer Group (Flying Tigers).
36 Thomas Roger Banister (1890–1955) was a member of the Chinese Customs Service. During 1931 and 1932 he was on special duty at the Inspectorate writing his surveys of Chinese trade in the preceding century, entitled 'A History of the External Trade of China, 1834–81' and 'Synopsis of the External Trade of China, 1882–1931'. During those two years, Banister also wrote his well-known account of China's Lights Service under the title *The Coastwise Lights of China: An Illustrated Account of the Chinese Maritime Customs Lights Service* (1933).
37 Willard Edward Annett (1895–?) was a member of the Chinese Customs Service. From April 1936 to September 1938 he served at the Inspectorate, Shanghai, as Pensions Chief Accountant and subsequently as Chief Accountant. He was promoted to Commissioner on 1 April 1937, and on 1 October 1938 was given charge of Ningpo.

38 Robert Hart (1835–1911) was the second Inspector General of China's Imperial Maritime Customs Service from 1863 to 1911.
39 Francis Aglen (1869–1932) was the third Inspector General from 1911 and was dismissed in 1927.
40 Hsu Tsu-shan (徐祖善; Xu Zushan; 1889–1957) was CMCS Coast Inspector. During 1922 to 1942, he served at Tientsin, I-chang and Hankou Customs, but when the war broke out Hsu returned to the Navy as a Major General. When the Chinese Civil War was over, he did not follow the Nationalist government but stayed in Mainland China.
41 Arthur Nicholas Young (1890–1984) was an American economist. He was the author of seven monographs, including *China's Economic and Financial Reconstruction* (1947), *China's Nation-Building Effort, 1927–37* and *The Financial and Economic Record* (1971). In 1929, he was an expert on public credit at the Commission of Financial Experts of the Chinese Government, and during 1929–1946 he was financial advisor for the Chinese government Government and the Central Bank of China.
42 Yang Min-hsin （楊明新; Yang Mingxin), Chinese Commissioner, was the Wuchow Commissioner during WWII and retired in 1947.
43 Fan Hao (范豪; Fan Hao), Chinese Commissioner, was appointed Hankow Commissioner after WWII in charge of the rehabilitation of the mid-stream of the Yangtze River.
44 R.C.P. Rouse was an English Indoor Assistant of the CMCS starting from 1923, and he was promoted to Commissioner of Foochow Customs in 1943.
45 Ying-chang Koo (顧應昌; Gu Yingchang, 1918–2011) was an economist. He was appointed to the ROC delegation at the United Nations in 1945 as technical attaché. After 1949, he taught economics at Michigan State University and Michigan University.
46 O. K. Yui (俞鴻鈞; Yu Hongjun; 1898–1960) was an economic and financial official of the Nationalist government. During the Second Sino-Japanese War, he was nominated the Deputy Minister of Foreign Affairs and Minister of Finance. After the war, he was appointed Governor of the Central Bank of China. In 1949, he went to Taiwan with the Nationalist Party and held the Governorship before he was appointed the Governor of Taiwan in 1953. He then became Premier of the Executive Yuan from 1954 to 1958.
47 Claude Forkner was a medical doctor at Peking Union Medical College Hospital.
48 John Herbert Cubbon (1887–?) was a member of the Chinese Customs Service. He assisted Stanley Wright in enlarging and revising the third edition of *China's Customs Revenue Since the Revolution of 1911*.
49 J.D. Campbell (1833–1907) joined the CMCS in 1862. He served in Peking as Chief Secretary and Auditor until October 1870 and was appointed Non-Resident Secretary in London in January 1874, remaining there until his death in December 1907. He acted as Hart's confidential agent in Europe, recruiting and examining foreign candidates for the Service, purchasing official stores, procuring apparatus for the lighthouses built by the Service, supervising the building of revenue (and other) cruisers required by the government, and carrying out negotiations entrusted to him.
50 Lott H.T. Wei (Wei Hsien-chang;韋憲章; Wei Xianzhang) was a government official. Between 1921 and 1927, Wei was assistant division manager of Nanyang Bros. Tobacco Co. Hankow for Hupeh, Hunan, Kiangsi, Honan & Szechuan. In 1927 he became advisor to the Hupeh stamp tax bureau. From 1927 to 1929, he was Chinese manager of Property at Butterfield & Swire Hankow. In 1929 he became Vice Director of the Central Mint in Shanghai.
51 Wu Teh-cheng (吳鐵城; Wu Tiecheng; 1888–1953) was a government official and Kuomintang Party Leader. Wu was elected as a member of the Kuomintang Central Executive Committee in 1929, and concurrently was a member of the Central Political

NOTES

Council. From 1932 to 1936, Wu served as the Mayor of Greater Shanghai and became Minister of Overseas Affairs in 1939.

52 David Ling-ken Kung (孔令侃; Kong Lingkan; 1916–1992), elder son of H. H. Kung, entered the Financial Ministry in 1936. After the outbreak of the War of Resistance, Kung moved to Hongkong and then became Madam Chiang's Personal Secretary in 1943. In 1948, Chiang Ching-kuo instructed to investigate Kung's Yangtze corporation on the charge of corruption. Kung moved his family and his assets to the US.

53 Also see Little's diary on 9 March 1951. During 1927 and 1929, Shanghai Commissioner Maze and Officiating IG Arthur Edwardes had a factional war for the post of IG-ship. Edwardes received the support of the British Foreign Office and the CMCS foreign staff and Maze received the support of the Nationalist government and the Chinese staff. Maze was finally appointed IG and in exchange for this favour he started to promote some outstanding Chinese assistants, e.g., Ting Kwei-tang and Hu Fu-sen. In addition, Maze also increased the salaries and promotion opportunities for the Chinese staff. This was why the Chinese staff was more loyal to Maze. However, the British staff resented Maze because they felt that the reason Maze came back to Chungking after he was released in 1942 was to collect his pension; they also felt that Maze did not care about the British staff's careers after he received his pension.

54 James M. Mead (1885–1964) was Democratic Senator for New York from 1938 until 1947. Mead was the Democratic candidate for Governor of New York in 1946, losing to Republican incumbent Thomas Dewey. After his defeat, Mead served on the Federal Trade Commission from 1949 to 1955.

55 Richard B. Russell (1897–1971) was an American politician from Georgia. As a Senator, he was a candidate for Democratic presidential nominee at the 1948 and 1952 Democratic National Conventions. He was a founder and leader of the conservative coalition that dominated Congress from 1937 to 1963.

56 R. Owen Brewster (1888–1961) was a Republican politician from Maine. Brewster served as Governor of Maine from 1925 to 1929, in the US House of Representatives from 1935 to 1941 and in the US Senate from 1941 to 1952.

57 Joseph W. Stilwell (1883–1946) was a United States Army four-star general known for service in the China-Burma-India (CBI) Theater during WWII. He became the Chief of Staff to Chiang Kai-Shek, served as the Commander of the CBI Theater responsible for all Lend-Lease supplies going to China, and later was Deputy Commander of the South East Asia Command. Due to pressure from China and Britain, Stilwell was recalled from his command by Roosevelt on 19 October 1944 and replaced by General Albert Wedemeyer.

58 Horace J. Seymour (1885–1978) was Ambassador of the United Kingdom to China from 1942 to 1946. Between April 1947 and July 1947, he was a member of the Franco-Siamese Boundary Commission in Washington, DC, and in December 1947 was appointed Chairman of the British Delegation to the Balkans Commission, based in Salonika, Greece.

59 Hoo Victor Chi-tsai (胡世澤; Hu Shize; 1894–1972) was a diplomat of Nationalist China and the first Chinese Assistant Secretary General of the United Nations, in charge of Trusteeship and Information from Non-Self-Governing Territories.

60 Victor Odlum (1880–1971) was a notable historian and supporter of British Israelism. He was a prominent member of the business and political elite of Vancouver, British Columbia, from the 1920s until his death. He was a newspaper publisher, a Liberal Member of the Legislative Assembly from 1924 to 1928, co-founder of the Non-Partisan Association in 1937, a temperance advocate, one of the first Directors on the board of governors that oversaw the new Canadian Broadcasting Corporation and a Canadian Ambassador.

NOTES

61 Sisley Huddleston (1883–1952) was a British journalist and writer. During the Second World War he was in Vichy France, taking French citizenship and writing in sympathy with the Vichy regime. He was imprisoned by the Free French in 1944 as a Vichy collaborator. He wrote a number of works, critical in particular of the Allied handling of the liberation of France.
62 According to the CMCS conventions, those members of staff who reached their retiring age could apply for 6 months' leave with full salary and get their full pensions without coming back to the Service. This was suspended because of the financial difficulties of the Chungking Inspectorate.
63 J. V. Porter, CMCS Commissioner, served as Assistant-in-Charge of the Dairen Custom House after the Mukden Incident as his former Commissioner, Japanese Fokumoto, retired from his post and switched to the side of Manchukuo. After Manchukuo seceded from Nationalist China, Porter went back to the Inspectorate General of Customs and worked under Maze until the outbreak of WWII in Europe.
64 Irene Mary Bewick Ward (1895–1980) was a British Conservative politician.
65 Gonion Edward Grimsdale (1893–1950) was a British Military Attaché to China during the Second World War. In 1942 he was appointed Military Attaché to the British Embassy at Chungking and in the same year was head of the British military mission in China; he retired in 1945.
66 Frederic Egglestone (1875–1954) was a lawyer, politician, diplomat and writer. In 1941 he was knighted and appointed first Australian minister to China. In 1944, Eggleston was appointed to the temporary position of Australian minister to the United States of America, succeeding Sir Owen Dixon. In 1946 he retired from active diplomacy and returned to Australia.
67 While he was the Officiating IG *ad interim*, Ting suggested that the Financial Ministry should issue the order to withdraw all high-ranking members of staff from the Wang Jingwei Customs Service. The deadline was on 31 December 1943. Before the deadline, if one could arrive in Free China he usually could get a promotion. This proposal was then approved by Financial Minister Kung.
68 Justin Brooks Atkinson (1894–1984) was an American theatre critic. He worked for the *New York Times* from 1925 to 1960. After the bombing of Pearl Harbor in December 1941, the *New York Times* sent Atkinson to the front lines as a War Correspondent in China, where he covered the war with Japan until 1945.
69 Lin Yun-kai: (林雲陔; Lin Yungai; 1881–1948) was a Chinese politician, banker and democratic revolutionary. In 1927, he became the Major of Canton and was promoted to President of the Guangdong government in 1931, following the lead of Chen Ji-tang. When Chen lost the fight in the Guangdong-Guangxi Incident, Lin left his post.
70 Liu Chi-wen (劉紀文; Liu Jiwen; 1890–1957) went to Chongqing when the Japanese army occupied Canton in 1938. In 1946, he was promoted to the Vice Minister of Audit. When the KMT lost China in 1949, Liu settled down in Taiwan and became the National Policy Advisor to the President.
71 The Chinese Medical Board (CMB) was established in 1914 by the Rockefeller Foundation, to develop the modernisation of public health in China.
72 On 8 September 1939, the Supreme National Defence Council of the Nationalist government had decided to combine the headquarters of the Central Bank, the Bank of China, the Bank of Communications and the Agricultural Bank of China and formed the Four-Joint General Office. The Office acquired the rights of issuing legal money from these four banks and centralized the power of currency issue on the Central Bank. Through strengthening the management of foreign exchange control, every application of governmental foreign exchanges was to be regulated and supervised by the Four-Joint Headquarters. Foreign exchanges were retrieved from the original four banks to be regulated by the Ministry of Finance. All foreign exchanges, currency and foreign currency were comprehensively controlled by the Ministry of Finance.

NOTES

73 Tseng Yang-fu (曾養甫; Zeng Yanfu; 1898–1969) was Director General of the Yunnan-Burma Railway in 1941. From 1943 to 1944, he was designated Minister of Comminutions. Between 1943 and 1945, Tseng was Chairman of the Engineer Commission of the National Military Council. In 1948, he became a member of the Central Executive Committee of Kuomintang, a member of Legislative Yuan, and President of the Chinese Engineers' Society and the Sino-Czechoslovakian Institute of Cultural Relations.
74 Randall Gould was Editor of the American-owned *Shanghai Evening Post and Mercury* and a veteran American newspaperman in China. On 25 June 1949, he ended this newspaper, stating that he could not run it if employees refused to accept his authority.
75 Fang Tu (方度; Fang Du) was the Canton Commissioner in 1949. Fang followed Little to Taiwan and was appointed Little's successor with Lo Ching-hsiang in 1950, but Fang controlled the real power of the Inspectorate. In 1955 Lo was retired; Fang was appointed IG and he was the first Chinese IG in history.
76 R.M.P. Bairnsfather served the Customs Service beginning in September 1920, and he was promoted to Commissioner of Tengchung Customs in October 1941.
77 Kuo-chen Wu (吳國楨; Wu Guozhen; 1903–1984) was a Chinese politician and scholar. He was considered as a pro-US liberal in the Nationalist Party. He served as Deputy Foreign Minister from 1943 to 1945. After WWII, Wu became the Mayor of Shanghai. Wu served as Governor of Taiwan from 1949 to 1953.
78 Sun Fo (孫科; Sun Ke; 1895–1973) was the son of Sun Yat-sen and a Chinese politician. Sun headed the Legislative Yuan from 1932 to 1948 and was Premier of the Executive Yuan in 1948. At the end of 1949, he exiled himself to Hongkong until 1951, moved to Europe from 1951 to 1952, and finally resided in the US from 1952 to 1965.
79 Pai Chung-hsi (白崇禧; Bai Chongxi; 1893–1966) was a Chinese general and a prominent Chinese Nationalist Muslim leader. He was the No. 2 leader of the Guangxi clique, which was the second largest faction in the Nationalist Party. He was the Minister of Defence from 1946 to 1948.
80 Morrie Depass (1895–1981) was a Colonel in the United States Army and a commanding officer of the Dixie Mission, an American observation mission to Yan'an, China, in 1944 to investigate and establish official relations with the Chinese Communists.
81 The Ting clique was headed by Ting Kwei-tang and some high-ranking Chinese officers in the CMCS. Most of these members had a long working history with Ting and were helped by Ting after WWII, as they had worked for Kishimoto Hirokichi during 1941 and 1945. The key members of the clique were Chang Yung-nien, Liu Ping-I, Tso Chang-chin, etc.
82 Chang-chin Tso (左章金; Zuo Zhangjin) served the Customs Service beginning in July 1926, and he was promoted to Commissioner of Kiaochow Customs in April 1944.
83 The American Seventh Army had liberated almost the entire south of France in August, including Marseille, and coordinated with French armies to attack the German troops which were stationed on the Massif des Vosges, in the northeast of France.
84 Cornelius Van der Starr (1892–1968) was an American businessman and operative of the Office of Strategic Services who was best known for founding the American International Group (AIG), a major corporation in the 21st century.
85 Philip Armand Hamilton Gibbs (1877–1962) was an English journalist and prolific author of books who served as one of five official British reporters during the First World War.
86 Arthur Thomas Quiller-Couch (1863–1944) was a British writer who published under the pen name of Q. Although a prolific novelist, he is primarily remembered for the monumental *Oxford Book of English Verse 1250–1900* (later extended to 1918) and for his literary criticism.
87 B. E. Foster Hall was British Commissioner of the CMCS. He was on leave when the Second Sino-Japanese War broke out and he chose to stay in the UK and joined the army after the outbreak of WWII. After the war, he was reinstated as Commissioner

NOTES

and stayed as Non-Resident Secretary in the London Office until the end of the Foreign Inspectorate in 1949. Then he worked closely with Little to restore the history of the CMCS.

88 Aleksandr Semyonovich Panyushkin (1905–1974) was Soviet Ambassador to the United States from 1947, transferring in July 1952 to Ambassador to China. He headed the First Chief Directorate (foreign intelligence) of the KGB from July 1953 to June 1955.

89 When Maze returned to Chungking from eastern Africa, T. V. Soong and H. H. Kung were both dissatisfied with Maze, as he did not prepare for moving the Inspectorate from Shanghai to Chungking.

90 Lin Shen (林森; Lin Sen; 1868–1943) was a politician and figurehead of the Nationalist government. The Japanese invasion of Manchuria prevented the civil war from erupting; however, it did cause Chiang to resign on 15 December. Lin was appointed in his place as Acting President and confirmed as President on 1 January 1932. When the Second Sino-Japanese War entered full swing in 1937, he moved to Chungking. He spurned all offers to defect and collaborate with the Japanese puppet government. He was the longest serving head of state in the ROC while it still held Mainland China.

91 Jean M. A. Fay was a French Assistant who joined the Customs in December 1913, and his last post was Pakhoi Commissioner until he retired in June 1944.

92 Lu Ping (盧斌; Lu Bin) Chinese Commissioner, was Ting Kwei-tang's close ally and best friend. He was transferred from the Inspectorate to the Chungking Custom House in 1941 by Maze to establish a shadow Inspectorate and to prepare for CMCS's evacuation. Before his arrival, the Chungking government had already appointed Tengyueh Commissioner C.H.B. Joly Officiating IG. Then he helped Joly to re-establish the CMCS in Free China. After the war, he was put in charge of the rehabilitation of the Tientsin Custom House.

93 Rabaul was the most important naval fortress of the Imperial Japanese Navy, the Combined Fleet, in the southwest Pacific Ocean. It was located on the northeast of New Guinea, near Bismarck Archipelago and New Britain Island. When the Japanese army occupied Bismarck Archipelago in 1942, Japan had fortified Rabaul as its biggest and most completed fortress and used it as its station to wage the attack on Australia and the Southeast Pacific. On 18 April 1943, the day that Japanese Commander-in-Chief of the Combined Fleet Isoroku Yamamoto's plane was shot down, it had taken off from Rabaul. When the Allies were planning to invade Rabaul, Japan still had a powerful force there, therefore the Allies changed their strategy from attacking Rabaul to isolating it. Massive airstrikes in December 1943 were intended to destroy Japanese combat forces though the result was not satisfying – only 6 battle cruisers and 52 warplanes were destroyed.

94 Louis Mountbatten (1900–1979) was a British statesman and naval officer. During the Second World War, he was Supreme Allied Commander South East Asia Command (1943–46). He was the last Viceroy of India (1947) and the first Governor General of the independent Dominion of India (1947–48), from which the modern Republic of India was to emerge in 1950.

95 When Allied forces successfully landed Sicily, Italy, in 1943, Churchill appointed Louis Mountbatten the Supreme Allied Commander South East Asia Command (SEAC) with promotion to Acting Full Admiral in August.

96 Eng Wen-hao (翁文灝; Weng Wenhao; 1889–1971) was a Chinese geologist, educator and politician. He was one of the earliest modern Chinese geologists and is regarded as the father of the modern Chinese oil industry in much of the literature. In 1948, he became the first Premier of the Executive Yuan. After the Nationalist Party was defeated in 1949, he fled to France, but he returned to China in 1951.

97 John K. Fairbank (1907–1991) was a prominent Harvard academic and historian of China. He published a number of academic and non-academic works on China. Fairbank

NOTES

established Harvard's Center for East Asian Research which was renamed in his honour after his retirement.

98   Jérôme Carcopino (1881–1970) was a French historian and author. He was elected to the Académie française, in 1955. From 1941 to 1942 he was minister of National Education and Youth in the government of Vichy France. He was a member of many archaeological and historical institutes in Europe.

99   Richard Dafydd Vivian Llewellyn Lloyd (1906–1983), better known by his pen name Richard Llewellyn, was a British novelist. During WWII, he rose to the rank of Captain in the Welsh Guards. Following the war, he worked as a journalist, covering the Nuremberg Trials, and then as a screenwriter for MGM.

100 The post of Deputy IG was abnormal in CMCS history as it only happened twice. As Ting stepped down from the post of OIG, Little had to award Ting with a more senior post. Hence, Ting became the most powerful DIG in the CMCS history, and his tenure was also the longest.

101 In 1934, Sheng Shicai (盛世才) was the *de facto* ruler of Xinjiang, though he still needed to consult with the Urumqi Soviet Consul General. Because Sheng did not have professional staff or proper insitutions that could supervise Chinese-Soviet trade smuggling caused a lot of loss of revenue and created many complicated conflicts. In order not to affect the relation between Xinjiang and Soviet authorities, Sheng had been continually requesting the Nationalist government to re-establish customs in Xinjiang. On 15 February 1944, Xinjiang customs were formally reestablished.

102 Ho Ying-ching (何應欽; He Yingqing; 1890–1987) was one of the most senior Nationalist generals and a close ally of Chiang Kai-shek. After the outbreak of the War of Resistance, Ho was appointed as Chiang's Chief of Staff. In 1944 Ho was appointed the General Commander of the Chinese Military Area. In 1946, Ho was sent to the United Nations Security Council as Director of the Chinese military delegation. One year later, he was called back to be a senior military advisor and regained the position of Defense Minister in 1948, witnessing the collapse of Nationalist China.

103 Hsu Kan (徐堪; Xu Kan; 1888–1969) joined the KMT and served in the Nationalist government in 1921. He was the minister of the Subsistence Department during 1941 and 1945. He took over Wang Yun-wu's position as Minister of Finance when Wang's policy failed disastrously; however, Hsu was unable to save the economy. In 1950, he followed the Nationalist government to Taiwan.

104 Feng Yu-hsiang (馮玉祥; Feng Yuxiang; 1882–1948) was a northern warlord and a Nationalist general. After the Second Sino-Japanese War began in 1937, he was Commander-in-Chief of the 6th War Area. After WWII, he travelled to the United States where he was an outspoken critic of the Chiang regime and of the Truman administration's support for it. He spent his later years supporting the anti-Chiang clique and the Communists, although he was never a Communist.

105 Huo Chi Chien (霍啟謙; Huo Qiqian), Chinese Commissioner, was the Chungking Commissioner after the outbreak of the Pacific War. He then became OIG Joly's Chief Secretary before Lu Ping's arrival. He was famous for his laziness and his extraordinary abilities.

106 Liu Ping-I (劉丙彝; Liu Bingyi), Chinese Commissioner, was Ting Kwei-tang's close ally. He deputed Ting who was the Chinese Secretary of IG Kishimoto. After Ting fled to Chungking in 1942, Liu stayed in Shanghai. After WWII, Liu was put in charge of the rehabilitation of the Customs affairs as the Dairen Commissioner, but he fled back to Shanghai in 1947.

107 What Little wrote about was the Third Moscow Conference (18 October–1 November 1943). After the Conference, American, British, Russian and Chinese foreign secretaries jointly announced the 'Moscow Declaration', which acknowledged the

NOTES

Declaration by the United Nations (announced on December 1942), insisted on their determination to fight the Axis Powers and agreed to establish the United Nations as soon as the war was over. This Conference reaffirmed China's status as one of the great powers.

108 Theodore Harold White (1915–1986) was an American political journalist and historian, known for his wartime reporting from China. During the war, White had come to know and respect Joseph Stilwell. White succeeded in seeing *The Stilwell Papers* through to publication. Later he wrote a book about China at war and in crisis, the best-selling *Thunder Out of China*.

109 William Langhorne Bond was the Vice President of the China National Aviation Corporation.

110 Sun Yat-sen (孫逸仙; Sun Yixian; 1866–1925) was a Chinese revolutionary and the first President and founding father of the Republic of China.

111 Seetoo You Chuan (司徒佑權; Situ Youquan) served in the service in February 1942 was Fourth Assistant A in the Chungking Custom House.

112 The 'Joly-Maze regime' refers to the period between January 1942 and 1 March 1943 while Joly was the OIG and Maze resumed his IG-ship.

113 Chang Yung-Nien (張勇年; Zhang Yongnian; 1893–1964) was one of the leaders of the Chinese staff in the CMCS. During the Second Sino-Japanese War he stayed in the Inspectorate General of Customs in Shanghai but managed to flee to Chongqing in November 1943. Afterwards he was made Staff Secretary. After the war, he allied with Ting Kwei-tang and fought for better treatment of the Chinese staff. When the Nationalist Party evacuated from Shanghai, he decided to stay in Shanghai with Ting and accepted the post of Deputy Commissioner of the Shanghai Customs station in the Peoples' Customs Service.

114 Chang's escape was rather interesting. He was initially stationed at Tientsin, and Kishimoto promoted him to Audit Commissioner and paid his trip to Shanghai. Chang took this opportunity to flee to Chungking. Kishimoto had been waiting for him for more than two months before finding out that Chang had already arrived in Chungking.

115 Peng Chung-wei (彭重威; Peng Zhongwei) was the Deputy Director General of Kuan-wu Shu in the Chungking government. Immediately after the outbreak of the Pacific War, Chungking needed to re-establish the Inspectorate but DG Loy Chang was still in Hongkong. Peng was appointed Acting DG and suggested appointing Tengyueh Commissioner Joly as Officiating IG.

116 Li Tong (李儻; Li Dang; 1888–1965) was the Director General of Kuan-wu Shu after Loy Chang. In 1948 he went over to the side of the Communists with Chen Chien and worked in the Hunan provincial government.

117 John Powell (1880–1947) was an American newspaperman and managing Director of China Press. He covered the outbreak of the Sino-Japanese War in Peiping and Shanghai in 1937 and later reported from Nanking and Central and South China until the outbreak of WWII. He edited *Who's Who* in China, 1926 and wrote the book *My Twenty-Five Years in China*, 1945.

118 Mansfield Freeman (1895–1992) was a Methodist minister. He was one of the original management group that started an insurance business in China that became the American International Group (AIG). He also was a prominent scholar of Chinese philosophy and a philanthropist.

119 Stella Benson (1892–1933) was an English feminist, novelist, poet and travel writer. In 1920 she went to China, where she worked in a mission school and hospital and met the man who would be her husband, James Anderson, an officer in the CMCS. Benson followed Anderson through various Customs postings including Nanning,

NOTES

Pakhoi and Hongkong, even though her writings on China sometimes put her at odds with the Customs Service leadership.

120 Franklin Delano Roosevelt (1882–1945), 32nd President of America, won a record four elections and served from March 1933 to his death in 1945. He was a central figure in world events during the mid-20th century, leading the United States during a time of worldwide economic depression and total war. A dominant leader of the Democratic Party, he built a New Deal Coalition that realigned American politics after 1932, as his New Deal domestic policies defined American liberalism for the middle third of the 20th century.

121 Winston Leonard Spencer-Churchill (1874–1965), British Conservative Prime Minister from 1940 to 1945 and again from 1951 to 1955, was regarded as one of the greatest WWII leaders. Churchill was also an officer in the British Army, a historian, a writer and an artist. He won the Nobel Prize in Literature.

122 Lu Pei Chang (魯佩璋; Lu Peizhang; 1890–1946) was born in Anhui and graduated from Nanking University. He joined the Nationalist government in 1929 as the Secretary to the Ministry of Industry and Commerce. In 1944 he was appointed the head of the Treasury and the Deputy Financial Minister.

123 The Sino-American-British Currency Stabilization fund was established in April 1941 with the purpose of stabilizing the official rate of exchange and maintaining the trade among the three countries. However, the fund was ended on 31 March 1944; the Management Committee of Foreign Exchange and the Central Bank took charge of its responsibilities.

124 Alf Hassel (1880–1956) was a Norwegian diplomat. From 1940 to 1945 he was Ambassador to Japan and Siam (Thailand); he also served as Ambassador to Chungking in 1942 and to China from 1943 to 1945. He was made Commander with Star in the Order of St. Olav in 1946 and was appointed as Minister to Stockholm, but had to relinquish the position due to poor health. From 1946 to 1950 he was assigned to the legation in Lisbon.

125 Kuang-pu Chen (陳光甫; Chen Guangfu; 1880–1976), a Shanghai-based Chinese banker and State Councillor. He was the founder of the first modern Chinese savings bank, a travel agency and the China Assurance Corporation Ltd. After the Communist revolution in Mainland China, K. P. Chen followed the Kuomintang-led government to Taiwan, though his Shanghai Commercial and Savings Bank was unable to re-establish its headquarters until 1954.

126 Cheng-ting Wang (王正廷; Wang Zhengting; 1882–1961) was a Chinese diplomat. He was Ambassador to the United States in 1936–38. He served in various minor government and party capacities during the war, but in 1949 stayed in Hongkong rather than go to Taiwan with Chiang Kai-shek's government.

127 John Maynard Keynes (1883–1946) was a British economist whose ideas have fundamentally influenced the theory and practice of modern macroeconomics and informed the economic policies of governments. He built on and greatly refined earlier work on the causes of business cycles, He is widely considered to be one of the founders of modern macroeconomics and the most influential economist of the 20th century.

128 On 26 December 1944, Rabaul was surrounded by Allied forces, and the Allies successfully retook one Japanese airport which was located on the northwest of New Britain Island, New Guinea (Rabaul was to the northeast of this airport). The Allies' action secured the sea route around New Britain Island and New Guinea.

129 After the Battle of Kursk, German armies were retreating from its eastern frontier. Since German forces no longer had the power to attack eastward, Soviet forces started to retake Ukraine. In the winter of 1943, the Soviets gathered 2.4 million soldiers and launched massive attacks westward, and soon successfully liberated Kiev.

NOTES

1944

1. The Customs Gold Unit was issued between 1931 and 1948. It could be used to pay customs duties and was widely used in the market only after 1942. One Gold Unit was equal to 20 legal money, and while the legal money was severely devaluating, the Customs Gold Unit was also affected by major fluctuations.
2. The Customs Gold Unit was devised by IG Frederick Maze after the heavy fall in the gold price of silver in 1929, so import duties were then levied on the gold basis, Haikwan Tael 1 = 1.5 CGU. See IG Circular No. 4025, 20 January 1930.
3. Ting-fu Tsiang (蔣廷黻; Jiang Tingfu; 1895–1965) was a historian and diplomat of the Republic of China. During his tenure at Tsinghua, he published the English-language *journal Chinese Social and Political Science Review* and mentored a number of historians in the study of Qing history, including John K. Fairbank. In 1945, Tsiang became Permanent Representative to the United Nations, and he subsequently also served as the Ambassador of China to the United States.
4. Chang Chen (張鎮; Zhang Zhen; 1899–1950) was a Major General and member of the Central Executive Committee of the Kuomintang. In 1939, he was Deputy Commanding General at Gendarmes Headquarters. Later, he became Commandant at the Gendarmes School, Director of the Chinese Boy Scouts, and Commanding General at Nanking Garrison Headquarters.
5. Yang Hsuen-cheng (楊宣誠; Yang Xuancheng; 1890–1962) participated in the Cairo Conference in 1943 and became Chiang's naval advisor. In 1948 he was transferred to the Taiwan provincial government.
6. Adrian Paul Ghislain Carton de Wiart (1880–1963) was a British Army officer who served in the Boer War, the First World War and the Second World War. He arrived in Chungking in early December 1943. For the next three years, he was involved in a host of reporting, diplomatic and administrative duties in the remote war-time capital. Carton de Wiart retired in October 1947, with the honorary rank of Lieutenant General.
7. Ernest William Hamilton (1858–1939) was a British soldier and Conservative politician who sat in the House of Commons from 1885 to 1892.
8. John Edward Masefield (1878–1967) was an English poet and writer and Poet Laureate of the United Kingdom from 1930 until his death in 1967. He is remembered as the author of the classic children's novels *The Midnight Folk* and *The Box of Delights* and poems including 'The Everlasting Mercy' and 'Sea-Fever'.
9. Geoffrey Arnold Wallinger (1903–1979) was a British diplomat and Ambassador to Thailand, Austria and Brazil.
10. Owen Mortimer Green (1876–1959) was *The Times* correspondent in Shanghai from 1910 to 1930, at one time Reuter's Far Eastern Editor and at the latter end of his life advisor and writer on Far Eastern affairs for the *Observer*.
11. Charles George Gordon (1833–1885), also known as Chinese Gordon, was a British army officer and administrator. He made his military reputation in China, where he was placed in command of the 'Ever Victorious Army', a force of Chinese soldiers led by European officers. In the early 1860s, Gordon and his men were instrumental in putting down the Taiping Rebellion, regularly defeating much larger forces.
12. Richard Morris Dane (1854–1940) had a career of great distinction in the Indian Civil Service, especially as Director General of Excise and Salt, and later took in hand the reform of the Salt Gabelle in China under the terms of the Reorganization Loan of 1913.
13. Auyang Ju (歐陽駒; Ouyang Ju; 1896–1958) was the Mayor of Canton in 1946. When the Nationalist Party lost Mainland China, he served the Nationalist government as a National Policy Advisor to the President in Taiwan.

NOTES

14 Gunther Stein was a German print journalist. Stein was correspondent in China for the *Manchester Guardian*, the *Christian Science Monitor* and the Associated Press.
15 Tu Ping-ho (杜秉和; Du Binghe; 1890–?) joined the Customs Service in 1913. Tu was promoted to Deputy Commissioner on 1 October 1934, and was transferred in 1937 to Ichang, where he was temporarily in charge. Tu had a highly specialised knowledge of Service accounts.
16 Quo Tai-chi (郭泰祺; Guo Taiqi; 1888–1952) was one of the technical delegates of China at the Paris Peace Conference, 1918–1919. In 1941, Quo was named to replace Wang Chung-hui as Foreign Minister. During his time as Foreign Minister, he negotiated an end to the special, extraterritorial rights exercised by the United States and United Kingdom in China since the mid-19th century. He also presided over the first session of the U.N. Security Council held in March 1946 in New York. In December 1947, Quo was appointed Chinese Ambassador to Brazil.
17 Ho Yao-tsu (賀耀祖; He Yaozu; 1889–1961) was appointed China's Ambassador to Turkey from 1934 to 1937 and then Governor of Gansu in 1937 and Mayor of Chungking in 1942. However, during these years he did not agree with Chiang's anti-communist policies and resigned as Mayor in 1945. In 1949 he joined the left wing of the Nationalist Party, the Revolutionary Committee of the Kuomingtang, and went over to the Communist camp.
18 *Vide* 20 August 1943 – Little then gave the correspondences to John Fairbank.
19 Antonius Hermanus Johannes Lovink (Tony) (1902–1995), former CMCS employee, was the last Governor General of the Dutch East Indies.
20 Shang Cheng (商震; Shang Zhen; 1888–1978) was an army officer. From 1929, he was Commander of the 32nd Army and member of the Peiping Branch Military Affairs Commission. In 1935, he was designated Chairman of the Hopei provincial government and Commander of the Peace Preservation Force of the Tientsin-Tangku area. Later, Shang became Chairman of the Honan provincial government.
21 Wang Chung-hui (王寵惠; Wang Chonghui; 1881–1958) was a jurist and Kuomintang leader. He became a member of the Central Supervisory Committee of the Kuomintang in 1929. In the following year, he was elected Judge of the Permanent Court of International Justice, and then sailed for The Hague, Holland, in April 1931. He returned to China in the summer of 1934, offering his good offices for a rapprochement between Nanking and Canton. Wang left China for The Hague in 1935 by way of Japan where he informally exchanged views with Japanese leaders on Sino-Japanese relations.
22 Han Li-wu (杭立武; Hang Liwu; 1903–1991) was a politician, political scientist, diplomat and social activist of the Republic of China. He contributed to ROC diplomatic efforts on international affairs, the protection of human rights and the salvation of refugees.
23 Harold George Nicolson (1886–1968) was an English diplomat, author, diarist and politician. He became Parliamentary Secretary and official Censor at the Ministry of Information in Churchill's 1940 wartime government of national unity, serving under Cabinet member Duff Cooper for approximately a year until he was asked by Churchill to leave his position; thereafter he was a well-respected backbencher, especially on foreign policy issues given his early and prominent diplomatic career. From 1941 to 1946, he was also on the board of governors of the BBC.
24 Hu Chung-nan (胡宗南; Hu Zongnan; 1896–1962) was a Nationalist four-star general and Chiang's favourite subordinate, together with Chen Cheng and Tang Enbo. After the retreat of the Nationalists to Taiwan in 1949, Hu served as the President's military strategy advisor until his death in 1962.
25 In 1915, Russia signed the Treaty of Portsmouth and the north of Sakhalin was ceded to Japan. Later, during the period when the Communist revolution was happening in Russia, Japan captured the whole region of Sakhalin. In 1925, Japan returned North

Sakhalin to Russia. According to the treaty, the Soviet Union transferred rights to explore for fossil fuels in the north of Sakhalin to Japan for 45 years. In the following 20 years, the rights of North Sakhalin became the key issue in Russia and Japan's diplomatic conflict. Japan's East Asia strategy was to stabilize the northern territory and invade towards the south. However, the Soviet Union wanted to avoid war on its eastern border. Therefore, the two countries wanted to make use of the issue of North Sakhalin to ease their diplomatic conflict, especially for Japan, which intended to buy North Sakhalin in order to acquire the oil resources on the island. As the Second World War broke out, there was a strategic shift between Japan and Russia, and Russia gained advantages over Japan during several negotiations. It was very difficult for Japan to keep dominance as before. In 1943, after the Soviet Union won the the battle of Stalingrad, Japan decided to sell the rights to North Sakhalin to maintain the neutrality between the two countries. The Soviet Union paid 5 million rubles every year, and in the following five years after the war, the Soviet Union offered 5,000,000 tons oil every year. On 30 March 1944, Russia and Japan signed a treaty on the rights of North Sakhalin in Moscow, which ended the conflict over that region.

26 Zinovi Pechkoff (1884–1966), Lieutenant General, joined the Free French Delegation as the Head in 1941. He was Head of the French Military Mission in China during 1943 to 1944, and French Ambassador Extraordinary and Plenipotentiary to China during 1944 to 1946.

27 This refers to the period from March to July in 1944, called the Battle of Imphal, which was waged by Japan. Imphal is located on the border between the eastern part of India and Burma. In 1942, the British army gave up Burma and fell back on India; Imphal was later built as a military and logistic supply base and had a high strategic value. In occupying Imphal, Japan cut the supply line of allied armies between China and India and used it as a stepping stone to invade India. On 8 March 1944, the Japan army was divided into three parts and waged formal attack on Imphal. However, the Commander of the Japanese army underestimated the unsuitability of the mountains surrounding Imphal for logistic supply. The Japanese army launched a fierce attack but then encountered supply problems. By April, the rainy season was approaching. It weakened the Japanese army's attack and further hampered supply. Meanwhile, with the help of air supply, the British army regrouped and launched a full-scale assault on the Japanese army, which eased the Imphal situation.

28 John Galsworthy (1867–1933) was an English novelist and playwright. He won the Nobel Prize in Literature in 1932.

29 Henry Wallace (1888–1965) was the 33rd Vice President of the United States (1941–1945), the Secretary of Agriculture (1933–1940) and the Secretary of Commerce (1945–1946).

30 Before he arrived in China, Vice President Wallace went to Siberia first, entered Sinkiang, and then arrived in Chungking on 20 June 1944. Wallace and Chiang mainly discussed that (1) President Roosevelt would treat the Nationalists and Communists equally, (2) the US had been invited by Stalin to reconcile the Sinkiang issue between China and the Soviet Union, and (3) the Stilwell issue. Due to this meeting, China and the US came to a consensus that Stilwell should be replaced, as he was disliked by both the Chinese and British generals.

31 Benjamin Greeley Ferris (1892–1982) was Joseph Stilwell's Deputy Chief of Staff.

32 The Marine Department was put in charge of the lighthouse service and the preventive (anti-smuggling) fleet before 1941. After the outbreak of the Pacific War, all the aforesaid service and fleet were left to the Wang Jingwei Customs Service.

33 Chang Pai Leh (張伯烈; Zhang Bolie), Chinese Commissioner, graduated from the Customs College. He was one of the most senior Commissioners. He was the first

NOTES

Chinese member of staff to reach the rank of Commissioner in a local Custom House. During WWII, he was Dean of the Customs College.

34 Hsieh Ping-hsin (謝冰心; Xie Bingxin; 1900–1999) was a left-wing writer and Wu Wen-tsao's wife. As a renowned writer, Hsieh excelled at describing social inequality and the beauty of nature. After the end of the Second World War, she was hired by Tokyo University as the first foreign female lecturer and taught Chinese literature there. When the Chinese Civil War was over, Hsieh Ping-hsin refused the invitation of Nationalist government and turned her loyalty to the Communist government which was built in Peking.

35 Henry Morgenthau (1891–1967) was the US Secretary of the Treasury under Roosevelt. He played a central role in organising US finances during WWII. He also played an increasingly major role in shaping foreign policy, especially with respect to Lend Lease, support for China, helping Jewish refugees and planning postwar reconstruction of Germany.

36 Chou Chung-yo (周鐘岳; Zhou Zhongyue; 1876–1955) was a government official, a State Councillor and Vice President of the Examination Yuan. He was Minister of Interior of the National Government from 1939 to 1944. Later he was a member of the Association for Preservation of National Cultural Antiques and the Ta-tung Society. In 1944, he was appointed Vice President of the Examination Yuan of the National Government.

37 Wang Shih-chieh (王世杰; Wang Shijie; 1891–1981) was a diplomat and academic in Nationalist China. He was Minister of Education, 1933–37, and Minister of Information, 1939–42 and 1944–45. After WWII he was appointed Foreign Minister by T. V. Soong and signed the Treaty of Friendship and Alliance with the Soviet Union in August 1945. In 1948 he stepped down as Foreign Minister. After the KMT retreated to Taiwan, he was named Secretary General to Chiang.

38 Edwin Sanders Perrin (1905–1946), Brigadier General (USAAF), was Deputy Chief of Staff of Headquarters of US Army Air Forces from 25 June 1943 to 29 April 1944.

39 Chen Cheng (陳誠; Chen Cheng; 1897–1965), together with Hu Chung-nan and Tang Enbo, formed the triumvirate of Chiang Kai-shek's most trusted generals during WWII. Chiang appointed Chen as Governor of Taiwan province in 1949. Chen became the Premier, the Vice President of the Republic of China and the Deputy Chairman of the Nationalist Party.

40 Wilfred Fang Po Ling (林芳伯; Lin Fangbo) was a newspaperman, Nanking correspondent of the United Press and later correspondent of Reuters at Canton.

41 Hsia Ting-yao(夏廷耀; Xia Tingyao; 1895–1949) was a member of the Chinese Customs Service. When the Second Sino-Chinese War broke out, Hsia was forced to leave and moved to inner China; he arrived in Chongqing in 1944 and became the first Chinese Inspector General at the Lanzhou Customs House. When the Second World War was over, he took over the Taipei Customs and stayed in Taiwan for three years. He returned to China in 1948 and died in March 1949.

42 The evacuation of the Loyang Custom House staff was because the Japanese military started the famous 'Operation Ichi-Go'. The operation began in April 1944 and ended in December 1944, and it was the biggest military campaign in the Second Sino-Japanese War. The aim of the operation was to eliminate all Nationalist troops on the Beijing-Guangdong railway and to destroy all Sino-American air force bases. In order to achieve the best military results, the operation was kept secret and neither the Nationalists nor the Communists were aware of it happening. Due to hyper-inflation, low morale and a disordered commanding system, the performance of the Nationalist army was unprecedentedly poor. The Imperial Japanese Army immediately took Henan, Hunan and Guangxi provinces and achieved its goals successfully. Compared to other countries' military performance in Europe, the Pacific and North Africa, the operation demonstrated every negative aspect of the Nationalist Party and Chiang Kai-shek.

43 M. M. Acheson joined the Customs Service in December 1925; he was Principal Assistant B from April 1940. He escaped from the Occupied Zone at this time.
44 E. A. Pritchard first served the Customs Service in May 1931; at this time he was in the Occupied Zone. After WWII, he was appointed Shanghai Commissioner to replace Ting Kwei-tang.
45 Mitchinaya (Myitkyina) here refers to the occupied airport of Mitchinaya, rather than the whole area. There were two airports in Mitchinaya, one in the north and one in the west. In April 1944, the Allies launched the battle of Mitchinaya. Sino-US allied troops occupied the west airport on 17 May. However, due to an underestimation of the enemy's strength, disagreement between the Chinese and US generals, lack of coordination between the ground and naval forces, the continuous reinforcement of the Japanese army, the offensive of the Allied forces in towns of Mitchinaya landed in a predicament. The battle of Mitchinaya did not end until August of the same year, when the Allied forces occupied the entire area.
46 Monte Cassino is in central Italy. It was the commanding height of the Gustav Line, a German defensive line. At the top of the mountain stood the medieval monastery of Cassino. As the Italian government surrendered to the Allied forces in September 1943, the Allies wanted to take Rome as soon as possible in order to end the war in Italy. Monte Cassino blocked the Allies' route from southern Italy to Rome. Allied forces launched four offensives with casualties exceeding 50,000 before eventually taking Monte Cassino. Only when the German commanding officer ordered his troops to withdraw from Cassino that the Allied forces eventually occupied the monastery, ending the battle.
47 During Operation Ichi-Go, Henan province suffered most seriously. Flooding in 1938, famine in 1942–1943 and the corruption of the Tang En-po troops made the local defence completely collapse.
48 Ronald Owen Hall (1895–1975) was an Anglican missionary Bishop in Hongkong and China in the mid-20th century. As an emergency measure during the Second World War, with China under Japanese occupation, he ordained Li Tim-Oi as the first woman priest in the Anglican Communion.
49 Soong Ching-ling (宋慶齡; Song Qingling; 1893–1981) was the second wife of Sun Yat-sen. She was a member of the Soong family and, together with her siblings, played a prominent role in China's politics prior to 1949. After the establishment of the People's Republic of China in 1949, she held several prominent positions in the new government, including Vice President of China, and travelled abroad in an official capacity several times during the early 1950s.
50 Soong Ai-ling (宋藹齡; Song Ailing; 1888–1973) was the eldest of the Soong sisters and the wife of H. H. Kung.
51 In April 1932, the Nationalist Party sanctioned the formation of the People's Political Conference and allowed the Conference to (1) bring out suggestions for the Nationalist government's interior and diplomatic polices, (2) create potential policies, and (3) supervise the government's administration. However, the Conference was purely consultative body, and the Nationalist government usually ignored its suggestions.
52 The Imperial Army of Japan launched Operation Ichi-Go to control the railway from Peking to Canton. The line from Peking to Hankow became the Army's phase one target, and Honan became its primary military goal. On 17 April, as Japanese motorised troops moved into the Central Plains of Honan, the defending Nationalist troops were completely incompetent, as they had been suffering seriously from famine, low morale and corruption. In mid-May, the Japanese troops controlled the whole province of Honan. Around 470,000 Nationalist soldiers surrendered and the Imperial Army achieved its phase one goal successfully on 25 May.

NOTES

53 After the first phase of Operation Ichi-Go, the Imperial Army marched along the railway and went to the south. The cities along the railway became its military objective, namely Changsha, Shangjao, Kukong, Wenchow and Foochow, and these cities were razed and ravaged.
54 Wu Wen-tsao (吳文; Wu Wenzao; 1901–1985) was a modern Chinese sociologist, anthropologist and ethnologist. In 1938 he founded the Department of Sociology of Yunnan University; after 1950 he served as a professor at the Central College for Nationalities. Wu promoted localization of sociology in China.
55 Wu Ching (吳青; Wu Qing; 1937–?) was the daughter of Hsieh Ping-hsin and Wu Wen-tsao. She was also a professor and was appointed as the deputy to the people's congress of the Communist Party, the People's Republic of China, in 1984.
    Wu Ping (吳冰; Wu Bing; 1935–2012) was the daughter of Hsieh Ping-hsin and Wu Wen-tsao. She had been a lecturer at Beijing Foreign Studies University. Her research interests lay in Asian American literature, English style, English writing and oral translation. She died in 2012.
56 Hsieh Ping-chi (謝冰楫; Xie Bing-ji) was Hsieh Ping-hsin's brother, son of Hsieh Bao-zhang.
57 The Bretton Woods Conference, formally known as the United Nations Monetary and Financial Conference, was a gathering of 730 delegates from all allied nations in Bretton Woods, New Hampshire, United States, to regulate the international monetary and financial order. The Conference was held from the 1–22 July, 1944. Agreements were executed that later established the International Bank for Reconstruction and Development and the International Monetary Fund.
58 J. A. O'Connor (1885–1952) was chief engineer for the US forces' China-Burma-India Theatre of Operations in 1944–1945.
59 David Dean Barrett (1892–1977) served more than 35 years in the US Army, almost entirely in China. Barrett played a critical role in the first official contact between the Communist Party of China and the United States government. Notably, he was Commander of the US Army Observation Group, also known as the Dixie Mission, to Yan'an, China, in 1944.
60 Hideki Tojo (1884–1948) was a general of the Imperial Japanese Army, the leader of the Imperial Rule Assistance Association and the 40th Prime Minister of Japan from 1941 to 1944. As Prime Minister, he was directly responsible for the attack on Pearl Harbor, which initiated war between Japan and the United States, although planning for it had begun before he entered office. After the end of the war, Tojo was arrested and sentenced to death for war crimes by the International Military Tribunal for the Far East.
61 Hengyang did not fall with Changsha at once. During the Battle of Hengyang, the Nationalist troops' performance was outstanding. The troops held the city of Hengyang for 42 days. It was the longest defence of a single city of the entire Second Sino-Japanese War.
62 Henri Philippe Pétain (1856–1951), generally known as Philippe Pétain, was a French general who reached the distinction of Marshal of France, and was later chief of state of Vichy France, from 1940 to 1944.
63 Between May and June 1944, Chiang's alleged association with a nurse called 'Chen' reached the point where rumours spread that Chiang's wife, Madame Chiang, had left China for Braziland begun divorce proceedings. However, historians have not come to an agreement with respect to the identity of Ms. Chen. Yang Tianshi, researcher at the Chinese Academy of Social Sciences, suggests that Ms. Chen is nothing but a synthesis of Chiang's female friends. Within the political and media circles in Chungking at the time, there had never been a specific identification of Ms. Chen. Chiang

NOTES

himself recorded that the scandal was closely related with the American side, especially the deadlock in his relations with Stilwell. In his private diary, Chiang bitterly complained that the scandal was an abominable conspiracy used by Washington to attack his personal authority, as well as the reputation and leadership of the Nationalist government.

64 Archibald T. Steele (1903–1992), an author and former Foreign Correspondent, was one of the first Western journalists to report from inside China in the early 1930s. In 1950 he was a co-winner of a George Polk award, given by Long Island University, for reporting on China for the *New York Herald Tribune*. In 1966, he wrote 'The American People and China'.

65 Gaston Marie Raoul de Sercey (1898–?) was in charge of the Chinese Overseas Remittances Department beginning in 1939. De Sercey's major contribution during the occupation was to provide as much relief as he could to POWs and internees, particularly those who had worked for the Chinese Maritime Customs and the important Hongkong firm of Jardine Matheson. After the war, he seems to have become a development banker, working for the International Bank for Reconstruction and Development.

66 Selwyn Speight (1908–1980) was an Australian journalist. He was appointed by the *Sydney Morning Herald* as War Correspondent in Chungking in November 1942. He reported on China's struggle against Japan during the Second World War.

67 Frank Dow Merrill (1903–1955) was an American Major General. From 1943 to 1944, he was Chief of the US Commanding General's Liaison Staff, South-East Asia Command. He was Deputy Commanding General of the China-Burma-India Theater of Operations from 1944 to 1945.

68 Chen Li-fu (陳立夫; Chen Li-fu; 1900–2001) was a Chinese politician. He was Educational Minister from 1938 to 1944. Along with his brother Chen Guofu, he formed the Central Club clique (CC clique), which was the most powerful faction of the civil service in the Nationalist Party.

69 Chen Kuo-fu (陳果夫; Chen Guofu; 1892–1951) was a Chinese politician and head of the CC clique.

70 Li Chai-sum (李濟深; Li Jishen; 1885–1959) was a former government official who played a leading part in the Fukien Independence Movement between 1933 and 1934. Li was reinstated in the KMT after the outbreak of the Sino-Japanese War, moved to Hongkong after VJ Day and carried out anti-Nanking activities. After he was expelled from the KMT, he became Chairman of the China Kuomintang Revolutionary Committee, an opposition group to Nanking. He went to Peiping from Hongkong in 1949 to participate in setting up a new democratic government in cooperation with Communists.

71 Donald Nelson (1888–1959) was an American business executive and public servant, serving as the executive Vice President of Sears Roebuck before accepting the position of Director of Priorities of the United States Office of Production Management (1941–1942). In 1942 Nelson became Chairman of the War Production Board (1942–1944) when it replaced the OPM. He later served for two years (1945–1947) as President of the Society of Independent Motion Picture Producers.

72 Patrick Hurley (1883–1963) was a US Major General, statesman and diplomat. He served as minister to New Zealand in 1942 and then went to the Soviet Union. Over the next two years, he visited the Near East, Middle East, China, Iran and Afghanistan on behalf of the President. He was appointed US Ambassador to China in 1944.

73 Walter P. McConaughy (1908–2000) was a career American diplomat. He worked in the US State Department and was posted to Hongkong around 1950. After returning to Washington to serve alongside Edwin M. Martin and O.E. Clubb in the Office of Chinese Affairs, he served as the Ambassador to Burma from 1957 to 1959.

NOTES

74 Baron Robert Rothschild (1911–1978) was a Belgian diplomat. He helped to draft the Treaty of Rome of 1957, which led to the foundation of the European Economic Community (EEC) in 1958. He was requested to go to China in 1944 and became the first Secretary at the Belgian embassy in Chungking, where he knew and grew to like Chou En-lai. After the Japanese surrender he went to Shanghai, where in 1946 he was appointed Consul General.

75 Li Tung-wha (李桐華; Li Tonghua) was Acting Deputy Commissioner of the Chinese Maritime Customs Service, Chefoo from 1934. During the War of Resistance, he was the Loyang Commissioner and was put in charge of helping his colleagues fleeing from Occupied China to Chungking.

76 Sheng Shih-tsai (盛世才; Sheng Shicai; 1897–1970) was the Governor of Sinkiang with the support of the USSR before 1942.Then he turned anti-Soviet, executing many Han Communists in hopes of securing the backing of the Kuomintang for his continued rule. The KMT removed Sheng in 1944, because he tried to get the support of the Soviet Union again, and appointed him Minister of Agriculture and Forestry. He fled to Taiwan along with the KMT at the end of the Chinese Civil War in 1949.

77 Lu Tso-fu (盧作孚; Lu Zuofu; 1893–1952) was a government official, as well as founder and general manager of Min Sheng Industrial Co., Chungking, from 1926. He was also a member and Commissioner of Reconstruction of the Szechuan provincial government beginning in 1935.

78 Chang Fa-kwai (張發奎; Zhang Fakui; 1896–1980) was a Chinese Nationalist general. He commanded the 4th War Area from 1939 to 1944, defending Guangdong and Guangxi against the Japanese and achieving a victory in the Battle of South Guangxi.

79 Carl Clinton Van Doren (1885–1950) was a US critic and writer. He won the 1939 Pulitzer Prize for Biography or Autobiography for *Benjamin Franklin*.

80 Wendell Lewis Willkie (1892–1944) was a corporate lawyer in the United States and the Republican Party nominee for President in 1940. Though he lost the presidential election, President Roosevelt appointed him as an informal Ambassador-at-large.

81 Lung Yun (龍雲; Long Yun; 1884–1962) was Governor and warlord of the Chinese province of Yunnan from 1927 to 1945. Immediately following the war, General Chiang Kai-shek moved against Long Yun and overthrew him in a coup. Long Yun escaped to Hongkong at the end of 1948 and joined the Kuomintang Revolutionary Committee. He went back to Yunnan in 1950, after the establishment of the People's Republic, and later became Vice Chairman of the National Defence Committee and Vice Chairman of the Administrative Council of Southwestern China.

82 Albert Wedemeyer (1897–1989) was an American Army Commander who served in Asia during WWII from 1943 to the end of the war. While in China during the years 1944 to 1945, he replaced Joseph Stilwell as Chiang Kai-shek's Chief of Staff and commanded all American forces in China. Wedemeyer supported Chiang's struggle against Mao Tse-tung and in 1947 President Truman sent him back to China to render a report on what actions America should conduct.

83 Douglas MacArthur (1880–1964) was an American five-star general and Field Marshal of the Philippine Army. He was Chief of Staff of the United States Army during the 1930s and played a prominent role in the Pacific Theater during WWII. He officially accepted Japan's surrender on 2 September 1945, aboard the USS Missouri anchored in Tokyo Bay, and oversaw the occupation of Japan from 1945 to 1951.

84 Princess Beatrice of the United Kingdom (1857–1944) was the fifth daughter and youngest child of Queen Victoria.

85 Chang Li-shang (張厲生; Zhang Lisheng; 1901–1971) was a Chinese politician and diplomat who served as Secretary General of the Kuomintang from 1954 to 1959. L.S.

Chang, as he was commonly known, played a key role in Nationalist China's political, economic, financial and foreign affairs as well as in Kuomintang affairs from the 1920s until his death in Taiwan in 1971.

86 Thomas Edmund Dewey (1902–1971) was the 47th Governor of New York (1943–1954). In 1944, he was the Republican candidate for President, but lost to President Franklin D. Roosevelt in the closest of Roosevelt's four presidential elections. In 1948, he was again the Republican candidate for President, but lost to the incumbent President, Harry S. Truman.

87 Hamilton Fish III (also known as Hamilton Fish Jr.; 1888–1991) was a soldier and politician from New York State. He served in the United States House of Representatives from 1920 to 1945. During that time he was a prominent opponent of United States' intervention in foreign affairs and a critic of President Franklin D. Roosevelt.

88 Clare Boothe Luce (1903–1987) was the first American woman appointed to a major ambassadorial post abroad. A versatile author, she is best known for her 1936 hit play *The Women*, which had an all-female cast.

89 Yu Pin (于斌; Yu Bin; 1901–1978) was a Chinese Cardinal of the Roman Catholic Church. He served as Archbishop of Nanking from 1946 until his death, having previously served as its Apostolic Vicar, and was elevated to the cardinalate in 1969.

90 Chou En-lai (周恩來; Zhou Enlai; 1898–1976), was the first Premier of the People's Republic of China, serving from 1949 to 1976. Chou served under Mao Tse-tung and was instrumental in consolidating the Communist Party's rise to power, forming foreign policy and developing the Chinese economy. He was also a skilled and able diplomat and served as the Chinese Foreign Minister from 1949 to 1958.

91 Tai Li (戴; Dai Li; 1897–1946) was a Chinese general. He led the Bureau of Investigation and Statistics during WWII.

1945

1 H. Horace Smith (1905–1976) was an American diplomat. He was the United States Ambassador to Laos from 1958 to 1960. In 1932 he was a US Vice Consul in Guangzhou, and in 1938 was a US Consul in Jinan.

2 Charles André Joseph Marie de Gaulle (1890–1970) was a French general, writer and statesman. He was the leader of Free France (1940–1944) and the head of the provisional government of the French Republic (1944–1946). In 1958, he founded the Fifth Republic and served as the 18th President of France, until his resignation in 1969.

3 Delvaux de Fenffe (1863–1947) was a Belgian politician of the Catholic Party. After World War I, he became a Royal Commissioner for the devastated regions in the provinces of Liege, Namur and Luxembourg. He became active in politics and was elected in 1926 as provincial senator for the Catholic Party in Luxembourg, a post he held until 1936.

4 John D. Sumner (1906–1931) got his doctorate from Northwestern University and taught economics at the University at Buffalo. The Nationalist government invited him to be economic advisor from 1937 to 1949.

5 Emily Hahn (1905–1997) was an American journalist and author. She was the author of 52 books and more than 180 articles and stories. She lived in Shanghai and Hong Kong between 1935 and 1943.

6 Eric Charles Hayes (1896–1951) was a British Army officer. He was appointed Head of the British Military Mission to China in 1945 and he was also the general officer who commanded British troops in China.

7 Stanley F. Wright was a Commissioner in the Chinese Customs and Francis Aglen's Personal Secretary. He wrote five books on the history of the CMCS.

NOTES

8   Emperor Shōwa (1901–1989) was the 124th Emperor of Japan, reigning from 1926 to 1989. He was the head of state under the limitation of the Constitution of the Empire of Japan during Japan's imperial expansion, militarization and involvement in WWII. After the war, he was not prosecuted for war crimes as many other leading government figures were, and his degree of involvement in wartime decisions remains controversial among historians to this day. During the post-war period, he became the symbol of the new state and Japan's recovery.
9   Benjamin H. Kizer (1878–1978) was a lawyer and a diplomat. After WWII he was the Director of the United Nations Relief and Rehabilitation Administration in China, and during the Cold War years he was an advocate of US diplomacy with the People's Republic of China.
10 George Hamden (1901–1998) was the Assistant Chief of Staff in the China Theater from 1944 to 1945.
11 Chaucer H. Wu (吳澤湘; Wu Zexiang; 1897–1973) was an editor and publisher of *China Voice* in 1932, and a member of the Treaty Commission, the Ministry of Foreign Affairs of the National Government from 1932 to 1935. In 1935, he became Special Inspector for Foreign Affairs, Szechuan and Sinkiang provinces.
12 Wellington Vi Kyuin Koo (顧維鈞; Gu Weijun; 1887–1985) was a Chinese diplomat and politician. He was one of China's representatives at the Paris Peace Conference of 1919 and he became Acting Premier twice in 1926 and in 1927. He also served as Ambassador to France, Britain and America. Koo was a participant in the founding of the League of Nations and the United Nations, and sat as a Judge on the International Court of Justice in The Hague from 1957 to 1967.
13 Lewis Mumford (1895–1990) was an American historian, sociologist, philosopher of technology and literary critic. He was particularly noted for his study of cities and urban architecture.
14 Tai En-sai (戴恩賽; Dai Ensai; 1892–1955), son-in-law of Sun Yat-sen, graduated from Columbia and started to serve Sun Yat-sen in the Southern Military Government in 1923. He was the Superintendent of Customs at the Canton Custom House in 1937 but held no further official post after 1938. In 1949, he moved back to Macao.
15 Leon Henderson (1895–1986) was the administrator of the Office of Price Administration from 1941 to 1942. He was replaced after the 1942 election and went into a career in business.
16 Ellis O. Briggs (1899–1976) was the Economic Counsellor of the US State Department in Chungking in 1945 and then the US Ambassador to Greece.
17 Kuniaki Koiso (1880–1950) was a general in the Imperial Japanese Army, Governor General of Korea and the 41st Prime Minister of Japan from 1944 to 1945.
18 Kantarō Suzuki (1868–1948) was an Admiral in the Imperial Japanese Navy, member and final leader of the Imperial Rule Assistance Association and the 42nd Prime Minister of Japan from 7 April to 17 August 1945.
19 John Gilbert Winant (1889–1947) was an American diplomat. He was appointed Ambassador to Great Britain in 1941 and US representative on the European Advisory Commission in 1943.
20 Harry S. Truman (1884–1972) was the 33rd President of the United States (1945–53). As the final running mate of Roosevelt in 1944, Truman succeeded to the presidency in 1945. Truman had a very negative opinion of the Nationalist Party, especially the Chiang, Soong and Kun families.
21 Percy Chen (陳丕士; Chen Peishi; 1901–1989) was a journalist and businessman.
22 James Theodore Marriner (1892–1937) was a US diplomat. He was assigned to Paris as Counsellor of Embassy and served as Chargé d'Affaires in 1931. He was then assigned as Consul General in Beirut in 1935.

NOTES

23 Paul Joseph Goebbels (1897–1945) was a German politician and Minister of Propaganda in Nazi Germany from 1933 to 1945. As one of Adolf Hitler's closest associates and most devoted followers, he was known for his zealous orations and deep and virulent antisemitism, which led to his strongly supporting the extermination of the Jews when the Nazi leadership developed their 'Final Solution'.
24 Karl Dönitz (1891–1980) was a German Admiral who played a major role in the naval history of WWII. In 1943, Dönitz achieved the rank of Grand Admiral and replaced Grand Admiral Erich Raeder as Commander-in-Chief of the Navy. After the death of Adolf Hitler and in accordance with Hitler's last will and testament, Dönitz was named Hitler's successor and Supreme Commander of the Armed Forces.
25 Apollon A. Petrov (1907–1949) was a Soviet diplomat and Ambassador to China. He was previously a member of the Russian Academy of Sciences where he specialised in ancient Chinese Taoist philosophy.
26 Jean-Baptiste Sabatier was a Commandant in the French Army and a Liaison Officer for NATO. He fought during the invasion of France at the outbreak of WWII in 1939.
27 Thomas Clayton Wolfe (1900–1938) was a major American novelist of the early 20th century. Wolfe wrote four lengthy novels, plus many short stories, dramatic works and novellas. He is known for mixing highly original, poetic, rhapsodic and impressionistic prose with autobiographical writing.
28 Wu Ting-chang (吳鼎昌; Wu Dingchang; 1884–1950) was a banker, journalist and founder of *Ta Kung Pao*.
29 *Ta Kung Pao* is the oldest privately run Chinese newspaper and was established in 1902. In the periods of late Qing and Nationalist China, Ta Kung Pao was liberal and openly criticized the KMT and CCP. After being suspended between 1952 and 1953, *Ta Kung Pao* became a national newspaper in Mainland China, but it was eventually dissolved due to the Cultural Revolution in 1966. In Hongkong, *Ta Kung Pao* is still active but controlled by the CCP and its political stance is considered as leaning towards the CCP.
30 Samuel Dashiell Hammett (1894–1961) was an American author of hard-boiled detective novels and short stories, a screenplay writer and a political activist.
31 Simon Bolivar Buckner (1886–1945) was an American army officer and Commanding General in Okinawa in 1945.
32 Yu Fei-peng (俞飛鵬; Yu Feipeng; 1883–?) served as Director of the China-Burma Administration in 1942, Director of the War Transport Administration in 1945 and Minister of Communications from 1945 to 1946.
33 Hallett Abend (1884–1955) was an American journalist. He was offered a job in 1926 as chief *New York Times* Correspondent in Peking as part of a six-months' vacation. He ended up staying 15 years and reported on the invasion of China by Japan. He wrote *Tortured China* and *Can China Survive?* His reporting of the 'Rape of Nanking' in 1937 exposed the extent of Japanese atrocities in the city.
34 Andrew Russell Pearson (1897–1969) was one of the best-known American columnists of his day, noted for his syndicated newspaper column 'Washington Merry-Go-Round', in which he attacked various public persons.
35 Louis Bromfield (1896–1956) was an American author and conservationist who gained international recognition, winning the Pulitzer Prize and pioneering innovative scientific farming concepts.
36 Whiting Williams (1878–1975) was co-founder of the Welfare Federation of Cleveland, a predecessor to the Community Chest and United Way charitable organizations, as well as an author of popular books and articles about labour relations during the early 20th century.
37 O. S. Lieu (Liu Hung-sheng) (劉鴻生; Liu Hongsheng; 1888–1956) founded the China Development Bank in Shanghai. He was also a philanthropist and founder of the following schools and hospitals: Tinghai Public School, Tinghai Girls' School and

NOTES

Tinghai Hospital at Tinghai, Chekiang, and the Tibet Road Hospital at Shanghai. He was a Director of the Chinese Red Cross Hospital.

38 Jonathan Mayhew Wainwright (1883–1953) was a career American army officer and the Commander of Allied forces in the Philippines at the time of their surrender to the Empire of Japan during WWII.

39 Silas Hardy Strawn (1866–1946) was a prominent Chicago lawyer and one of the named partners at the law firm of Winston & Strawn. In 1925, US President Calvin Coolidge named Strawn as one of two American delegates to the Special Conference on American Relations with China, held in Beijing. Strawn was also Chairman of the Chinese Extraterritoriality Commission.

40 Chester William Nimitz (1885–1966) was a Fleet Admiral of the United States Navy. He played a major role in the naval history of WWII as Commander-in-Chief, United States Pacific Fleet, and Commander-in-Chief, Pacific Ocean Areas, for US and Allied air, land and sea forces during WWII.

41 George Carleton Lacy (1888–1951) was an American Methodist missionary and the last Methodist Bishop in Mainland China. In 1941 Lacy was elected Bishop of the China Central Conference and was assigned to Foochow. Lacy's tenure as Bishop was set to end in 1949, but the advent of the Communist government made it impossible to hold a general conference or elections.

42 Liu Chieh (劉鍇; Liu Jie; 1906–1991) was a Chinese diplomat. He served as the counsellor and minister of the Chinese Embassy, Washington, from 1940 to 1945; as deputy Secretary General of the Chinese Delegation to the San Francisco Conference on International Organization in 1945; as Administrative Vice Minister for Foreign Affairs from 1946 to 1947; and as Chinese Ambassador to Canada from 1947.

43 Louis Wilson Maddox (1891–1956), Brigadier General, was Chief Finance Officer of the Services of Supply in the South-West Pacific Area between 1942 to 1943. From 1943 to 1945 he was Chief Finance Officer of US Army Forces in Far East. He retired in 1946.

44 Chiang Mon-lin (蔣夢麟; Jiang Meng-lin; 1886–1964) was a notable Chinese educator, writer and politician. Jiang was General Secretary of the Executive Yuan of the Republic of China from 1945 to 1947. He was also Chairman of the Sino-American Joint Commission on Rural Reconstruction in the late 1940s and 1950s.

45 Lo Ching-hsiang (羅慶祥; Luo Qingxiang) was the Preventive Secretary of the Inspectorate General. He followed Little from Shanghai in April 1949 and moved to Taiwan in 1950. He was chosen by Little as his successor with Fang Tu.

46 Tseng Kuang-chin (曾擴情; Tseng Kuoqin; 1894–1983) was a member of the Central Executive Committee of the Kuomintang and Director of Party Affairs in Szechuan. He served as councillor of the Political Department, Military Affairs Commission in 1941. In 1945, he became Director of the Political Department, Central Military Academy. From 1946 he was Director of the Political Department Generalissimo's Headquarters in Chungking and later became Secretary General of the same headquarters.

47 William Johnston Keswick (1903–1990) was Chairman of the Shanghai Municipal Council during the crises leading to the Pacific War. Early on in the war, Keswick was appointed chief of the British Special Operations Executive (SOE) based in London. After joining the British Army, he saw service in the Middle East before returning to participate in the Normandy landings as part of the 21st Army Group.

48 Kuo Yu-yung (郭有容; Guo Yourong) joined the CMCS in 1923 and was appointed Deputy Commissioner at the Shanghai Custom Hosue in 1947.

49 Thomas Cassin Kinkaid (1888–1972) served as an Admiral in the USN during WWII. He built a reputation as a 'fighting admiral' in the aircraft carrier battles of 1942 and commanded the Allied forces in the Aleutian Islands campaign.

NOTES

50 Lewis Barton Combs (1895–1996) was a US admiral and engineer who helped found the United States Naval Construction Battalions, known as the 'Seabees', during WWII.
51 Westray Battle Long (1901–1972) was Second Director of the Women's Army Corps.
52 Ting Yao-chen (丁耀琛; Ding Yaochen), Ting Kwei-tang's eldest son, joined the CMCS in 1941. He asked for sick leave in June 1947 and he passed away from TB in the same year.
53 Frank Tillman Durdin (1907–1998) was a Foreign Correspondent for the *New York Times*. During his career, Durdin reported on the Second Sino-Japanese War (1937–1945), the collapse of European colonial rule in Indo-China, and the emergence of the People's Republic of China. He was the first American journalist granted a visa to re-enter China in 1971.
54 Milton E. Miles (1900–1961) was a Vice Admiral in the United States Navy who served in WWII as head of Naval Intelligence operations in China, and later was second-in-command of the Sino-American Special Technical Cooperative Organization.
55 Russell Edward Randall (1902–1992) was Brigadier General and Deputy Commanding General of the 10th Air Force in India from July 1944 to September 1944. From September 1944 to October 1945, he was Commanding General of the 312th Fighter Wing in China.
56 Li Chang-cho (李長哲, Li Changzhe), native of Shanghai, joined the CMCS in 1929 and made Deputy Commissioner in 1946.
57 Allan George Mossop (1887–1965) was a British Judge of South African origin who served in China. He was the Chief Judge of the British Supreme Court for China from 1933 to 1943. His appointment as Judge was formally terminated in 1943 after the Sino-British Treaty for the Relinquishment of Extra-Territorial Rights in China was ratified. Mossop returned to China in 1946 as an advisor to the British Embassy.

Appendix I

1 In 1942, Sinkiang Governor Sheng Shih-tsai suspected the Soviet Union of attempting to overthrow his provincial government, so he decided to end the relationship with the Soviet Union and turned to establishing a relationship with the National Government. In 1944, the Soviet Union supported Sinkiang nationalists in an uprising against KMT rule. Apart from encouraging the uprising and creating a border conflict between China and Soviet Union, Sheng also aimed at seizing control of Sinkiang. The National Government, sent troops to suppress the riot, and raised a diplomatic protest against the Soviet Union. However, the Soviet Union not only refused to stop supporting the uprising but also blamed it on the National Government, saying that it provoked the border conflict. All this happened during the war period. In order to avoid a breach between anti-Axis powers, the United States attempted to mediate, but without success. The conflict between China and the Soviet Union over the border issue was not over until the Chinese Communists established control over Sinkiang in 1949.